Synge and His Influences:
Centenary Essays from the Synge Summer School

Synge and His Influences:
Centenary Essays from the Synge Summer School

Edited by Patrick Lonergan

Carysfort Press

A Carysfort Press Book in association with Peter Lang

Synge and His Influences:
Centenary Essays from the Synge Summer School
edited by Patrick Lonergan
First published as a paperback in Ireland in 2011 by
Carysfort Press Ltd
58 Woodfield
Scholarstown Road
Dublin 16
Ireland

ISBN 978-1-78874-854-4

© 2011 Copyright remains with the author.

Typeset by Carysfort Press Ltd

Cover design by eprint

This book is published with the financial assistance of
The Arts Council (An Chomhairle Ealaíon) Dublin, Ireland

Caution: All rights reserved. No part of this book may be printed or reproduced or utilized in any form or by any electronic, mechanical, or other means, now known or hereafter invented including photocopying and recording, or in any information storage or retrieval system without permission in writing from the publishers.

For Nicholas Grene

The editor and publisher gratefully acknowledge the financial assistance and support of the Department of Arts, Sport and Tourism.

Additional financial support was provided by the Grant-in-Aid of Publication Fund at National University of Ireland, Galway.

ACKNOWLEDGEMENTS

In 2009, I was approached by what was then the Department of Arts, Sport and Tourism (now known as the Department of Tourism, Culture and Sport), which wished to mark the centenary of Synge's death by supporting a publication in his honour. I want to thank Ministers Mary Hanafin and Martin Cullen for supporting this venture, and especially want to convey my gratitude to Mr Peadar Caffrey, who gave strong backing to this book throughout all stages of its preparation.

The Grant-in-Aid of Publications fund of National University of Ireland, Galway also provided assistance. I am grateful too for a period of sabbatical leave from NUI Galway, part of which was spent completing this book.

In addition to marking the centenary of Synge's death, this volume seeks to celebrate the second decade of the Synge Summer School. I am very grateful to Adrian Frazier (director in 2001 and 2002) and Tony Roche (director from 2004 to 2007) for supporting this publication: both have been (as always) very generous with their time and advice. I'm also grateful to the contributors, most of whom spoke at the 2007, 2008 and 2009 Schools. I must also acknowledge the many scholars, artists, and theatre practitioners who have contributed to the School since 2001: they are listed at the end of this book, and I regret that it was not possible to include more of their papers.

I am very grateful to Gavin Quinn and Andrew McLellan of Pan Pan Theatre company for allowing me to use an image from their Chinese-language version of *The Playboy of the Western World* for the cover of this book. Their production was one of the most exciting recent events in Irish theatre, and the image reminds us brilliantly that we still have much to learn from Synge's plays.

In his characteristically modest afterword, Adrian Frazier comments that any director of an Irish summer school is always in danger of killing it off. Summer schools are an important – indeed, a unique – feature of Ireland's cultural landscape, but their viability and existence has been in doubt for most of the last decade. As the person who has attempted to kill the Synge Summer School 'for a third time' this decade (following Adrian and Tony), I've become very aware that the continuing existence of Ireland's summer schools is entirely a result of the enthusiasm and commitment of local communities. The dedication of the Synge Summer School Committee is the primary reason that so many people come back to Rathdrum from one year to the next. I am very grateful to Nick Kirwan, Liz Elkinson, Joan Kavanagh, Enda Fitzpatrick, Jill McCarthy, Michael Brennan, and Elizabeth Tottenham.

Lilian Chambers, Dan Farrelly and Eamonn Jordan of Carysfort Press have been a pleasure to work with, as always. I am also very grateful to Rachael Kilgallon. And as ever I must thank Therese and Saoirse Lonergan.

I must also thank Nicholas Grene, who founded the Synge Summer School and who has done so much to promote the appreciation and understanding of Synge's work. It's worth recording that almost half of the contributors to this book came to the Synge Summer School for the first time when they were graduate students. Without exception, all of them have spoken of the warmth of the welcome they received there, and of the inspirational quality of the Schools that Nicky directed. This is just one of the many ways in which he has had an enormously positive impact on countless students and scholars, myself included. It gives me, the Synge Summer School committee, and all the contributors to this book great pleasure to dedicate this book to him.

Patrick Lonergan, Galway, 2010.

TABLE OF CONTENTS

Acknowledgements	ix
About the Synge Summer School	xiii
Foreword	xv
Anthony Roche	
Introduction	1
Patrick Lonergan	
**1	The Poeticizing of Synge**	7
Ann Saddlemyer	
**2	Censorship and Self-Censure in the Plays of Synge**	33
Ben Levitas	
**3	Synge, Evolutionary Theory, and the Irish Language**	55
Mary Burke	
**4	Synge's Things: Material Culture in the writings of Synge**	73
Paige Reynolds	
**5	The Best Field Worker: Synge and Irish Folklore**	93
Eilís Ní Dhuibhne	
**6	Fair Play Synge**	111
Mark Phelan	

7 | **Synge, Anarchism, and the European Avant-Garde**   133

Shaun Richards

8 | **The Translator's Playwright: Karel Mušek and Synge**   153

Ondřej Pilný

9 | **Well, Well, Well: A Question Of 'Piety'**   181

Richard Pine

10 | **Synge and Tom Murphy: Beyond Naturalism**   199

Alexandra Poulain

11 | **Living With Ghosts: Synge and Marina Carr**   215

Emilie Pine

12 | **Re-Location and Re-Locution: Adapting Synge**   225

Melissa Sihra

13 | **Evolving *Playboys* for the Global World**   245

Sara Keating

14 | **Re-Writing Synge's *Playboy* – Christy's Metamorphosis, A Hundred Years On**   259

Bisi Adigun

Afterword   269

Adrian Frazier

Synge Summer School, 2001 to 2010   275

Texts Cited   279

Contributors   291

Appendix   295

Index   301

ABOUT THE SYNGE SUMMER SCHOOL

The Synge Summer School was established in 1990 by Professor Nicholas Grene. It meets in Rathdrum, Co Wicklow each year, offering participants the chance to enjoy lectures and seminars on Synge and Irish drama in one of Ireland's most beautiful counties. The school is open to all, welcoming academics, teachers, students, researchers, theatre practitioners (amateur and professional), and theatre enthusiasts of all kinds. Every year, participants travel to the school from all parts of Ireland, and from many countries throughout the world. While there is a full academic programme, involving a series of seminars, lectures and an optional drama workshop, there is also a lively social programme, which includes a tour of Wicklow, a trip to the Abbey Theatre, and many other events.

The current Director of the School is Patrick Lonergan (National University of Ireland, Galway). Past directors of the School include Nicholas Grene (Trinity College Dublin), Adrian Frazier (NUI Galway) and Anthony Roche (University College Dublin).

www.syngesummerschool.org/

Synge Summer School Committee, 2010

Nick Kirwan (Chairman)

Liz Elkinson (Secretary)

Joan Kavanagh

Enda Fitzpatrick (Treasurer)

Jill McCarthy

Michael Brennan

Elizabeth Tottenham

FOREWORD

Anthony Roche

At the end of the first decade of the twenty-first century, *Irish Times* theatre critic Peter Crawley considered the range of theatre offered on Irish stages in that ten years and concluded that John Millington Synge was the greatest contemporary playwright. He based this judgement not only on the magnificent accomplishment of the Druid Theatre Company's staging of the entire official canon but also on the diversity of Synge stagings by other Irish theatre makers. Pan Pan Theatre Company produced a resolutely contemporary *Playboy of the Western World* in Chinese Mandarin while Roddy Doyle and Bisi Adigun moved a Nigerian Christy Mahon to the exotic landscape of west Dublin. As Fintan O'Toole put in when reviewing *DruidSynge*, the playwright, 'abused and appropriated during his lifetime, and treated with a curious mixture of awe and neglect thereafter, almost a century after his death has finally been given his due.'

Synge's achievement has not been accomplished by the theatrical innovation of stage productions alone but by the activities of contemporary scholars. 2009 was the centenary of Synge's death and Nicholas Grene, Professor of English at the playwright's *alma mater* Trinity College, Dublin, convened a conference there to celebrate that event. He invited Declan Kiberd, W.J. McCormack and myself to join him on a panel to discuss what had first got us interested in Synge and what shape that interest had taken. Writing in *The Irish Times* some weeks later, Adrian Frazier was struck by the centrality of Synge to a whole generation of scholars. In my own case I am acutely aware of the degree to which Synge informed my subsequent exploration of contemporary Irish drama. Declan Kiberd and I had both been undergraduates in Trinity in 1971, the centenary of Synge's birth, and spoke that day of the impact this had had on each of us and our subsequent decision to write a PhD on Synge, Declan at Oxford with Richard Ellmann, myself at the University of California with Vivian Mercier. Of Nicholas Grene's many contributions over the years to developing our understanding of Synge, not the least was his decade of acting as first director of the Synge Summer School, held in Rathdrum near his own family home in Ballinaclash (mentioned several times in *The Well of the Saints*). Under the inspiration of the local committee who have sustained it over the years, the Synge Summer School has worked to increase awareness of how much of Synge's writing is centred on Wicklow, the site of his ancestral home, and how eclipsed this has been in the public's perception by an overemphasis on the Aran Islands. The essays in this collection all derive from that annual gathering, and I thank the volume's editor and the School's current director, Patrick Lonergan, for the opportunity to open this volume. Adrian Frazier, Patrick and myself have been the School's directors in the first decade of this century, and the volume itself is in many ways one of the most appropriate means of examining the richness and complexity of Synge's achievement and legacy.

There has not been a single-authored monograph on the playwright since Mary C. King's *The Drama of J.M. Synge* in 1985. While this may be regretted, the fact that there have been multi-authored volumes in ever-growing number seems to me appropriate for a writer whose work evokes such a wide range of contexts (dramatic, philosophic, linguistic, political, ethnographic, etc.) and whose influence has not only been pervasive in the past hundred plus years but has spread in so many directions, forward into contemporary Irish drama, outward into other languages and cultures. When his official biographer James Knowlson asked Samuel Beckett whose work had most influenced his, the octogenarian playwright murmured only one word in response: 'Synge.'

The perception of Synge in Ireland has been bedevilled from the start by the 'authenticity' debate. At Yeats's urging, Synge sourced his play *The Shadow of the Glen* in a story he heard on the Aran Islands; and his Preface to *The Playboy of the Western World* is keen to stress the authenticity rather than the inventiveness of his language. But it increasingly seems to me that the charges brought against Synge and his work by the nationalists on the score of 'foreign influence' were all true. As a student of comparative literatures,

Synge would only have been too aware of the debt of the *Shadow* to the Widow of Ephesus story, but he had to keep silent in the face of Arthur Griffith's charge. The answer was not either/or but both/and. If Yeats advised Synge to give up Racine and go to the Aran Islands, the latter did so with Racine in his back pocket, as *Riders to the Sea* makes clear. During rehearsals of *The Well of the Saints*, Willie Fay charged that the play was far too Left Bank in its derivation; but if it was, it was also a dramatization of the debates between St Patrick and Oisín, in Douglas Hyde's view the closest ancient Irish literature came to a drama. W.J. McCormack's 2000 biography, *Fool of the Family*, makes clear how important were Synge's first two years in Germany, away from Dublin and home for the first timer. He read the plays of Ibsen (in German) and frequently attended the theatre. Although never directly stated, it may well be that Synge had never gone to a theatre before he left Dublin (in line with the rest of his family). But McCormack displays a hankering for Synge to remain on the Continent and has no great *grá* for the decision to go to the Aran Islands. The crucial conjunction, however, may well have been the interleaving of the five annual visits to the Arans from 1898 to 1902 with the three year experiment of the Irish Literary Theatre initiated by Yeats and Lady Gregory. Synge attended (and wrote about) the first and the last, and was particularly taken with Douglas Hyde's *Casadh an tSúgáin/The Twisting of the Rope* and its development of what Nicholas Grene has termed the 'stranger in the house' motif – which Synge was to make so much his own. When the three year experiment ended, Synge was waiting, with his first two one-act plays. In Germany, he had come into contact with a national culture and drafted an outline of his first Irish play (never written). With the development of the nascent Irish national theatre, he was well placed and more than ready to lay out the template for a national theatre, securely Irish in its sources yet nourished by an awareness of parallels with world culture. This volume shows how that far-seeing achievement has continued to unfold across time.

INTRODUCTION

Patrick Lonergan

The centenary of Synge's birth was celebrated in 1971 with the publication of several important studies of his work. There were new collections of essays, edited by S.B. Bushri and Maurice Harmon. Ann Saddlemyer produced an edited edition of the letters of Synge and Molly, Robin Skelton and James Kilroy both published short books about elements of Synge's life, and Nicholas Grene produced a catalogue of the Synge papers that had been acquired by the library of Trinity College Dublin.

Many of those books are now recognised as having contributed in important ways to the development of the field – yet when he came to review them in 1974, Robert Hogan thought they 'raise[d] some salient problems about the state of Anglo-Irish scholarship and perhaps of literary scholarship in general'.[1] His view was that almost everything worth saying about Synge had already been said, and he suggested that 'It might well be time for a critical moratorium on Synge':

> The problem of Synge is not that difficult, and Irish scholars may be in danger of working a few authors to death. If there are any major Synge projects left, they are a Collected Letters, an annotated bibliography, and any biography to supersede the Greene-Stephens book and make use of new material. If Irish scholars turn their attention to other figures, as they should, there remains the danger of puffing ... Synge is perhaps the Scylla of the author who is overworked [by scholars], and [Jack B.] Yeats the Charybdis of the author who is hardly worked at all. If Irish studies is to prosper, some discrimination and judgment will be needed to steer a sensible course. (1038)

Hogan's remarks now seem difficult to understand. Of course, at that time he couldn't have foreseen how the study of 'Anglo-Irish Literature' (as it was then called) would change – influenced first by the development of a stronger critical tradition within Ireland itself, then by the impact of critical theory, and finally by a move into the interdisciplinary field of Irish Studies. In judging Hogan's remarks, we do have the privilege of hindsight, but it's probably fair to state that he was also simply incorrect – as would be proven with the publication of important monographs on Synge by Nicholas Grene, Declan Kiberd, Toni O'Brien Johnson, and others during the period 1975 to 1985.

That new scholarship was matched by new approaches to staging Synge's plays, notably by Galway's Druid Theatre. That company began life on 3 July 1975 with a production of *The Playboy of the Western World*. Rather like Hogan, Druid's founders had considered Synge over-familiar and tired: they had chosen his play not as something exciting and new, but as an Irish classic that might resonate with a tourist audience. Yet as they rehearsed, they were struck by the power and strangeness of Synge's plays, and they resolved to return to them at the earliest opportunity. They did so many times over the subsequent years. In 1982, for instance, they gave what is still regarded as the definitive *Playboy*, presenting that play's sexuality and violence with an unflinching realism. And they would later stage all of Synge's works (with the exception of *When the Moon Has Set*) together under the banner of *DruidSynge*, an event that was hailed by Fintan O'Toole as 'one of the greatest achievements in the history of Irish theatre' when it premiered in 2005.[2]

Internationally, Synge would prove an inspiration for writers everywhere. Most famously, Mustapha Matura would relocate the action of *The Playboy* to Trinidad in his 1984 *Playboy of the West Indies* – while in 2009, Philip Roth published *The Humbling*, a short novel that enters into playful dialogue with Synge, not least through naming one of its characters Pegeen Mike. In writing such works, Roth and Matura find themselves part of a long tradition of literary respondents to Synge: one that includes Brecht, Lorca, Derek Walcott, Joseph O'Connor, John McGahern, and many others (including, as Melissa Sihra points out in this book, the fascinating Ugandan playwright Erisa Kironde).

These three forces – academic scholarship, theatre production, and literary composition – all came together to ensure that by 2009, the centenary of Synge's death, it would be impossible to claim that nothing more could be said about his life or work. The biography that Hogan called for had been realised in 2000 when W.J. McCormack gave us *Fool of the Family*, a book that debunked many of the myths about Synge's life. It also proved that we need to know much more about Synge's relationships with European culture, with religion, and with the history and culture of Ireland. Since that book's arrival, the study of Synge has been carried out in a surprising variety of ways. There have been dazzlingly imaginative re-readings of Synge in Declan Kiberd's *Irish Classics* (written before *Fool of the Family* but also published in 2000) and Susan Cannon Harris's *Gender and Modern Irish Drama* (2002). And there have been meticulously careful archival reconstructions of the Irish Literary Revival and Synge's place in it by Chris Morash's *History of Irish Theatre* (2002), Ben Levitas's *Theatre and Nation* (2002) and P.J. Mathews's *Revival* (2003). A great many other books and articles have sought to present new perspectives on Synge, and many of them inform the essays in this volume.

As Anthony Roche remarks in his foreword, Synge is now so strong a presence in Irish drama that he seems like a contemporary playwright. As Ireland entered a period of startling transformations from 1995 onwards, Synge's plays would be used to anchor the country's sense of self. Patrick Mason's *Well of the Saints* would triumph in Dublin, Galway, Paris, Perth and Edinburgh in 1995 and 1996 – a time when Ireland was just beginning to reconsider its relationship with the rest of the world. In 2001, partly in response to McCormack's rooting of Synge in Europe, the Abbey's Artistic Director Ben Barnes would hire the director Niall Henry to offer a new perspective on *The Playboy*. Known for his indebtedness to European performance practices, Henry stripped back the play to its essence, performing it on an almost bare stage and casting radically against type to force audiences to forget everything they thought they knew about Synge. In 2004, Barnes himself would direct *The Playboy*, in an overambitious production that would soon come to symbolise the Abbey's faltering centenary celebrations and its looming bankruptcy. Shortly afterwards, in 2005 and 2006, *DruidSynge* would be seen by audiences throughout Ireland, and in Edinburgh, New York, and Japan.

In that contrast between Druid's global success and the Abbey's near collapse, we might find a metaphor for the state of Irish society at that time. Small, flexible entities like Druid could achieve success on an international stage with apparent ease, yet our national institutions were clearly failing us, overburdened with bureaucracy and lacking in leadership. Just as the Irish government would bail out the Abbey in 2005, deeming it 'too big to fail', so would it consider itself obliged to bail out Ireland's banks in 2008. In doing so, they revealed that the 'gallous story' of the Celtic Tiger period was a fantasy designed to mask the 'dirty deeds' of bankers, politicians, property developers, and regulators. Synge's warnings about the dangers of self-delusion seemed more pertinent than ever.

Synge's plays could also be used to consider new ways of thinking about what it means to be Irish – and what it might mean to write an Irish play. Just as Druid would bring Synge to Asia, Pan Pan Theatre company brought a Chinese version of Synge back to Ireland in December 2006 (an event discussed in more detail in this volume by Sara Keating), performing it before an audience that included a substantial presence from Dublin's Chinese community. And a few months later, the Nigerian dramatist Bisi Adigun and Irish writer Roddy Doyle would collaborate on a new version of *The Playboy*, which opened at the Abbey during the 2007 Dublin Theatre Festival. Sadly, the future of that production was placed in doubt when a legal dispute arose about the issue of copyright and royalties – proving, perhaps, the ongoing power of Synge to excite controversy. Bisi Adigun contributes an essay to this volume in which he describes the process of writing the play with Doyle, and calls its opening night 'one of the most joyous moments of my life'. The later dispute is, he points out, a 'story for another day' (and, of course, we must remember that it's a story that has two sides, as all disputes inevitably will).[3] If the modern-day *Playboy* has now been overshadowed by a disagreement, we should not lose sight of the intercultural promise it seemed to offer. In an Ireland that seems ever more divided, it's important to be reminded of Synge's focus on the dignity of the outsider.

It's important, also, to be reminded that Synge did not just reflect upon his own society; he also anticipated much that would follow. In his contribution to this volume, Ben Levitas points out that Synge's treatment of censorship (and self-censorship) would become far more relevant after his death than it was during his lifetime. Synge would also become an important guiding influence for future Irish writers, among them Brian Friel (as Richard Pine illustrates), Marina Carr (as is shown by Emilie Pine), and Tom Murphy (as discussed by Alexandra Poulain).

Synge's influence on Ireland and its writers is important – but so too are the writers and countries that influenced him. Here again McCormack's biography is an important starting-point for the contributors to this volume, allowing Mary Burke to consider the interplay of Darwinism, botany and the Irish language in Synge's imagination – and being used by Shaun Richards to consider Synge's time in Europe and, in particular, his awareness of anarchism. Just as Europe influenced Synge, so would Synge influence Europe, as Ondřej Pilný illustrates in his case study of Czech productions of Synge in Prague. And we must also be aware of Synge's poetic influences: not just figures such as Dante but, as Ann Saddlemyer reminds us, contemporaries like the fascinating American poet Agnes Tobin.

Synge's influence on fields other than literature and drama is also important. For Éilís Ní Dhuibhne, he is an exemplary folklorist, someone with an ability to 'empathize with other people, to "get under their skins"', as all anthropologists (and most great writers) should. Mark Phelan draws out this feature of Synge's work in his exploration of popular and material culture in nineteenth-century rural Ireland – an argument developed from a different perspective by Paige Reynolds, who uses Synge's work to understand the culture where Phelan uses the culture to understand Synge. In both cases, as with all of the essays in this book, influence moves in both directions, allowing us to understand what shaped Synge, but also allowing us to consider how contemporary forces can influence our re-reading and re-staging of Synge's works.

All of the essays in this volume were delivered for the first time at the Synge Summer School, and I have invited the authors to retain (where possible) the sense that their papers were written to be spoken aloud and then discussed by a lively and engaged audience. There are areas of shared concern in the essays, but there are also intriguing divergences, in terms of scholarly methodology as well as theme. Brought together, what these essays aim to show is not just that there is much more to say about Synge – but that there are many different ways of talking about him, staging him, and being influenced by his legacies.

---

[1] Robert Hogan, 'Review. John Synge and Jack Yeats'. *Journal of Modern Literature*. 3:4 (April 1974) (1031-38): 1031.

[2] Fintan O'Toole, 'Bringing Death to Vivid Life'. *The Irish Times*, 19 July 2005: 10.

[3] At the time of writing, the dispute remained unresolved. A report in *The Irish Times* provides an account of the differing opinions in the matter. See Mary Carolan, 'Copyright breach claim over modern production of "Playboy" at Abbey'. *The Irish Times*. 18 May 2010. Fintan O'Toole offers a critique of the case in an opinion column 'Theatre Has Nothing to Declare but an Innate Uncertainty' in *The Irish Times*, 22 May 2010.

1 | THE POETICIZING OF SYNGE

Ann Saddlemyer

When I announced the title of this paper, a friend's first response was, 'what an ugly word!' It was even more jarring in its original form, 'the poeticization of Synge', though perhaps still more accurate. Since I am no linguist or rhetorician, I do not intend to delve deeply into the analysis of language – that has been done well and thoroughly by Alan Bliss, Nicholas Grene, Toni O'Brien Johnson, Declan Kiberd, Mary King, and others.[1] Rather, I am interested in exploring the process by which the playwright discovered his individual voice, created his own kind of poetry in which to express that voice, and achieved a distinctive style, what he called the 'portrait of one's own personality, of the colour of one's own thought' – or 'strengthening' by 'making personal'. So this paper falls somewhere between biography and criticism, exploration and meditation.

Synge's first published work did not promise much in terms of the personal or the original. A sonnet accepted by *Kottabos* when he was a twenty-one-year old Trinity student, it begins:

> O river could'st thou make response in words
> what questions I should ask of olden time!

and goes on to lament the

> changes since have crept o'er all thy glen
> And now a thrifty nation needs must strive
> To grow rich wheat where nought then lived but game.[2]

(One wonders how the earnest young Synge would have reacted to the Celtic Tiger or global warming.) Not surprisingly, that same year, two versions of a longer conversation in verse between the poet and a mountain flower were kindly but firmly rejected by the editor of the *Irish Monthly*. So – how did he get from the sentimental moralizing of 'Glencullen' and 'A Mountain Creed' to the hard concrete immediacy of this poem, so praised by Yeats?

A Question

> I asked if I got sick and died, would you
> With my black funeral go walking too,
> If you'd stand close to hear them talk or pray
> While I'm let down in that steep bank of clay.
>
> And, No, you said, for if you saw a crew
> Of living idiots, pressing round that new
> Oak coffin – they alive, I dead beneath
> That board, – you'd rave and rend them with your teeth.

Or, written in the same month (October 1908), this crisp translation from the thirteenth-century German of Walter von der Vogelweide?

> I never set my two eyes on a head was so fine as your head, but I'd no way to be looking down into your heart.
>
> It's for that I was tricked out and out – that was the thanks I got for being so steady in my love.
>
> I tell you, if I could have laid my hands on the whole set of the stars, the moon and the sun along with it, by Christ I'd have given the lot to her. No place have I set eyes on the like of her; she's bad to her friends, and gay and playful with those she'd have a right to hate. I ask you can that behaviour have a good end come to it?

T.S. Eliot once commented that the kind of poetry he himself needed as an adolescent writer, to teach him the use of his own voice, 'did not exist in English at all; it was only to be found in French'.[3] And it is interesting that when Synge turned from the study and practice of music to that of literature, his first attempts at self-expression beyond those early Wordsworthian hymns to nature were in the languages he was studying at the time – first in German (the draft of a play), then in French (essays of various kinds). When he considered the necessity of earning a living, it was as a journalist, optimistically as a leader writer on Irish literature for French newspapers. Probably he was influenced by his closest friend in Paris, Stephen MacKenna, a journalist who would later translate Plotinus; at any rate, when he bought a typewriter, it was to take to

Paris. Another early ambition was more exotic. Perhaps inspired by the romantic history of Lafcadio Hearn, whom his brother-in-law claimed as a cousin, he contemplated going to Japan. He even went so far as to commission his brother Samuel, who was about to embark as a medical missionary in China, to enquire about work as an interpreter on liners to the Far East. Whether Sam dissuaded him or his mother convinced him such a life would be unsuitable, we will never know; instead Synge enrolled in language courses at the Sorbonne (concentrating on Petrarch and French literature) and then moved on to Rome and Florence to further his study of Italian. Once back in Paris he exchanged language lessons and even joined a weekly debating society to encourage his public voice, scrupulously entering in his diary the number of times he spoke. And all the time, he continued his efforts to place articles on his travels and reading, though with limited success.

Well, we all know what happened then. Through a network of Irish exiles in Paris, Synge encountered W.B. Yeats, who was fired with enthusiasm for both 'a Celtic and Irish school of dramatic literature' and the Aran Islands. It is quite possible that this new acquaintanceship inspired Synge's next course at the Sorbonne, a study of Irish and Homeric civilizations, but it eventually led to his first trip to Aran two years after that meeting and, ten months after that, a journey to Brittany. On an early visit to Aran, he began experimenting with a translation of 'The Fate of the Children of Uisneach', but although he had studied Irish (and Hebrew) at Trinity College, he seems to have drawn the line at attempting to write anything in Irish apart from a few letters. Instead, he continued to pursue a life reporting on his experiences, achieving some modest success in Irish newspapers and journals with stories of Aran and the occasional book review.

Although we know that he was soon – though cautiously – involved in Yeats and Lady Gregory's plans for what would become the Irish Literary Theatre, Synge did not give up his room in Paris until he had completed the manuscript of *The Aran Islands* and submitted two plays to Willy Fay's Irish national dramatic company (soon to be superseded by Yeats and Gregory's organization). Nor did he cease studying European literature. In the late 1890s, he had shown two impressionistic pieces to MacKenna, 'Vita Vecchia' and 'Étude Morbide'; after completing *The Playboy* in 1907, he returned to these early works and began to revise them. A year later, when leaving his papers for Yeats to go through after his death, he wrote ambivalently: 'the other early stuff I wrote, I have kept as a sort of curiosity but I am anxious that it should not get into print ... I do not want my good things destroyed, or my bad things printed rashly'.[4] Clearly he needed to have that 'early stuff' heard, if not published.

The titles of these early works reflect both his literary studies and his musical ambitions. 'Vita Vecchia' ('the Old' – or rather, 'Later – Life') is modelled on – and a response to – *La Vita Nuova* ('the New' – or 'Early Life'), the earliest known work by Dante, whom Synge doubtless studied at the Collegio Romano in 1896. 'Vita Vecchia' (also entitled 'the Vale of Shadow') follows in miniature Dante's pattern of prose interspersed with poems; and, like the *Nuova*, his 'Vecchia' blends biography and allegory, reciting a series of dreams or, perhaps more accurately, dream-visions. Dante was recording his first glimpse as a nine-year-old boy of Beatrice, the idealized figure who haunted his dreams, his life, and that great work, *The Divine Comedy*. What is apparently the latest version of Synge's heavily annotated and incomplete draft begins: 'A young girl of the Roman Catholic Church spent nine weeks in the house where I lodged when I was studying music in Germany'.[5] That combination of Catholic faith, the number nine, artistic study and 'desolate faithfulness' to an unnamed young girl of great beauty, purity, and goodness suggests just how closely he was influenced by Dante. Synge goes further in complexity than his Italian model, however – three women are included in his narrative of loss. As W.J. McCormack says in his biography of Synge, it is fruitless to attempt to identify the women in this series of impressions (though many have tried);[6] more recognizable are the descriptions of the Wicklow hills he worshipped in his childhood and his distress at the briefness of the cycles of the natural world, themes that would remain with him for the rest of his life.

'Vita Vecchia' is made up of poems (fourteen in one version, eight in another) connected by prose passages which are at times straightforward narrative, reflecting recognizable incidents from Synge's experiences in France, Italy, and Ireland, and at other times dream-like visions of unattainable women. Again and again, this unfinished composition returns to a haunting celebration, not of the unapproachable 'white star-like' woman he sees a number of times, but of the 'wonderful glory' of the Irish countryside. Although the work was never completed, when Synge returned in 1907 to this 'series of dreams to my later life' he revised some of the poems included in it – but once again decided against publication. His first editor Yeats agreed, and so 'Vita Vecchia' remained in manuscript form until the publication of the *Complete Works* in the 1960s. (A fine description of the state of the manuscripts and transcription of two of the fullest drafts of 'Vita Vecchia' has been published by Ruth Connolly and Alex Davis in the Trinity College *Long Room Journal*.[7])

Synge's next 'Imaginary Portrait', 'Étude Morbide', written while he was living in Paris, again reflects his current interests. 'Vita Vecchia' reflected his admiration for Dante and the study of Italian (and also perhaps in its alternation of prose and poetry the medieval French *Aucassin et Nicolette*, another favourite and – as Declan Kiberd has pointed out – medieval Irish romances like the tales of the 'Three Sorrows' and the Sweeney narratives[8]). 'Étude Morbide' on the other hand is influenced by his reading of contemporary French writers such as Huysmans, Mallarmé, Baudelaire, Maeterlinck, and the legendary Villiers de l'Isle-Adam. (You will recall that Villiers' *Axel* had affected Yeats profoundly when he began to write his plays; Synge arrived in Paris after the production with its famous declaration, 'As for living our servants will do that for us', but the symbolist drama it heralded was still very much in the air.) It also signals Synge's eclecticism – Spinoza, Herbert Spencer, the Stoics, the mystics, and Thomas à Kempis, from whom he quotes in an unpublished dialogue between the saint and Rabelais.

Even the title – 'Étude' – reminds us of the artistic movements of the time: think of Claude Debussy, whose Impressionist compositions exemplified the transition from the late Romantic to twentieth-century modernist music and were inspired by the Symbolist movement in literature (settings of poetry by Verlaine, Baudelaire, and Mallarmé and the opera *Pelléas and Mélisande*, based on Maeterlinck's drama). Debussy's own *Études* were written later, but the form, a short musical composition emphasizing a particular technical skill and usually for a solo instrument, would have been familiar to Synge as a music student. I am sure that, like all earnest pianists, he practised Czerny's *Études* (still in vogue when I studied piano), though he would have been aware of the transformation of the form by later composers from Chopin up to the present day.

Although written as a series of diary entries, 'Étude Morbide' is closely related to 'Vita Vecchia', reaching beyond autobiography towards fantasy: once again, the hero is a violinist involved with more than one woman, who records his dreams and anguish at failing as an artist, and seeks solace in nature. But now it is not the Wicklow hills that provide comfort to the overwrought narrator but a journey to Finisterre, the northwestern part of Brittany which Synge had visited after his first trip to Aran.

In his instructions to Yeats, Synge insisted that this early 'morbid thing about a mad fiddler in Paris, which I hate' not be published.[9] He may have preserved 'Étude Morbide' because it is so closely related to his first completed play, *When the Moon Has Set*, the script he first submitted to Yeats and Lady Gregory as early as 1901; and his first play is already present in 'Vita Vecchia': 'At this time I began a long poem in blank verse about a nun who was set free from her bondage ... and met and married a person, who represented myself'.[10] *When the Moon Has Set* is more overtly autobiographical than either 'Vita Vecchia' or 'Étude Morbide', for it reflects Synge's anguish over the rejection by his first love Cherrie Matheson and, as Nicholas Grene and W.J. McCormack have shown, draws on tales of the inhabitants of Wicklow. But the ideas and musical motifs threaded through the 'Vita' and 'Étude' and all the versions of *When the Moon Has Set* have their origin in notebook jottings dating from Synge's first year in Paris, 1895.

That Synge kept all three, along with other early poems marked 'Reserved' and 'Biographical Matter only not to be printed as literary work' as well as other scattered scenarios and dramatic fragments, indicates how strongly he felt about self-preservation. An early draft of his preface to *Poems and Translations*, the last volume he was to see through the press (though he died two weeks before its publication) included this self-conscious and revealing defence:

> In publishing the following verses and sketches I am doing what I have sometimes decided it would be better to leave undone. They were written from five to eight years ago and, as is obvious enough, in Paris among all the influences of the so-called decadent and symbolist schools. Still I think as a man has no right to kill one of his children if it is diseased or insane, so a man who has made the gradual and conscious expression of his personality in literature the aim of his life, has no right to suppress himself any carefully considered work which seemed good enough when it was written ... To burn what one has written without giving at least one chance of existence is a sort of intellectual suicide against which one's instinct [cries] out ... At the moment of creation the balance of the critical and creative impulses which works in the forming of any artistic

production is the essential artistic element of the writer's temperament.[11]

The letter with which he submitted his poems for Yeats's assessment reinforces this ambivalent attitude:

> I do not feel very sure of them, yet enough of myself has gone into them to make me sorry to destroy them, and I feel at times it would be better to print them while I am alive than to leave them after me to go God knows where.[12]

The well-known published Preface is more confident, though there is a suggestion of the 'decadent and symbolist schools' in his description of the poetry of 'these days' being 'usually a flower of evil or good', and even in the assurance that 'it is the timber of poetry that wears most surely, and there is no timber that has not strong roots among the clay and worms'.[13]

Although in those early years he attempted both poetry and a play in German, Synge never contemplated writing verse in French; that language was reserved for his journalism. Where the young Eliot found endorsement, Synge found the French alexandrine 'strange, rigid and monotonous. I know that many passages written in this metre are truly beautiful and artistic but on account of its rhyming I don't think it is convenient for a long poem'.[14] 'Convenient' for Synge seems to mean appropriate to himself only or, as he was to jot down in a notebook, a work of art 'must have been possible to only one man at one period and in one place'.[15] Consider the phrase in his draft preface quoted above: the artist's job is to make 'the gradual and conscious expression of his personality in literature the aim of his life'. That early voice of his works in Paris, though self-consciously dismissed later as 'a sort of curiosity', was the first tentative step towards expression of his own personality. This meant not only in choice of subject but in style. It shows forth in passages in *When the Moon Has Set*, not in the stilted 'proper' speech of the hero, but in Bride, the young servant girl:

> She'll be coming in a minute I'm telling you, and let you be taking your own rest. You're wanting it surely, for we were thinking it's destroyed you'd be driving alone in the night and the great rain, and you not used to anything but the big towns of the world.[16]

While still at work on *When the Moon Has Set*, Synge had seen W.G. Fay's actors perform '*une pièce charmante*' in Irish, Douglas Hyde's

Casadh an tSúgáin ('The Twisting of the Rope', 1901). About the same time he reviewed Lady Gregory's *Cuchulain of Muirthemne*, praising her first extended use of what would become known as 'Kiltartanese':

> The Elizabethan vocabulary has a force and colour that make it the only form of English that is quite suitable for incidents of the epic kind, and in her intercourse with the peasants of the west Lady Gregory has learned to use this vocabulary in a new way, while she carries with her plaintive Gaelic constructions that make her language, in a true sense, a language of Ireland.[17]

But although in Synge's early play the setting and country speech recalls Wicklow, unlike Gregory's characters who are rooted along the Clare/Galway border, the Anglo-Irish artist-hero of *When the Moon Has Set* still longs for Paris.

The voice is stronger when it shelters in country speech – as in this unpublished ballad of the 1890s where in an encounter on the back roads of Wicklow a tramp argues that it is better to go to the workhouse than steal his way into the Glencree reformatory:

> That I'm jist goin' to the House
> Jist goin' to be a pauper
> To axe her gracious Majesty
> For a life of meal and torper.[18]

If Robin Skelton is correct in assigning the 'Ballad of a Pauper' to the mid-1890s when Synge was in his early twenties, such efforts in south Dublin dialect are unique, and too imitative of the style of the stage Irishman to be sufficiently what he would later call 'personal'. As late as 1902, while working on the early drafts of *Riders to the Sea*, *The Shadow of the Glen*, and even *The Tinker's Wedding*, he was still sufficiently influenced by nineteenth-century poetic drama to attempt two plays in blank verse: *A Vernal Play*, in which shepherds and maidens meet in the glens of Wicklow to admire the beauty of trees, flowers and sunsets, and *Luasnad, Capa and Laine*, based on a tale from Geoffrey Keating's *The History of Ireland*, where all the characters perish in the waves. Clearly he had read both Villiers's *Axel* and Yeats's *The Shadowy Waters*. A third effort, *The Lady O'Conor*, its plot taken from one of Pat Dirane's stories on Aran, also began in verse, but by 1904 had shifted uneasily to a prose somewhere between *The Shadow of the Glen* and *The Playboy of the Western World*. He did not turn his attention to verse-writing again for at least two years.

His search for *le mot juste* continued, however. Still caught up in aesthetic impressionism, his earliest published response to Aran depends on the vocabulary of Walter Pater: the words 'intense', 'curious', 'strange', 'luminous', 'magnificent', 'wonderful brilliancy', 'inconceivable', even 'delicious', frequently appear, and in his notebooks he acknowledges Pater's insistence on finding 'everything in the instant'.[19] On his first visit to the furthermost west of Ireland, he remarks on the 'affinity between the moods of these people and the moods of varying rapture and dismay that are frequent in artists, and in certain forms of alienation'.[20] As he is rowed over to Inishmaan from the larger island, he writes of the 'moment of exquisite satisfaction to find myself moving away from civilisation in this rude canvas canoe of a model that has served primitive races since men first went on the sea' (57). As with the 'grey poteen, which brings a shock of joy to the blood', Synge's impressions on his first two visits to Aran are charged with a Hopkins-like sensibility: 'there is hardly an hour I am with them that I do not feel the shock of some inconceivable idea, and then again the shock of some vague emotion that is familiar to them and to me' (113). Almost rhapsodic evocations of his own emotional response ('one of the moods in which we realize with immense distress the short moment we have left us to experience all the wonder and beauty of the world' [139]) are broken by matter-of-fact descriptions of island life and his remoteness from it when, like the old story-teller Pat Dirane, he provides 'minute details to show that he was actually present' (72). *The Aran Islands* concludes with the bare statement, 'The next day I left with the steamer' (184).

I need not labour the impact Synge's journeys to Aran made on his plays. Sufficient that 'the shock of new material', as he admitted himself, first in Paris and more irrevocably in the west of Ireland, created the style of language and story-telling we now recognize as his alone. And here comes that ugly word from my title, employed not by the poet Yeats but by his painter father John Butler Yeats, renowned for his portraits:

> The Irish peasant mind is not common, is indeed so interesting that the peasants in the west of Ireland can enjoy themselves in solitude, poeticized, if I may use such a word, by their religion, by their folk lore, and by their national history, and by living under a changeable sky which, from north to south and from west to east is a perpetual decoration like the scenery in some vast theatre ... Synge spoke of their poetical language, and ranked it above any written in his plays.[21]

Synge's teachers on Aran confirmed Pater's well-known assertion that all art aspires towards the condition of music; he would take that dictum as his own. When he meets his first guide, old Mourteen, he describes how the story-teller 'sat down in the middle of the floor and began to recite old Irish poetry, with an exquisite purity of intonation that brought tears to my eyes though I understood but little of the meaning' (56). The old woman in whose cottage he lived recited verses from Douglas Hyde's *Love Songs of Connacht* (1893) 'with exquisite musical intonation, putting a wistfulness and passion into her voice that seemed to give it all the cadences that are sought in the profoundest poetry' (112). On a later visit he was counselled by an old net-mender on Kilronan pier: 'A translation is no translation ... unless it will give you the music of a poem along with the words of it' (149). I have discussed elsewhere the musical form of *Riders to the Sea* and the contrapuntal/harmonic structure of his later plays.[22] Sound and feeling must work upon each other – but how does one translate that combination into words?

Ever since his days as an aspiring journalist, Synge had been intrigued by the challenge of translating the style and thought of one mind and language into another. Rumour has it that during his first months in Paris he collaborated with a friend on a translation of *Intentions*, Oscar Wilde's collection of theoretical essays and dialogues. We do not know whether that plan ever materialized, but contemplating the project alone would have sharpened his own concern with the question of style, which he described as the 'portrait of one's own personality of the colour of one's own thought',[23] and the relationship between personality and the natural world, 'possible to only one man at one period and in one place'.[24]

Synge therefore first deliberately 'translated' himself, and then as Declan Kiberd has pointed out in *Synge and the Irish Language*, became an accomplished, sensitive translator of others. The language in his first six plays heightens the qualities of the speech he heard on Aran and on the Wicklow roads, while remaining true to the thought behind it. (His training as a musician and a keen ear for rhythm and pattern enabled precision, even in what Toni O'Brien Johnson has called 'the clash of incompatibles';[25] sometimes of course he did not have to do anything more but quote selective phrases he heard.) Despite Yeats's attempt to memorialize his friend to suit his own needs, Synge's Abbey colleague was perceptive when he claimed, 'Perhaps no Irish countryman had ever that exact rhythm in his voice, but certainly if Mr Synge had been born a countryman, he would have spoken like that'.[26] The language he gives his characters is a deliberate creation, but it suggests a living, vibrant speech.

The 'shock of new material' led in a bare four years to the plays that culminated with *The Playboy of the Western World*. Then came another shock to the senses: during that time he fell deeply in love with the actress whom he himself coached (in the role of the Tramp) as Nora Burke in *The Shadow of the Glen* and who, triumphantly, became Pegeen Mike. In almost daily letters and frequent walks in the Wicklow hills Synge's courtship of young Molly Allgood became more and more intense; in 1906 he sent these lines (not included in the *Collected Works*) commemorating their artistic partnership and his delight in finding love at last:

> To you Bride, Nora, Kathleen, Molly Byrne,
> I of my age have brought the pride and power,
> And seen my hardness in your sweetness turn
> A new delight for our long fame a dower.
> And now you bring to me your young girl's pride,
> And sweeten with your sweetness all my days,
> Telling me dreams where our red lips have cried
> The long low cry that folds all earthly praise.
> And so in all our lot we hold a mart
> Of your young joy and my too gloomy art. [27]

While on Inishmaan Synge had observed that 'one is forced to believe in a sympathy between man and nature'.[28] That sympathy now became translated in his relationship with Molly: 'we both have a poetical strain in us,' he wrote to her:

> and we should take care of it – as one takes care of some rare flower in one's garden, that dies easily and leaves one the poorer forever. You feel as fully as anyone can feel all the poetry and mystery of the nights we are out in – like that night a week ago when we came down from Rockbrook with the pale light of Dublin shining behind the naked trees till we seemed almost to come out of ourselves with the wonder and beauty of it all. Divine moments like that are infinitely precious. [29]

This letter was written in 1906, and it is significant that he speaks here not as a playwright, but as a poet. In the early works, including *When the Moon Has Set*, the heroes are musicians; the simplicity and internal rhythms of *Riders to the Sea* depend upon a musical structure. But from *The Shadow of the Glen* on, that persona has been replaced by the poet: the Tramp who sings so sweetly of the joys of nature (and in whose role Synge wooed Molly); the zesty vulgar rhapsodies of the irrepressible old tinker woman Mary Byrne; the seductive urgings of blind Martin Doul; and of course, Christy Mahon, poet par excellence, who not only tells his story 'lovely' but wins 'a fiddle was played by a poet in the years gone by'.[30]

However, not since his Paris days does Synge appear to have thought of himself as a poet, until late in 1906 when his courtship of Molly became serious:

> I send you three of the old verses you may like to have them for old time's sake though you must not take them as specimens of my verse writing. They were really improvisations. Two others I have about you are better, but you could not read them they are so much pulled about ... Remember they are not particularly good examples of my verse although my heart is in them. [31]

Still he remained uneasy about his skills: 'I wish you'd read a lot of verse. I want some one who can tell me when if ever my verses are good. That is a thing I cannot do for myself and I've got to find out'.[32] Eventually he showed some of his poetry to John Masefield, who would later declare that 'Those who want to know what he was in himself should read the poems. The poems are like the man speaking. They are so like him that to read them is to hear him'.[33] And, as we have seen, when Synge finally realized he was dying, they were nervously submitted to Yeats.

Synge would have been delighted with Masefield's verdict, for in most of these mature verses, as in *Deirdre of the Sorrows*, he was 'pouring out [his] heart' to Molly; they were indeed 'the man speaking'.[34] While writing the preface to accompany these poems he condemns false poetic diction and material of the very kind he was guilty of writing in the 1890s. Now what was essential to 'vital verse' were humour and a 'poetic feeling for ordinary life', both qualities singularly lacking in such works as 'Vita Vecchia', 'Étude Morbide', and *When the Moon Has Set*. 'It may almost be said', he writes in his final artistic testament, 'that before verse can be human again it must learn to be brutal'.[35] And elsewhere:

> What is highest in poetry is always reached where the dreamer is leaning out to reality, or where the man of real life is lifted out of it, and in all the poets the greatest have both these elements, that is they are supremely engrossed with life, and yet with the wildness of their fancy they are always passing out of what is simple and plain. [36]

To Molly he commented, 'You are more interested in the natural and human side of art than in the very exalted or poetical ... That is as it should be, and I am the same I think'.[37] And many of his love poems reflect that, such as 'In May':

> In a nook
> That opened south,
> You and I
> Lay mouth to mouth.
>
> A snowy gull
> And sooty daw
> Came and looked
> With many a caw;
>
> 'Such,' I said,
> 'Are I and you,
> When you've kissed me
> Black and blue!'

When submitting his poems to Yeats, he explained his own evolving aesthetic. 'I am most interested now in my grim[m]er verses, and the ballads, (which are from actual life)'.[38] Two of those 'grimmer' poems – the ballad 'Danny' and the famous 'Curse' ('To a sister of an enemy of the author's who disapproved of *The Playboy*') – were rejected by a nervous Lolly Yeats, publisher of the Cuala Press. These and two others – 'The 'Mergency Man' (just as bloodthirsty and outrageous in language as 'Danny') and the love poem 'In Kerry' were restored by her brother for the first trade edition of *Poems and Translations*, published by Maunsel a year after the limited Cuala edition. There Yeats also added the bitter 'I've Thirty Months', precisely dated by Synge 25, ix, 1908 (59), written after his book was with Lolly's typesetters:

> I've thirty months, and that's my pride,
> Before my age's a double score,
> Though many lively men have died
> At twenty-nine or little more.
>
> I've left a long and famous set
> Behind some seven years or three,
> But there are millions I'd forget
> Will have their laugh at passing me.

Synge's selection for that first publication included only two love lyrics, and began with 'Queens':

> Seven dog-days we let pass
> Naming Queens in Glenmacnass,
> All the rare and royal names
> Wormy sheepskin yet retains:
> Etain, Helen, Maeve, and Fand,
> Golden Deirdre's tender hand,
> Bert, the big-foot, sung by Villon,
> Cassandra, Ronsard found in Lyon.
>
> Queens of Sheba, Meath and Connaught,
> Coifed with crown, or gaudy bonnet;
> Queens whose finger once did stir men,
> Queens were eaten of fleas and vermin,
> Queens men drew like Monna Lisa,
> Or slew with drugs in Rome and Pisa.
> We named Lucrezia Crivelli,
> And Titian's lady with amber belly,
> Queens acquainted in learned sin,
> Jane of Jewry's slender shin:
> Queens who cut the bogs of Glanna,
> Judith of Scripture, and Gloriana,
> Queens who wasted the East by proxy,
> Or drove the ass-cart, a tinker's doxy.
> Yet these are rotten – I ask their pardon –
> And we've the sun on rock and garden,
> These are rotten, so you're the Queen
> Of all the living, or have been.

Written with a strong dose of ironic humour, 'Queens' in style and language is an implied criticism of the well-known translation from Villon by Dante Gabriel Rossetti (who had published not one but two versions of Dante's *La Vita Nuova*). Synge's poem runs very close to the last two stanzas of Rossetti's version, entitled 'Ballad of the Dead Ladies':

> White Queen Blanche, like a queen of lilies,
> With a voice like any mermaiden –
> Bertha Broadfoot, Beatrice, Alice,
> And Ermengarde the lady of Maine –
> And that good Joan whom English-men
> At Rouen doom'd and burn'd her there –
> Mother of God, where are they then? –
> But where are the snows of yester-year?
>
> Nay, never ask this week, fair lord,
> Where they are gone, nor yet this year,
> Except with this for an overword –
> But where are the snows of yester-year?

Nor did Synge have any qualms about expressing publicly his view of the more anaemic art of some of his Irish contemporaries:

The Passing of the Shee

After looking at one of A.E.'s pictures.

> Adieu, sweet Angus, Maeve and Fand,
> Ye plumed yet skinny Shee,
> That poets played with hand in hand
> To learn their ecstasy.
>
> We'll search in Red Dan Sally's ditch,
> And drink in Tubber fair,
> Or poach with Red Dan Philly's bitch
> The badger and the hare.

Although Rabelais was called up in defence of *The Playboy*, and a version of Ronsard's epitaph on that great novelist and physician appears in one of Synge's poems, it was to the fifteenth-century poet, thief, and vagabond François Villon that Synge most frequently turned when seeking examples of the strong writing, the 'romance of reality' he now thought essential to poetry. In his early notebooks, Villon is his benchmark for 'the wonder of world set against the misery of age and death'.[39] Villon's poem 'The Beautiful Helmet Maker', becomes Synge's relentless 'An Old Woman's Lamentations' with the vivid description: 'That's what's left over from the beauty of a right woman – a bag of bones, and legs the like of two shrivelled sausages going beneath it'.[40] 'Prayer of the Old Woman, Villon's Mother' (previously translated by Rossetti and Swinburne), movingly reflects the original ballad, 'Lady in heaven, Empress here on earth' without the weaknesses he found in most contemporary lyric poetry (Yeats apparently excepted, though Yeats was never certain just what Synge thought of him).

That first edition of Synge's *Poems and Translations* also included Colin Muset's ironic, self-mocking complaint to his patron, which begins 'I'm getting old in your big house, and you've never stretched your hand with a bit of gold to me, or a day's wages itself'.[41] Added by Yeats to the trade edition of *Poems and Translations* the following year are two other representatives of the 'strong roots among the clay and worms'. Earlier I quoted Synge's translation from the thirteenth-century German minnesinger Walter von der Vogelweide, whose works he sought out on his final visit to Germany just months before his death (it is interesting but probably not relevant that Martin Luther translated one of Vogelweide's songs). From the cache of manuscripts Synge left him, Yeats also selected a translation from the early nineteenth-century Italian poet, scholar, and philosopher Giacomo Leopardi, contemporary of Schopenhauer. It may only be coincidence that both Villon and Leopardi are mentioned in Wilde's *Intentions*, which Synge certainly knew even if he did not work on the rumoured French translation. His version of Leopardi's lovely song 'To Silvia' includes only the first three stanzas, which Yeats thought a fitting conclusion to Synge's entire volume:

> Are you bearing in mind that time when there was a fine look out of your eyes, and yourself, pleased and thoughtful, were going up the boundaries that are set to childhood?
>
> That time the quiet rooms, and the lanes about the house, would be noisy with your songs that were never tired out; the time you'd be sitting down with some work that is right for women, and well pleased with the hazy coming times you were looking out at in your own mind.
>
> May was sweet that year, and it was pleasantly you'd pass the day.
>
> Then I'd leave my pleasant studies, and the paper I had smudged with ink where I would be spending the better part of the day, and cock my ears from the sill of my father's house, till I'd hear the sound of your voice, or of your loom when your hands moved quickly. It's then I would set store of the quiet sky and the lanes and little places, and the sea was far away in one place and the high hills in another.
>
> There is no tongue will tell till the judgment what I feel in myself those times.

With the exception of Colin Muset, whose complaint he rendered in both verse and prose, all of these translations – or rather versions – are written in prose, about the same time he was struggling to find a new voice for what became his last play, *Deirdre of the Sorrows*. In fact, some of the phrases used in the translations turn up in the play. Rather too casually, he had explained that *Deirdre of the Sorrows* was 'an experiment chiefly to change my hand'; 'it would be amusing to compare it with Yeats' and Russell's but I am a little afraid that the "Saga" people might loosen my grip on reality.'[42] He continued:

> when one comes to deal with them they seem very remote; one does not know what they thought or what they ate or where

they went to sleep, so one is apt to fall into rhetoric. In any case
I find it 'an interesting experiment', full of new difficulties, and
I shall be the better, I think, for the change.[43]

But I do not believe that either *Deirdre* or the translations of Petrarch, Dante, Villon, and others of this later period can be dismissed as merely 'five-finger exercises', despite his protestations. Admittedly, Synge did not search far for his models; like Muset, Leopardi and Villon were popular in the late nineteenth century. He is for example bound to have read Robert Louis Stevenson's short story about Villon, 'A Lodging for the Night'. And the 1901 play *If I Were King* was adapted from a novel of the same name by Justin Huntly McCarthy, of the well-known Irish political family. (In this romance, Villon is appointed by the King of France, Louis XI, to be Constable of France for a week. The 1925 operetta *The Vagabond King* is also based on this play, which has been filmed three times and made Villon so popular he even appears in *Archie and Mehitabel*.) It may well have been the very popularity of these European poets that led Synge to attempt translation from the original to his own voice, as far as possible from the 'poetry of the lyrical boy', the phrase with which he dismissed most contemporary poetry (again, Yeats excepted). But when Synge turned to the translation of Petrarch and Dante, he did not always adopt the convention of the courtly lover, nor did the impulse first come from Molly Allgood.

Ten years after writing 'Vita Vecchia' with its echoes of Dante, he wrote to her, 'I think I'll teach you Italian too so that you may be able to read the wonderful love poetry of these Italian poets Dante, and Petrarch, and one or two others'.[44] Inevitably, that led to a rewriting of that love-poetry in his own voice, influenced however by the voice of a different woman, one just as beautiful as Molly, but an artist of a different stripe. Who was she?

During the winter of 1904, while Synge and Lady Gregory were busy establishing the Irish National Theatre Society in Dublin, Yeats was on a lecture/reading tour of North America. While in San Francisco he made the acquaintance of the American poet Agnes Tobin, a wealthy and stunningly beautiful woman roughly his age who had found his play *Deirdre* 'a revelation'. In return she gave him a copy of her translations of ten sonnets and a canzone from Petrarch. Yeats was effusive in his praise:

> I delight in your Petrarch. I have read it over & over. It is full of wise delight ... a thing of tears & ecstacy especially that long

lyric at the end ... You have style, loftiness & your little book is the best thing I have found here ... they have in them not only the words which were taken from Petrarch, but in your own rhythm and vocabulary a certain ecstacy, a certain elevation.[45]

When he returned to England Yeats sent a copy of her translations to Arthur Symons: 'I think them very delicate, very beautiful, with a curious poignant ecstasy, and would have written about them but for my ignorance of Italian'.[46]

Agnes Tobin was no stranger to London, or to the company of poets. Daughter of a wealthy San Francisco banker, she was a frequent visitor to Europe and by the mid-1890s had become an intimate friend of the poet Agnes Meynell (who wrote the preface to Tobin's first book of translations) and her circle. By the time Yeats met her she was already friends with Joseph Conrad, who later dedicated *Under Western Eyes* 'To Agnes Tobin who brought to our door her genius for friendship from the uttermost shores of the West'. And thanks to Yeats's introduction, she became a loyal supporter of Symons, especially during his years of mental illness. Yeats continued to praise her work to others, claiming 'You are the greatest poet of America since Whitman'.[47] Later she would claim responsibility for Yeats's Civil List pension and become a devoted friend to his former lovers Florence Farr and Maud Gonne, who described her as an 'amusing talker' and 'the most glorious of human creatures'.[48] Her portrait by Augustus John, another close friend, shows her graceful, arched neck, downcast eyes, and masses of rippling hair; her nickname in England was 'Lily'.

Exactly when Agnes Tobin entered Synge's orbit is not documented. It may have been as early as March 1904 when his first two plays were performed in London; more likely, it was the following year when the Abbey Theatre returned to England in November 1905. They were certainly on closer terms by September 1906 when, back in Dublin, the company gave a copyright performance of Tobin's translation of Racine's *Phaedra*, which had been commissioned the previous year by Mrs Patrick Campbell but whose promised 'sumptuous production' never materialized. For a year or so, the directors contemplated including it in the Abbey repertoire. (Interestingly, among Synge's papers is a scenic breakdown of Racine's plays.) On the occasion of the copyright performance, the grateful author gave a dinner to the company, at which Synge did not hide his attraction for Molly. 'I shall never forget how beautiful that dear girl looked at dinner with her wreath'

Tobin wrote him the next day – 'it was something to burn candles before'.⁴⁹ Synge in turn wrote to Molly, 'Isn't Miss Tobin nice? I have to go to Waterford with her tomorrow for the day ... she wants to see the place as some of her people come from there and she does not like going alone, so she asked me to go with her'.⁵⁰ Another letter assures Molly, 'There is not of course the remotest sign of flirtation about us but I like her greatly, and value her friendship'.⁵¹ By now, Tobin was addressing him in her letters as 'My dear Friend'.

The two poets had much in common, especially their love of languages: she read and spoke French, German, Italian, and Spanish; read Latin and studied Greek at Stanford; at sixteen translated Schiller's *Mary Stuart*; and made her first visit to Paris about the same time Synge did, thereafter travelling widely in France and Italy where she became friends with some of the leading writers of the day. After the *Playboy* fracas, she urged him to write verse 'and take a rest from play writing'. But she also used her many powerful connections to try to get his work produced in America; she may have been responsible for the invitation by the American benefactor John Quinn – who through her initiative purchased manuscripts of both Symons and Conrad – that Synge take a rest cure in the United States.

In his turn, Synge advised her on the punctuating and proofreading of her translations; certainly by late 1906, he was reading Tobin's Petrarch – probably her recently published third volume – alongside the original texts he had previously studied in Paris ten years earlier almost to the day, and immediately began his own translations.

Here are examples of the renderings from Petrarch, first in Tobin's verse:

Sonnet X

> When all her golden beauty did unclose
> In Love's great noon and glory of desire,
> Slipping her sheath, and yearning higher, higher,
> Laura, my life, did leave me to my foes,
> And living, lovely disembodied, rose
> To the white wicket and the shimmering choir.
> Ah, why does not that 'last day' come and tire
> My soul for Heaven? – that last day one knows
> But as the first in Heaven. The same way
> That all my thoughts go, and as feather light,
> My soul would rise, a pilgrim keen and gay.

> Why must I wait, dear Christ? Why must I stay?
> Bitter and ever bitterer grows the fight.
> Had I but died three years ago today![52]

Synge's prose version is entitled 'He wishes he might die and follow Laura':

> In the years of her age the most beautiful and the most flowery, – the time Love has his mastery – Laura, who was my life, has gone away leaving the earth stripped and desolate. She has gone up into the Heavens, living and beautiful and naked, and from that place she is keeping her Lordship and her rein upon me, and I crying out, Ohone, when will I see that day breaking that will be my first day with herself in paradise?
>
> My thoughts are going after her, and it is that way my soul would follow her, lightly, and airily, and happily, and I would be rid of all my great troubles. But what is delaying me is the proper thing to lose me utterly, to make me a greater weight on my own self.
>
> Oh, what a sweet death I might have died this day three years to-day!

Here, Agnes Tobin after 'Sonnet LXXIV':

> The glorious angels, and those blessèd ones
> The citizens of Heaven, the first day
> My Lady enters there do block her way;
> Marvelling greatly, each to see her runs:
> 'What light is this? And what new beauty suns
> Its strangeness here?' They to each other say.
> Because a thing so gemmed, in such array,
> Has never come before. From sext till nones
> Preening herself, content with her new home,
> She shines the whitest-burning seraph down;
> But now and then the undazzled eyes will roam,
> The bird-bright head will turn, the jewelled gown
>
> Rustle and shimmer like to moonlit foam;
> She waits for me: and, oh, I come – my Crown!

Compared with Synge's 'Laura waits for him in Heaven':

> The first day she passed up and down through the Heavens, gentle and simple were left standing, and they in great wonder, saying one to the other: –

> 'What new light is that? What new beauty at all? The like of herself hasn't risen up these long years from the common world.'
>
> And herself, well pleased with the heavens, was going forward, matching herself with the most perfect that were before her, yet one time, and another, waiting a little, and turning her head back to see if myself was coming after her. It's for that I'm lifting up all my thoughts and will into the Heavens, because I do hear her praying that I should be making haste forever.

Without denying Agnes Tobin's achievement (and there is no record of what he thought), Synge has taken an entirely different path: the unapproachable is made familiar, the general become individual; most of all, the formal transformed to the colloquial in a free and vital mood. 'I only care for personal lyrical modern poetry and little of that,' he wrote while dismissing historical drama.[53] In realizing that it was necessary that he himself move on, he understood that poetry – and poetic drama – must change. 'For the present the only possible beauty in drama is peasant drama, for the future we must await the making of life beautiful again before we can have beautiful drama. You cannot gather grapes of chimney pots'.[54] A draft Preface to *The Tinker's Wedding*, which he was also revising in 1907, insists that 'when a work is rich and unique it must be taken freshly and directly from life, and it must be many-sided, so that it has a universal quality'.[55]

It is clear from his translations, written at the same time as *Deirdre of the Sorrows* and his later poetry, that Synge had found a solution similar to Petrarch's own. I do not know whether he had read Petrarch's defence of translation to Boccaccio: 'I quote the authors with credit, or I transform them honourably, as bees imitate by making a single honey from many various nectars'. Or, in another letter to Boccaccio:

> A proper imitator should take care that what he writes resembles the original without reproducing it. The resemblance should not be that of a portrait to the sitter – in that case the closer the likeness is the better – but it should be the resemblance of a son to his father'.[56]

Compare Synge's comments in his Preface to *Poems and Translations*: 'The translations are sometimes free, and sometimes almost literal, according as seemed most fitting with the form of language I have used'.[57]

But he also realized that what he had achieved could easily fall into bathos: Gerald MacNamara's *The Mist that Does Be on the Bog* (1909), a parody of *The Shadow of the Glen*, appeared very quickly after the first production, and many later imitations are rightly dismissed as 'Synge-Song'. When his German translator Max Meyerfeld asked for a simple transliteration of *The Well of the Saints,* Synge replied rather doubtfully:

> I can do a few pages at first, and then any particular passages that you find difficult. I do not think you will find the general language hard to follow when you have done a few pages, as the same idioms are often repeated, and the purely local words are not very numerous. However I perfectly understand that it will be a difficult language to translate.[58]

James Joyce, who considered *Riders to the Sea* 'the work of a tragic poet' and frequently chanted Maurya's final speech, wisely translated the play into standard Italian, trying to follow the original rhythms as closely as possible.[59]

Most successful have been artists who recognized his innovations and took their own way. Derek Walcott admits his play *The Sea at Dauphin* (1954):

> is modelled completely on *Riders to the Sea* ... As a young writer coming out of the Caribbean, all those models which are obvious didn't bother me because I had the same thing Synge had: a totally new language, a totally new set of rhythms, and a totally new people in a sense. [60]

And Mustapha Matura, whose adaptation *Playboy of the West Indies* (1984) gave him 'a wonderful opportunity to use the Trinidadian language of the period' recalled 'the richness and metaphorical power of the way people spoke' in his childhood. 'People don't seem to use language in the same metaphorical and magical way with that ironic sense of humour these days'. [61]

Remember the old net-mender's advice in *The Aran Islands*: 'A translation is no translation ... unless it will give you the music of a poem along with the words of it' (149). And perhaps most successful of all has been recognition from musicians. Vaughan Williams's operatic transformation of *Riders to the Sea* required only one additional line. Most recently the Yorkshire composer Gavin Bryars, fascinated with the sonnet form, discovered Synge's translations of Petrarch. The result has been seventeen madrigals, the first eight of which were first performed in Christ Church Cathedral in Dublin and the next nine in the Glen Gould studio in Canada. Not surprisingly, he is contemplating setting Deirdre's final soliloquy to music because of its 'strong Petrarchan feeling'.

Yeats was to admit of his colleague's achievement, 'In the arts he knew no language but his own'.[62] But I hope Synge would be pleased with this circling back to the music of his own beginnings.

---

[1] Alan J. Bliss, 'The Language of Synge' in *J. M. Synge Centenary Papers*. Edited by Maurice Harmon (Dublin: Dolmen Press, 1972). Nicholas Grene, *Synge: A Critical Study of the Plays* (London: Macmillan, 1975). Toni O'Brien Johnson, *Synge: The Medieval and the Grotesque* (Gerrards Cross: Colin Smythe, 1982). Declan Kiberd, *Synge and the Irish language*. 2nd ed (London: Macmillan, 1993). Mary C. King. *The Drama of J. M. Synge* (Syracuse: Syracuse University Press, 1985).

[2] J.M. Synge, *Collected Works, Volume I: Poems*. Edited by Robin Skelton (Gerrards Cross: Colin Smythe, 1982): 3.

[3] T.S. Eliot, *On Poetry and Poets* (London: Faber, 1957): 252.

[4] J.M. Synge, *Collected Letters, Volume 2*. Edited by Ann Saddlemyer (Oxford: Clarendon Press, 1984): 155.

[5] J.M. Synge, *Collected Works Volume II: Prose*. Edited by Alan Price (Gerrards Cross: Colin Smythe, 1982): 16.

[6] W.J. McCormack, *The Fool of the Family: A Life of J.M. Synge* (London: Weidenfeld and Nicholson, 2000): 156.

[7] Alex Davis and Ruth Connolly, 'J. M. Synge's "Vita Vecchia": An Autobiographical Palimpsest'. *The Long Room*, 50-51 (2005): 46-63.

[8] See Kiberd, *Synge and the Irish Language*.

[9] Synge, *Letters Volume 2*, 155.

[10] Synge, *Prose*, 19n.

[11] Synge, *Poems*, xiii-iv.

[12] Synge, *Letters 2*, 195.

[13] Synge, *Poems*, xiii and xxxvi.

[14] J.M. Synge, *Letters Volume 1*. Edited by Ann Saddlemyer (Oxford: Clarendon Press, 1983): 25n.

[15] See Synge, *Prose*, 349.

[16] J.M. Synge, *Collected Works, Volume III: Plays 1*. Edited by Ann Saddlemyer (Gerrards Cross: Colin Smythe, 1982): 157.

[17] Synge, *Prose*, 368.

[18] Synge, *Poems*, 8.

[19] Ann Saddlemyer, '"A Share in the Dignity of the World": J.M. Synge's Aesthetic Theory' in Robin Skelton and Ann Saddlemyer (editors): *The World of W.B. Yeats* (Seattle: University of Washington Press, 1965) (207-19): 215.

[20] Synge, *Prose*, 74.

[21] John Butler Yeats, *Early Memories: Some Chapters of Autobiography* (Dublin: Cuala Press, 1923): 81

22 Ann Saddlemyer, 'Synge's Soundscape' in *Interpreting Synge: Essays from the Synge Summer School, 1991-2000*. Edited by Nicholas Grene (Dublin: Lilliput Press, 2000): 176-91.
23 Saddlemyer, 'Dignity', 211-12.
24 See Synge, *Prose*, 349.
25 Johnson, *Synge: The Medieval and the Grotesque*, 171.
26 Synge, *Plays 1*, 64.
27 Quoted in J.M. Synge, *Letters to Molly*. Edited by Ann Saddlemyer (Cambridge: Belknap Press of Harvard University Press, 1971): xiv.
28 *Prose*, 75
29 Synge, *Letters 1*, 268.
30 Synge, *Plays 2*, 145.
31 Synge, *Letters 1*, 244-5.
32 Synge, *Letters 1*, 321.
33 John Masefield, *John M. Synge: A Few Personal Recollections with Biographical Notes* (New York: Macmillan, 1915): 11.
34 Synge, *Letters 2*, p 80.
35 Synge, *Poems*, xxxvi.
36 Synge, *Poems*, xv.
37 Synge, *Letters 1*, 267.
38 Synge, *Letters 2*, 195.
39 Saddlemyer, 'Dignity', 211.
40 Synge, *Poems*, 80.
41 Synge, *Poems*, 82.
42 Synge, *Letters 2*, 56.
43 Synge, *Letters 2*, 122.
44 Synge, *Letters 1*, 267.
45 Qtd. in W.B. Yeats, *Collected Letters Volume III, 1901-1904*. Edited by John Kelly and Ronald Schuchard (Oxford: Oxford University Press, 1994): 545-6.
46 W.B. Yeats, *Collected Letters, Volume IV, 1905-1907*. Edited by John Kelly and Ronald Schuchard (Oxford: Oxford University Press, 2005): 144.
47 Yeats, *Letters IV*, 436.
48 Maud Gonne and W.B. Yeats, *The Gonne-Yeats Letters*. Edited by Anna MacBride White and A. Norman Jeffares (Syracuse: Syracuse University Press, 1994): 271.
49 Qtd. in Synge, *Letters to Molly*, xix.
50 Synge, *Letters 1*, 205.
51 Synge, *Letters 2*, 255.
52 Quotations from Agnes Tobin are from *Agnes Tobin: Letters, Translations, Poems With Some Account of her Life*. 400 copies were privately printed by the Grabhorn Press for John Howell, San Francisco, 1958.

53 Synge, 'Historical or Peasant Drama' in J.M. Synge, *Playboy of the Western World and Other Plays* (Oxford: World's Classics, 1998): 149.
54 Synge, *Plays 2*, 394.
55 Synge, *Plays 2*, 291.
56 See Reed Way Dasenbrock, *Imitating the Italians* (Johns Hopkins University Press, 1991).
57 Synge, *Poems*, xxxvi.
58 Synge, *Letters 1*: 115.
59 James Joyce, *Occasional, Critical and Political Writing*. Edited by Kevin Barry (Oxford: World's Classics, 2002): 209.
60 Derek Walcott, *Conversations with Derek Walcott*. Edited by William Baer (Jackson, Mississippi: University Press of Mississippi, 1996): 24
61 Qtd. in Paul F. Botheroyd, 'Ireland and the Caribbean, Two Caribbean Versions of J.M. Synge's Dramas', in *Perspectives on Irish Drama and Theatre*. Edited by Jacqueline Genet and Richard Allen Cave (Gerrards Cross: Colin Smythe, 1991): 88.
62 W.B. Yeats, *Autobiographies*. Edited by W.H. O'Donnell and D.N. Archibald (New York: Scribner, 1999): 378.

2 | CENSORSHIP AND SELF-CENSURE IN THE PLAYS OF J.M. SYNGE[1]

Ben Levitas

Consoling the much put-upon Priest in *The Tinker's Wedding*, J.M. Synge's ferocious old traveller Mary Byrne softens into momentary sympathy at his lot: 'It's destroyed you must be' she says, 'hearing the sins of the rural people on a fine spring'.[2] Here set out, with an energetic economy, are some of Synge's central concerns. The phrase relates moral codes to sexual behaviour, setting the religious sense of transgression against spring-induced natural urges. It also offers the dynamics of confession as a licensed expression, operating within socially sanctioned circumstances and to a select audience. The image operates as a kind of minor metatheatrical gesture, calling imagined audiences to attend their parallel experience, as they suffer to be told Synge's shameful stories of country folk, and take upon themselves the task of censure. The phrase turns the confessional into the smallest theatre in Ireland and requires the theatre likewise to be a space of judgement. Between them, Synge acknowledges knowingly that in the Ireland of his time, his drama had little room to manoeuvre, but that its tight space was capable of binding in the theatricalities of reception.

This metadramatic dimension of Synge's work constantly locates the theatre as a material art, bridging society and culture: its self-awareness carries an insistence linking sex and violence to their licence, and that licence to the specifics of social relations. The performative process of confessional exchange requires that it remain part of corporeal relations. Responding to Mary Byrne, the priest, clearly exhausted by his unendingly redemptive labour, is thrown into relief against the energy of the 'rural people' who, in addition to their physical trials, have still the capacity for temptation. As the priest agrees, 'It's a hard life, I'm telling you, a hard life' (19).

The Tinker's Wedding was an apt vehicle for such expansive pith. In September 1905, W.B. Yeats declared its performance and publication 'too dangerous at present',[3] and Synge did not disagree with this evaluation. He knew that the play was 'too immoral for Dublin'.[4] Indeed, in composing a play in anticipation of rejection, Synge was taking the measure of acceptability. In a pre-revolutionary Ireland rapidly fixing Catholic identity as a key aspect of cultural difference, Synge's tale certainly tested the bounds of tolerance. But, through emphasis upon occluded issues of desire and conflict, it did so with a pointedly progressive emphasis on the way in which class and gender difference amplify the alienation felt by cultural outsiders, whether tramps, poets or, in this case, 'tinkers'. For Synge's imagined marginalia, the consensual impulse to conform forms a denial, masking widening fracture. In performance, however, this process is exposed, as the imposition of consensus is forced to manifest itself as a category of censorship.

The Tinker's Wedding, as a title, holds this irony concisely: the 'tinker', a label with connotations of the economically straitened, socially indecent, and culturally marginal, is placed in conjunction with demands of decency and social convention – the wedding. Drawn to the proprieties of a respectable life, Sarah Casey's attempt to marry Michael Byrne is frustrated by a fundamental problem: the sacrament is beyond her means. She strikes a deal with the Priest, who settles for 'a crown along with the ten shillings and the gallon can' Michael Byrne is making, but the bargain is always vulnerable to the 'heathen' appetites of Mary, who takes the can to sell for drink. Once denied purchasing power, Sarah tries menacing the priest, each threat comically pushing her further out from the codes of behaviour to which she aspires. The theme and function of the play thus combine, as the action at this point also pushes the possibility of its performance out of reach of Irish acceptability.

If, as has been said, the Travellers are Ireland's 'Other',[5] Synge does not merely invite the audience to partake of their traducement. Rather he appropriates their marginality to the other marginality of avant-garde performance, linking their assumed energy to the dynamism of the banned. In the final coup de grace, the three finally turn on the Priest, tying and gagging him, binding a sack over his head. Mary Byrne chides him to reflect upon the error of his ways, 'the way you'll not be so airy again going to rob poor sinners of their scraps of gold' (47), and makes the priest's release – and survival – conditional upon an oath not to report them. The social censor is thus himself silenced, if only until he finds his loophole: 'I've sworn not to call the hand of man upon your crimes to-day; but I haven't sworn I wouldn't call the fire of heaven from the hand of the Almighty God. [*he begins saying a Latin malediction in a loud ecclesiastical voice.*]' (49).

The play thus ends with a recognition that the coming cultural power lay with the Church, not the theatre (or the Travellers). It posits its own defeat in an imagined double denunciation, echoing offstage and on. In anticipating final failure, the play censures its own tendency for naïve confrontation. These ironies are further embellished by the fact that the audience for which the play was intended was discreetly denied the possibility of a performance. Merely reading the published product brings the work closer to the nature of a private confessional than to a public hearing, muting the themes of trespass the play explores. It is the possibility of physical, public embodiment that shows the play's power as being rooted in display rather than evocation.

Usefully, this returns us to the importance of construing Synge as a writer for the stage, not just the page. It is the action of binding and gagging, not the verbal threat, that provokes. And in pushing the play beyond the pale, Synge also pushed it across the footlights. The ever-present issue of his works' troubled reception continually insisted on the recognition of social agency rather than artistic autonomy. Yeats and Lady Gregory, in censoring Synge, were forced into priestly restriction rather than an embrace of stylized peasant bohemia. Imagining audience outrage, they had to adopt a shared taboo; if anyone was to be gagged it was the playwright rather than the Priest. Cultural pragmatics won out over aestheticism. Launching the Abbey, Yeats had been proud of the new theatre's capacity to resist the agitprop imperatives of radical nationalists, declaring that there would be 'no propaganda but that of good art'.[6] Here, though, was a case of no art being the best propaganda available.

However exceptional in its provocation, Synge's interrogation of conventionality in *The Tinker's Wedding* is notably typical of his work in a number of respects. It considers notions of piety, respectability, and acceptance. In testing the dynamics of conventionality, it fixes on the nature of sexual relations and of violence. The examination of morality is typically done in the context of the material struggles and 'hard' lives of those depicted. That depiction, insisting on the physical ('hard') fact of performance as a social act, acts to offset the transformative capacity of imaginative, poetic power. Further, it is all accomplished with one reflexive eye on the way the wider social dynamics of reception resonate with the action, doubling up the drama of censure and consensus with the theatrical issues of convention and censorship.

It is worth noting the international dimensions of such subjects. Synge's capacity to strain the patience of a particular Irish audience has been so thoroughly scrutinized that it is easy to forget that the questions raised thereby extended far beyond Irish attitudes. Bourgeois anxieties regarding public access to inappropriately indiscreet displays were meat and drink to what claimed the title 'modern drama', and it is a commonplace that for the European avant-garde, the public ban, the theatre riot, or indeed sheer unperformability were often considered as badges of success rather than symptoms of failure. Such changes in aesthetic intent put legislators on their mettle, as issues of artistic integrity impacted upon the social perception of legitimate expression – particularly regarding 'obscenity' – in the early decades of the twentieth century. This was by no means confined to Britain; by 1910, a French initiative produced a conference in Paris to draw up an international convention to regulate the distribution of obscene publications, which roped in the United States, Britain, Germany, Austria-Hungary, and Russia. This was the beginning of a complex process in which modern states legislated for categories of the acceptable, while anxiously noting that modernist strategies often purposely violated them.[7] Both the UK and Ireland had, well into the latter stages of the twentieth century, stringent laws operating literary censorship. But it is worth noting the interesting contrast that evolved: in the Irish Free State and Republic tight restriction of publications coexisted with a theatre that was given relative freedom (despite occasionally falling prey to clerical influence, particularly in the 1950s); whilst in Britain the theatre was more closely monitored than any other form.[8] Postcolonial Ireland preserved the conditions which had given Irish theatre practice curious exemption under British rule. In Ireland, British rule had anomalously offered no official state censorship. The jurisdiction of the Lord Chamberlain did not extend to Dublin, which was regulated through the altogether cruder means of the Lord Lieutenant issuing – and potentially rescinding – specific theatre patents. In Britain, by contrast, a strict stage censorship, established in 1737, continued until 1968. In the first decade of the twentieth century, Ibsen's *Ghosts*, Shaw's *Mrs Warren's Profession*, and Wilde's *Salome* (along with *Oedipus Rex*) were all held to be unworthy of public exposure. The gap was demonstrated during the *cause célèbre* that was G.B. Shaw's *The Shewing Up of Blanco Posnet*, a play forbidden in England but defiantly performed by the Abbey in 1909. As Yeats and Lady Gregory had guessed, the removal of licence by the agencies of British power in Ireland was, by then, rendered politically non-viable: an indication of the crudity of the mechanism in place. Such measures were ill suited to Liberal Home Rule sensibilities, which were generally disposed to greater freedom both for Ireland *and* for the theatre (at least until the First World War stiffened attitudes).

Defence of artistic freedom nevertheless had a potent influence on figures of the Irish Revival; in 1907, Synge (still smarting from the *Playboy* riots), Yeats, and Shaw had joined with seventy-one other writers in signing an open letter condemning the British censor.[9] Such common cause started early for those (Shaw, Wilde, Yeats) who were rooted in London. Hostility to censorship was built into the development of radical opinion, included within a broad remit of subversion at the Imperial centre. Not all such approaches were consistent. Critiques of the Lord Chamberlain and his role in censoring the stage in Britain could produce very different expressions of what might constitute the 'Freedom of the Theatre'. William Archer, one of the champions of 'New Drama', campaigned against the Chamberlain's Office as a Nannying institution which inhibited the mature development of discerning public taste:

> At present the public feels little or no responsibility for the morals of the stage; but the deliberate abolition of the censorship by the representatives of the people would be, in effect a formal engagement on the part of the said people to assume the charge which, rightly considered, is inalienably theirs. The mere sense of responsibility is an education and when once the public is awakened to its responsibility, I am very much deceived if, in any average audience, there would not be a clear majority on the side of decency .[T]he public, the true censor, is always on the spot, and its authority no one can evade.[10]

If uttered in a spirit dedicated to the emancipation of theatre practice, Archer's promotion of audience authority is here offered as a reassurance to the powers-that-be that overtly coercive restriction is unnecessary, given the security of hegemonic systems of thought. The democratic possibilities suggested in Archer's analysis are self-consciously progressive, but his construction of an audience as a generically average public, inclined to uphold conventional decencies, fundamentally construed the democratic possibilities of the theatre in consensual terms. An audience can be trusted to uphold social norms, whereas more turbulent aspects of the democratic process – the conditions of dissent, disturbance, fracture, conflict, and contestation – are reassuringly kept in abeyance.

A more stringently polemical approach to the question was posited by Shaw, a fellow campaigner for greater freedom in the theatre, whose work regularly fell foul of the censor's judgement. Shaw, absorbing the impact both of the Parnell scandal and the London debut of *Ghosts*, identified such theatrical struggles in *The Quintessence of Ibsenism* in more combative terms:

> The point to seize is that social progress takes effect through the replacement of old institutions by new ones; and since every institution involves the recognition of the duty of conforming to it, progress must involve the repudiation of an established duty at every step.[11]

In place of the 'people' and the 'public', we are given the 'social' and the 'institution'; and in place of 'responsibility', we have 'repudiation'. A mature theatre culture, Shaw suggested, is to be characterized not by convention, but by unconventionality. Identifying Ibsen as an archetypal pioneer, he posits that unpleasant plays provide the opportunity of revealing accepted standards as false. With progress, he suggested, the unacceptability of the play will be transferred to the convictions, previously held, that once opposed it. This conception of the theatre considered its generation in dialectical terms, insisting the question of censorship to be political rather than simply moral. However, it also construed that dialectic in terms of a kind of instructive antithesis, in which the pioneer-artist is granted new licence on the grounds of special status. The censor is to be divested of its power, but rather than being transferred to the audience, it is delivered to the author – which from Shaw's point of view was no bad thing. As he declared to a parliamentary committee in 1909: 'the toleration of heresy and shocks to morality on the stage, and even their protection against the prejudices and superstitions which necessarily enter largely into the morality of public opinion, are essential to the welfare of the nation'.[12] On the one hand, Shaw suggests that the theatre is inevitably mired in social substance, on the other that its art should be awarded an autonomy that carries it above the combat. The alternatives aired by Archer and Shaw were played out differently again in the context of the absence, as it were, of an Irish censor. As Joan Fitzpatrick Dean has demonstrated, the politics of censorship and censoriousness in Ireland were a complex weave that brought in questions of nationalist aesthetics, artistic licence, issues of class and gender, as well as religious sensibilities and colonial jurisdiction.[13] The ambivalent relationship with state control of theatre in Britain often gave Ireland greater freedom, while posing a series of unsettling questions for its nascent sense of statehood.

Which returns us to J. M. Synge. The reception of Synge's work by Abbey audiences has received sustained scrutiny in recent times.[14] Their 'horizons of expectation' have been repeatedly scanned. The best of this work records a rich variety of responses – rather than a simply polarized opposition between Protestant Anglo-Irish art house authors and patriotically pietistic patrons constrained by idealized notions of the Catholic Gael. The debates and discussions which emerged in the formative years of the national theatre(s) were thoroughly involved with a politics of representation that recognized the importance of that politics in the struggle for independence; but it also involved other emancipatory currents – regional, generational, socialist, feminist – that cut across the national question. Synge's work reflexively participated in such discussions. Central to that debate, fixed on what kind of Ireland a free Ireland might be, was that sense of censorship explored by Archer, contested by Shaw, and elaborated by W.B. Yeats. The capacity of the Irish urban Catholic middle (and lower middle) class to flex its muscle in the Revival theatre expressed a liberated sense of its powers, an attitude that bode well for the nationalist cause. A new demos was in the making. In its confident anticipation that its powers of censure could be formalized with independence, however, the marginalized, critical challenges produced by radical voices were potentially threatened. As is well documented, Synge's provocative effect on the progress of the Irish Revival began with the very first production of his work, *The Shadow of the Glen*, in 1903. From the start of the play, Nora's confidential intimation that her apparently dead husband 'was always cold, every day since I knew him ... and every night, stranger' signals Synge's intent to restore, as he put it, 'the sex element to its natural place'.[15] By the time Nora is forced out at the end of the play, to a life on the roads with a romantically eloquent tramp, the natural place of this 'sex element' has been firmly established in controversy: it is a key issue and energy in the repudiation of duty and convention. Synge is plainly on the Shavian side of the argument: the Ibsenite echoes in the play are clear, and apparently mobilized to make manifest the author's intention to disrupt social norms.[16] W.B. Yeats certainly took the play as a cue to assert this theatre as above, or beyond, reproach: '[W]e must learn', he wrote, 'that beauty and truth are always justified of themselves ... They judge and are above judgement'.[17] Crucially, however, Synge freights the romantic ideal of bohemian release with a darker cargo: the material recognition of the facts of poverty and privation. It is sensual physicality that connects these apparent oppositions. Nora Burke's sexual appetites are tempered with a certain tough cynicism: 'if it's a power of men I'm after knowing,' she confesses to her suitor, 'they were fine men, for I was a hard child to please, and a hard girl to please [*she looks at him a little sternly*] and it's a hard woman I am to please this day' (49). Adultery is a calculated release from a marriage dictated by economic necessity, and Nora counts out her dowry '*listlessly, in little piles on the table*' (49) to demonstrate that finance is always in play. Likewise, although the deathbed pretence of Dan Burke is all the more comic because his health is clearly preternaturally robust, this is established as an irony given a brutal environment where nothing can be heard but 'the wind crying out in the bits of broken trees were left from the great storm' (49). By rights, he should be dead by now. The tragic vulnerability of life in *Riders to the Sea* shadows this comedy from the start.

Throughout this sexual drama, language is salted with realism, as much as it is mobilized as a romantic, liberating force. Nora undercuts the tramp's seductive evocations of nature with the wry supposition that 'it's myself will be wheezing that time with lying down under the heavens when the night is cold'. '[B]ut', she concedes, 'you've a fine bit of talk, stranger, and it's with yourself I'll go' (57). The action onstage reiterates this ambivalence. The tramp's most commanding register emerges at the point of ejection, focused upon and framed by the doorway: a portal controlled by the master of the house. Warm language offers a small night fire to huddle by rather than a glorious new dawn. What sexual freedom is gained comes at the cost of social exclusion. The fact that the patriarch is not dead at all emphasizes the point that oppressive structures are not simply dispatched and forgotten, but endure in the absence of those expelled.

The prolonged controversy that met this play, and its denunciation as unrepresentative slander upon the good name of Irish womanhood, has been thoroughly examined elsewhere.[18] I would note here only that the reception shifts Synge toward more complex outcomes in subsequent plays. Although *The Shadow of the Glen* is shadowed by future struggle, it finally exudes emancipatory confidence. As Synge became more aware of the hostility to his work, however, the balancing of an awareness of his own vulnerability to criticism evolves into a theatrical working-through of the role of his art in influencing Irish life. Synge does not relinquish his need to upset or challenge; his discussions of sensual imagination move toward an enquiry into the presumptions of artistic imagination. And once again, this examination emerges in a materialist underpinning of rhetoric and fantasy.

A key text here is that fable of alienation, *The Well of the Saints*, particularly the second act, in which Martin Doul, the blind beggar given sight, rejects his wife to woo Molly Byrne. For this central act in the play, Synge shifts from a comic to a sombre idiom, and sets his scene at the smithy, where the once itinerant tramp is struggling with his new role as a labourer. Finding himself able-bodied, Doul discovers his worth is now determined less by abstract humanity than by the exchange value of his labour. Timmy the blacksmith declares, 'Working hard? I'll teach you how to work hard, Martin Doul'.[19] In a short dialogue this reiteration of the word 'hard' includes within its ambit labour, difficulty, durable objects and objective acknowledgement of the world's suffering. Doul responds: '(*Taking stick*) That's a hard terrible stick, Timmy'. And again: 'It's a hard thing for a man to have his sight, and he living near to the like of you [*he cuts a stick and throws it away*], or wed with a wife [*cuts a stick*], and I do be thinking it should be a hard thing for the Almighty God to be looking on the world, bad days' (105). The elaboration of work, physically performed, in terms of such various hardships, prepares the way for a more sensual physicality. The scene moves on to Martin Doul's explanation of his revelation in seeing the gap between Molly's physical beauty and his own decrepitude. It is, he says: 'the like of little children do be dreaming after in the dark night that its in grand houses of gold they are, with speckled horses to ride, and do be waking again, in a short while, and they destroyed with the cold, and the thatch dripping, maybe' (113). For Doul's expression of the polarities of fantasy and reality, Synge engages social simile – pinned by the rhyme of gold with cold – to describe the personal, abrupt trauma of revelation the character has experienced.[20]

In more than one sense, Martin Doul *realizes* what he is missing. The effect is to pull in unrequited passion as an element of alienated social experience, a kind of double denial. Again, the conjunction insists that the question of physical desire, being material, always includes the sexual as part of a socially constructed set of possibilities. The connection is maintained as Martin Doul continues the imaginative return to comfort via his fantasies of Molly Byrne:

> Lying down across a sop of straw, and thinking I was seeing you walk, and hearing the sound of your step of a dry road, and hearing you again, and you laughing and making great talk in a high room with dry timber lining the roof' (113).

Molly Byrne, scandalized and impressed by the ability to deploy such imaginative power, is drawn in to spur him on: [*half invitingly*]. 'It's a fine way you're wanting to pay Timmy the smith ... and it's not his *lies* you're making love to this day, Martin Doul' (115).

Martin Doul's 'making love' to Molly Byrne involves a poetic register, rooted in the newly seen. In this literal assertion of artistic vision, beauty is freshly minted when the eye of the beholder is renewed. Doul emphasizes that his sense of Molly Byrne's beauty can, through a poetic language giving that marvel form, make Molly's own image unfamiliar to herself. But the coin of this beauty is two-sided: the defamiliarization is both an opportunity for Byrne to re-imagine her position, and an assertion of an objectifying gaze:

> **DOUL.** [*seizing the moment that he has her attention*]. I'm thinking by the mercy of God it's few sees anything but them is blind for a space (*with excitement*). It's few sees the old women rotting for the grave, and it's few sees the like of yourself [*He bends over her*], though it's shining you are, like a high lamp would drag in the ships out of the sea.
>
> **MOLLY BYRNE.** [*shrinking away from him*]. Keep off from me, Martin Doul. (117)

The disjuncture stresses the significance of staging and its relation to the themes apparent in the text. Synge's instructions for Martin –

his seizing of Molly's attention; his excitement; his bending over her – provoke Molly Byrne's response of '*shrinking away*'. The body language thus acts to counterpoint the poetic language, challenging Doul's attempt to lyrically project an amorous conviction upon the object of his desire. In so doing, it draws the attention back to the potential of construing aspects of sight and blindness as elements of the performed and the censored. '[I]t's few sees anything but them is blind for a space' imaginatively deploys the idiomatic meaning 'a period of time' with an added connotation of renewed spatial awareness. Alteration over time reveals the social dimensions of space, and historicizes the options available for the censure of perceived 'truths', as well as facts to which we prefer to remain blind – not to mention whatever social agencies act to delimit our sight.[21]

Molly's rejection of Martin Doul acknowledges that solipsistic fantasy is vulnerable to the shifting gaze of the theatre audience, that the idealized vocal powers of the tramp in *The Shadow of the Glen* are no longer bewitching in their capacity to override alternative perceptions (in this case the woman pursued). Here physical action contests the lyrical, and with metatheatrical percussion: the scene reflexively acknowledges Synge's hubris in expecting to woo and win the audience. Seamus Deane's criticism of a process by which, 'mesmerized by an eloquence we concede the imagination a radical autonomy' is thus overtly anticipated and arrested.[22] Molly, tellingly, is only '*half-mesmerised*' (117). What engenders resistance to Synge's powers of persuasion is their tendency to alienate rather than seduce. What repulses is Martin Doul's need to reify the object of his desire into something irreducible, not merely the young and not rotting, but that which is permanent, constant, and heroic: an unchanging beacon to the lost.

The Well of the Saints airs Synge's sense of complicity in the structures of power he intends to critique. The idea or ideal expressed, the desire to share vision, is always snared in the material processes that allow it form. We are reminded at the beginning of the play that only a saint can deliver redemption unblemished: 'for I'm told the holiness of the water does be getting soiled by the villainy of your heart, the time you'd be carrying it, and you looking round on the girls, maybe' (79). Whatever Synge delivers to his audience will be flavoured with something of his self, soured, perhaps, by the hands that carry it. Yet this is no mere corruption: it asserts a dialectic in which the ideal is itself redeemed by the vibrancy of ephemeral, physical being. Synge's sketch for a dialogue between Rabelais and Thomas à Kempis offers an early model of the carnivalesque: 'At a fair also with ale and the sound of fiddles and dancers and the laughter of fat women the soul is moved to an ecstasy which is perfection and not partial'.[23] In *The Well of the Saints,* this perfect 'laughter of fat women' is also interrogated. Molly Byrne carries the holy water to the church, and perhaps into it seeps something of her own effervescent thrill in life. But it takes on some of her shallowness too. What the dialectic illuminates is that to designate the physicality of the peasant as joyful is to idealize it, to abstract it from the very properties that allow pleasure in the first place. Synge, like Martin Doul, is in danger of leaning over the object of his desire, idealizing it as a studied joy, and missing the lack of reciprocation. Catching himself in the act, as it were, he has to step back. Rabelais also upbraids à Kempis: 'You had all the poor and the vanquished who having nothing on the earth looked for treasure in Heaven'.[24] In this light, aspiration to the ideal emerges from the brutalities of deprivation, and the danger is twofold: that a saintly rejection of the physical world alienates the idealist from its delights, but that a sinner's idealization of its delights requires acquiescence in its brutalities. Synge, as a keen reader of Marx, knew that his alienated pull toward the lives he depicts was not innocent – it also involved an interest – and that his social and political place in Ireland bound him tightly to its cultural economy.[25] This, for all his Ascendancy history, is Synge as an anticipator of Brecht.[26]

Two key moments in the last act of *The Well of the Saints* bring this conjuncture into sharp focus. The first is the delight in rediscovered rapport as Martin and Mary Doul reconnect. Blind again, the two express themselves in a language free from the nets of proof, evocative, giving voice to the expectant imagination, enjoying hope in what will become comely: her white hair, his 'silken, streamy beard' (131). The second is a sharp moment struck at the point when the saint returns to threaten this happiness by restoring their sight for good: '*He raises can. Martin Doul with a sudden movement strikes the can from Saint's hand and sends it rocketing across stage*'(147). The shift is from speech to action: if the first mode invites joyful, comic restoration, the second slams the physical fact of performance back into the equation, invoking disruption and rejection.

The swift shock abruptly jolts the utopian dream back to the dimensions of the stage. Thereafter, the ensuing dramatization of ejection, in which the couple are driven out by their erstwhile community, swiftly completes the play in raw immediacy. The audience are brought into tight proximity with the instinct to silence, while the fantasy of a new life to 'the south' tempts the Douls to new peril. As Timmy says, that way lies 'a power of deep rivers with floods in them where you do have to be lepping the stones and you going to the south, so I'm thinking the two of them will be drowned together in a short while, surely' (151). Sympathy may be drawn to the rich, sustaining delusions of Martin and Mary; but the end also marks the likely consequence of their refusal to adjust to the material dimension. Reality will recognize them, if they do not recognize reality.

Central to this crucial caveat in our response to the couple is Martin Doul's aggressive poetic register, used first to best the Saint in a rhetoric of the senses, then to deny his wife a considered choice of whether to be cured, and finally to paint a glowing image of their new destination: 'a soft wind turning round the little leaves of the spring and feeling the sun' (149). Mary, like Nora before her, has a clearer notion of what the journey will entail: 'a slough of wet on one side and a slough of wet on the other, and you going a stony path with a north wind blowing behind'(151). The socially combative rebellion of Martin Doul thus echoes the tramp of *The Shadow of the Glen*, but he is less easy to fix as an emancipatory figure. Martin's arrogation of authority over his wife echoes his assertion of desire over the figure of Molly, tying his own moral impulse to a tendency to project his will upon others, less than mindful of their needs as opposed to his own. In the context, the terse instruction by a choric 'people' to 'Go on from this' (149) is both an indictment of coercive consensus, and an acceptance of a shared capacity for imposition. This, in performance, provides an ambivalent message for critics tempted to censor an author already inclined to self-censure.

At the start of *The Well of Saints*, Mary Doul instructs her husband to hide the raw material from which they make rush-lights from the inner fibre of the plant: 'Let you put the pith away out of their sight' (75). Synge's concern for what happens when his pithiness is left plain is, with deft wordplay, linked in to processes of production both economic and theatrical.[27] Predictably, the production of the play met with bitter criticism. Joseph Holloway had written to Frank Fay beforehand: 'Billingsgate no matter how clothed in imagery of diabolical cleverness remains Billingsgate and never can become anything else; and when linked with irreverence it becomes quite intolerable to an Irish audience'.[28] The *Freeman's Journal* condemned the 'jargon of profane familiarity', and Sinn Féin founder Arthur Griffith designated it 'pure whitechapel'.[29] As ever with Synge, the combination of violent and lyrical language was disconcerting. A Billingsgate 'clothed in imagery' can claim the brutal force of bad language while stepping clear of mere cliché. And for such critics, since filthy speech conflated associations of working-class vulgarity with the colonizer's marketplace, its combination with Irish cadences was doubly disturbing.

Moreover, Synge's capacity to unsettle drew power from his capacity to combine direct language, poetic cadence, and dramatic symbol. His language is embedded in action, and audience objection found each reinforcing the other. During the *Playboy* riots, one interviewer insisted that the problem was not that he called a spade a spade: 'the complaint is, Mr. Synge, that you call it a bloody shovel'.[30] That distinction calls to mind the hinge upon which *The Playboy* changes direction, namely the appearance of Christy's father, Old Mahon, in act two, and his exchange with Widow Quin:

> **MAHON.** I want to destroy him for breaking the head on me with the clout of a loy. [*He takes off a big hat, and shows his head in a mass of bandages and plaster, with some pride.*] It was he that did that, and amn't I a great wonder to think I've traced him ten days with that rent in my crown?
>
> **WIDOW QUIN.** [*taking his head in both hands and examining it with extreme delight*]. That was a great blow. And who hit you? A robber maybe?
>
> **MAHON.** It was my own son hit me, and he the divil a robber or anything else but a dirty, stuttering lout.[31]

As Mahon explains, no spade, or shovel, did the damage. It was a loy. From the opening of the play, Synge's insistence on the cultural specificity of the weapon fixes the action in the particular. Naming the tool of rural Irish labour makes the violence socially and economically determined. It is no weapon of choice, but the instrument of circumstance. And with the introduction of its target, Mahon's head, the loy gains new weight. As several witnesses to the first production would vouch, this point marks the place at which the mood of the audience shifted from indulgence to discomfort, before evolving into downright hostility.[32] From this moment, we are made acutely aware of a 'dirty deed' forcing its way into the 'gallous story' told thus far. The brutal evidence of violence, the exaggeratedly bloody bandage, offers an overtly physical counterpoint to Christy's lyrical elaborations. As a corresponding phrase, 'dirty, stuttering lout' confirms the impact by insisting on a return to the real world that reins in Christy's speech to a haltering dumbness. It was no coincidence that this juncture of language and image of violence was the precise point that Arthur Griffith thought most important to censor as 'the foulest language we have ever listened to from a public platform'.[33] Griffith actually misheard the word 'stuttering' as something altogether more obscene, and the projection of sexual disgust upon the misheard is only further testament to the provoking, sickening insistence of the formative past. When the father appears, the allegorical possibilities are narrowed, and a generalized violence is forced into specific form, with identifiable victims and known localities. To anticipate a sexual connotation is an acknowledgement of the degree to which the physical facts of sex, procreation, and family are bound in with the social violence that marks boundaries of difference defining gender, class, and nation.

Similar processes are in operation in the crucial scene where the action became unbearable to the first Abbey audience, that gap between the second strike of the loy and the father's second survival. This, the lynching episode, quickly rendered the play as unplayable. It is marked by two critical junctures. The first is a famous sexual image, and an odd juxtaposed action:

> **CHRISTY.** It's Pegeen I'm seeking only, and what'd I care if you brought me a drift of chosen females, standing in their shifts itself maybe, from this place to the Eastern World.
>
> **SARA.** [*runs in, pulling off one of her petticoats*]. They're going to hang him. [*Holding out petticoat and shawl.*] Fit these upon him and let him run off to the east. (167)

The potency of Christy's declaration has been much analysed as a deftly ironic evocation conjuring the sexually wanton image to emphasize chastity, prompting an outrage at licentiousness at the moment when it is denied. The corresponding image of Christy's cross-dressing, using Sara's surrendered undergarment, is no less notable however. This transgression obviously tests the conservative allocation of gender roles, already challenged by the feistiness of Pegeen and the Widow Quin. The fantasy of the harem is paired with over-romantic delusion, though neither can match the contingent gender roles of real live men or women.

But there is another possible dimension to the image, thrown up by Peter Hart's analysis of the social roots of youth culture in the Irish Volunteers. The wearing of women's clothes by local male youths (along with the wearing of clothes inside out, with faces masked, blackened, or rouged, and legs bound with hay or straw) was a feature of festival days in Irish folk culture. Particularly on Skelling Night (Shrove Tuesday), gangs of Straw Boys would ridicule the transgressive to impose a carnival coercion. Bachelors, old maids, adulterers, difficult drunks, and lusty widows were all targets.[34] Such groups often established the social ties underlying the revolutionary bands that formed the Irish Republican Army. Christy's suggestive drag can be interpreted as a further layering of inversions and coercions that resonates with the attempt at social censoring of *The Playboy*. Christy's supposed purity of intent is echoed by his dress, but the attempt to 'shift' his gender and escape retribution only returns him to the uniform of the young male intent on policing communal conformity.

The image thus invites consideration of Christy's revolutionary potential. Straw Boys were ambiguous forces, coercive in their targets, subversive in their rowdiness. Just as Synge had drawn upon social trespass in *The Tinker's Wedding* to break a theatrical taboo, the echo of the Boys' presence in *The Playboy* appropriates a folk unruliness to the theatrical idiom. This dynamic is further elaborated in the closing image of the sequence, in which Pegeen lifts the 'lighted sod' to Christy's leg.

PEGEEN. [*coming over*]. God help him so. [*Burns his leg*]

CHRISTY. [*kicking and screaming*]. Oh, glory be to God! (171)

The spare contrast between the brutality of the action and the twin providential injunctions constitutes an extreme polarity. At one end, the contact is metaphorically and literally grounded. The scorching turf, like the loy and the petticoat/shift, is both domestically specific and politically resonant: the lighted sod had been a common symbol of the Land War. It carries, therefore, connotations of resistance as well as of home and hearth. At the same time, deploying the blasphemy of religious language at a moment of unholy torture brings into tight proximity the detachment of the divine and the immediacy of physical harm. This is doubled up with Pegeen's sudden renunciation of intimacy ('a strange man is a marvel' [169]). With that estrangement comes a jarring replacement of pleasure with pain, forcing the moment of rejection to recognize in its violence a sublimation of repressed sexual attraction.

Synge's calculated provocation in *The Playboy* did more than expose his audiences' own sexual repression, and force them to sublimate their own desires as defensive outrage. The language of Synge's theatricality is always assertive in its testing interplay between the ideal and real, and always alert to the ambiguous powers of concerted action. As in *The Well of the Saints*, the commentary operates in a metatheatrical dimension as well as a thematic one. Provoking the riot, Synge's incitement brings his audience into the play, completing the explosive action by engaging his public in a common manifestation of staged ideas. In one sense, this is prototypically avant-gardist. In a draft letter to Stephen MacKenna in 1904, Synge suggested that:

> I think the Law-Maker and Law Breaker are both needful in society – as the lively and volcanic forces are needed to make the earth's crust inhabitable – and I think the Law-Maker is tending to reduce Ireland or parts of Ireland to a dismal morbid hypocracy [sic] that is not a blessed unripeness.[35]

By this logic Synge finds himself happily thrown into the company of the socially transgressive tinkers, tramps, and outlaws he imagines providing Ireland's energy for change. On the other hand, Synge's physical symbols are always carefully selected for their evocation of social struggles. Such denotations detonate within any easy, romanticized associations. Bringing the audience in as protagonists draws attention to the relationship between the stage and the auditorium, and notice to the demarcations of power explicit in the physical space of the Abbey Theatre. In this sense, *The Playboy* is the most overt attempt to dramatically acknowledge his social and cultural position in what Ronan McDonald has described as an 'art of guilt'.[36]

To recognize Synge in the playboy Christy, is to identify Synge with a character whose expectant anticipation of a 'romping lifetime' shouts a return to the line of shift-clad females he had once declined as empty fantasy. If the author is to be redeemed from his tendency to objectify, it begs an interruption to the process of alienation the play describes. This is not a one-way street: scrutiny of Synge's self-aware social class position is demanded, but at the price that the audience scrutinize their own implication in other systems of control. The possibility that the dialectic between the real and idealized Ireland may in this context emerge as a lived dynamic between play and spectators enjoins all participants in an expanding theatre of censorship.

If *The Playboy* is the most dynamic of Synge's explorations, *Deirdre of the Sorrows* is in many respects the most ameliorative. Unfinished as it was, it suggests a type of rapprochement following the contest of 1907. Venturing into a mythic domain, Synge softens (at least at first) the rougher aspects of his work. The romanticism of the 'natural', as it characterizes sexual spirit, is certainly more idealized in this partly-formed play. Lavarcham's opening description of Deirdre as 'her like was made to have her pleasure only' seems a new exercise in objectification:[37]

> [S]he's little cause to mind an old woman when she has the birds to school her and the pools in the rivers where she goes bathing in the sun. I'll tell you if you seen her that time, with her white skin, and her red lips, and the blue water and the ferns about her, you'd know, maybe, and you greedy itself, it wasn't for your like she was born at all (187-89).

Here, as Lavarcham paints it for Conchubor's benefit, is the innocently sexual, but mediated for the voyeur. Modestly, Deirdre's body is soluble within nature; her colour complements a perfect palette – white skin, red lips, blue water – while the languid vowels (school, pool, bathing) draw out the scene's sensuality. The greediness Lavarcham notes is shared, perhaps, between the old for the young and the male for the female, and this ambiguity allows tension to enter the image. Still, the mythic frame, in restricting the realist grit of earlier plays, brings the evocation perilously close to sentimental eroticism. Even Joseph Holloway considered that, despite Synge's 'ruck of muck', Molly Allgood's Deirdre was 'an exquisite embodiment of the simple child of nature'.[38]

Nevertheless, Synge's insistence on the bruising interruptions of a less forgiving climate acts on his characters as on himself: idylls, as Deirdre finds out in act two, are only suspensions of disbelief. The final act of *Deirdre of the Sorrows* combines a dual return to two earlier endings: *Riders to the Sea* and *The Shadow of the Glen*.[39] Here, the heroine, rather than sceptically accepting new life, embraces a shared death:

> It was sorrows that were foretold, but great joys were my share always; yet it is a cold place I must go to be with you, Naisi, and its cold your arms will be this night that were warm about my neck so often. It's a pitiful thing Conchubor, you have done this

night in Emain; yet a thing will be a joy and a triumph to [the] ends of life and time (269).

Trapped by the voracious Conchubor, Deirdre's romantic wish is for immortality in myth: 'the way there will be a story told of a ruined city, a raving king and a woman will be young for ever' (267). But in the telling, Synge's play returns the immortal to the temporal moment. Deirdre's longing for immediate warmth opposes the coldness of her mythic monument, which stands exposed as scant compensation for the loss of life-in-love. Her refuge in the tragic gesture thus doubly recognizes Conchubor's material power, which governed what was treasured as well as what was lost. Deirdre's and Naisi's idealized, idyllic, and utopian moment only existed in temporary release, much as Nora Burke enjoyed her imagined freedom from Dan before he sat up. Equally, if the theatre remains content merely to provide that release, it necessarily conspires to return us afterward to our unaffected brutal realities. The final, materially grounding truth – of that open grave on stage – deepens the sense in all Synge's work that the word cannot endure above, beyond, or outside the physical world.

In that misgiving is evidence both of his commitment to disruption, and a refusal to assume the Shavian, or Yeatsian, authority to instruct. After his death in 1909, such radical nationalist voices as Patrick Pearse, Thomas MacDonagh, and P.S. O'Hegarty picked up on the provocative sensibility in Synge as an element of their revolutionary intent. Yet, perhaps in drawing the Abbey battles and Synge into their heroic embrace, they inadvertently contracted the germ of Synge's reflexive self-questioning. When the dynamic socialist-revivalist W.P. Ryan reviewed the new collected works in 1911, he reckoned a performance of *The Tinker's Wedding* would mark 'a piquant test of Ireland's sense of humour'. With Synge's characters, he suggested, 'we are borne far from convention, make-believe, and moral cowardice, into something of raciness, grimness, fearlessness, romance and spaciousness of older Gaeldom'.[40]

Yet Synge's influence was, like his works, more than literary. The spaciousness Ryan notes emerges in Synge's insistent sense of physical performance, and with it, his social impact. Forcing the Abbey battles brought his plays into a dimension of the radical politics of the revolution and left a legacy that was a material, theatrical possibility: that relative freedom the theatre enjoyed once the Free State, and finally the Republic, had found their form. It was a contribution to the democratic possibilities of the new Ireland. Synge's specificity, linking the sexual to the physical to the material, locates his drama not in a set of universalizing codes of liberation, but on location. Fixing his plays on axes of contestation that insist on their particularity, it demands an open politics. He opposes the censor, but shares the displaced authority between the audience and himself.

---

[1] This is a revised version of an article that originally appeared as 'Censorship and Self-Censure in the Plays of J.M. Synge', *Princeton University Library Chronicle* (Special Issue): 68.1-2, Autumn 2006.

[2] J. M. Synge, *Collected Works, Volume IV: Plays 2*. Edited by Ann Saddlemyer (Gerrards Cross: Colin Smythe, 1982): 19. Further references will be cited by page number in the text.

[3] W.B. Yeats, *The Collected Letters of W. B. Yeats, Volume IV, 1905-1907*, edited by John Kelly and Ronald Schuchard (Oxford: Oxford University Press, 2005): 190. Not until 1971 would the Abbey stage the play for the first time (although it was produced in 1909 in London).

[4] In a letter (March 1, 1906) to Max Meyerfield, tempting him to produce the play in Berlin. *The Collected Letters of John Millington Synge*, Volume 1, 1871-1907, edited by Ann Saddlemyer (Oxford: Clarendon Press, 1983): 148.

[5] Mary Burke, 'Eighteenth-Century European Scholarship and Nineteenth-Century Irish Literature: Synge's *Tinker's Wedding* and the Orientalizing of Irish "Gypsies" in *The Irish Revival Reappraised*. Edited by Betsey Taylor FitzSimon and James H. Murphy (Dublin: Four Courts Press, 2004).

[6] W.B Yeats *Samhain: An Occasional Review* (Dublin: Sealy Bryers and Walker, September 1903): 4.

[7] Norman St John-Stevas, *Obscenity and the Law* (London: Secker & Warburg, 1956).

[8] St. John-Stevas, 178.

[9] Steve Nicholson, *The Censorship of British Drama 1900- 1968*, vol. 1 (Exeter: University of Exeter Press, 2003): 44-5.

[10] William Archer, *About the Theatre: Essays and Studies* (London: Fisher Unwin, 1886): 166-7, 168.

[11] George Bernard Shaw, *The Quintessence of Ibsenism* (London: W. Scott, 1891): 94.

[12] Shaw's submission to the Joint Select Committee of 1909 was not accepted by them as a statement, and was therefore subsequently paraphrased by him (under protest) as part of a letter to the *Times*, 2 August 1909. *Censorship and Licensing (Joint Select Committee): Verbatim Report of the Proceedings and a Full Text of the Recommendations* (London: The Stage, 1910): 203.

13 Joan Fitzpatrick Dean, *Riot and Great Anger: Stage Censorship in Twentieth Century Ireland* (Madison: University of Wisconsin Press, 2004).
14 David Cairns and Shaun Richards, 'Reading a Riot: the "Reading Formation" of Synge's Abbey Audience', *Literature and History* 13, 2 (Autumn 1987): 219 -37. Adrian Frazier, *Behind the Scenes: Yeats, Horniman, and the Struggle for the Abbey Theatre* (Berkeley and Los Angeles: University of California Press, 1990). Lionel Pilkington, *Theatre and State in Twentieth Century Ireland: Cultivating the People* (London: Routledge, 2001).
15 J.M. Synge, *The Shadow of the Glen* in *Collected Works Volume III: Plays 1*. Edited by Ann Saddlemyer (Gerrards Cross: Colin Smythe, 1982): 35. Further references will be cited by page number in the text. The second quotation is from a letter by Synge to his friend Stephen MacKenna. See *Letters 1*, 74.
16 See Christopher Murray, *Twentieth Century Irish Drama: Mirror up to Nation* (Manchester: Manchester University Press, 1997): 69-74.
17 W.B. Yeats in *United Irishman*, 4 April, 1903.
18 Susan Canon Harris, *Gender and Modern Irish Drama* (Bloomington: Indiana University Press, 2002): 71-8. Ben Levitas, *The Theatre of Nation: Irish Drama and Cultural Nationalism, 1890-1916* (Oxford: Oxford University Press, 2002); P.J. Mathews, *Revival: The Abbey Theatre, Sinn Fein, The Gaelic League and the Co-operative Movement* (Cork: Cork University Press, 2003).
19 J. M. Synge, *The Well of the Saints* in *Plays 1*, 105. Further references will be cited by page number in the text.
20 For Synge's emphatic use of simile, as opposed to metaphor, see Grattan Freyer, 'The Little World of J.M. Synge', *Politics and Letters* 1, 4 (1948): 50-52; and Ronan McDonald, *Tragedy in Irish Literature: Synge, O'Casey, Beckett* (London: Palgrave, 2002): 55.
21 Mikhail Bahktin's concept of the 'chronotope' has resonance here, particularly as applied by Maria Shevtsova. See for example, 'Sociocultural Performance Analysis', *New Approaches to Theatre Studies and Performance Analysis*. Edited by Gunter Berghaus (Tubingen: Max Niemeyer Verlang, 2001): 48-49.
22 Seamus Deane, *Celtic Revivals: Essays in Modern Irish Literature 1880-1980* (London: Faber and Faber, 1985): 58.
23 J. M. Synge, 'A Rabelaisian Rhapsody', a draft in *Plays 1*, 185.
24 Synge, *Plays 1*, 184.
25 W. J. McCormack, *Fool of the Family: A Life of J.M. Synge* (London: Weidenfeld and Nicholson, 2000): 143.
26 For further elaboration of this association, see Anthony Roche, 'Synge, Brecht, and the Hiberno-German Connection', *Hungarian Journal of English and American Studies*, 10.1-2 (2004): 9-32.
27 Mary C. King, *The Drama of J. M. Synge* (Syracuse University Press, 1985): 106-7.

[28] Quoted in Robert Hogan and James Kilroy, *The Modern Irish Drama: A Documentary History, Vol. 3, The Abbey Theatre: The Years of Synge 1905-1909* (Dublin: Dolmen Press, 1978): 16.

[29] See 'Irish National Theatre, Synge's New Play', *Freeman's Journal*, 6 February 1905 and 'All Ireland', *United Irishman*, 11 February 1905.

[30] *Dublin Evening Mail*, 28 January 1907.

[31] J. M. Synge, *Collected Works Volume IV: Plays 2*. Edited by Ann Saddlemyer (Gerrards Cross: Colin Smythe, 1982): 121. Further references will be cited by page number in the text.

[32] The change was marked by Padraic Colum, *The Road Round Ireland* (New York: Macmillan, 1926): 211-12; and Maire Nic Shiublaigh, *The Splendid Years* (Dublin: J. Duffy, 1955): 81-2. See also Nicholas Grene, *Synge: A Critical Study of the Plays* (London: Macmillan, 1975).

[33] Arthur Griffith, *Sinn Féin*, 2 Feb. 1907.

[34] Peter Hart, *The I.R.A. and its Enemies: Violence and Community in Cork 1916-1923* (Oxford: Clarendon Press, 1998): 178-79.

[35] *Letters 1*, 76. See also Gale Schricker Swiontkowski, 'The Devil and Auld Mahoun: Exposing the Trickster Archetype in Synge's Christy Mahon by Way of Rushdie's Muhammad/Mahound' in Alexander G. Gonalez (editor): *Assessing the Achievement of J.M. Synge* (Westport, Conn.: Greenwood Press, 1996): 163.

[36] McDonald, *Tragedy in Irish Literature*, 54.

[37] J. M. Synge, *Plays 2*, 183. Further references will be cited by page number in the text.

[38] Joseph Holloway, *Joseph Holloway's Abbey Theatre: A Selection from his Unpublished Journal Impressions of A Dublin Playgoer*. Edited by Robert Hogan and Michael J. O'Neill (Carbondale: Southern Illinois University Press 1967): 135.

[39] I am beholden here, as elsewhere in this article, to *DruidSynge*, all six of Synge's plays directed by Garry Hynes and performed as a single cycle by the Druid Theatre Company in 2005 and 2006. Hynes's direction made explicit, particularly at the close of *Deirdre*, Synge's echoed images and strategies.

[40] W.P. Ryan, 'A Singer 'O the Green', *Daily Chronicle*, 4 February 1911.

3 | SYNGE, EVOLUTIONARY THEORY, AND THE IRISH LANGUAGE

Mary Burke

Shortly after *The Playboy of the Western World* row in 1907, Synge wrote 'Can We Go Back into Our Mother's Womb?' a short prose piece predicting that any attempt to revive the Irish language would and should fail, which he subtitled 'A Letter to the Gaelic League By a Hedge Schoolmaster'. The baldly provocative opening paragraph of the letter, which was included in an early handwritten draft, was excised from a later typed version:

> Much of the writing that has appeared recently in the papers takes it for granted that Irish is gaining the day in Ireland and that this country will soon speak Gaelic. No supposition is more false. The Gaelic League is founded on a doctrine that is made up of ignorance, fraud and hypocrisy. Irish as a living language is dying out year by year – the day the last old man or woman who can speak Irish only dies in Connacht or Munster – a day that is coming near – will mark a station in the Irish decline which will be final a few years later.[1]

The organization Synge referred to was co-founded in 1893 by Eoin MacNeill and Douglas Hyde for the purpose of preserving the language in areas where it was still spoken. However, by the late 1890s, when the movement had gained huge popularity amongst political and cultural nationalists alike, stress began to be laid upon the more ambitious aim of spreading Irish as a means of general social intercourse. Thus, Synge's attempt to tone down the rhetoric of his original opening paragraph suggests that he was aware that his attitude to the revival of Irish was out of step with the mainstream Anglophone cultural nationalist movement, which was, on the whole, enthusiastic in its support of Gaelic League aims in the early years of the twentieth century, despite some caveats.[2] (At first glance, Synge's attitude seems almost in keeping with the disdain for Irish displayed by certain Unionist Trinity College Dublin dons of the Revival period, or with the young James Joyce's mockery of the Gaelic League's mission in a lecture delivered in the same year that 'Can We Go Back into Our Mother's Womb?' was drafted.[3]) Moreover, the excising of the original opening also suggests that Synge must have seriously considered publishing the open letter, though 'Can We Go Back into Our Mother's Womb?' was never made public.

The tone of what became the opening paragraph of the typed draft is only marginally less confrontational:

> There was never till this time a movement in Ireland that was gushing, cowardly and maudlin, yet now we are passing England in the hysteria of old women's talk ... Was there ever a sight so piteous as an old and respectable people setting up the ideals of Fee-Gee because, with their eye's glued on John Bull's navel, they dare not be Europeans for fear the huckster across the street might call them English (399-400).

At the close of 'Can We Go Back into Our Mother's Womb?' Synge qualifies that when he refers to 'this credo of mouthing gibberish' he speaks 'not of the old and magnificent language of our manuscripts, or of the two or three dialects still spoken, though with many barbarisms, in the west and south, but of the incoherent twaddle that is passed off as Irish by the Gaelic League' (400). However, the effect remains that of a whole linguistic tradition assigned to the ash-heap of history.

Synge studied Irish at Trinity College, had improved his ability in the language on the numerous trips he took to Aran and Kerry, and was a writer whom Declan Kiberd's *Synge and the Irish Language* established as having been deeply immersed in his country's native language and literary tradition. Indeed, in a deeply class-conscious and sectarian Victorian Ireland – one in which Synge must have been marked as upper-middle-class and Anglo-Irish the moment he opened his mouth to talk in English – speaking in Irish almost certainly functioned for Synge as a welcome escape from the labels that defined him. So why did he vehemently predict the disappearance of a language that he loved and could eventually speak with no small fluency?

The handful of critics who have commented in passing on 'Can We Go Back into Our Mother's Womb?' have tended to see its antagonism as emerging from the fact that in the wake of the *Playboy* controversy, Synge was detested by many members of the Gaelic League for his perceived attack on rural Irish values.[4] However, this is too shallow an analysis, since Synge had displayed antipathy towards the Gaelic League years before the *Playboy* riots. The events concerned may have lent a vitriolic edge to Synge's language in his 1907 piece, but he had already predicted that the Gaelic League's efforts would ultimately be fruitless in 'The Old and New in Ireland', an article written five years earlier for *Academy and Literature*:

> The Gaelic League with the whole movement for language revival is so powerful that it is hard to think it will pass away without leaving a mark upon Ireland, yet its more definite hope seems quite certain to end in disappointment ... English is likely to remain the language of Ireland, and no one, I think, need regret the likelihood.[5]

Moreover, Synge excised the following unkind passage originally included in a draft of 'The Old and New in Ireland': 'Most of us have a certain satisfaction when we read the productions of the Gaelic League that these writers use a language that is not intelligible outside their club-room doors' (383). In addition, a satirical scenario drafted by the dramatist during 1905, which suggested that the Ireland of the future would only successfully rid itself of the English language by cutting out the tongues of every member of its population, is an obvious attack on the organization concerned.[6]

Nevertheless, in that same year, Synge wrote a series of twelve articles for the *Manchester Guardian* on the poverty-stricken Congested Districts of the western seaboard. In 'Possible Remedies', the final article of the series, he praises the Gaelic League's attempts to stem the flow of emigration from the region, but pessimistically concludes that 'one fears that when the people realize in five, or perhaps in ten, years that this hope of restoring a lost language is a vain one the last result will be a new kind of hopelessness.'[7] Despite the fact that Gaelic League members were very vocal in their condemnation of Synge's work in the early years of the twentieth century, he appreciated the zeal of the organization even as he doubted the advisability of its aims. Scholars of Synge's work generally concur that the author's depictions of Irish life in his prose writings suggest him to have been a sensible and shrewd observer whose instinctive idealism was always tempered by scepticism. As such, the disconcertingly belligerent tone of 'Can We Go Back into Our Mother's Womb?' indicates that, in tracing the letter's disproportionately violent language, it might be productive to look beyond motives grounded in the ongoing spats the Gaelic League had with Synge and his supporters regarding his plays.

Brian Ó Conchubhair's ground-breaking 2009 study *Fin de Siècle na Gaelige: Darwin, An Athbheochan agus Smaointeoireacht na hEorpa* situates the Gaelic Revival within the broad contexts of contemporaneous European intellectual, social, and literary trends.[8] I will presently demonstrate that one of these influential movements – evolutionary theory – suggested to Synge that Irish was destined for extinction. Ó Conchubhair argues that the entwined issues of the perceived degeneration of the Irish 'race' and the threatened loss of the native language were commonly linked through the prism of Darwinism in the Revival period. In *Primitivism, Science, and the Irish Revival*, Sinéad Garrigan Mattar makes a tantalizing but brief reference to 'Can We Go Back into Our Mother's Womb?' in a broader analysis of Synge and primitivism:

> For Synge, a return to the Irish language on a national level was an attempt to defy the most basic laws of evolution: Irish society had set its foot on the path of modernization, and progress was inevitable. The loss of the language ... could not be reversed.[9]

My analysis will build upon Garrigan Mattar's statement and Ó Conchubhair's analysis by demonstrating that Synge's understanding of evolutionary theory (and particularly of Herbert Spencer's widely misapplied phrase, 'survival of the fittest') suggested to him that a linguistic tradition rooted in 'a small island placed between two countries which speak [English]' was not fit for survival.[10] The references to evolutionary theory and social Darwinism in Synge's writings will be examined and brought to bear upon the attitude to Irish displayed in 'Can We Go Back into Our Mother's Womb?' as will the fact that, in writing of the language traditions of Ireland, Synge deploys the vocabulary of early nineteenth-century linguistics, which depicted language as an organism that grows and decays. For an author forever affected by his traumatic initial encounter with Darwin, the understanding that Irish was a biological entity – and that as such it was subject to the laws of evolution – was potentially alarming.

Synge was born in 1871, the year in which Charles Darwin published *The Descent of Man*, and W.J. McCormack's biography of the dramatist opens by situating the writer in a period in which evolutionary theory was popularly understood to epitomize the disruption of traditional living patterns by industrialization, urbanization, and technological advance. The adolescent Synge began a consecutive reading in September 1895 of Darwin's *On the Origin of Species* (1859), its successor, *The Descent of Man*, and the work of Herbert Spencer, then at the zenith of his reputation.[11] The evolutionary implications of Synge's concept of the inevitable extinction of a language seemingly less than fit for the modern era become credible when one attends to the psychic and spiritual wound that such reading material inflicted upon the future playwright, as described in 'Autobiography':

> When I was about fourteen I obtained a book of Darwin's. It opened in my hands at a passage where he asks how can we explain the similarity between a man's hand and a bird's or bat's wings except by evolution. I flung the book aside ... Till then I had never doubted ... I had of course heard of atheists but as vague monsters that I was unable to realize. It seemed that I was become in a moment the playfellow of Judas. Incest and parricide were but a consequence of the idea that possessed me.[12]

Evolutionary theory generated a consciousness of a universe ruled by randomness and existential hopelessness, as evinced in a passage from 'Étude Morbide', a veiled autobiographical account of the playwright's early manhood:

> I have been reading Herbert Spencer and my creed is now very simple. Humanity has evolved from the conditions of the world, and will return to the nothing it has come from. Each separate life is but a ripple on the waves – a blade of grass on the roadside. For those who fail, there is no hope.[13]

This lack of hope for the evolutionarily unfit recalls the reference in 'Possible Remedies' to the 'hopelessness' that will ensue once the west of Ireland poor realize that the Gaelic League's efforts to revive Irish are bound to fail. Later in life, Synge remained profoundly impressed by the similarity between 'a man's hand and a bird's or bat's wings' referred to in 'Autobiography'. Edward Stephens was struck by the atypical intensity and abruptness with which his uncle questioned him as to whether he had noticed a case containing 'the skeleton of a man's hand, a monkey's paw, and a bat's wing' on a visit to the Dublin Museum in 1902.[14] In addition, Synge links his adolescent loss of religious faith in the face of evolutionary theory to the passing away of naiveté in socio-political matters by recording that, in the wake of encountering Darwin, his allegiance switched from 'the Kingdom of God' to the 'kingdom of Ireland'.[15] Interestingly, Yeats similarly constructs the predominantly Protestant-led Revival as a compensatory response to evolutionary theory: 'deprived by Huxley and Tyndall, whom I detested, of the simple-minded religion of my childhood, I made a new religion, almost an infallible Church of poetic tradition'.[16] A traumatic reaction to Darwin's theory was generally more of a Protestant than a Catholic phenomenon in Ireland and, moreover, Synge came from a strict evangelical tradition on both sides of his family, so his more extreme reaction to Darwin may be situated within both his family's religious culture and the broader Irish evangelical response to evolutionary theory.[17] Yeats later found comfort in mysticism: a middle-class liberal Protestant background such as his may have predisposed a resistance to the seemingly nihilistic Darwinian view of life Synge succumbed to, since the evangelical view of a Manichean world was rather close to the outlook of the evolutionist, as suggested by Huxley:

> The doctrines of predestination; of original sin; of the innate depravity of man and the evil fate of the greater part of the race; of the primacy of Satan in this world ... faulty as they are, appear to me to be vastly nearer the truth than the 'liberal' popular illusions that babies are all born good...[18]

As Weldon Thornton so astutely notes in *J. M. Synge and the Western Mind*, 'Darwin did not give Synge new facts, so much as he gave him a new way of looking at things he already knew'.[19] The religious resonance of the title 'Can We Go Back into Our Mother's Womb?' – that very question is used to express doubt regarding the Christian doctrine of the necessity of being 'born again' in John 3:4[20] – indicates that for Synge, the belief that Irish cannot survive becomes enmeshed with his foundational refutation of his evangelical rearing on encountering Darwin.

Neither 'Étude Morbide' nor 'Autobiography' was published during Synge's lifetime, but their vocabulary of social Darwinism is also evident throughout the works that appeared before Synge's death. A passage in 'A Landlord's Garden in County Wicklow' (1907) concerning the 'tragedy' of the 'dwindling' landlord class pivots on the unspoken and perhaps unspeakable word 'extinction', a term used mainly in relation to the history of British landed families prior to its hijacking by palaeontology and evolutionary theory.[21] In the essay concerned, Synge's own class is – to use the common nineteenth-century concept derived from the popular (mis)understanding of Darwinism – degenerating and emasculated to the point that it is unable to reproduce enough to guarantee survival:

> The desolation of this life is often of a peculiarly local kind, and if a playwright chose to go through the Irish country houses he would find material, it is likely, for many gloomy plays that would turn on the dying away of these old families, and on the lives of the one or two delicate girls that are left so often to represent a dozen hearty men who were alive a generation or two ago ... Wherever [the descendants of these people] are, they do not equal their forefathers.[22]

A discarded note toward 'A Landlord's Garden in County Wicklow' remarks that despite its achievements during the eighteenth century, the Ascendancy was doomed because it lacked the 'seed' of 'future life' (231). Synge's consideration of the issue of the enfeeblement of his class constitutes a distorted echo of Darwin's discussion of natural selection in *On the Origin of Species*:

> The theory of natural selection is grounded on the belief that each new variety ... is produced and maintained by having some advantage over those with which it comes into competition; and the consequent extinction of the less-favoured forms almost inevitably follows ... a few of the sufferers may often long be preserved, from being fitted to some peculiar line of life, or from inhabiting some distant and isolated station, where they have escaped severe competition.[23]

In addition, Synge, whose brothers and brothers-in-law were conventionally successful, invokes the ubiquitous Victorian utilization of the phrase 'survival of the fittest' in 'The Vagrants of Wicklow' (1906) to explain the failure of the artist in comparison with his conformist siblings:

> In the middle classes the gifted son of a family is always the poorest – usually a writer or artist with no sense for speculation – and in a family of peasants, where the average comfort is just over penury, the gifted son sinks also, and is soon a tramp on the roadside.[24]

Moreover, in *Playboy*, the earth is stalked by a Victorian freak show procession of those who do not score high on the evolutionary scale: 'Red Linahan, has a squint in his eye, and Patcheen is lame ... the Mad Mulrannies ... lost in their wits. We're a queer lot these times'.[25] In this post-Darwin dramatic universe, where a professed father-slayer is almost married off to his former wet nurse, the floodgates certainly are opened to something like the 'incest and parricide' feared by the adolescent Synge.

In 1827, Franz Bopp, the founding-father of comparative linguistics, wrote: 'Languages must be regarded as organic bodies, formed in accordance with definite laws; bearing within themselves an internal principle of life, they develop and they gradually die out.'[26] In 'The Evolution of the Concept of "Linguistic Evolution" in the 19th and 20th Century', Brigitte Nerlich notes that early nineteenth-century linguists such as Bopp routinely described language as an organism that grows and decays. That view culminated in August Schleicher's mid-century work on the Indo-European languages and his attempt to establish their so-called 'family tree' in a study published concurrently with Darwin's *On the Origin of Species*. In 'The Old and New in Ireland', Synge utilizes this established convention of language-as-organism to link the loss of Irish in the long-Anglicized east of Ireland to the emergence of Revival-era Anglo-Irish literature, a loss that he implies does not bode well for the contemporaneous emergence of Irish-language literature from the west and south:

> While the new *blossom* due, if these views are correct, to the final *decay* of Irish among the national classes of Leinster was beginning to open, the *old roots* in Munster and the West began also to put out a *new growth*. Some of this new Irish work has considerable value, but what, one cannot but ask, will be its influence on the culture of Ireland? Will the Gaelic *stifle* the English once more, or will the English *stifle* the new hope of the Gaels? (emphasis added) [27]

Of course, in a post-Darwin world, the implication of the discourse of language as living organism is that certain fragile branches on the language tree must ultimately wither away; the contemporary Irish language culture of Munster and Connacht may disappear just as Leinster Irish before it died off. Interestingly, the early nineteenth-century linguists referred to by Nerlich borrowed the term 'evolution' (as understood before Darwin, of course) from the biological sciences to describe language growth or transformation. Thus, in deploying botanical vocabulary to discuss contemporary Irish language culture in 'The Old and New in Ireland', Synge simultaneously invokes the laws to which all organisms were seen to be subject in a post-Darwin universe. The crux of Synge's argument in the excised opening paragraph of 'Can We Go Back into Our Mother's Womb?' is that 'Irish as a *living* language is dying out year by year' (399, emphasis added). This implies that the Gaelic League is keeping a feeble organism alive by artificial means, but if nature is left to take its course, then a tongue that is no longer fruitful, useful, or able to adapt to contemporary conditions is destined to die out, in the manner of the Ascendancy class doomed to extinction due to its lack of 'seed':

> As long as these old people who speak Irish only are in the cabins the children speak Irish to them – a child will learn as many languages as it has need of in its daily life – but when they die the supreme good sense of childhood will not cumber itself with two languages where one is enough. It will play, quarrel, say its prayers and make jokes of good and evil, make love when it's old enough, write if it has wit enough, in this language which is its mother tongue. This result is what could be expected beforehand and it is what is taking place in Ireland in every Irish-speaking district.[28]

Since it could almost have been written to account for the linguistic scenario Synge details above, Darwin's description of the process of natural selection (mentioned above) bears repeating: 'a few of the [less-favoured forms] may often long be preserved, from being fitted to some peculiar line of life, or from inhabiting some distant and isolated station, where they have escaped severe competition', but 'extinction ... inevitably follows'. The most striking aspect of this prediction of the extinction of Irish by a writer who loved and studied the language is its note of acceptance of the necessity of the disappearance of the native tongue.

This is in keeping with the view of Darwin, who saw extinction as commonplace and indispensable to evolutionary change: 'The extinction of species and of whole groups of species ... almost inevitably follows on the principle of natural selection; for old forms will be supplanted by new and improved forms' (475). Synge speaks of the inevitable dying away of his own class in 'A Landlord's Garden in County Wicklow' in a dispassionate tone and is equally saturnine in contemplating the fate of a language that he had spent years mastering. In light of Synge's deployment of botanical vocabulary to discuss the threatened language of Irish in 'The Old and New in Ireland', it is worth noting too that the piece's opening description of rarefied cultivation gone to sterility, rot, death and overgrowth in the abandoned landlord's garden of the title evocatively sets the scene for Synge's cool musings upon the withering of the Anglo-Irish branch of the Irish family tree:

> Just inside the gate, as one entered, two paths led up through a couple of strawberry beds, half choked with leaves, where a few white and narrow strawberries were still hidden away. Further on was nearly half an acre of tall raspberry canes and thistles five feet high, growing together in a dense mass, where one could still pick raspberries enough to last a household for the season. Then, in a waste of hemlock, there were some half-dozen apple trees covered with lichen and moss, and a few dying plum trees, a dead pear tree, and a large fuchsia filled with empty nests. A few lines of box here and there showed where the flower-beds had been laid out, and when anyone who had the knowledge looked carefully among them many remnants could be found of beautiful and rare plants. Under the east wall there was the roof of a green-house, where one could sit and watch the birds and butterflies, many of which were not common.[29]

Synge's implicit pairing in his short prose writings of the native language and what he refers to in 'A Landlord's Garden in County Wicklow' as the country's 'highly-cultivated aristocracy' as two 'beautiful and rare plants' destined for extinction is ultimately a refutation of the kind of contemporary ultra-nationalist criticism that saw his class as being in Ireland but not native to Ireland.

Synge was not the only Revival-era speaker of Irish to invoke the vocabulary of evolutionary theory in speaking of Irish. However, when a sometimes combative promoter of the language revival like Patrick Pearse utilizes such vocabulary, as in the title 'The Language that Was Nearing Extinction and the Professors' (a fable he wrote for *An Barr Buadh* satirizing the controversies among enthusiasts as to what constituted 'good' grammar[30]), its humour is predicated on the assumption that to predict the extinction of what then seemed to be a newly flourishing language was hilarious. Nevertheless, Pearse, who is often remembered by critics of the Revival only for his antipathy to the Anglo-Irish literary movement, utilizes botanical vocabulary in the manner of Synge when conceding that English and Irish would eventually have to co-exist peacefully:

> Ní ceart dúinn a dhearmad go bhfuil an Béarla ann, agus go mbeidh sí i n-úsaid ag Gaedhealaibh de réir deallraimh an fhaid agus beidh sé i n-úsaid ag na Sasanachaibh féin ...' San

toisg is fearr, beidh dá theanga againn feasta, agus is fiú an bheirt acu do *shaothrú* go dichellach. [It is not right for us to forget that English is here and that it will, it seems, be used by the Irish as long as it is used by the English themselves ... In the best sense we will have two languages from now on, and it is worthwhile to *cultivate* both of them to the best of our ability]. (Emphases added)[31]

As noted above, it is in considering this issue of the possibility of the co-existence of English and the native language in the Irish cultural sphere in 'The Old and New in Ireland' that Synge most repetitively deploys botanical metaphors. He wrote the piece in 1902, the year in which he began the first draft of *The Tinker's Wedding* and was also working on *Riders to the Sea* and *The Shadow of the Glen*; that is to say, this is the period in which he was developing the distinctive literary Hiberno-English for which he has long since been celebrated. The implication of the vocabulary that Synge uses to discuss the contemporary linguistic status of Ireland ('blossom', 'decay', 'old roots', 'new growth') is that the heightened Hiberno-English of his plays is a vigorous hybrid that is the result of the grafting of an Irish language shoot onto the stronger stock of English. In Darwinian terms, Hiberno-English is the 'new and improved form' that inevitably replaces the outmoded 'old forms' of enfeebled Irish and what Synge considered to be the inadequate English of a colonized people. The popular concept of the perfected nature of the hybrid plant underlines Synge's previously discussed reference to Hiberno-English in 'The Old and New in Ireland', in which he states that the writing being done in English that is inflected by Irish possesses 'sureness and *purity of form*' (emphasis added).[32] Just as Synge and Pearse diverge in their sense of the appropriateness of utilizing the concept of extinction in relation to the Irish language, Synge here deviates from the commonplace Gaelic League attitude that any mixing of Irish or English language or culture enervated rather than revitalized the indigenous tongue. As Douglas Hyde famously sets out to demonstrate on the opening page of 'The Necessity for De-Anglicizing Ireland' (1892), the 'failure of the Irish people in recent times has been largely brought about by the race ... ceasing to be Irish without becoming English'. Synge's argument in 'The Old and New in Ireland' is far subtler than simply suggesting that Standard English will replace the native tongue or the country's flawed English; rather, he posits that in previous generations in Ireland, the gradual transition from Irish to English meant that neither language was spoken or written well, but that the recently emerged literary dialect incorporating the best of both linguistic cultures would prove to be an alternative to both:

> With the present generation the linguistic atmosphere of Ireland has become definitely English enough, for the first time, to allow work to be done in English that is perfectly Irish in its essence ... A generation or two ago ... writers who lived close to the soul of their country were kept back by the uncertainty of her linguistic sense, and nearly always failed to reach the finer cadences of English ... roughness of the spoken language – when it is not a primitive roughness – leads, or tends to lead, to burlesque writing.[33]

In a draft of that article, the ever-modest Synge praises Yeats as 'the first writer who has written in an Irish spirit with a full appreciation of English rhythms', for which it seems, 'he has been attacked over and over by the Gaelic enthusiasts because he writes in English' (383).

According to Robert Keefe's 'Literati, Language, and Darwinism', the 'primacy of language' as carrier of recoverable cultural truth, an idea promulgated by early nineteenth-century linguistics, came 'under the assault of Darwinism' by the century's close. In particular, *The Descent of Man*, with its surmise that human language evolved when primeval man imitated the mating calls of 'other animals', 'pulled the ontological base out from under early Victorian conceptions of language'.[34] *The Shadow of the Glen* expresses this post-Darwin disintegration of the boundary between the human voice and that which apparently emerges from animal/nature:

> **TRAMP.** It was no lie, lady of the house ... I was passing below on a dark night the like of this night, and *the sheep were lying under the ditch and every one of them coughing, and choking, like an old man*, with the great rain and the fog ... Then I heard *a thing talking – queer talk*, you wouldn't believe at all, and you out of your dreams, – and 'Merciful God,' says I, 'if I begin hearing the like of that *voice out of the thick mist*, I'm destroyed surely'. (emphases added)

The implication of Keefe's reading of language after Darwin is that Revival-era Irish language enthusiasts possessed the assurance of the pre-Darwin era in the capacity of language to carry essence or truth. For Pearse, Irish was 'indelibly stamped with the personality of the nation ... We cannot come into touch with the language without coming into touch with the mind of the nation, nor can we come into touch with the mind of the nation otherwise than through its language.'[35] Synge, on the other hand, was liberated by his reading of evolutionary theory from any such illusions. For this post-Darwin lapsed evangelical, no one language could be privileged over another since *all* languages had endured the Fall.

So, how did the Irish language fare in the century after Synge's lifetime? The leaders of the Gaelic League were amongst those who structured the post-Independence state's Irish language policy. After initial enthusiasm, and despite the implementation of mandatory study of Irish at all levels of education and an emphasis on ability in the language within the public sector, by the latter part of the century there was 'not even one exclusive domain of life where one absolutely need[ed] Irish, or where one would benefit from using Irish only'.[36] Indeed, the compulsory nature of post-1922 policy seemed to engender resentment toward Irish in many. Speaking of the decade after Irish independence in an otherwise positive article on the revival of Irish during the twentieth century, language activist Donald Caird notes:

> There was abroad in [the 1930s] a common view amongst the school boys and girls of Dublin that the Irish language was something invented in some obscure department of the Civil Service for the specific affliction of the youth of Dublin – a sort of Danegold imposed upon the dwellers of the Pale to punish them, if not for their treachery, at least for their lack of enthusiasm in relation to the maintenance of Ireland's cultural heritage.[37]

Ironically, the very success of the Gaelic League in its early years may actually have indicated that the hope that Irish might once more be a widely-used mode of social intercourse was doomed, since its initial revitalization 'was made possible precisely by the elements of progress – namely improvement in communications, a postal service, national newspapers and higher education – which threatened the very survival of the language'.[38] Although Synge's use of a distinctive brand of Hiberno-English in his plays implicitly advocates for a poetic dialect in which the essence of Irish might be revitalized by crossing with English, he never directly addresses the issue of the survival of the Irish language in his drama. However, this issue is made explicit in the work of a contemporary playwright who self-consciously builds upon the literary Hiberno-English of his predecessor:

MAG. [Irish] sounds like nonsense to me. Why can't they just speak English like everybody else?

MAUREEN. Why should they speak English?

MAG. To know what they're saying.

MAUREEN. What country are you living in? [...] It's Irish you should be speaking in Ireland.

MAG. Except where would Irish get you going for a job in England? Nowhere ...

MAUREEN. If it wasn't for the English stealing our language, and our land, and our God-knows-what, wouldn't it be we wouldn't need to go over there begging for jobs and for handouts?

MAG. *(Pause.)* Except America, too ... If it was to America you had to go begging for handouts, it isn't Irish would be any good to you.[39]

In this scene from his 1996 play *The Beauty Queen of Leenane*, Martin McDonagh writes of the hard-nosed attitude toward the Irish language of certain contemporary inhabitants of Leenane with the benefit of hindsight, of course, which draws attention to the prescience of the earlier dramatist. In his foundational consideration of Synge and the native language, Kiberd concludes that, in the wake of a state language policy that amounted to artificial life support, the dramatist's 'grim predictions' vis-à-vis the lexical impoverishment and decline in the number of speakers of 'living' Irish 'were fulfilled'.[40] If Synge's prose masterpiece, *The Aran Islands*, gradually yields to an accepting despair regarding the encroachments modernity is making into island society, then he displays a greater degree of hope concerning the linguistic future of Ireland. Yes, the native language in its purest form is destined for extinction, but not before the beautiful but threatened native plant is grafted onto the imported English root to produce a vital hybrid of both languages. In contemplating the future of Irish, Synge ultimately overcomes the nihilism that evolutionary theory had imparted in him during his youth; 'pure' Irish might become extinct, but its rhythm and energy would survive in the literary Hiberno-English of *Playboy* and its ilk.

---

[1] J.M. Synge, 'Can We Go Back into Our Mother's Womb?' *Collected Works Volume II: Prose*. Edited by Alan Price (Gerrards Cross: Colin Smythe, 1982): 399. Subsequent quotations are included in the text.

2 For instance, in the December 1904 issue of *Samhain*, W.B. Yeats suggested that Gaelic League-endorsed Irish-language drama was beginning to be dominated by propaganda, to the detriment of more artistic plays. *Explorations* (London: Macmillan, 1962): 135-36.

3 For an account of the clash of the Gaelic League with Dr. John Pentland Mahaffy of Trinity College Dublin, see P.J. Mathews, 'Hyde's First Stand: The Irish Language Controversy of 1899' *Éire-Ireland*, 35:1 (2000): 173-187; 'The League organizes festivals, concerts, debates and social gatherings at which the speaker of *Beurla* (that is, English) feels like a fish out of water, lost in the midst of a crowd chatting away in a harsh, guttural tongue. Often on the streets groups of young people may be seen to pass speaking Irish perhaps a little more emphatically than is really necessary. The members of the League correspond in Irish and on many occasions the poor postman, unable to read the address, has had to turn to the head of his section for help in unravelling the problem'. James Joyce, 'Ireland: Island of Saints and Sages'. *James Joyce: Occasional, Critical and Political Writing*, ed. Kevin Barry (Oxford: Worlds Classics, 2002): 109-10.

4 Declan Kiberd, *Synge and the Irish Language*. Second Edition (London: Macmillan, 1992): 2.

5 Synge, 'The Old and New in Ireland', *Prose*, 385.

6 Synge, 'Deafmutes for Ireland', *Prose*, 218-19.

7 Synge, 'Possible Remedies', *Prose*, 341

8 The title of the book translates as '*Darwin, the Language Revival and European Intellectual Thought*'. I wish to thank Brian Ó Conchubhair for graciously discussing his work with me in great detail and at short notice when I was completing this article. See Brian Ó Conchubhair, *Fin de Siècle na Gaelige: Darwin, An Athbheochan agus Smaointeoireacht na hEorpa* (Indreabhán: Cló Iar-Chonnachta, 2009).

9 Sinéad Garrigan Mattar, *Primitivism, Science, and the Irish Revival* (Oxford: Clarendon Press, 2004): 154.

10 Synge, *Prose*, 385.

11 Vivian Mercier, *Modern Irish Literature: Sources and Founders*. Edited by Eilís Dillon (Oxford: Clarendon, 1994): 215.

12 Synge, *Prose*, 10-11. I discuss the manner in which Synge's understanding of evolutionary theory shapes his depictions of Travellers ('tinkers') and Aran Islanders in 'Evolutionary Theory and the Search for Lost Innocence in the Writings of J.M. Synge' in *The Canadian Journal of Irish Studies* 30: 1 (2004): 48-54 and in Chapter 3 of *'Tinkers': Synge and the Cultural History of the Irish Traveller* (Oxford: Clarendon Press, 2009): 96-133.

13 Synge, *Prose*, 29.

14 Stephens Typescript, 1495, quoted in Synge, *Prose*, 11f.

15 Synge, *Prose*, 13.

16 Yeats, *Autobiographies* (London: Macmillan, 1955): 115-16.
17 The Irish churches generally struggled with the purported dismissal of Christian values by evolutionists, rather than Darwin's core tenets, and discussions of John Tyndall's controversial address to the Belfast British Association for the Advancement of Science meeting in 1874 suggest that his manifesto that religion must acquiesce to science had a delayed but profound effect on north of Ireland evangelical Protestantism, making it impossible 'for at least a generation' for the Belfast religious community 'to find any rapprochement with Darwinian biology' of the sort effected elsewhere. David Livingstone, 'Darwin in Belfast: The Evolution Debate,' in *Nature in Ireland: A Scientific and Cultural History*. Edited by John Wilson Foster and Helena C.G. Chesney (Dublin: Lilliput, 1997): 395, 403.
18 T.H. Huxley, quoted in James Moore, *The Post-Darwinian Controversies* (London: Cambridge UP, 1979): 349.
19 Weldon Thornton, *J. M. Synge and the Western Mind* (Gerrards Cross: Colin Smythe, 1979): 42.
20 'Jesus answered and said unto him, verily, verily, I say unto thee, except a man be born again, he cannot see the kingdom of God. Nicodemus saith unto him, how can a man be born when he is old? Can he enter the second time into his mother's womb, and be born?' (John 3:4).
21 Gillian Beer, 'Darwin and the Uses of Extinction' *Victorian Studies* 51: 2 (2009) (321-31): 321.
22 Synge, *Prose*, 231.
23 Charles Darwin, *On the Origin of Species* (London: Murray, 1859): 320-322.
24 Synge, *Prose*, 202.
25 Synge, *Collected Works Volume IV: Plays 2*. Edited by Ann Saddlemyer (Gerrards Cross: Colin Smythe, 1982): 59.
26 Franz Bopp, quoted in Brigitte Nerlich, 'The Evolution of the Concept of 'Linguistic Evolution' in the 19th and 20th Century', *Lingua* 77: 2 (1989): 101-12.
27 Synge, *Prose*, 385. I wish to thank to Christina Wilson and Ellen Cotter Wilson for their advice regarding botanical vocabulary.
28 Synge, *Prose*, 399.
29 Synge, *Prose*, 230.
30 Raymond J. Porter, 'Language and Literature in Revival Ireland: The Views of P.H. Pearse,' *Modern Irish Literature: Essays in Honor of William York Tindall*. Edited by Raymond J. Porter and James D. Brophy (New Rochelle, N.Y.: Iona College Press, 1972) (195-214): 200. The translation of Pearse's Irish-language title is Porter's own.
31 Patrick Pearse, 'Nuaidheacht' (News): *Fáinne an Lae* 24 February 1900: 57, quoted in Philip O'Leary, 'Uneasy Alliance: The Gaelic League Looks at the 'Irish' Renaissance', in Audrey S. Eyler and Robert F. Garratt (editors): *The Uses of the Past* (Newark: University

of Delaware Press; London and Toronto: Associated University Presses, 1988): 155.
32 Synge, *Prose*, 384.
33 *Prose*, 384-5
34 Robert Keefe, 'Literati, Language, and Darwinism' *Language and Style* 19: 2 (1986) (123-38): 131.
35 P.H. Pearse, 'What Is a National Language?' *An Claidheamh Soluis*, 28 January 1905, 6-7.
36 Annette Storgaard Jorgensen, 'Mission Impossible? An Account of the Role of Schooling in the Revival of Irish' in *Student Foreign Language Projects at RUC* (Roskilde: Roskilde Universitetscenter, 1988): 16-39.
37 Donald Caird, 'A View of the Revival of the Irish Language' *Éire-Ireland*, 25: 2 (1990) (96-108): 96.
38 Greta Jones, 'Contested Territories: Alfred Cort Haddon, Progressive Evolutionism and Ireland,' *History of European Ideas* 24.3 (1998): 204.
39 Martin McDonagh, *The Beauty Queen of Leenane and Other Plays* (New York: Vintage, 1998): 8.
40 Kiberd, *Synge and the Irish Language*, 223.

4 | SYNGE'S THINGS: MATERIAL CULTURE IN THE WRITINGS OF SYNGE

Paige Reynolds

What are things? The answer to this seemingly straightforward question has intrigued scholars of late, and in particular scholars from a variety of disciplines who have been interrogating in a school of criticism dubbed 'thing theory' the relationship between subject (we humans) and object (those material items in the world). These analyses focus on the circulation and consumption of goods, as well as examining how people use material objects to create meaning and identities. Much of this work recovers the historical context and meaning of particular objects – one can imagine, for instance, an essay that examines the manufacture, distribution, and reputation of the loy in order to explain better its literal and symbolic meanings for the first audiences of Synge's *The Playboy of the Western World*. More recently, analyses of material culture have taken a more theoretical turn, asking us to consider the 'thing' – a word that Bill Brown employs not to describe an inert object, but rather an article exposing the dynamic relationship between subject and object.[1] If modern times have insisted on a clear divide between people and objects, Brown and others employing 'thing theory' insist these boundaries are in fact porous, if they exist at all.[2] 'Thing theory' thus challenges or complicates readings of material culture that regard objects as strictly oppressive, and consumption as a threat to autonomy. It encourages us instead to celebrate objects, according to Sherry Turkle, as 'thought companions, life companions' and to bring more nuance to our readings of the material matter scattered about everyday life.[3]

The recent critical attention awarded to material culture presents exciting opportunities for thinking about Synge's body of work and, more particularly, about Synge's things. Through this lens, we can trace his representations of and engagement with material culture to learn about his perceptions of Ireland and his times. In *The Aran Islands*, Synge replicates the Revival's unabashed celebration of authentically Irish material culture, but in doing so he invests all objects, even those mass-produced, with inspirational or liberating qualities. In that study, as well as in *Riders to the Sea* and *The Playboy of the Western World*, he undermines any reductive understanding of things to reveal the complex roles they play in the lives of his seemingly 'primitive' western characters. In particular, Synge uses things to demonstrate how material culture affords women a glimpse of lives richer and more empowered than the painfully austere and constrained ones depicted in his drama.

The historian Toby Barnard has identified ways that material culture in Ireland is unique, citing in particular the practical difficulty in recovering artefacts in order to reconstruct the Irish past. He contends that these difficulties are exacerbated by an 'ideological resistance' in Ireland to material culture, stemming from a history in which most lived in poverty and many died of famine.[4] As Barnard establishes in his study of possessions in Stuart and Hanoverian Ireland, objects in Irish culture were tethered to the binaries that divided colonial culture more generally, including those between English and Irish, Protestant and Catholic, colonizer and colonized.[5] He describes the performative function of objects in Ireland – their capacity to register social status publicly – and he reveals how possessions in the eighteenth century exacerbated the divide between affluent Protestants and the Catholic majority in Ireland. These objects in Ireland became, early on, devices that – like theatrical props or costumes – signalled publicly an individual's national, political, social, and religious identifications, a point confirmed by the work of Claudia Kinmonth on material culture in rural Ireland.[6]

The suspicion of things was a logic embedded in the cultural nationalism of late nineteenth- and early twentieth-century Ireland. The cultural revival of this period aggressively touted its antipathy toward things, partially to differentiate Ireland from its colonizer, England, a country heavily identified with industry, with the mass production and consumption of material goods. Anti-materialism offered the Revivalists a logical ideological weapon in their struggle against imperial culture, given the practical facts that England was rich and Ireland was poor, and that trade laws made Ireland a dumping ground for English commodities while interfering with Irish exportation. Thus, a core principle of Revivalism positioned and privileged the 'spiritual' nature of Ireland against and above the sordid 'material' character of England. These ideals are captured by many Revivalist texts, including W.B. Yeats's 'The Lake Isle of Innisfree'. This poem, published in 1892, reflects the ideals of the Revival by celebrating human labour (building a cabin, farming beans, harvesting bees) over the mass production of the factory. It lionizes the Irish countryside as opposed to the city (the poet escapes 'the roadway' and 'pavements grey' for the natural beauty and calm of Innisfree), and privileges the spiritual over the material (peace is obtained by a retreat into imagination, a move away from the outside world of material things).

But the Revival did not simply reject things out of hand. There was, in fact, a Revivalist conception of Irish things that celebrated native crafts and industry as the antidote to the shoddy, mass-produced English objects infecting Irish culture. Whether the limited-run art books of the Cuala Press, the fashion and other forms of Irish manufacture celebrated in the feminist journal *Bean na hÉireann*, or the traditional dress advocated by Arthur Griffith and donned by Maud Gonne and others, the 'authentic' things of the Revival offered consumers, frequently imagined as women, an alternative to the corrupt English commodities littering Ireland. In his writing, Synge picks up on the refrain of anti-materialism rife in Revivalist thinking, as well as on the Revival's celebration of 'authentic' Irish wares that might prevail in the market over mass-produced English commodities. Yet he also brings to light the more complex – and sometimes contradictory – attitudes regarding material culture that characterized early twentieth-century Ireland.

In *The Aran Islands*, Synge shares his observations of western life accrued during visits to the islands between 1898 and 1901. His reckoning of life on these Atlantic islands marches in step with Revivalist logic by applauding the anti-modern and the anti-material, while allowing for any celebration of the primitive. He celebrates the objects produced by the islanders, writing:

> In Aran even manufacture is of interest. The low flame-edged kiln, sending out dense clouds of creamy smoke, with a band of red and grey clothed workers moving in the haze, and usually some petticoated boys and women who come down with drink,

forms a scene with as much variety and colour as any picture from the East.[7]

The manufactured objects of this 'most primitive' (53) culture are at a far remove from those produced in the industrial west of England, and Europe more generally, and this picturesque scene of production is described impressionistically – not through the realism of a Dickens or Gaskell. Manufacture in Aran is orientalized and met with forbearance, even admiration, as is commerce, when Synge observes without judgement that islanders sell pampooties and maidenhair ferns as souvenirs to the summer tourists (52).

Throughout his study of the Aran Islands, Synge portrays things as anodyne, even beneficial. He observes:

> Every article on these islands has an almost personal character, which gives this simple life, where all art is unknown, something of the artistic beauty of medieval life. The curaghs [sic] and spinning-wheels, the tiny wooden barrels that are still much used in the place of earthenware, the homemade cradles, churns, and baskets, are all full of individuality, and being made from materials that are common here, yet to some extent peculiar to the island, they seem to exist as a natural link between the people and the world that is about them. (58-9)

This passage reflects the premises articulated by the German philosopher Martin Heidegger, whose writings are seminal to thing theory. Heidegger distinguishes between mere objects, which are mass produced and useful, and the charisma of the thing, which is made by human hands and untouched by technology.[8] Synge here lauds the Heideggerian 'thing': as pure reflections of a 'simple life', these 'articles' concretize the abstract values Synge espouses. Each is made by hand; each is unique, native, and individual; all employ materials distinct to the island.

These items identified by Synge – curaghs, spinning wheels, wooden barrels, earthenware, cradles, churns, and baskets – have a utilitarian function tied directly to the labour of the island's inhabitants. Yet these objects 'exist' not merely for utility, which would reduce them to an object. They also provide a register of the 'natural link between the people and the world that is about them', which makes them a thing. Modernity removes the intimacy between person and object, but this primitive Aran culture laudably reinstalls that bond – or more accurately, never relinquishes that connection. The 'almost personal character' of material objects gives life on the Aran Islands 'artistic beauty', albeit an austere one.

In the securely 'primitive' context of the Aran Islands, even mass produced commodities can shed their strictly negative associations. For instance, Synge commends the important function these 'things' serve in the sociability of the islands. Gifts facilitate his intimacy with the community, a fact demonstrated by his description of the 'great excitement' generated by 'some little presents' of folding scissors, a strop, and 'some other trifles' that he brings the islanders (106). From Synge's perspective, these gifts from the 'modern' world do not corrupt the 'primitive' island, but instead cement community relations. When he describes the delight the islanders take in viewing his photographs, he fixates on their unfamiliarity with these mechanically reproduced objects and thus authenticates their status as primitive subjects. But he simultaneously reveals that these modern things can bring together people in shared space and time and facilitate social interaction; the affect and intimacy generated by these photographs invite him, a modern subject, into this primitive community.

To further authenticate the integrity of the islanders, Synge records additional instances in which they fail to understand objects of the outside world and creatively repurpose them as a consequence. For instance, his watch fails to satisfy locals seeking the hour because its mode of time keeping is unfamiliar to them. Nonetheless, they wrest their own meaning from modern things: Pat Dirane requests a clock as a gift from Synge, saying with it 'they wouldn't forget me, and wouldn't a clock be as handy as another thing, and they'd be thinking of me whenever they'd look on its face' (67). This, of course, confirms once more the pure, primitive status of the islanders who resist the temporal order of the modern world and regard the clock instead as a register of personal and communal history. The clock now functions not as a timekeeper, but instead as a portrait of Synge, a souvenir of his visit to the islands. The status of the clock as souvenir instils it with the power 'to authenticate a past or otherwise remote experience and, at the same time, to discredit the present'.[9] This reckoning of souvenirs articulated by Susan Stewart suits the utopian world of things concocted by Synge. Whether the pampooties and ferns taken from the island by tourists or the strops and clocks introduced into the island by Synge, souvenirs deny the present moment of modern material culture.

The islanders are not the only ones who repurpose things. Synge contends that the native objects of the islands offer him short-term access to the islanders' authenticity. When his own shoes fail to keep him steady and on pace during walks around the island, his hosts make him pampooties, which 'consist simply of a piece of raw cowskin, with the hair outside, laced over the toe and round the heel with two ends of fishing-line that work round and are tied above the inset' (65). Just as he translates Irish into English, he translates this unfamiliar thing to his readers, identifying the values of the island culture through his description of this simple, organic, hand-made shoe.

In great detail, Synge describes his care of the boots and how he must learn to walk in them. Initially, he bruises his heels when he walks in the pampooties 'as one does naturally in a boot' and recovers only when 'after a few hours' he 'learned the natural walk of man, and could follow my guide in any portion of the island' (65). The provocative reiteration of the term 'natural' in this passage suggests that the ordinary but contrived behaviour demanded by the city and its shoes actually harms him on the island, and that his new pampooties require him to adopt a walk instinctive to humans, a 'natural walk' that can be 'learned' anew in only a few hours. The thing here requires an adaptation of behaviour, which in turn brings man closer to his natural state. As he insists, the 'absence of the heavy boot of Europe has preserved to these people the agile walk of the wild animal, while the general simplicity of their lives has given them many other points of physical perfection' (66). In addition, Synge attributes the remarkable dancing on the island to the 'lightness of the pampooties' (153) – not the innate talent of the islanders. For Synge, the thing explains the difference between the authentic islander and the corrupted modern subject, a premise holding great promise for those seeking authenticity, since by obtaining these objects, they gain immediate access to the desired natural state.

Thing theory explores the variable relationship between subject and object, a dynamic that appears throughout Synge's reckoning of material culture on the islands. He describes the return of a curragh 'towing a large kitchen table that stood itself up on the waves and then turned somersaults in an extraordinary manner' (138). He adopts the logic of the island, allowing mundane objects magical qualities, and he infuses this table with life by personifying it. This moment recalls the moment in Marx's *Capital* (1867), when Marx describes 'commodity fetishism' as the way consumers ignore or deny the human labour that produces objects. Marx regrets that value is located in commodities themselves rather than in the labour that creates them: he explains that when wood becomes a table, and when a table enters the market and becomes a commodity, the table magically takes on a life of its own: 'it stands on its head, and evolves out of its wooden brain grotesque ideas far more wonderful than if it were to begin dancing of its own free will'.[10] Synge likely encountered this passage while travelling Europe and studying at the Sorbonne, and here he echoes Marx and similarly imbues a table with life, allowing it to dance.[11] But nature makes Synge's table dance, not the illusions of capitalism. Throughout *The Aran Islands*, labour power generally remains with the person who made the native thing, not with the thing itself.

By studying *The Aran Islands*, we can derive a sense of how Synge regarded the material culture of the islands, and what that tells us about his values. While he sanctions primitive objects bearing the trace of human labour, and thus reaffirms familiar Revivalist discourse about objects, he refuses to condemn modern, mass-produced commodities. In the appropriate context, they too can validate and promote the anti-colonial ideas of Irish cultural nationalism. This reading of the 'things' of Synge's cultural anthropology – his collection of folklore and anecdote – invites us to think about the representation of things in his drama.

Any understanding that we have of things in drama is complicated by their status as props, as objects that convey meaning on the stage in addition to their role as symbols in the text of the play. In his book *The Stage Life of Props*, Andrew Sofer defines the prop as 'a discrete, material, inanimate object that is visibly manipulated by an actor in the course of performance'.[12] Props are set pieces used in dramatic action, ones that make literal the symbols in the written text. They carry, according to Sofer, three levels of meaning: they have a literal meaning (think again of Christy's loy on stage: this is a fake spade), a connotative meaning (that represents an actual spade), and a symbolic meaning (that symbolizes male authority, rebellion against the patriarch, and such). The fluid nature of the prop means that it plugs easily into the flexibility 'thing theory' associates with objects. As well, props help us to understand better the seriousness with which Synge regarded material culture. For instance, he famously insisted that props for *Riders to the Sea* come from the homes of friends from the Aran Islands in order to have provenance that was 'immediate' and authentic.

There is something to be said about things in all of Synge's work, but the remainder of this essay focuses on *Riders to the Sea* and *The Playboy of the Western World*, in part because they offer a provocative critique of gender and material culture in the early twentieth-century Ireland of Synge's imagination.

Riders to the Sea opens in the cottage kitchen of Maurya and her family, a space cluttered with the devices needed to eke out a living from the harsh natural conditions of their western island home – nets, oilskins, spinning wheel. The objects in this play are supercharged with meaning, in part because they are scarce due to the stark poverty from which the characters suffer. Thus the new boards standing against the kitchen wall are conspicuous because they are the most precious things Synge presents to the audience. These boards convey the triple meaning that Sofer describes: the boards are literally real boards, connotatively boards to build a coffin, and symbolically a means of telegraphing the prominent place of death in this home and community.

As in *The Aran Islands*, the easy passage in this culture between the worlds of the material and the spiritual shapes how these characters regard objects. As the play opens, Nora and Cathleen have obtained a package of clothes, which they fear may have belonged to their missing brother, Michael, who is presumably lost at sea. In this play, things are transformed into texts, revealing once more the easy converse between thing and language on the islands. Nora and Cathleen have been given a bundle by the priest, the shirt and stocking of a drowned man, which they fear may have belonged to Michael. Nora and Cathleen must 'read' the shirt's flannel and the stocking in order to identify their brother. The shirt's fabric – of which there are 'great rolls ... in the shops of Galway' – allows for misreading;[13] it holds a promise that Michael survived and that this mass-produced material might have been worn by another drowned fisherman. But the handmade stocking, which Nora knitted with 'three score stitches, and I dropped four of them' (15), seals their suspicions of their brother's death. The distress upon discovering this truth leads Nora to embrace the clothes and exclaim: 'And isn't it a pitiful thing when there is nothing left of a man who was a great rower and fisher, but a bit of an old shirt and a plain stocking?' (17). In a culture that esteemed the spiritual over the material – think here of a different Michael's willing revocation of his wedding dowry for the glorious march to death in Yeats and Gregory's play *Cathleen ni Houlihan* (1902) – this moment is significant. For a flash, death reduces a man to ordinary things, rather than immediately glorifying his spirit; in their grief, these women's instinct is not to turn to the spirit for relief, but to the material for truth.

In *The Aran Islands*, things are imbued with magical powers, a quality attributable in part to long-standing spiritual beliefs. When Pat warns Synge to put a sharp needle beneath the collar of his coat in order to protect himself from fairies, he maintains that this banal object is infused with incredible power, the authority to ward off evil (80). Like this needle, the objects in *Riders to the Sea* are charged with meaning that well exceeds their actual value. When Bartley wants to take the rope in their home to act as a harness, Maurya refuses, insisting that it will be needed to lower Michael's body into the grave should it wash ashore. Yet Bartley takes the rope, insisting that he needs it for a halter. This ordinary rope, placed on the wall because the pig with the black feet was eating it, becomes infused with ritual meaning. It becomes the umbilical cord linking Maurya to her last living son, a cord he pulls off the wall and takes from his home and his mother. Like other ropes in Irish drama – ranging from the untwisted rope in Douglas Hyde's *Casadh an tSúgáin* (1901), to the rope that cannot restrain Christy in *Playboy*, to the rope that does not hang Lucky and Estragon in Beckett's *Waiting for Godot* (1955) – this rope fails.[14]

The relationship to things in *Riders* is gendered. In *The Aran Islands*, women are the ones who make souvenirs for the tourists, who buy materials, and who drive a good bargain. In *Riders*, women are precluded from the system of buying and selling. When Bartley suggests that Cathleen sell the pig with the black feet if she can obtain a good price, Maurya snaps, 'How would the like of her get a good price for a pig?' (9). Maurya is sceptical about exchange due in part to the mammoth losses she has suffered. Toward the end of the play, she gives a literal catalogue of the men she has lost at sea: a husband, a husband's father, and her six sons, including Bartley and Michael. As Maurya observes, 'There does be a power of young men floating round in the sea' (23). This moment again refuses the Revivalist logic in which death is a triumph, in which the loss of the material to obtain the spiritual renders a net gain – a logic that would be espoused by George Russell (AE), Padraic Pearse, and other poets of this period. Instead, for women like Maurya, death is strictly about loss.

Because Maurya refuses the 'payoff' of male sacrifice – the exchange of an Irishman's life for the greater good – she refuses exchange in any context. When Bartley prepares to leave for the market to sell his horse, she asks, 'what is the price of a thousand horses against a son when there is one son only?' (9). In *The Aran Islands*, Old Pat shares a story about the young man O'Conor who seeks to marry the daughter of a wealthy farmer; the girl's father demands her weight in gold, and O'Conor is refused when his pile of gold weighs less than the daughter after both are placed on the balance scale. This tale acknowledges that money, in this case gold, is a medium of exchange valued primarily in the logic of capitalism because it can be converted into something else. That is, we do not value a gold coin strictly as a thing – for instance, because its form would serve well as the steering wheel of a toy car or because it bears the portrait of someone famous; we value the symbolic power of the gold coin because it has exchange value and can be converted into something else. Yet this tale strangely insists on the present thing-like quality of both the gold and the girl by privileging their status as objects that bear weight; both women and currency are objectified, reduced merely to weighted objects placed on a balance scale, a sinister equation that nonetheless attempts to deny the rules capitalism has established for monetary exchange.

In *The Aran Islands*, the girl and the gold for different reasons should be impervious to objectification, to being reduced to mere things considered equivalent and therefore readily exchangeable and interchangeable. Maurya resists a similar process of objectification and exchange when she imagines a thousand horses weighed against one son. For Maurya, nothing can outweigh the value of her only remaining son. When she refuses Bartley her blessing as he goes to the market, Maurya refuses to participate not only in a market economy that requires her son risk his life for money, but also in this system of equivalence and exchange between things. Thus, as Bartley leaves, Maurya withholds her blessing – basically the only 'thing' she has as a woman in a household so bereft of material goods.

In the introduction to *The Aran Islands*, Synge insists the book offers 'a direct account of my life on the islands, of what I met with among them, inventing nothing, and changing nothing that is essential' (47). Here, he ascribes to his writing the attributes of the things produced by the Aran inhabitants: his words similarly are a direct product of his experience, use native material, and maintain the essential nature of the islands. Given the powerful link that Synge establishes between things and language, Maurya's perplexing refusal to bless Bartley invites a provocative reading of the gift. The French sociologist Marcel Mauss describes the gift as a reciprocal relationship; the bond between the giver and gift creates a social bond with the obligation to reciprocate.[15] As he notes, this is an important distinction in a market economy, where objects can be sold and become alienated from their original owner. So gift exchange, for Mauss, represents a form of mutual interdependence that promises to exist outside of a market economy. This logic of interdependence, and the wish for an idyllic space outside the market, is evident in the gifts Synge describes in *The Aran Islands*. But in *Riders to the Sea*, Synge complicates the simple bonds Mauss describes between the person who awards the gift and the person who receives it, in part, I would argue, to demonstrate further the limitations placed on women in the island culture.

In *Given Time: 1. Counterfeit Money*, Jacques Derrida regards the gift as a paradox, and contends that a gift cannot appear as a gift; if it is identified as such, it enters a cycle of repayment and debt. The gift is the impossible:

> the one who gives it must not see or know it either; otherwise he begins, at the threshold, as soon as he intends to give, to pay himself a symbolic recognition, to praise himself, to approve of himself, to gratify himself, to congratulate himself, to give back to himself symbolically the value of what he thinks he has given or what he is preparing to give.[16]

Derrida contends that any pre-existing bond (family, political, economic, friendship) means that the gift is not spontaneous, and is therefore not a gift.

For Derrida, there is no gift, only exchange, so the true gift is the gift of nothing, the gift of time. The gift functions as a gift only if it is free of self and desire, a form of 'absolute forgetting' that is impossible in the gift economy. This notion of the gift and the impossibility of absolute forgetting explain further why Maurya refuses to bless her son. By withholding her blessing from Bartley, she rejects the illusion of mutual interdependence characterizing the gift system described by Mauss and Derrida. She will not grant Bartley her blessing because the gift is a sham, an impossibility. Derrida writes

> For there to be gift, not only must the donor or donee not perceive or receive the gift as such, have no consciousness of it, no memory, no recognition; he or she must also forget it right away [*à l'instant*] and moreover this forgetting must be so

> radical that it exceeds even the psychoanalytic categoriality of forgetting ... We are speaking here of an absolute forgetting – a forgetting that also absolves, that unbinds absolutely and infinitely more, therefore, than excuse, forgiveness, or acquittal. (16)

Maurya cannot and will not forget what she has given the sea, as evidenced by her careful catalogue of all the men whom she has loved and lost. She recognizes that her blessing to Bartley cannot be a gift, and she must withhold it; in doing so, she refuses to absolve, to excuse, to forgive, and to acquit.

Maurya's subversion of island values does not end there. In *The Aran Islands*, Synge conjures a utopia where things are positively tethered to the individuals who created them, in contrast to the modern, industrialized world of alienated labour beyond its borders. But the sea has the power to rip these things away, to swallow and destroy, and perhaps later disgorge, them. Thus Maurya actually prefers the way material objects circulate beyond the island: 'In the big world the old people do be leaving things after them for their sons and children, but in this place it is the young men do be leaving things behind for them that do be old' (13).

Maurya's seemingly perverse relationship to material culture, which also explains why she forgets to acquire nails for the coffin, sheds light on the anguished conclusion of *Riders*. She closes the play by asserting:

> Michael has a clean burial in the far north, by the grace of the Almighty God. Bartley will have a fine coffin out of the white boards, and a deep grave surely. What more can we want than that? No man can be living for ever, and we must be satisfied (27).

This moment, read traditionally as a moment of relief for Maurya, one in which she can finally find a measure of peace because she has nothing left to lose, fails to satisfy – unless it conveys Maurya's fury. In this moment, she rejects the promise of eternal life, refuses the promises offered by Catholic and national celebrations of the spirit. Her question, answered literally, is unfathomable. Of course she can want more than a clean burial for one son and a fine coffin for another. The final line ironically suggests that a female desire for 'more' might be good, that it might offer a way to see things beyond the limits imposed here – by poverty, by place and situation, by gender, by nature. Maurya can imagine a 'big world' beyond the island, a more 'natural' world where things are willed from the old to the young. Yet the utter impossibility of obtaining 'more' on this destitute island prevents Maurya from articulating her entirely reasonable desires as anything more than a rhetorical question.

Things play an equally critical role in *The Playboy of the Western World*. *Playboy* opens in a shebeen, a space that serves two functions as private home and as a public space providing goods to the local community. In the first scene, Pegeen slowly and carefully writes an order to Mister Sheamus Mulroy, Wine and Spirit Dealer, Castlebar, reading:

> Six yards of stuff for to make a yellow gown. A pair of lace boots with lengthy heels on them and brassy eyes. A hat is suited for a wedding-day. A fine tooth comb. To be sent with three barrels of porter in Jimmy Farrell's creel cart on the evening of the coming Fair to Mister Michael James Flaherty. With the best compliments of the season. Margaret Flaherty.[17]

The opening scene of *Playboy* is misleading. The curtain rises on a setting described as 'very rough and untidy' (57), but we encounter first this neatly articulated list of seemingly frivolous goods, niceties that intimate Pegeen's refinement. Pegeen, introduced here as Margaret, appears a young woman enraptured by the acquisition of pretty things and acutely aware of her own femininity. Of course, the obstreperous heroine is soon cursing her father, maligning Shawn Keogh, and physically threatening Christy with a broom. Importantly, this first scene demonstrates her connection to and conversation with the outside world, represented by a merchant in Castlebar. Like Maurya in *Riders*, Pegeen uses things to imagine another place, an alternative to the claustrophobic Mayo community that oppresses her. Only one element of this opening scene reflects the actual power dynamics of the play: Pegeen's father Michael alone holds the authority to receive these goods, despite the fact that she orders them and likely does the work to pay for them.

For all of the cognitive dissonance generated by this first scene, it makes great sense in the context of the play as a whole because it introduces a world rich with material objects. All three acts of *The Playboy of the Western World* open by focusing on things. Act one begins with Pegeen's wedding order; act two begins with Christy cataloguing all of the items in the shebeen; and act three begins with Philly and Jimmy marvelling over varieties of skulls and bones.

In act two, left alone in the shebeen, Christy cleans Pegeen's boots as he counts to himself the jugs on the dresser:

Half a hundred beyond. Ten there. A score that's above. Eighty jugs. Six cups and a broken one. Two plates. A power of glasses. Bottles, a schoolmaster'd be hard set to count, and enough in them, I'm thinking to drunken all the wealth and wisdom of the County Clare' (95).

For Christy, Mayo promises a world of plenitude, even excess. In act one, Pegeen's bridal order suggests her desire to be somewhere and someone she is not. But here, Christy's attention to objects reveals that this shebeen is just where he wants to be. This scene also demonstrates that an attachment to everyday objects and domestic pleasures is not simply the domain of women. The overt fascination with domestic things admittedly feminizes Christy, but it simultaneously debunks any notion of a strictly gendered response to things: in *Playboy*, things speak to and about both men and women.

As act two continues, Susan, Nelly, Honor, and Sara enter the shebeen and offer Christy gifts: while Pegeen is seeking out goat's milk for his tea, Sara brings him a brace of duck eggs, Susan brings him a pat of butter, Honor brings him a little cut of cake, and Nelly brings him a little laying pullet (99). Mauss claimed that gifts cement community relations, but they also serve in *Playboy* as bait. The girls want intimate contact with this local celebrity, and they are willing to pay to obtain that attention. This act soon provides a second instance of bribery masquerading as gift exchange, when Shawn comes to the shebeen with the Widow Quin in order to ask Christy to leave Mayo. He offers Christy 'half of a ticket to the Western States!' (113), and further promises 'my new hat', 'my breeches with the double seat', and 'my new coat ... woven from the blackest shearings for three miles around' (113-115). He also promises 'my blessing and the blessing of Father Reilly itself, maybe, if you'll quit from this and leave us in the peace we had till last night' (115). The gifts are a mix of native and foreign goods, material objects and ephemeral blessings. Christy recognizes these things for what they are – not gifts, but 'bribery for to banish me' (115). To this Shawn replies, 'Let you not take it badly, mister honey, isn't beyond the best place for you where you'll have golden chains and shiny coats and you riding upon hunters with the ladies of the land' (115). Again, the outside world is portrayed as temptingly rich with opulent goods.

Throughout Synge's body of work, women are revealed to have a complex relationship with material culture and consumption. In *The*

Aran Islands, he describes the arrival of a pedlar, whom he suspects must be German or Polish, to the island:

> He opened his wares on the slip as soon as he landed, and sold a quantity of cheap knives and jewellery to the girls and younger women. He spoke no Irish, and the bargaining gave immense amusement to the crowd that collected round him (138).

Synge continues, 'I was surprised to notice that several women who professed to know no English could make themselves understood without difficulty when it pleased them' (138) – here, objects enable translation, even facilitate it. One local girl even warns the pedlar that his rings are overpriced in a Gaelic construction.

The women in *The Aran Islands* control the bargaining process, and in the second act of *Playboy*, the Widow Quin similarly commands the social dynamics surrounding things. She recognizes the seductive nature of the tactile, and encourages Christy to don the clothes Shawn offers. By touching these things, putting on these clothes, Christy comes to recognize them as a costume, as a further chance to alter his identity, to enhance his appeal, and to attract Pegeen. Shawn offers a ewe for her assistance, but she ups the ante by asking for 'the red cow you have and the mountainy ram, and the right of way across your rye path, and a load of dung at Michaelmas, and tubary upon the western hill' (117). Shawn agrees and adds that if she were to marry Christy, he would include:

> the wedding-ring I have, and the loan of a new suit, the way you'd have him decent on the wedding-day ... two kids for your dinner, and a gallon of poteen, and I'd call the piper on the long car to your wedding from Crossmollina or from Ballina. I'd give you ... (117).

In *Playboy*, Synge portrays Shawn as a snivelling coward beholden to the Church, which implies that he is an unsuitable match for Pegeen. But in light of the equation offered in *The Aran Islands*, in which the balanced weight on a scale between a woman on one side and the gold offered by her suitor on the other seals a marriage promise, Shawn is revealed here to be deeply in love. His offer to the Widow Quin is remarkable not only because of its sheer bounty, but also because of its fathomless nature – Quin literally has to interrupt Shawn to make him stop offering her things. As well, Shawn appears as invested as Pegeen in the material goods necessary for a wedding. He has a clear and well articulated sense of the requirements for a nice ceremony; he recognizes and has acquired the necessary goods.

Despite the fact that Synge invites us to disdain Shawn, he portrays Shawn through these things as a man whose desire to marry Pegeen is profound and who shares her interests, if only in wedding swag. It may appear that Synge seeks to reduce his characterizations to those binaries beloved by Revivalist thinking – Christy's facility with poetry is good, Shawn's materialism is bad – but that simple reduction fails here, just as it fails in *The Aran Islands*.

This is confirmed by the fact that things greatly contribute to Christy's apotheosis. In *A Room of One's Own* (1929), Virginia Woolf attributes the paucity of works of literary genius by women in part to a lack of access to material goods: their lack of a private room in which to write, their lack of tasty meals to stimulate intellectual conversation. Before he arrives in Mayo, Christy suffers from a similar material deprivation, but his stories take on new, enhanced forms each time he gains access to better things. His narrative becomes richer and more detailed after he receives the gifts from the local girls in act two, and his language is enhanced further when he appears outfitted in Shawn's natty new clothes. As Christy asserts, 'From this out I'll have no want of company when all sorts is bringing me their food and clothing, the way they'd set their eyes upon a gallant orphan cleft his father with one blow to the breeches belt' (119). Christy associates the pleasure of material goods with the pleasure of his new community, and his increasingly sumptuous language reveals a similar association between things and poetry.

Concerned that Pegeen might reject him when she discovers that Old Mahon lives, Christy despairs this possible loss: 'Amn't I after seeing the love-light of the star of knowledge shining from her brow, and hearing words would put you thinking on the holy Brigid speaking to the infant saints' (126-127), to which the Widow Quin replies, 'There's poetry talk for a girl you'd see itching and scratching, and she with a stale stink of poteen on her from selling in the shop' (127). Here, Christy speaks the language of an advertising agent, sprucing up his commodity with elaborate, complimentary, and even inaccurate language that hints once more at the threat of female objectification. At the same time, he reveals his own desires, how they have been so stimulated he cannot see the object of his desire for what she really is. Widow Quin is, as it were, not buying it. Christy replies, 'It's her like is fitted to be handling merchandize in the heavens above' (127). Pegeen is portrayed as a salesgirl, someone selling wares – on earth, or in heaven. As in *The Aran Islands* and *Riders to the Sea*, Synge stages a world characterized by an easy converse between the material and spiritual realms.

The Widow Quin promises Christy a life outside of this market economy, but he has no interest. She offers him the idyllic existence portrayed in Yeats's 'Innisfree' with 'nice jobs you could be doing, gathering shells to make a whitewash for our hut within, building up a little goose-house, or stretching a new skin on an old curagh I have' (127). This is the authentic life lionized in *The Aran Islands* and other Revivalist tomes, but Christy wants the salesgirl and the stuff. Seeing she cannot seduce him with this bucolic fantasy, the Widow Quin returns to the language of the market that Christy has learned to embrace and quickly determines to drive a hard bargain, asking him for 'a right of way I want, and a mountainy ram, and a load of dung at Michaelmas' (131) – the same goods she requested earlier from Shawn – if she comes to his aid in his efforts to secure Pegeen. He agrees. As in *The Aran Islands*, the women in Synge's world drive the best bargains.

Like acts one and two, act three opens with a close focus on material culture. Here, Philly and Jimmy contemplate what might happen should the skull of Christy's father be unearthed by a farmer digging for potatoes. This prompts Jimmy to ask, 'Did you never hear tell of the skulls they have in the city of Dublin, ranged out like blue jugs in the cabin of Connaught?' (133). Even as Jimmy describes these skulls as a spectacle strictly for entertainment, the venerated skulls also suggestively recall sacred relics, most obviously those physical remains on public display, such as the right arm of St. Francis Xavier currently at the Church of Gesù in Rome. The skulls fuse Catholic belief and cultural display, but both Jimmy and Philly lack the proper reverence for these objects: Jimmy marvels at the promised 'show' of skulls in Dublin, and Philly describes his childhood pastime of playing with the bones of a man in a graveyard, where he would 'put him together for fun' (135).

Synge may lampoon the sacred qualities of ritual objects in this scene, but he adamantly maintains the inherent humanity of these remains. When Philly insists of these 'shiny bones' that 'you wouldn't meet the like of these days in the cities of the world' (135), Old Mahon enters and replies immediately, 'You wouldn't, is it? Lay your eyes on that skull, and tell me where and when there was another the like of it, splintered only from the blow of a loy' (135). Old Mahon draws attention back to the thing's point of origin in the human body, to the skulls and bones. He links the thing to the person, and in doing so, refuses the impulse of Jimmy and Philly to regard human remains as akin to mass produced objects, as things that are bountiful and available for play – even as Old Mahon's insistence on the unique quality of his own skull seems oversold.

The deluge of things that help to transform Christy into the Playboy of the Western World continues after he wins the local games. After his victory, the crowd yells, 'Here's his prizes! A bagpipes! A fiddle was played by a poet in the years gone by! A flat and three-thorned blackthorn would lick the scholars out of Dublin town!' (145). These are not gifts like the girls' foodstuffs or bribes like Shawn's new hat and coat; they are prizes Christy has earned for his stellar performance. And these are the things of art – the bagpipes of a musician, the fiddle of a poet, and the blackthorn of a scholar replace the murderous farmer's loy. But as Christy tells Pegeen, 'the crowning prize I'm seeking now' is her promise to wed him (147). After winning these prizes, Christy's language moves into poetry hyperspace, and Pegeen agrees to marry him. She can marry quickly, not because permission from Father Reilly has arrived, the dispensation that Shawn deemed necessary for a wedding, but because, as Pegeen announces, 'I, with my gowns bought ready, the way that I can wed you, and not wait at all' (149). Christy replies, 'It's miracles, and that's the truth' (151). On one hand, the 'miracles' refer to his fated meeting with Pegeen, but on the other they conflate the fact of her gown – its readymade nature and its fortuitous acquisition – with a miracle, a Christian supernatural event.

After Christy is revealed to be a liar and accused of killing his father a second time before the villagers, the material objects from the play take on a different meaning. The comparison of Pegeen to an objectified 'drift of chosen females' (167) stirs anger; the clothes, here a petticoat and shawl, are intended to conceal Christy rather than to celebrate him; the ticket out of Mayo is no longer a bribe, but an endeavour to save his life. Christy fails to understand how these things have changed. If the villagers can quickly acclimatize to his shifting reputation, Christy fails to grasp readily how these objects function in this new climate of antipathy. As they pressure him to leave Mayo, he refuses and insists 'for she will wed me surely, and I a proven hero at the end of all' (167), a misreading of the situation.

In the play's conclusion, Christy's flight from Mayo and Pegeen's bereavement are no longer tied to things; the language of the play's final moments turns to activities and abstractions. It seems that

Christy can leave Mayo only when he accepts that the gifts the villagers offered were never just gifts; when Christy recognizes the obligations inherent in their gifts, he finally grasps the true nature of the community and his misreading of their generosity. That knowledge frees him to leave. But it remains true that Christy, thanks to the same community, has come to see himself as a 'hot commodity', suggesting that he has internalized the logic of the market. But as in *Riders,* the woman, here Pegeen, is left behind, bereft, and trapped in her same harsh environment.

Much of Synge's writing supports our understanding of Revivalist ideologies of the thing: mass-produced material objects from England are bad; hand-crafted objects from Ireland are good. However, his writing reveals that surprising nuances lurk within this reductive binary. In both *Riders* and *Playboy,* as well as in *The Aran Islands*, there are moments when things – especially modern things in the wider world, less primitive and authentic objects – advance the interests of the community, as well as grant individuals moments of authority and autonomy. Things offer Synge's female characters a flash of hope, a mirage different from their destitute reality. Just as cultural nationalism promised political independence through the manufacture and consumption of Irish goods, and made these promises largely to women, these plays intimate that characters can obtain a similar personal freedom through things. However, in Synge's work, this promise, glimpsed briefly by women, can be fully realized only by the male hero, a poet like Christy Mahon.

My thanks to Susan Cannon Harris, Patrick Lonergan, and the participants of the 2009 Synge Summer School for responses to earlier versions of this essay.

[1] Bill Brown, 'Introduction,' *Things*. Edited by Bill Brown (Chicago: University of Chicago Press, 2004): 1-22.

[2] A rash of recent books and essays investigates the place of things in literature and culture. Recent work examining things in modern Irish literature includes Elizabeth Inglesby, 'Expressive Objects: Elizabeth Bowen's Narrative Materializes', *Modern Fiction Studies* 53:2 (Summer 2007). Special Issue on Elizabeth Bowen, ed. Susan Osborn: 306-333. Paige Reynolds, 'Colleen Modernism: Modernism's Afterlife in Irish Women's Writing', *Éire-Ireland* 44:3-4 (Fall/Winter 2009) 94-117. Stephen Watt, *Beckett and Contemporary Irish Literature* (Cambridge: Cambridge University Press, 2009): 40-49.

See also *Éire-Ireland* 46:1-2 (Spring/Summer 2011). Irish Things: Special Issue on Irish Material Culture. Edited by Paige Reynolds.

3 Sherry Turkle, 'Introduction: The Things That Matter,' *Evocative Objects: Things We Think With*. Edited by Sherry Turkle (Cambridge, MA: MIT Press, 2007): 9.

4 Toby Barnard, *A Guide to Sources for the History of Material Culture in Ireland, 1500-2000* (Dublin: Four Courts Press, 2005): 16.

5 Toby Barnard, *Making the Grand Figure: Lives and Possessions in Ireland, 1641-1770* (New Haven: Yale University Press, 2004).

6 Claudia Kinmonth, *Irish Country Furniture, 1700-1950* (New Haven: Yale University Press, 2003); Claudia Kinmonth, *Irish Rural Interiors in Art* (New Haven: Yale University Press, 2006).

7 J.M. Synge, *Collected Works II: Prose*. Edited by Alan Price (Gerrards Cross: Colin Smythe, 1982): 77. Subsequent references appear in the text.

8 Martin Heidegger, 'The Thing,' *Poetry, Language, Thought*. Translated by Albert Hofstadter (New York: Harper Perennial, 2001): 161-184.

9 Susan Stewart, *On Longing: Narratives of the Miniature, the Gigantic, the Souvenir, the Collection* (Baltimore and London: Johns Hopkins University Press, 1984): 139.

10 Karl Marx, 'The Fetishism of Commodities and the Secret Thereof' *Capital, Volume 1*. Translated by Ben Fowkes (New York: Penguin Classics, 1990): 163-164.

11 W.J. McCormack identifies several instances of Synge's musings on Marx found in notebooks, diaries, and letters. See *Fool of the Family: A Life of J. M. Synge* (London: Weidenfeld and Nicholson, 2000): 42, 143, 185.

12 Andrew Sofer, *The Stage Life of Props* (Ann Arbor, MI: University of Michigan Press, 2003): 11.

13 J.M. Synge, *Collected Works III: Plays 1*, Edited by Ann Saddlemyer (Gerrards Cross: Colin Smythe, 1982): 15. All future references appear in the text.

14 Sofer provocatively links the failure of the rope in *Godot* to other failed moments in modern drama (190).

15 Marcel Mauss, *The Gift: The Form and Reason for Exchange in Archaic Societies*. Translated by W. B. Halls (New York: W. W. Norton, 1990).

16 Jacques Derrida, *Given Time: 1. Counterfeit Money* Translated by Peggy Kamuf (Chicago: University of Chicago Press, 1992): 14.

17 J.M. Synge, *Collected Works IV: Plays 2*. Edited by Ann Saddlemyer (Gerrards Cross: Colin Smythe, 1982): 57. All future references appear in the text.

5 | THE BEST FIELD WORKER: SYNGE AND IRISH FOLKLORE

Éilís Ní Dhuibhne

> The women wear red petticoats and jackets of the island wool stained with madder, to which they usually add a plaid shawl twisted round their chests and tied at the back. When it rains they throw another petticoat over their heads with the waistband around their faces, or, if they are young, they use a heavy shawl like those worn in Galway. Occasionally other wraps are worn, and during the thunderstorm I arrived in I saw several girls with men's waistcoats buttoned round their bodies. Their skirts do not come much below the knee and show their powerful legs in the heavy indigo stocking with which they all are provided.
>
> The men wear three colours: the natural wool, indigo, and a grey flannel that is woven of alternate threads of indigo and the natural wool.[1]

The level of detail in this, Synge's description of the dress of the Aran islanders, is such that the garments in question could easily be copied using the designs described. The detailed account of clothes was partly motivated by Synge's appreciation of their beauty, and perhaps to some extent by his attraction to some of the people who wore the outfits. His deep, personal appreciation of both is not something he hides:

> The dull red of the petticoats especially if surmounted by a deep blue shawl is more quietly fair than any peasant costume I have met in Europe ... What has guided the women of grey-brown western Ireland to clothe them in red? The island

without this simple red relief would be a nightmare fit to drive one to murder in order to gloat a while on the fresh red flow of blood. (54n)

While this, and several of Synge's observations, are speculative and impressionistic, he is at least as often clinically objective in his descriptions of many aspects of folk life. His precision in such accounts partly reflects his photographic eye. Synge *is* a camera, if less self-consciously than Christopher Isherwood in *Goodbye to Berlin*. The level of detail in his notes on boats, clothes, kelp gathering, houses, and other aspects of daily life on Aran is greater than that in most post-Flaubertian flaneuristic literary descriptions, or even than that in actual photographs, such as those Synge himself took. The comparison it instantly and distinctly evokes is with the writings of ethnographers, anthropologists, or folklorists.

Since noticing the ethnographical quality in Synge's descriptions, I have discovered that others had commented on this quality in his writing. Declan Kiberd, for instance, in his chapter on Synge in *Irish Classics*, comments on Synge's anthropological tendency in *The Aran Islands*, noting that he had read Fraser's work, and posing the question: 'Was Synge in fact an anthropologist *avant la lettre*?'[2] Brian Ó Conchubhair, in a lecture on Synge delivered at the Royal Irish Academy in September 2009, observed that Synge had been influenced by lectures at the Sorbonne given by the philologist and Celticist, De Jubainville.[3] David Kiely, in his 1994 biography, writes that Synge read the works of the folklorist Anatole Le Braz, who wrote about the folklore of Brittany, and attended a lecture by him at the Sorbonne in 1897.[4]

It is reasonable to conclude that Synge's meticulous note-taking and detailed descriptions of folklife on the Aran Islands were influenced by his reading of scholarly and ethnographical works, and by exposure to the ideas and methods of folklorists, such as Le Braz. His awareness of folklore and ethnology sharpened his eye and his pen, and ensured that *The Aran Islands*, and his other travel writings, were richer and more interesting as social and historical documents than might otherwise have been the case. What is even more interesting to consider is how this ethnological sensibility nourished his skill as a playwright.

Most of Synge's plays are based to a greater or lesser extent on sources originating in Irish oral tradition: that is, in folklore. Sean Ó Súilleabháin's short and informative article 'Synge's Use of Irish Folklore', included in the *Synge Centenary Papers* published in

1971, is still the most comprehensive survey of Synge's use of folklore.[5] Ó Súilleabháin notes that *The Playboy of the Western World, The Well of the Saints, The Tinker's Wedding,* and *Riders to the Sea* all have roots directly in oral tradition. That is to say, Synge heard the stories, or parts of the stories, told by storytellers, usually in the west of Ireland. His receptivity to these tales, legends, and anecdotes was that of a folklorist. As Ó Súilleabháin puts it:

> He preferred, in his wanderings in parts of Ireland, to mix and converse with ordinary people rather than the upper classes. Thus farmers, shepherds, fishermen, tramps and tinkers form the majority of the people whom he met. He was an unflagging notetaker, always jotting down words, phrases, snatches of song and other items of lore, which served as material for his written works. (18)

Ó Súilleabháin also noted that Synge's prose writings were rich repositories of ethnographic data:

> His prose writings concerning Wicklow, Mayo, Connemara, Mayo and Kerry are very rich in documentation about social and economic conditions, and are useful sources for historians, ethnologists, and sociologists. (18)

Ó Súilleabháin, however, regretted that he didn't have the scope to deal with that aspect of Synge's work in his article, which focused on the relationship of the plays with folktales and legends.

The play which draws most exactly on a story from oral tradition, and for which we have the best source trail, is *The Shadow of the Glen*, which was first performed on 3 October 1903. There is not much mystery about Synge's source for the play. He heard the story on which it is directly based on Inis Meáin in May or June 1898, during his first visit to the Aran Islands.[6] The storyteller was Pat Dirane – a man of about eighty, who lived in 'a miserable hovel' not far from the house where Synge stayed, McDonaghs'. Although Synge used pseudonyms for most of the people he described in his book, in order to protect their privacy, he did not change Pat Dirane's name – probably because Pat died very soon after Synge met him, and before he published anything relating to him.

Even before he came to Inis Meáin, Synge had known about Pat Dirane. Synge's mentor on Inismore, Mairtín Ó Conghaile ('Mourteen') had told him that there would be an old man on Inis Meáin with many stories to tell him. Mairtín himself was a well known storyteller whose stories had been heard by everyone who visited Inismore – Holger Pedersen, W.B. Yeats, Jeremiah Curtin, and Patrick Pearse among them. His recommendation was reliable.

Synge met Pat Dirane a few days after he arrived on Inis Meáin. He describes the first encounter vividly:

> When I was going out this morning to walk round the island with Michael, the boy who is teaching me Irish, I met an old man making his way down to the cottage. He was dressed in miserable black clothes which seemed to have come from the mainland, and was so bent with rheumatism that, at a little distance, he looked more like a spider than a human being.
>
> Michael told me it was Pat Dirane, the story-teller old Mourteen had spoken of on the other island. I wished to turn back, as he appeared to be on his way to visit me, but Michael would not hear of it.
>
> 'He will be there by the fire when we come in,' he said; 'let you not be afraid, there will be time enough to be talking to him by and by'.
>
> He was right. As I came down into the kitchen some hours later old Pat was still in the chimney-corner, blinking with the turf smoke (60-1).

Pat then told Synge a story in English, which Synge called 'The Unfaithful Wife', and which was a version of an international folktale known to folklorists as 'The Wager on the Wife's Chastity' (AT 882) – a story which Synge recognized as an international tale even if he did not use that term, writing that 'it gave me a strange feeling of wonder to hear this illiterate native of a wet rock in the Atlantic telling a story that is so full of European associations', and he goes on to mention literary versions of the same story, by Shakespeare, Boccaccio, and Ruprecht of Wurzburg, also referring to a 'somewhat similar' Scottish oral version collected in Campbell's *Popular Tales of the Western Highlands* (65).[7]

While folklorists these days don't usually refer to their informants as 'illiterate natives of a wet rock' (and this is an unusual sort of phrase for Synge himself to use), the entire account of his first meeting with Pat Dirane, who was to be such a key informant for him, is reminiscent of similar accounts by contemporary folklorists. For instance, Ray Cashman gives similarly detailed accounts of his meetings with his various informants in his book, *Storytelling on the Northern Irish Border*.[8]

After the first meeting, Pat Dirane established a practice of coming to McDonaghs' cottage and telling stories to Synge there.

This is an interesting reversal of the normal way of doing things: most often, where an outsider is interested in collecting stories from an oral narrator, the collector goes to the storyteller's house. It seems clear from the information Synge gives us about Pat Dirane's house – namely that it 'a little tint', in Pat's own words, and 'a miserable hovel', in Synge's (100)– that the reason for the reversal of the procedure was that the storyteller's house was too uncomfortable. There is perhaps a hint that Pat got some food at McDonaghs' cottage as well, since he seemed to visit around dinner time. He was very badly off. An indigent bachelor in his eighties, he belongs to what the Danish folklorist, Bengt Holbek, recognized as the typical socio-economic group of oral storytellers in late nineteenth-century Denmark. Examining the informants of the great Danish collector, Evald Tang Kristensen, who collected extensively in West Jutland in the 1880s, he found that most of Kristensen's informants of fairytales were poor peasants, some of them smallholders or tradesmen, but the majority were landless labourers, so poor that they could not afford to marry.[9]

Pat appears to have belonged to this class. And he had another characteristic of many storytellers, although Synge does not connect this with his narrative ability or with his repertoire of tales: he was a migrant worker. 'He spoke English with remarkable aptness and fluency, due, I believe, to the months he spent in the English provinces working at the harvest when he was a young man,' writes Synge (61).

Synge notes Pat Dirane's history as a migrant worker in connection with his good English, but this background would have played a role in Dirane's development as a storyteller. Travelling men – for instance, tailors, who moved from parish to parish plying their trade – have traditionally more opportunities for learning new stories than those who stay at home.

It is not exactly clear how Pat Dirane's storytelling progressed after his first encounter with Synge: the sequence of time is not precisely described in *The Aran Islands*, and dates are not given for the narration of individual tales. But it seems that Pat visited the McDonaghs most days, if not every day, around dinnertime. Synge writes: 'As I came in she was busy getting ready my dinner, and old Pat Dirane, who usually comes at this hour, was rocking the cradle' (69). (There follows a careful description of the design of the cradle.) If Pat Dirane told a story or stories every day, which is possible and perhaps even likely, Synge did not record them all. However, on a day probably not long after the first documented story was told, he took down a second story from him. This is the tale Synge called 'The Unfaithful Wife', and it is the story which is the source of *The Shadow of the Glen.*

The Aran Islands provides a very full and vivid description of the circumstances in which the story was told. As usual, the setting was the McDonagh kitchen. There was another lodger in the house over these few days: a nine-month-old baby, a grandson of the McDonaghs. His mother was away at a fair in Galway – on a trip which lasted for several days, a sort of holiday, one assumes. It is interesting that a woman, and a mother of a baby at that, would have gone to the fair at this time. So the baby was being looked after by his grandparents, and by Pat Dirane, and by Synge himself, on occasion. He seems to have dominated life in the house, as babies do. He was teething, and became ill, refusing the bottle:

> The baby is teething, and has been crying for several days. Since his mother went to the fair they have been feeding him with cow's milk, often slightly sour, and giving him, I think, more than he requires. (70)

On the day the *Shadow of the Glen* story was told, he had taken a turn for the worse:

> This morning, however, he seemed so unwell they sent out to look for a foster-mother in the village, and before long a young woman, who lives a little way to the east, came in and restored him to his natural food.
>
> A few hours later, when I came into the kitchen to talk to old Pat, another woman performed the same kindly office, this time a person with a curiously whimsical expression. (70)

This is fascinating material, providing us with a luminous insight into the life of the island. There are not many accounts by folklorists of the detail of child-rearing, at this date or later. That women were prepared to breastfeed their neighbour's child, on a casual basis to help the child, is not something I would have been aware of, even though I have collected a good deal of information about childbirth and the care of babies from women in Kerry.

As the baby was being nursed by the person with the whimsical expression, Pat, presumably sitting close to her, told the story:

> Pat told me a story of an unfaithful wife, which I will give further down, and then broke into a moral dispute with the visitor, which caused immense delight to some young men who

had come down to listen to the story. Unfortunately it was carried on so rapidly in Gaelic that I lost most of the points. (70)

So we find out that there were also a few young men listening to the story. Thus we have an excellent vivid picture of the storytelling context: the woman nursing the baby, Synge, some young men, and possibly Mrs McDonagh sat around the fire, listening to Pat Dirane's tale.[10]

What is most likely Synge's transcription of Pat's story survives as Manuscript 4337, tucked into the back of the *Shadow of the Glen* manuscript in Trinity College library. The version of the story published by Synge in *The Aran Islands* differs from the manuscript only in a few minor instances, where he tidied up the English, which bears the marks of hasty writing, probably from dictation, in the manuscript. An exact transcription of the manuscript has been published by Ann Saddlemyer, as follows:

> One day I was travelling on foot from Galway to Dublin and the night came down on me when I was but a bit out of the town I was wanting to get into for to pass the night. The rain was falling and it was growing so dark I turned aside into an old house without a roof so that the walls would give me a bit of shelter. As I was looking round me I saw a light about fifty [feet] from me in some bushes. Thinkin' I'd be better in any sort of a house than there I crossed out over the wall and got up against the wall to look into the window. I saw a dead man laid out on a bed and candles lighted and a woman sitting up watching by him. I felt startled like when I seen him but it was rainin' hard and I said to myself in [my] mind that if the man was dead he'd do me no harm. With that I knocked at the door and [a] woman opened to me.
>
> 'Good even' ma'am,' says I.
>
> 'Good even' kindly stranger,' says she 'come in out [of] the rain'.
>
> So she took me in and told me how her husband was dead and she watching by him. After she brought me into the parlour it [was] a fine clean house and gave me a cup of tea putting a cup with a saucer under it on the table in front of [me] with good sugar and bread. A while later I came back to the kitchen where the dead man was lying out on the table and when I sat down she gave me a fine new pipe off the table and a drop of spirits then says she
>
> 'Are you afeard to be alone with himself stranger'
>
> 'Bedad then I'm not ma'am,' says I. 'He thats dead can do no hurt'.

With that she told me she wanted to go out and say to her friends that her husband was after dyin' on her and she left me then and locked the door after her.

I smoked one pipe and I leaned out and took another off the table and was smokin' it with my hand on the back of the chair the way you are yourself in this moment, God bless you, well, I was lookin' on the dead man and I thought he lifted his eyes. Then I was afeard and I looked at him still and he opened his eyes right open and looked at me.

'Don't be afeard, stranger' says the dead man. 'I am not dead at all in the world. Come here and help me up and I'll tell you all about meself'. So I went up to him and took the sheet off of him and I saw how he'd a fine clean shirt on his body, and fine flannel drawers. Then says he

'I've got a bad wife so I let on to be dead the way I'd catch her at her goings on'.

Then he got two fine sticks he had to keep down his wife and he put the two down at each side of him, and lay down again as if he was dead. In half an hour the woman came back and a young man along with her. Well she gave him his tea and told him he was tired and would be right to go in and lie down in the bedroom. The young man went in and the woman sat down beyond me to watch by the dead man. A while [after] she stood up and 'Stranger' says she 'I am going to get the candle out of the young man's bedroom. The young man will be asleep by now'.

She went into the bedroom and stayed there.

Then in a little while the dead man got up and took one stick and gave me the other and when we went in he saw them and he hit the young man with the stick so that his blood lept up and hit the gallery. That is my story.[11]

It seems to me that this story, as contained in the manuscript, is a fairly faithful documentation of the words of the storyteller, as faithful as you could achieve when writing from dictation or very recent memory of the story – and it was told, as I think there is every reason to believe, in English.[12]

The 'Tale of the Unfaithful Wife', as Synge called it, is a version of a story which is popular in Ireland and Scotland, although not collected elsewhere as far as is known. It has been classified as AT 1350, 'The Loving Wife', in *The Types of the Irish Folktale*, the standard index of Irish folktales.[13] In a previous article dealing with this folktale, I analysed the stories listed by Sean Ó Súilleabháin under this tale type.¹⁴ I don't want to enter into the details of that analysis here but the conclusion was that of the some 100 stories listed under this title in *The Types of the Irish Folktale,* forty-eight versions belong to the same type as the story told by Pat Dirane. That is to say, forty-eight variants of the story type told by Pat – more or less identical to his as far as plot is concerned, although varying in details – have been recorded, some by writers but the majority by the folklore collectors of the Irish Folklore Commission, all of which are available in the manuscripts of the National Folklore Archive, University College Dublin. The story was occasionally called 'The Man Who Pretended to be Dead' by the collectors who recorded and transcribed it and it is possible that storytellers also referred to this tale by that name, which is the title I shall use from now on.

So at least forty-eight versions of 'The Man Who Pretended to be Dead' had been collected in Ireland by 1966, when Sean Ó Súilleabháin and Reidar Th Christiansen published their index of Irish tale types. This constitutes a very substantial number of archived versions. Since the collected material is usually the tip of the iceberg of oral tradition, and one can assume that many more stories were told than were ever collected, the quantity of archived versions indicates beyond any reasonable doubt that Pat Dirane's story was very well known and popular in Irish oral tradition.

The earliest version of the tale referred to in *Types of the Irish Folktale* pre-dates Synge's by a few years – it is published in Jeremiah Curtin's *Tales of the Fairies and of the Irish Ghost World,* which came out in 1895.¹⁵ His version is called 'Maggie and the Dead Man'. Synge does not seem to have been aware of it, although he was certainly aware of Jeremiah Curtin's work, and mentions him and his collection of stories in *The Aran Islands.*¹⁶ Given that Synge fails to comment at all on this story's history in *The Aran Islands* (as he does on the story of 'The Unfaithful Wife'), he was probably not aware that 'The Man Who Pretended to be Dead' – or 'The Unfaithful Wife', as he called it – was a well known tale. The latest version listed in *Types of the Irish Folktale* was collected in Dromard in Longford in 1955, and I have collected a version as late as 1987. By far the vast majority of the versions known were collected in the 1930s, however – the heyday of the Irish Folklore Commission, founded in 1935.

The story has a fairly wide distribution: it has been most frequently collected in Galway, Donegal, and Kerry, but also in

Mayo, Sligo, Carlow, Longford, Wexford, Clare, Cork, Tipperary, Limerick, and Tyrone.

No less than ten versions were collected in Galway, in the 1930s, all in Connemara. None has been recorded on the Aran Islands, but this reflects the fact that little collecting was carried out by the folklore collectors of the Commission on the islands, which, as far as oral narrative is concerned, belong in any case to the same tradition zone as Connemara.

A complete listing of all the versions can be found in my article on this tale in *Bealoideas*. In fact there is not a huge amount of regional variation in this tale type, although certain details change from place to place: for instance, in Donegal versions of the story, the visitor to the house who helps the husband beat up the lover is rewarded for his efforts with money or the offer of a job, a motif which does not occur elsewhere. In Galway and Mayo versions, the weapons used by the husband to beat up the lover is always a stick, or even, more curiously, two sticks, as in Pat Dirane's version, whereas in Cork it is a shotgun or an axe. In Kerry, the protagonist, the traveller, is usually a woman. And so on.

A very interesting aspect of the story is that many versions are told in the first person, just as Pat Dirane's story is. In relation to Dirane's version, Synge comments on this:

> In stories of this kind he always speaks in the first person, with minute details to show that he was actually present at the scenes that are described.
>
> At the beginning of this story he gave me a long account of what had made him be on his way to Dublin on that occasion, and told me about all the rich people he was going to see in the finest streets of the city (72).

Unfortunately, Synge did not take down in detail this introduction to Pat's story. In telling it in the first person, however – in pretending to have been a participant in what he knew was a fictional story – he was conforming to tradition, particularly to the Connacht tradition as far as this story is concerned. No less than four Galway versions and three from Mayo are told as first person narratives, as are two Kerry and one Donegal version. In several of the Connacht versions, the first person narrator is a seasonal migratory worker on his way home from his seasonal work, just like Pat Dirane. In no version is the narrator or protagonist on his way to or from Dublin, as in Pat Dirane's version. Pat's inclusion of Dublin in his story was probably in deference to Synge, a Dubliner, or to show off to Synge that he too had been to Dublin. In all other respects, however, Pat Dirane's version of 'The Man Who Pretended to be Dead' parallels the other Galway versions. It is a full and authentic version of this migratory story. Pat had probably heard it told in the first person by somebody else, either on Inis Meáin or in Galway or on his travels – it is the kind of story which might be told as a warning to people going on long journeys, where they would sometimes require shelter at the houses of strangers, or to boast about the adventures and dangers experienced on such a journey. Of course its main function is to thrill and frighten the listeners; it is not unlike modern horror fiction, or modern legends such as 'The Ghost Hitchhiker' or 'The Hatchet Hitchhiker', which have a similar mixture of functions.[17] (In connection with this comparison, one might add that in several of the first person narratives, the adventure is set in the storyteller's youth. Many terrifying modern legends with a warning function concern teenagers or students.)

It belongs to a sub-genre of old traditional stories which are fairly realistic (thus lending themselves to the device of first person narration) but also macabre or grotesque. The landscape of this story, with its mixture of realistic and surreal images, of terror and amusement, of the banal and the unexpected, is not unlike the territory of the dream. And the crepuscular setting – captured by Synge in what is one of his most suggestive titles – adds to this effect. One wonders if even the storytellers – using the first person to give an account of an entirely fictional event wrapped up in what was, for many of them, as for Pat Dirane, a true memory of travelling as migratory labourers alone in the countryside – hint, among all their other suggestions, that it was all an eerie dream?

Since there is some scholarly scepticism about Synge's Irish oral source for *The Shadow of the Glen*, it may be useful to quote another version of the story told by a Galway narrator. This is a translation of a version told by Colm Ó Maolliadh, Leitir Meallain, Connemara, on 2 March 1942, and collected by Proinnsias de Búrca. This version is entitled simply 'A Scéal Féin', his own story.

> I have a little bit to tell you now about something that happened to me when I was a young fellow. I left home foolishly and I was over there in the place they call County Clare, going to harvest potatoes. But I wasn't able to harvest them very well at the time. I'd be picking at them and that sort of thing. I wasn't there for long when I became homesick and I was going home again. I left a place we call Mionlach, about twenty-four miles east of Galway, at midnight. I was going

along not knowing where I was going, since there was nobody with me but the dead of night, until I came to a place they call Goirtín an Airgead. I called in to a house then, because there was a good bit of the night left, and I asked for lodgings. There was nobody inside but a woman whose husband was dying in the settle bed. There wasn't a boy or a child there, just the man and his wife. She said she would be glad if I came in at that moment, that she wanted to go to the neighbours, because her husband was dying. I wouldn't be much good to her at this point. But of course I was afraid when she said she had to go to the neighbour leaving me inside the house. I would have much preferred to go with her. All the same I was tired and as well as that I was hungry ... and I was thinking ...

[*changes the cylinder, there is a gap and he starts again*] But anyway she stood up as soon as I came in. I was kind of tired and I sat down all right. The man was dying. He let out one big sigh, he closed his mouth himself, and his two eyes. He stretched out his two hands and his two feet. I didn't know what would be happening to a person who was just about to die or who was dying. But she knew it. She had seen them dying before. 'He's gone now,' she said. 'I suppose he is,' said I. 'Stay there for a quarter of an hour,' she said. 'I haven't far to go'. I was going to jump up to get out of there. But she had no sooner said the word than the door was closed and the lock on it. I was a prisoner. There was no way out except through the window and there was only one little tiny window that nothing bigger than a dog would get through. If I broke the window, it's true that I was so small then that I might have got out of it.

She stayed away for a good long time. As soon as she went out, the boyo came to me. 'Go down,' he said to me. 'I'm not dead at all yet, don't be afraid. In the room,' he said, 'there is a cupboard and take the butter dish that is in it'. I was afraid of him. I went down and got the butter dish from the cupboard that was in the room, a little awful room. 'Do you see now,' he said, 'that little gallery up there? See if there is a big blackthorn stick there'. I went up and I got the stick, a big stump of a blackthorn stick that was nearly a quarter stone weight, and knobs on it. I gave it to him. He put it under the pillow and under the bed. 'Go up now to the dresser,' he said, 'and bring down the cake that's there'. I went to the dresser and got the cake. He took it and cut it, a huge big chunk at first, two halves, and then he made two halves again of those, two slices down the middle, and he put nearly an inch and a half of butter on it. And he told me to go and get a big mug of milk ... he ate and drank, and then I left the cake back. As soon as that was done the boyo lay back and he was dying again.

Soon the girl returned, a big huge redhaired man with her. 'By dad,' said the redhaired man, 'he's kicked the bucket at last. We've been watching him a long time'. 'Now', said she, 'isn't this just what we wanted? He's out of the way now'. 'He is,' said he. All she did was go to the kettle and hang it up. When the kettle boiled and all sorts ready, and they talking and chatting to one another, and me sitting down, I got up to go out. 'Oh,' said she, 'don't stir till morning. It's not worth your while. You are as well off staying with us till morning'. I was making a thief of myself all right ... Who would not believe that I had eaten the bread and the butter and everything? As soon as she had made the tea she went to the cake, and half or more of it had been eaten. She asked me if I had eaten it and I denied it. Then she went to the butter dish and half the butter was gone, or more. 'Oh,' she said, 'who would do that? Isn't the butter gone too? There was half a bowl here when I went out. I don't know what to do. I'm not sure if a bit was taken from the bread before I left but I know nothing had been taken from the butter. So I suppose that you ate both the bread and the butter'. 'By dad I did not,' I said. 'You did', she said. They were giving out to me. What did the boyo do but jump up out of the bed, the blackthorn stick in his hand. He hit the red headed man and knocked him down. He hit him again and knocked him. He made for the door which was open or half open – it wasn't locked at this point. And as soon as the fuss and the fighting and the hullabaloo started I ran off myself, I got out of there and went off ...[18]

The above version has plenty in common with Pat Dirane's, as have most of the other forty-eight Irish versions. It is clear that Synge's version of the tale, as preserved in his manuscript and in *The Aran Islands*, is a full and faithful representation of the oral tale.

Usually writers who base their stories on oral tales manipulate them considerably in order to serve their own purposes. While storytellers do not know tales off by heart, and every individual narration is to some extent a unique work, writers are more likely than oral narrators to make significant alterations to their source material, sometimes with good results and sometimes cheapening and ruining a good story.[19] How did Synge use the story he collected from Pat Dirane in his play, *The Shadow of the Glen*?

He changes the setting, from an anonymous place between Galway and Dublin to a more specific location in the Wicklow Mountains. He gives names to the characters, who are functionaries in the oral tale, and he attributes stronger personalities to them:

Dan the husband is mean; the lover, Michael Dara, is cowardly. He calls the narrator a 'tramp'. I suppose Pat Dirane, like the migratory workers who told this story and who play this role in it, were tramps from a certain point of view, and Synge's tramp is noble and good, but it is not a description the storyteller, or any seasonal labourer, would have appreciated.

The main alteration Synge makes in the story is, of course, in the ending and in his moral attitude to it. Every oral version ends violently: the lover and the wife are beaten up, thrown out of the house, or murdered. Sometimes the wife is thrown out with the lover so it is possible that they go off together after the story. The scenario in which the tramp – the storyteller – teams up with the wife is Synge's unique invention. In the oral stories, the tramp character always sides with the betrayed husband; they are almost invariably of the same opinion, that the wife and her lover are at fault. This is also the point of view taken by the majority of the storytellers. They tell this story as a comic and frightening tall tale, and/or as a misogynistic story. It is interesting to speculate that the young woman who engaged in a moral dispute about the story with Pat Dirane might have held the same moral view as Synge – that is, that she would have had sympathy with the wife. Peig Sayers, who told a version of this tale in 1943, displays a certain amount of understanding for the plight of the younger woman married to an old man.[20] But her compassion is unusual.

Synge transformed the message of the play by adding a surprising twist to the end and by developing the characters beyond the flat ciphers or role fillers which populate this, as all, oral tales. Yet in many respects he remained surprisingly faithful to his source, even in quite small details. The house of Dan and Nora, for instance, is 'the last cottage at the head of a long glen'.[21] Pat Dirane's version is set in a house outside a town, hidden in trees, and in all versions the house is in a remote spot, as required for the scary atmosphere and plot (so there can be no easy escape for the narrator – he or she is trapped, like a hitchhiker in the car of a serial killer). In the play, the tramp is attracted to Nora and Dan's house by the light, just as in Dirane's version. In the play, Nora invites the tramp in out of the rain, which is exactly what the wife does in Pat Dirane's story.

Perhaps the most significant trait borrowed from the source is the mood of the play, its mixture of comedy and tragedy, realism and the gothic, light and dark (which are in fact also mirrored in the lighting of the play, and the story – it is shadowy, and moves from dark to light and light to dark). Among the many criticisms the play received, most of which seem all the more remarkable when one realizes how closely based on popular Irish tradition the play is, was that it mixed tragedy and comedy too freely. Daniel Corkery wrote that 'the outstanding weakness of the play, however, is the ... too rapid transition from mood to mood that occurs in it'.[22] A later commentator commended the play for being a 'tragically hearted farce' and describes it as a new type of English drama, imported by Synge from France'.[23] However, it is absolutely clear that this mixture of comedy and tragedy, farce and earnestness, terror and humour, is present in Pat Dirane's story and indeed in every single version of this story. It depends for its effectiveness on a mixture of seemingly conflicting moods and emotions, teetering on the border of terror and hilarity – a region occupied by many Irish stories. Synge introduced this particular medley of contradictory moods to the stage directly from the McDonaghs' kitchen on Inis Meáin, adding pathos and pity to the intoxicating mix.

In remodelling Pat Dirane's story for the stage, reinterpreting it, seeing the situation from the point of view of the wife rather than of the husband, Synge was doing what all oral storytellers felt free to do with the story types available to them. But he does not tamper all that much with the structure or cast of the original story, which, for all its apparent simplicity, provides scope for the narrator to emphasize one point of view or the other – hence the moral dispute which immediately broke out in the kitchen on Inis Meáin as soon as the story was told. It is a story, and by no means the only one, which poses a question rather than implicitly giving an answer (who is most at fault in this unhappy marriage?).[24] Synge, by making Dan old and miserly, points the finger of blame at the husband. But in versions of the story where the husband is neither miserly nor old, the situation is less clear. And, no matter what slant the writer or teller of the story takes, it remains open to audience dispute – which *The Shadow of the Glen* duly experienced, in the spate of protests by Arthur Griffith and others. That the play had the power to provoke such a reaction is not really surprising, given that we know the original story told by Pat Dirane had provoked its own lively 'moral dispute' in the summer of 1898, in a cottage on Inis Meáin. (What a pity Synge did not understand the rapid Irish in which the dispute was rapidly carried out! One wonders if that very dispute, understood or not, encouraged his interest in the play – he had advance proof of the story's capacity to engage and arouse an audience.)

That Synge had attended lectures on anthropology before visiting Aran and writing his diary and travelogue suggests that his interest in the detail of regional dress, boats, architecture, and so on, was motivated by scholarly considerations. All evidence indicates that he documented folklife and folklore with remarkable accuracy and fidelity. In short, in the field, he worked like a folklorist. His methods were not dissimilar from those of early folklorists such as Carl Wilhelm Von Sydow or Robin Flower or any of the later scholars who spent long periods in the west of Ireland. And indeed one might add that his method had even more in common with the observer-participation methodology of more contemporary anthropologists, as exemplified by, for instance, Ray Cashman, or Helena Wulff in *Dancing at the Crossroads*.[25]

The personal experience, the personal element, in ethnographic research, tended to be ignored by earlier generations of scholars, but forefronted in later studies, where the observers admit that they are part of the process – and that they like what they do. Scholars visit the islands, the remote Gaeltacht regions, for scholarly reasons. But they also like visiting those regions. They enjoy staying in small cottages, eating country food, walking, and above all they feel happy and at home in the company they find. They respect it. They love their informants. Scholarship, which is essentially objective and scientific, is in fact usually mixed with more subjective and emotional factors. This is most definitely the case where folklore, ethnology, and anthropology are concerned, although it is true of many other scholarly disciplines.

Synge was, as Kiberd notes, an anthropologist *avant la lettre*, and he recorded what he saw with reasonable accuracy, but he was also emotional in his reactions – as Kiberd also notes, commenting, for instance, on the blend of empiricism and romanticism in his personality, a blend which is common in folklorists and ethnologists – thankfully.[26]

Like the fieldwork of such scholars, Synge's careful observation of the lives and lifestyles of the people he visited in the west of Ireland was a form of love. The greatest fiction, and even more so, the greatest drama, depends on the ability of the artist to empathize with other people, to 'get under their skins'. Iris Murdoch, in her work on the philosophy of writing, remarks that the essence of art is love, and that 'Love is the perception of other individuals ... the extremely difficult realization that something other than oneself is real'.²⁷ 'Anthropology', like most such terms, has many definitions, the loosest of which in the OED is 'the science of humankind, in the widest sense'. 'Folkloristics', 'ethnology', and 'anthropology' are words which are used loosely in popular parlance (even as brand names for clothes and furniture) but they also have precise scholarly definitions. All these studies have as their ultimate objective the study of people, people other than the self who is studying them. Arguably then all good playwrights and novelists – according to Iris Murdoch's criteria – are anthropologists of a kind.

Synge, to an exceptional degree, was a scientific, painstaking, and loving observer and documenter of other peoples' lives and stories. This close observation, using classic ethnographical methods – probably partly consciously and partly spontaneously – gave him insight into the minds and hearts of others: as Kiberd writes, 'He cannot claim the islands: rather they have possessed him, and may yet speak through him, helping him to express a life of his own that has not found expression' (439). Synge found his raw material in the oral tradition of the Aran Islands. The islands gave him plots and characters, which is no small gift. It is likely that he also learnt valuable lessons about the craft of storytelling, of drama – that narrators such as Pat Dirane were his creative writing teachers, as it were. Clearly all of this was crucially important for his writing. But his empathy with the islanders and his insight into their hearts and souls was possibly even more essential for his development as an artist. And this empathy is something which he shares with the most dedicated anthropologists, ethnologists, and folklorists.

---

1 J.M. Synge, *Collected Works Volume II: Prose*. Edited by Alan Price (Gerrards Cross: Colin Smythe, 1982): 59. Subsequent references appear in the text.
2 Declan Kiberd, *Irish Classics* (London: Granta, 2000): 434.
3 Dr Brian Ó Conchubhair, 'Vernacular and Dialectical Languages in the European and Irish Fin de Siècle'. Lecture given at the symposium on the Fin de Siècle, Royal Irish Academy, 4 September 2009.
4 David M. Kiely, *John Millington Synge, A Biography* (Dublin: Gill and Macmillan, 1994): 17
5 Seán Ó Súilleabháin, 'Synge and Irish Folklore' in Maurice Harmon (ed), *J.M. Synge Centenary Papers* (Gill: Dublin, 1972). References appear in the text.
6 A fuller discussion of Synge's source in folklore for *The Shadow of the Glen* is available in my article, 'Synge's Use of Popular Material in

The Shadow of the Glen', Bealoideas, Journal of the Folklore of Ireland Society, 1990: 141-80.
7 His reference is to J.F. Campbell, *Popular Tales of the West Highlands* (London: Gardner, 1890).
8 Ray Cashman, *Storytelling on the Northern Irish Border, Character and Community* (Bloomington: Indiana University Press, 2009).
9 Bengt Holbek, *Interpretation of Fairytales* (Helsinki, 1987). Folklore Fellows Communications 239., 146 ff.
10 In *Synge, A Biography*, Kiely writes that the McDonaghs' house was a post office, which would explain why it received so many visitors.
11 J.M. Synge, *Collected Works, Volume III: Plays 1*. Edited by Ann Saddlemyer (Gerards Cross: Colin Smythe, 1982): 254-5.
12 See Éilis Ní Dhuibhne, 'Synge's Use of Popular Material in *The Shadow of the Glen'*, Bealoideas, 1990, 141-80, for discussion of language in which the story was told by Pat Dirane.
13 Reidar Th Christiansen and Seán Ó Súilleabháin, *The Types of the Irish Folktale* (Dublin, 1966).
14 See Ní Dhuibhne, 'Synge's Use of Popular Material'.
15 Jeremiah Curtin, *Tales of the Fairies and the Ghost World* (London, 1895). The story had been previously published by Curtin in *The Sun*, 1893.
16 Synge, *Prose*, 50. Synge's informant on Inismore mentions that Curtin complained that he made money from his stories. It would be interesting if one of these was a version of our story. But Curtin's version of 'The Man Who Pretended to Be Dead' was collected in the Dingle area. It differs from Pat Dirane's in several respects, not least in being told in the first person by a woman, Maggie Doyle – Kerry variants tend to be told by and about women.
17 See Éilis Ní Dhuibhne, 'Dublin Modern Legends: an intermediate Type List', *Bealoideas* (1983): 55–69.
18 NFC 802, pp 98-108. My translation.
19 See, for instance, Chaucer's use of AT 1186, 'With His Whole Heart', in *The Friar's Tale* – Éilis Ní Dhuibhne, 'Ex Corde', *Bealoideas* (1980): 86–134
20 NFC 908,273. Collected from Peig Sayers in May 1943 by Seosamh Ó Dálaigh.
21 Synge, *Plays 1*, 31.
22 Daniel Corkery, *Synge and Anglo-Irish Literature* (Cork, 1931): 126.
23 J. Thorning, *En moderne irsk dramatiker* (Copenhagen, 1921).
24 A good example of a 'question' story is 'Which Was The Noblest Act?' the basis of Chaucer's *Franklin's Tale*.
25 Helena Wulff, *Dancing at the Crossroads* (Oxford, 2008).
26 Kiberd, *Irish Classics*, 421.
27 Cited in James Wood, *The Broken Estate* (New York: Picador, 1999): 181.

6 | FAIR PLAY SYNGE

Mark Phelan

> An intelligent peasant, who was brought to see the acting at the Dublin theatre, declared on his return: 'I have now seen the great English actors, and heard plays in the English tongue, but poor and dull they seemed to me after the acting of our own people at the wakes and fairs'. [1]

The origins of the Irish Revival and the advent of modern Irish drama can be traced back to the extraordinary efflorescence of fieldwork by nineteenth-century antiquarians, historians, philologists, and mythologists of Celtic folklore and folk traditions – material which subsequently became both source and subject for cultural production, especially in the drama of W.B. Yeats, Lady Gregory, J.M. Synge, *et al.* Although scholarship examining the origins and impact of the Irish Revival is as vertiginous as it is voluminous, one relatively neglected seam quarried in recent years by scholars is the influence of primitivism on the Irish Revival. A product of profound cultural anxiety, given the rapid changes precipitated by modernization, primitivism played a crucial role in the development of Revivalist politics and aesthetics, as well as the dramaturgy of modern Irish drama. Primitivism also played a pivotal role in the development of international modernism. As James Knapp reminds us, Synge and Gauguin's visits to Brittany in the late nineteenth century were of seminal importance for both Irish *and* European art as they were the 'starting point for their artistic experiments [that were] so important to the Modernist movements in literature and the arts which were just beginning to take shape'.[2] From the exotic, elemental Brittany and sophisticated café culture of Paris, these avant-garde emissaries moved to new shores: Gauguin to the South Pacific, Synge to the wild west of Ireland.

Sinead Garrigan Mattar makes an important distinction between romantic and modernist primitivism. The former is reliant on Rousseau's model of the noble savage; the latter is moulded in the image of the savage god: a counter-representation generated by scientific developments as Darwinian theory decommissioned the idea(l) that 'primitive' peoples lived in a prelapsarian condition of 'naturalness' from which Western society had fallen, so that 'the degenerationist model behind the noble savage was transformed into an evolutionary one'.[3] And, indeed, Yeats and Synge's use of folklore and representations of the Irish peasantry reproduce both forms of primitivism. Yeats's early work was inspired by and infused with a romantic primitivism (though his later work is more modernist) whilst the advent of anthropology allied to some pioneering fieldwork in the Aran Islands locates Synge in the modernist primitivist mode. Declan Kiberd suggests Synge was 'an anthropologist *avant la lettre*', that his sojourn in the western seaboard was his *Triste Tropiques*, with the playwright even equipped like Lévi-Strauss with notebooks, typewriter, and camera (with which he took perhaps the first photographs of the Great Blaskets).[4] In many aspects, *The Aran Islands* is an exemplar of early anthropology: part ethnographic documentary, part autobiography, its primitivist gaze provides a platform for his critique of the ruthlessness of 'progress'.

Primitivism appealed to Yeats and Synge as a means of escape from the vicissitudes of modernity, industrialization, 'civilization' – all of which were axiomatically associated with Anglicization. It also was an aesthetic strategy to distance themselves from mass-produced popular culture. However, the irony is that the very sources and subjects of their folkloric-ethnographic-anthropological interest – fairs, folktales, patterns, keens, wakes, music, dancing – *were* intrinsically part of popular peasant culture. Paradoxically, the vitality of peasant popular culture and its inimicality with modernity (to which it was vividly, even violently, opposed) had originally attracted Revivalist figures like Yeats and Gregory. But it also caused them considerable problems, because the same saturnalian aspects of Irish society that they sought to idealize had previously been used to authorize colonial representations of the Irish as pre-modern, savage, ungovernable, irrational, brutish. For Yeats and other Revivalist artists and authors, if Ireland was to be represented anew, the rowdy, Rabelaisian nature of folk culture had to be rarefied. And if its carnivalesque peasant world of wakes, patterns, and fairs was to appear on the national stage, its Dionysian essence had to be disciplined by an Apollonian aesthetic (as too, did their audiences).

Synge, however, later came to reject this Revivalist strategy of representing the peasant, as expressed in the revelatory poem, 'The Passing of the Shee' (printed in full in Ann Saddlemyer's essay in this collection). Its epigraph explains how the poem is precipitated by Synge's contemplation of a picture by George Russell (AE) (whose painting and poetry embodied the most esoteric excesses of the Revival) and provides a stage from which Synge can gently renounce his affiliation with this particular form of Revivalist art. The first stanza bids farewell to the Celtic mists and myths that suffused Revivalist poets and artists (like AE and the younger Synge), whilst the second announces the poet's new inspiration and allegiance as he communes not with legend but with the lived experience of peasants and poachers. This simple two-stanza structure reveals the sudden rupture between the Revivalist representations of a romantic Ireland that is violently contrasted with a vital peasant culture of fairs, vagrancy, poaching, and drinking.

It is this disjuncture that I wish to examine further in this essay: the riotous reality of peasant popular culture in the context of its Revivalist representation. For the purposes of this essay, I have chosen to examine this in disjuncture relation to the representation and the reality of fair day in Ireland.

Fair Day and Fair Play(s)

> A fair, a patron or other public meeting seldom concludes without a pitched battle, and the loss of three or four lives. [5]

The music, songs, and stories of Irish folk culture are littered with references to fairs and markets, testifying to the central role they played in the social and cultural life of rural Ireland. They were important social occasions, not just for trade but also for the transmission of cultural histories, memories, music; for courtship and conflict; for recreational relief from the ardours of rural life. Many fair days have ancient origins, dating back to pre-Christian times, and many were organized according to special dates in the pastoral year. The harvest festival is perhaps the most famous, hailing from pagan celebrations of the *Lúnasa* festival which usually comprised gatherings on hilltops, or by lakes, rivers, or holy wells such as those that inspired Brian Friel's masterpiece *Dancing at Lughnasa* (1990) and informed Máire MacNeill's magisterial study *The Festival of Lughnasa* (1982), in which she traces how this pagan tradition became incorporated into Christian celebrations of Patrons and Feastdays. Today some still exist, albeit in the vitiated touristic version of Ould Lammas Fair in Ballycastle or Puck Fair in Killorglin.

However, the fires which smoulder in the backhills of 1930s Donegal in Friel's play are themselves literal and figurative references to the hazy borders between tradition and modernity. The blend of Christian pieties and pagan practices in these fairs and festivals reveals the vestigial traces of an earlier culture. With mention of Friel, it is perhaps fitting to consider *The Memoirs of the Ordnance Survey of Ireland* – Ireland's Domesday book – which sheds fascinating light on the pervasive occurrence of fairs and their profound impact on local life. It also illuminates why these events were much more than mere economic events. As a certain Lieutenant Lancey observes, the local peasantry 'have very little amusement or recreation',[6] especially as 'cock fighting, hurling and dancing are declining' – comments which resonate with Synge's words seventy years later in Kerry:

> Here [at Puck Fair] there were a number of people who had come in for amusement only ... a crowd is as exciting as champagne to these lonely people, who live in long glens among the mountains.[7]

It is the same with the blind piper of Padraic Colum's play who pleads to be allowed to attend the fair just so that he can 'be out in the day and to feel the throng moving about, and to be talking to the men that do be on the roads'.[8] However, the propensity for fairs to be disrupted by faction fighting (discussed below) causes Lancey to complain about their frequency, citing fifteen annual fairs in Fintona, Co. Tyrone, in addition to weekly markets, as symptomatic of this excess. He writes that those fairs:

> too frequently offer a temptation to the idler quitting their work, of which he is ever ready to avail himself, and the town overflows on those occasions with persons who have no business whatsoever to transact. The number of fair days could very advantageously be curtailed, as tending only to riot and disturbance and being profitable only to the spirit dealer and distiller, but what is the positive loss on these occasions? Look at the crowds of idlers who frequent the fairs throughout

Ireland with no object but amusement. How much valuable time is lost?[9]

In contradistinction to this colonial representation of fair days is the work of Charles McGlinchey: a Donegal weaver, tailor, and life-long bachelor whose oral history recalls the 'tale' end of a traditional way of life, in a narrative that was given to fellow Inishowen man, Patrick Kavanagh (whose recordings were later edited by a more recent resident of Ireland's northernmost peninsula: Brian Friel). Geographically and generationally liminal, McGlinchey was the last of his family line; his reminiscences luminously record the local customs, traditions, and histories of communities that inhabit the *mise en scène* of Friel's *oeuvre*, and provide a rich oral history of the local fair at Pollan, one of the largest in the north of Ireland, and which took place on 29 June and 10 October up until 1812:

> The people gathered from all airts and parts, and the green was black with people and standings and play-actors of all kinds. It was a cattle, horse, and sheep fair, but there was great drinking and dancing and singing carried on too. All the mentioned girls of the three parishes were there, and many a match and wedding was settled at the same fair of Pollan.[10]

McGlinchey recounts stories of how a notoriously predatory local landlord, Colonel McNeill, used to carry off local girls who were sometimes rescued by local men such as the formidable Séimí Airis McCole, 'a mentioned man with the stick' (53); and he relates how after one fair 'some Ardagh men felled him [McNeill] with a stone on the head and Eoin Airis McCole castrated him with an old hook'. His recitation of oral tradition of fairs is related not only in story form but also in folk song, notably in several verses of *Pléarnáca na bPollan* ('Pollan Revels'): a muscular musical account of the carnivalesque nature of these occasions dating back to the mid-eighteenth century:

> On returning up from the fair of Pollan,
> I'm asleep and don't waken me.
> With the rise of the moon and the breaking of dawn,
> I'm asleep and don't waken me.
> My singing and shouting and noise will be heard there,
> Heaps of big curses as if 'twas a dragon,
> My throat will not silence, except while drinking, till the morning,
> I'm asleep and don't waken me.
>
> Going over the bridge at the end of my spree
> I'm asleep don't waken me.

> There will be hundred of lumps on top of my head,
> I'm asleep don't waken me.
> My hat and my coat will be around me in tatters,
> My scarf and my shirt will be sundered in ribbons
> And my shoulders black as soot with batterings and blows,
> I'm asleep don't waken me.[11]

In this account – as with so many other songs about fairs and wakes – such revels, ructions, and riots are part of the event itself. Moreover, the motif of sleeping and waking reflect the seasonal cycles of the fairs, the ritual of mummers' plays (which embody these cycles of death and regeneration), and the wider performative culture of wakes and patterns.

In 1810 John Gamble disapprovingly noted the prevalence of 'club law' at Irish fairs,[12] whilst in 1812, another English traveller, Daniel Dewar, disdained not only the proliferation of fairs in Ireland but their propensity to 'present a scene of perfect confusion and intemperance, which is seldom finished without an engagement with the shillela [sic]'[13] – something the author eponymously insists is one of the *Causes which have Retarded the Moral and Political Improvement of Ireland*. Few Revivalists would have disagreed with Dewar's otherwise imperialist purview of their country. However, whilst Revivalist organizations and a resurgent nationalist movement in Ireland contested colonial attitudes to, and representations of, the Irish as congenitally violent, the hard historical facts reveal that homicide rates were far higher in Ireland than in England, whilst there were also enormous cultural differences in attitudes towards violence in Ireland.

This prevalence of violence and the difference in prevailing cultural attitudes towards it are refracted in *Playboy*: 'where now will you meet the like of Daneen Sullivan knocked the eye from a peeler, or Marcus Quinn … got six months for maiming ewes'[14]; or Jimmy Farrell who 'hanged his dog from the licence and had it screeching and wriggling [for] three hours' (73), or Sara Tansey, who 'yoked the ass cart and drove ten miles to set your eyes on the man bit the yellow lady's nostril on the northern shore' (97). Pegeen Mike too, is 'a fine, hardy girl would knock the head of any two men' (63) and Widow Quin is assumed by everyone to have killed her husband, whilst the central character of Christy is famously elevated for slaying his da, Old Mahon, who has also been in and out of the asylum 'for battering peelers or assaulting men' (85).

Ian O'Donnell attributes the high levels of lethal violence in late nineteenth-century Ireland to the 'persistence of "recreational" violence',[15] whilst Carolyn Conley highlights how disproportionate levels of violence (nearly half of almost 2,000 homicides between 1866 to 1892 in her dataset) derived from mostly drink-related altercations – 'melancholy accidents' where honour was at stake.[16] This widespread culture of 'recreational' violence meant that the (often shambolic) legal system could not sentence perpetrators with severe penalties and often could not even convict, as tolerant juries generally accepted such actions and pleas that perpetrators did not intend to kill their victims, who were sometimes blamed for having weak skulls: 'I put it to you in fairness, me lord, that if he had a very thin skull, the fair of Cappawhite was no place for him'.[17]

Whilst the Fair at Cappawhite was notorious for violent disturbances, it by no means had the worst reputation, as the infamous Donnybrook Fair literally became a byword for riotous ructions and was condemned (and celebrated) in myriad ways through music, song, literature, painting, poetry, parliamentary enquiries, sermons, and travelogues. *The Parliamentary Gazetteer* of 1845 described the Donnybrook Fair as 'a perfect prodigy of moral horrors' and stated that its vulgar dissipation brought disgrace upon:

> not Ireland alone but civilized Europe. It far surpassed all other fairs in the multitude and grossness of its disgusting incidents of vice; and, in general, it exhibited such continuous scenes of riot, bloodshed, debauchery, and brutality, as only the coarsest taste and the most hardened heart could witness without painful emotion.[18]

The hysterical tone of this moral condemnation became increasingly commonplace and eventually led to the closure of the Fair in 1855, although by this stage its infamy had deterritorialized the word 'Donnybrook' to signify any wild, unruly, drunken riot involving intoxicated Irishmen, whether at home or abroad. Images from *Punch* and *Harper's Weekly* of simian-featured, shillelagh-swinging Irishmen with unhealthy predispositions for drinking and fighting forged the enduring stereotype of the Stage Irishman of the popular theatre.

In these rituals (and their representation), drink and violence were often presented as revivifying and restorative, as reflected in peasant folklore and popular culture (songs, music, music hall, patterns, wakes etc.). However, they were later regarded as degenerative and debilitating by an increasingly hegemonic alliance of (otherwise incongruous) modernizing institutions and Revivalist organizations: Catholic and Protestant Churches, Father Mathew's Temperance movement, O'Connellite nationalism, Young Ireland, the Land League, the Gaelic League, the Co-operative movement, the Gaelic Athletic Association, the Abbey Theatre, and the state itself. This internal donnybrook between a pre-Famine culture of fairs and factions against the modernizing, monopolizing powers of the state and political nationalism could have only one victor, and the latter's triumph was almost absolute.

'Donnybrooks' were symptomatic, for the broader nationalist movement, of everything that was wrong with Ireland: both internally in terms of its citizens' behaviour and the way in which this became synecdochic for the country as a whole. In supplanting the signified with the signifier, the 'donnybrook' became the very symbol of Ireland that Revivalists sought to dismantle, and their success in so doing was widely acclaimed. The only regret expressed for the extinction of this tradition I could find comes, curiously, from a clergyman: Canon George Birmingham. 'The faction fights are over, but have we gained greatly?' he asks.[19] This lonely voice reverberates in the recordings and collections of the Folklore Commission, whilst a more muted threnody for this vital folk culture can be found in theatrical form in the work of M.J. Molloy, Bryan MacMahon, John B. Keane, Friel, Tom Murphy, and of course, John Millington Synge.

The world of the fairs, races, wakes, and weddings infuses all of Synge's drama, which captures the comic commingling of commerce and carnival that characterized Irish fairs. *The Shadow of the Glen* opens with the tramp travelling from Aughrim fair before his fateful visit to Nora Burke's cottage; *The Playboy of the Western World* opens with Pegeen Mike enumerating a list of products (including plentiful supplies of porter) to be sent to Michael James Flaherty 'on the evening of the coming fair' (57); *The Well of the Saints* opens with Martin and Mary Doul bickering over a missed opportunity to beg coppers from those 'after passing to the fair of Clash';[20] *The Tinker's Wedding* opens on the eve of a local fair for which its eponymous protagonists are bound as part of their itinerant travels from horse fairs in Wicklow to horse racing in Arklow; the widow Quinn imagines herself and the Playboy of the western world listening to 'the penny poets singing in an August fair' (87); and in the tragic *denouement* of *Riders to the Sea*, Maurya's last surviving son is drowned as he sets sail from Inishmaan 'with the horses to the Galway fair'.²¹

In his ethnographies of the Aran Islands, Wicklow, and Kerry, Synge records visiting fairs in Aughrim and the famous Puck Fair in Kerry. Before fair day, he falls 'in with tramps and trick characters of all kinds, sometimes single and sometimes in parties of four or five' (264) who are travelling to the fair, and mixes with the throngs of farmers, hawkers, and livestock as they travel into the Puck Fair, passing '[j]ust outside the town, near the first public-house, blind beggars ... kneeling on the pathway, praying with almost Oriental volubility for the souls of anyone who would throw them a coin' (265) – which obviously sets the scene for his *Well of the Saints*. Similarly, in 'At a Wicklow Fair', he joins with the 'curious' concourse 'one always meets in these fairs, made up of wild mountain squatters, gentlemen farmers, jobbers and herds ... tinkers ... tramps and beggars' who provided the *dramatis personae* for his plays.²²

To a lesser degree, fairs appear in other Revivalist dramas, notably Padraic Colum's *Thomas Muskerry* (1910) and *The Fiddler's House* (1907), whilst in Douglas Hyde's 1904 play, *An Cleamchnas* (*The Matchmaking*), two small farmers negotiate marriage terms for their children, though the son of one is absent, having come home late from the fair. In Rutherford Mayne's *The Turn of the Road* (1906), William Granahan, pious paragon of Presbyterian respectability, is embarrassed by his wife, who recalls how he once came home from the fair, full drunk on top of a bread-cart. Fairs feature more fleetingly in Yeats's drama. *The Unicorn from the Stars* (1907) makes mention of the 'troop of beggars. Bringing their tricks and their thieveries they are to the Kinvara Fair'.²³ The fair at Ballina is repeatedly referenced in *Cathleen ni Houlihan* (1902) in commercial terms of trade and transaction, connecting this materialistic, economic public sphere with the personal through the eldest son Michael's arranged marriage – thus setting up the nationalist-Revivalist narrative whereby Michael rejects his *paramour*, parents, and the bourgeois values associated with his marriage to follow the French at Killala. There is an elliptical reference to Puck Fair in *Purgatory* (1938), whilst in one scene of *The Death of Cuchulain* (1939), the material world of a 'Fair Day in Ireland' is contrasted with the mystical dance of Emer around the severed head of her lover Cuchulain.

In Padraic Colum's *The Land* (1905), strong farmer Murtagh Cosgar appeals to his son, with whom he is in heated argument, to rein in their anger:

> **MURTAGH COSGAR.** Stop. We can have kindness in this. We needn't be beating each other down, like men at a fair.
>
> **MATT.** We're not men at a fair. May God keep the kindness in our hearts.[24]

Fairs also feature in Lady Gregory's drama: in the *Travelling Man* (1910), the woman of the house is home alone as her husband has travelled to the *Samhain* fair; in *The Rising of the Moon* (1907), an escaped rebel prisoner pretends to a policeman (who is on the lookout for him) that he is merely an itinerant musician 'going the roads and singing in fairs';[25] and in *The Poorhouse* (1907), Paudeen berates Colum for the time he 'lay for three hours of the clock in the middle of the street [on] a fair day ... red drunk' until peelers brought him 'to the barracks'.[26] Her comedy, *Spreading the News* (1904), is set on a fair day and opens with the following fascinating exchange:

> **MAGISTRATE.** So that is the Fair Green. Cattle and sheep and mud. No system. What a repulsive sight!
>
> **POLICEMAN.** That is so, indeed.
>
> **MAGISTRATE.** I suppose there is a good deal of disorder in this place?
>
> **POLICEMAN.** There is.
>
> **MAGISTRATE.** Common assault?
>
> **POLICEMAN.** It's common enough.
>
> **MAGISTRATE.** Agrarian crime, no doubt?
>
> **POLICEMAN.** That is so.
>
> **MAGISTRATE.** Boycotting? Maiming of cattle? Firing into houses?
>
> **POLICEMAN.** There was one time, and there might be again.
>
> **MAGISTRATE.** That is bad. Does it go any farther than that?
>
> **POLICEMAN.** Far enough, indeed.
>
> **MAGISTRATE.** Homicide, then! This district has been shamefully neglected! I will change all that. [27]

This excellent index of the carnivalesque energies, violent excesses, and agrarian insurgency that characterized fair days is all the more significant for their utter absence in Gregory's depiction of an Irish fair which is shorn of these anarchic, atavistic elements, to serve up instead a harmless comedy about idle gossip. In contrast to this are the exchanges between the cantankerous paupers of *The Poorhouse*. That play is a study of companionship and interdependence, set in a bleak poorhouse where two elderly, immobile inmates are confined to their beds, from which they feud incessantly, fantasizing about further beatings they would give to one another if they could only reach one another:

> **PAUDEEN.** (*gnashing his teeth at him*) It's finely I'd leather your bones now if I could rise up, but remember, you vagabond, the fine welting I gave you thirty years ago at the fair of Dunmore, that left your stump of a nose crushed and broken from that out.[28]

In much the same way that Synge's Mayo villagers celebrate violence, Paudeen exults in the 'fine welting' issued, exhibiting none of Murtagh and Matt Cosgar's reticence about violence, for there is little of their 'kindness in our hearts', or in the thousands of other faction fighters like him for that matter.

After his travels through Wicklow and Kerry, Synge would have been familiar with the 'gallous stories' of famous faction fighters and the propensity for factions to clash at fairs and patterns. Although massively in decline by the late nineteenth century, factions still sporadically clashed with one another and this martial culture was preserved in the music and memory of local lore. Indeed, one famous ballad, written around the same year as Synge's birth, alludes to this tradition:

> 'Twas the 24th of June the day before the fair.
> When Ireland's sons and daughters in crowds assembled there.
> The young and the old, the brave and the bold, they gathered to sport and kill.
> 'Twas a curious combination beneath the cross of Spancil Hill.

Whilst nostalgia, homesickness and sentimentality are staples of Irish emigrant songs – of which 'Spancil Hill' is one of the most celebrated – many (mistakenly) find this music mawkish. But what is memorialized in this instance is not some idealized 'auld sod' – for this is no saccharine sentimentalized 'Ireland' but a savage, Syngean culture and community. The date invoked by the author is 24 June: fair day, St. John's Eve, where on the same date in 1834, factions called the Coleens and Lawlor-Black Mulvihills 'gathered to sport and kill' in the pastoral setting of Ballyeagh Strand, Co. Kerry, which was soon transformed into a bloody bucolic battlefield strewn with the bodies of dozens dead and several hundreds injured.[29] Involving almost 3,000 armed men, this engagement was one of the 'the most sanguinary faction fights that ever disgraced this unhappy country' as even the *American Railroad Journal and Advocate of Internal Improvements* reported.[30] Indeed, more were killed and wounded in this altercation than in all the nationalist rebellions of the century. Yet, aside from a few fleeting references and a single article in a local history magazine,[31] it has been almost entirely ignored by historians and other scholars.

Faction fights like these involved small localized armies, hundreds, even thousands strong. Consequently, faction fighting was rarely spontaneous in nature, with confrontations taking place at predetermined dates and venues, especially fairs, patterns, races, and matches – as well as weddings, wakes, and funerals.[32] Fighting was often 'conducted on business-like principles';[33] for instance, one report describes 'parties coming from separate quarters [who] brought with them carts filled with straw to serve as ambulances'.[34] The reasons for their feuding baffled the authorities of the time, and were often attributed to arcane, even trivial causes, although invariably many of them emanated from territorial disputes and the impugning of family notions of honour. The fight itself, however, became ritualized and recreational. Factions themselves were formally organized entities with members swearing oaths of allegiance 'to stand by each other at all fairs and patrons',[35] and they often had their own emblems, music, chants, accoutrements, and bars.[36] Connected by clan, parish, or politics, the factions clashed at markets, fairs, races, patterns, and festivals and boasted an extraordinary variety of names and aliases. Phillip Robinson lists the Billy Smiths, Billy Welters, Blackfeet, Caravats, Carders, Fraternals, Freemasons, Moonlighters, Plishers, Precursors, Queen's Boys, Ribandmen, Rockites, Shamrocks, Shanavests, Slating, Terry Alts, Thrashers, Three Year Olds, the Four Years Olds, Whiteboys, Whitefeet, and Widgeons or Northerners.[37] To that list could be added the Bawns, Bootashees, Bogboys, Blue Belt Boys, Oakboys, Steel Boys, Gate and Pudding Lane Boys, Liberty Rangers, Lawlor-Black Mulvihills, Black Hens and Magpies, Moll Doyle's Children, Moyle Rangers, Paudeen Gar's Boys, Polleens and Gows, Gumminses, Ormond Boys, Pallets, Guag Boys, Graces, Cooleens,

Coffeys, Chalkers, Keevaghs, Darrigs, Dowsers, Dingers, Grainshees, Tubbers, Thrashers, Rightboys, Reaskawallaghs, Resoultys, Gortacloughs, Houghers, Shaskans, and the Kinnegad Slashers, amongst myriad others.

Leaders of the factions were often colourful, charismatic figures such as 'Caravat Hanley' whose heroic demeanour and dandified dress gave the name to his faction as he flung his caravat to his followers from the scaffold whilst trading sartorial insults with his arch enemy 'Paudeen Gar' over his raggedy shanavest (waistcoat). Caravat Hanley was hanged in 1805 in Clonmel though he lived long in folk memory as a 'flamboyant dandy who strutted about by day openly sporting a "blunderbuss and a brace of pistols"'.[38] Factions and parishes held great pride in their local champions, like Seamus Mór Hartnett, who squeezed water out of the head of a blackthorn that had been seasoned for seven years up a chimney;[39] giant Bill O'Dwyer from Galbally, 'known to his friends as Bottom, who could walk into the enemy stronghold of Mitchelstown with his two bulldogs, Cull and Colonel, who he said were a match for the devil',[40] 'Great Big Mick Foley' memorialized in an 1837 ballad;[41] and legendary faction fighter Matt Ganley, who was even hired to guard mail coaches from Boyle to Sligo Town. Often these formidable individuals would fight one another in single combat before the rest of the faction engaged one another. There are even accounts of factions recruiting champion stick fighters from other baronies and counties to challenge the leading faction fighter of their local rivals. Indeed, champions themselves would travel great distances on their own volition to measure themselves against other renowned stick fighters whose reputations travelled beyond their faction and fiefdom via honorific songs,[42] some of which were folk precursors to later English versions that became popular, such as 'Mush Mush' which celebrated the champion faction fighter, Billy McGee:

> Oh, me fame went abroad through the nation,
> An' folks came a-flockin' to see
> An' they cried out, without hesitation
> 'You're a fightin' man, Billy McGee!'
> Oh, I've cleaned out the Finnegan faction
> An' I've licked all the Murphys afloat,
> If you're in for a row or a ruction,
> Just tread on the tail o' me coat.[43]

Such encounters are also recorded by Carleton, notably in 'The Battle of the Factions' in which the narrator's grandfather – 'a powerful *bulliah batthagh* in his day' – encounters his rival 'big Mucklemurray, who stood before him the greater part of an hour and a half, in the fair of Knockimdowney – for both factions were willing to let them try the engagement out, that they might see what side could boast of having the best man'.[44] Little over a half-century later, however, the status of such fighters has dramatically changed, as is evident from the fate of James Reynolds, 'one of the most famous faction leaders'[45] in Longford, who cuts a forlorn figure in post *fin de siècle* Ireland; expiring in exile in a bleak Cavan workhouse in 1903 after being banished from his hometown for his constant faction fighting. His fate reveals much as to how this martial culture was crushed by modernity.

One explanation for the celebration of faction fighters is that Ireland's ancient myths and martial culture had long valorized violence in extolling champions' extraordinary feats of strength, courage, and skill, as reflected for example in Ossianic lays, a vital performative aspect of popular oral culture. Another crucial contributing factor is touched on inadvertently by Lieutenant Lancey in the *Ordnance Survey Memoirs of Ireland*, when he observes of the parish of Clonmany, Co. Donegal that it comprises 'an industrious people for about six months in the year. The other six they do nothing except a few who occasionally fish'.[46] There was not a lot of work available for young men, a problem compounded by local dependence on potato crops, which required so little work beyond sowing and harvesting that potato drills were christened 'lazy beds'. It is little wonder, in light of Lancey's observation cited earlier that the peasantry had 'very little amusement or recreation' (50), that faction fighting also became a form of recreational release. This culture of recreational violence was practised and accepted widely, according to Conley, who argues that this is reflected in the statistic that forty-one percent of all Irish homicides between 1866 and 1892 were 'recreational in origin'.[47] Faction fighting was largely the cause of such carnage and yet was regarded as a traditional form of sport. Ireland's ancient martial culture also contributed to a situation in which the faction fights became agonistic recreational contests.

Synge's poetry, drama, and prose trace the contours of this culture, the most obvious example being Christy's elevation as a champion whose heroic actions and sporting achievements are celebrated by his adopted community. Synge's awareness of how communities can valorize violence is also evident in his poetry, notably in his depiction of the life and death of the eponymous anti-hero of his poem 'Danny':

> There's not his like from Binghamstown
> To Boyle and Ballycroy,
> At playing hell on decent girls,
> At beating man and boy.
>
> He's left two pairs of female twins
> Beyond in Killacreest,
> And twice in Crossmolina fair
> He's struck the parish priest.[48]

Eventually 'a score I'm told and nine' of Erris men beat Danny to death, but not before he leaves a number of his assailants battered and bloody. The violence of the poem was such that Elizabeth Yeats excluded the poem from the Cuala Press edition of Synge's poems, but in many ways it connects the poetics and performance of violence of Synge's theatre with that described in his travelogues of Kerry and Wicklow. Synge describes how, when races were held at high tide near Dingle in Kerry, hundreds thronged sandhills and milled around booths selling apples, cakes, and porter whilst roulette men and 'a number of the usual trick characters' entertained the public and others danced polkas in the dunes to melodeons.[49] When Jennet races were held they 'delighted the people' but subsequent disputes over who had won 'nearly ended in blows'. Later in the evening 'news had been coming in of the doings in the sandhills, after the porter had begun to take effect' and night had fallen:

> 'There was great sport after you left,' a man said to me in the cottage this evening. 'They were all beating and cutting each other on the shore of the sea. Four men fought together in one place till the tide came up on them, and was like to drown them; but the priest waded out up to his middle and drove them asunder. Another man was left for dead on the road outside the lodges, and some gentleman found him and had him carried into his house, and got the doctor to put plasters on his head. Then there was a red-headed fellow had his finger bitten through, and the postman was destroyed for ever'. 'He should be,' said the man of the house, 'for Michael Patch broke the seat of his car into three halves on his head'. (275)

This provides the inspiration for the races in which Christy Mahon proves his athletic prowess 'bringing bankrupt ruin on the roulette man, and the trick-o'-the-loop man, and breaking the nose of the cockshot-man, and winning all in the sports below' (133). It also provides the context in which Christy's violence with the loy could have been tolerated had it not been for the fact his victim was his father. Intoxicated by his victories on the seashore and 'drenching with sweat' (145) when Christy confronts Shawn Keough for Pegeen's hand, threatening to 'add a murder to my deeds to-day' (155), he is advised to head for the 'foreshore if it's fighting you want' where such violence is licensed as part of the day's sport and 'the rising tide will wash all traces from the memory of man' (155).

In honour of his heroic feats in 'racing and lepping and licking the world', Christy is awarded a 'three-thorned blackthorn that would lick the scholars out of Dublin town' (145): a gift ghosted with the legacy of faction fighting. Such a blackthorn was no shillelagh – a term coined by tourists and travellers – nor would it resemble the kitsch sticks hawked to hikers and tourists today. This was a fighting weapon: a *cleigh alpeen.* They came in a range of sizes, from eight to ten foot wattles to the more standard three foot alpeens, as well as smaller *kipeens;* short sticks used for close-quarters combat that could be easily concealed. They were usually forged from blackthorn, oak, and ash, though one champion faction fighter's weapon was made from holly that had been seasoned in brandy. Other accounts claim that whitethorn was never used as it could infect any wounds it inflicted. Fighting sticks were the subject of considerable love and labour. In his entertaining though sometimes suspect books, John Hurley draws extensively on Carleton's stories to describe some of the processes whereby *bata,* as he calls them, were prepared by the peasantry.[50] All sticks were carefully selected and cut with the ballroot attached to provide the bulbous business end of the weapon and William Wright's observation that, 'the shillelagh, like the poet, is born, not made'[51] is verified by other accounts, whereby particularly promising growths of blackthorn were jealously guarded and protected by those hoping to harvest the prospective weapon.[52] Once selected, sticks were trimmed of thorns, though sometimes several were left for either decorative affect or deadly effect, before the weapon underwent a long process of seasoning, with sticks 'sometimes tempered in a dung-heap ... others in slack-lime',[53] though the most common process of all was for them to be rubbed with butter or oil before being seasoned up chimneys for several months. Though butter and train oil were often used, claims that a special oil derived from boiling cows' feet was especially effective in seasoning alpeens.

One extraordinary account of this process is given by Wright, in which he describes how Emily Brontë's Irish uncle Hugh prepares a 'shillelagh' with which he allegedly intends to slay the anonymous reviewer who penned a scathing review of *Jane Eyre*:

> the first act was to dig up the blackthorn carefully, so that he might have enough of the thick root to form a lethal club. Having pruned it roughly, he placed the butt end in warm ashes night after night to season. Then when it had become sapless and hard he reduced it to its final dimensions. Afterwards he steeped it in brine, or 'put it in pickle,' as the saying goes; and when it had been a sufficient time in the salt water, he took it out and rubbed it with shamois and train oil for hours. Then came the final process. He shot a magpie, drained its blood into a cup, and with the lappered blood polished the blackthorn till it became glossy black with a mahogany tint. The shillelagh was then a beautiful, tough, formidable weapon, and when tipped with an iron ferrule was quite ready for action.[54]

Carleton also gives a detailed description of how fighting sticks were fashioned, seasoned, wielded and prized by combatants,[55] all of which transforms our understanding of the scene in *Playboy* when Christy is presented, as a champion, with a 'three-thorned blackthorn that would lick the scholars out of Dublin town' in honour of his sporting prowess (145).[56] The Folklore Commission also contains testimonies of how fighters christened their sticks with names like *Bás San Saggart* (Death Without a Priest) and *Leagadh Gan Eirí* (Down and Out),[57] and in a George Moore's novel, a faction fighter of the 'Two-Year Olds' christens his stick 'The Murrigan', meaning 'great queen' for 'she is the queen of the fair this many a day'.[58] Patrick Logan also recalls a 'famous maker of fighting sticks' from his childhood who christened sticks 'Rid the Lane', 'Dead with One Stroke' and 'No Opinion for Nine Days': the latter meaning that no medical prognosis was possible for a full nine days following a blow from this formidable stick.[59]

Any consideration of the frequency and ferocity of faction fights and the fact that these epic altercations often involved hundreds, and sometimes thousands of combatants, adds an entirely different valency to Synge's valedictory 'Preface' to *Playboy*. 'Anyone who has lived with real intimacy with the Irish peasantry will know that the wildest sayings and idea in this play are tame indeed' (53). He was right. Irish-Ireland claims that the Irish were not violent – as they had been *mis*represented in Synge's play – seem ludicrous in light of Carleton's accounts of faction fights and of a peasantry who exulted in violence as do Synge's Mayo villagers, who embrace 'a man did split his father's middle with a single clout' (157).

Less than a year after the founding of the Irish Literary Theatre, in his introduction to William Carleton's stories, Yeats stated that:

> The history of a nation is not in parliaments and battlefields, but in what people say to each other on fair-days and high-days, and in how they farm, and quarrel and go on pilgrimage. These things Carleton recorded.[60]

These things too Synge grandiloquently recorded in his brief but brilliant body of work. Fair play.

---

[1] Lady Francesca Speranza Wilde, *Ancient Legends, Mystic Charms, and Superstitions of Ireland* (London: Ward and Downey, 1888): 154.

[2] James Knapp, 'Primitivism and Empire: John Synge and Paul Gauguin', *Comparative Literature* 41:1 (1989): 52-68, 53.

[3] Sinead Garrigan Mattar, *Primitivism, Science and the Irish Revival* (Oxford: Oxford University Press, 2004): 5.

[4] Declan Kiberd, *Irish Classics* (London: Granta, 2000): 434.

[5] Thomas Crofton Croker, *Researches in the South of Ireland: Illustrative of the Scenery, Architectural Remains, and the Manners and Superstitions of the Peasantry; with an Appendix Containing a Private Narrative of the Rebellion of 1798* (Dublin: John Murray, 1824): 230.

[6] Angélique Day and Patrick McWilliams (editors): *Ordnance Survey Memoirs of Ireland: Parishes of County Tyrone 1 1821, 1823, 1831-6* vol. 5 (Belfast: Institute of Irish Studies, 1990): 50.

[7] J.M. Synge, *Collected Works Volume II: Prose*. Edited by Alan Price (Gerrards Cross: Colin Smythe, 1982): 265.

[8] Padraic Colum, *Three Plays: The Fiddler's House, The Land, Thomas Muskerry* (Boston: Little, Brown and Co., 1916): 148.

[9] Ordnance Survey, 72

[10] Charles McGlinchey and Brian Friel, *The Last of the Name* (Dublin: Collins, 2007): 51. Subsequent references appear in the text.

[11] *The Last of the Name*, 55-6. The ballad itself was composed by the poet Denis O' Donnell from Ballyliffin who was banned from attending the fair and locked in his room where he composed the 'Pollan Revels'.

[12] John Gamble, *Sketches of History, Politics and Manners: Taken in Dublin and the North of Ireland in the Autumn of 1810* (London: C Cradock and W Joy, 1811): 206.

[13] Daniel Dewar, *Observations on the Character, Customs, and Superstitions of the Irish and on Some of the Causes which have Retarded the Moral and Political Improvement of Ireland* (London: Gale and Curtis, 1812): 153-4.

14 J.M. Synge, *Collected Works Volume IV: Plays 2*. Edited by Ann Saddlemyer (Gerrards Cross: Colin Smythe, 1982): 59. Subsequent references appear in the text.
15 Ian O'Donnell, 'Lethal Violence in Ireland, 1841-2003: Famine, Celibacy and Parental Pacification', *British Journal of Criminology* 45:5 (2005): 1.
16 Carolyn A. Conley, *Melancholy Accidents: The Meaning of Violence in Post-Famine Ireland* (New York & Oxford: Lexington Books, 1999).
17 Dr J. Dowling cited by Patrick O'Donnell, *The Irish Faction Fighters of the 19th Century* (Dublin: Anvil Books, 1975): 51.
18 E. Estyn Evans, *Irish Folk Ways* (Mineola, New York: Dover Publications Incorporated, 2000): 256
19 George Birmingham, *The Lighter Side of Irish Life* (London and Edinburgh: T.N. Foulis, 1914): 44
20 J.M. Synge, *Collected Works, Volume III: Plays 1*. Edited by Ann Saddlemyer (Gerrards Cross: Colin Smythe, 1982): 71.
21 Synge, *Plays 1*, 5.
22 Synge, *Prose*, 226.
23 W.B. Yeats, *Collected Works: The Plays* (New York: Scribner, 2001): 213.
24 Padraic Colum, *The Land* in *Three Plays*, 128.
25 Lady Gregory, *The Rising of the Moon* in *Seven Short Plays* (Dublin: Maunsel, 1911): 88.
26 Lady Gregory, *The Poorhouse* in *Collected Plays 4: Translations, Adaptations and Collaborations* (Gerrards Cross: Colin Smythe, 1979): 297.
27 Lady Gregory, *Seven Short Plays*, 3-4.
28 Lady Gregory, *Collected Plays 4*, 297-8.
29 Estimates vary from around twenty to those wildly claiming two hundred perished, though certainly hundreds were injured. James H Murphy, *Ireland: A Social, Cultural and Literary History, 1791-1891* (Dublin: Four Courts Press, 2003): 35
30 'Dreadful Affray and Wholesale Slaughter in Kerry', *American Railroad Journal and Advocate of Internal Improvements*, 9 August 1834, 491.
31 Eamon Browne, 'Faction Fighting in Kerry, Ballyeagh Strand 1834' *Kerry Archaeological and Historical Society Magazine*. 9 (1998): 39-42.
32 See O'Donnell, *Faction Fighters*, 22, 77, 99, 185; John P. Harrington, *The English Traveller in Ireland. Accounts of Ireland and the Irish Through Five Centuries* (Dublin: Wolfhound Press, 1991): 228; Frank Sweeney, *The Murder of Connell Boyle, County Donegal, 1898* (Dublin: Four Courts Press, 2002): 19.
33 *The Irish Times*, 22 June 1878.
34 *The Irish Times*, 24 June 1880.

35 Paul E. W. Roberts, 'Caravats and Shanavests: Whiteboyism and Faction Fighting in East Munster, 1802-11' in *Irish Peasants: Violence and Political Unrest, 1780-1914*. Edited by Samuel Clark and James S. Donnelly Jr (Madison: University of Wisconsin Press, 1983): 64-101; 79.
36 O'Donnell, *Faction Fighters*, 25.
37 Phillips, 'Hanging Ropes and Buried Secrets', *Ulster Folklife*, Vol. 32, 1986, 4. Several of the groups enumerated by Robinson are actually agrarian secret societies and political groupings, and though they are not factions *per se*, their membership and activities were often blurred.
38 Roberts, 70.
39 Kevin Danaher, *In Ireland Long Ago* (Cork: Mercier Press, 1964): 125.
40 O'Donnell, *Faction Fighters*, 49.
41 See Michael Houlihan *Puck Fair. History and Traditions* (Limerick: The Treaty Press, 1999): 145
42 Patrick Lyons records James O' Flynn's account of Páidín Geárr, a champion stick fighter who lived near Clonmel, being challenged by 'the leading champion of the Thurles region' who 'set out on his quest ... a modern knight-errant ... a stiff journey of ten Irish miles' to challenge Páidín to fight him' and the 'resulting spree lasted three days'. 'Miscellanea', *Béaloideas* Vol. 13, No. 1-2 (1943): 270.
43 This song later became a hit for the Clancy brothers and, appropriately, features in the soundtrack of John Ford's *The Quiet Man* (1953)
44 William Carleton, *Traits and Stories of the Irish Peasantry*, vol. 1 (Dublin: William Curry Jun. and Co., 1843): 116
45 'Fair Play in Lanesboro, but no Faction Fighting', *Irish Times*, 14 January 1999.
46 *Ordnance Survey* vol. 38. 17.
47 Carolyn Conley, 'The Agreeable Recreation of Fighting', *Journal of Social History*, 33:1 (1999): 57-72; 59.
48 J.M. Synge, *Collected Works Volume 1: Poems*. Edited by Robin Skelton (Gerrards Cross: Colin Smythe, 1982): 56.
49 J.M. Synge, *Prose*, 274.
50 John W. Hurley, *Shillelagh: The Irish Fighting Stick* (Pipersville: The Caravat Press, 2007) and *Irish Gangs and Stick-fighting in the Works of William Carleton* (Pipersville: The Caravat Press 2006).
51 William Wright, *The Brontes in Ireland: Or Facts Stranger than Fiction* (London: Hodder and Stoughton, 1893): 284-5.
52 See Chapter 16 of George Moore's *The Story-Teller's Holiday* (Privately printed for subscribers only by Cumann Sean-eolais na h-Eireann, 1918)
53 Tyrone Power, *The Lost Heir and the Prediction* (New York: J and J Harper, 1839): 427

54 Wright, 284-5.
55 William Carleton, see 'The Party Fight and Funeral' in *Traits and Stories*, esp. 184-5; 212-215.
56 For Bruce Stewart, Christy's exultation in violence and joyous boast that he is 'master of all fights' marks his 'newly-won prowess as a faction fighter'. '"The Bitter Glass": Postcolonial Theory and Anglo-Irish Culture: A Case Study', *The Irish Review*. 25 (Winter, 1999 – Spring, 2000): 40.
57 O'Donnell, *Irish Faction Fighters*, 65.
58 Moore, *The Story-Teller's Holiday*, 68.
59 Patrick Logan, *Fair Day: The Story of Irish Fairs and Markets* (Belfast: Appletree Press, 1986): 103.
60 Yeats, 'Introduction', *Stories from Carleton* (London: Walter Scott, 1899): xvi.

7 | SYNGE, ANARCHISM, AND THE EUROPEAN AVANT-GARDE [1]

Shaun Richards

As is well known, Synge made several journeys to the Aran Islands, experiences recorded in the journal which forms such an important insight into the value-system which informed his plays. What is perhaps less well known, and certainly less commented on, is the fact that he was an equally frequent visitor to Paris in these years. In fact his Paris period ran from before, and continued after, his Aran Islands visits, starting in 1895 and ending in 1903, with the Aran Islands being largely an autumn destination – and then only for a few weeks at a time – while Paris was chosen essentially for the winter into spring, the rest of the year being taken up between Dublin and Wicklow. Unfortunately, and frustratingly, in terms of literary history at least, we have no Parisian equivalent to his Aran Islands journal. Indeed, as W.J. McCormack observed in his biography of Synge, *The Fool of the Family*, 'Pathetically little of his Paris experiences can be recovered',[2] and Synge never referred to the milieu of artistic experiment and political radicalism by which he was surrounded during his time there.

My suggestion is that we can very usefully make connections between Synge's work and this radical European milieu: connections which, if not supported by hard evidence such as a journal so as to become 'fact', will still enable us to add to our understanding of his plays. And we need to remember that Synge was much more than a tourist in Europe; he spoke both French and German, and while his social circle in Paris does appear to have been largely made up of Irish exiles, he did attend lectures at the Sorbonne – in modern French literature – and clearly could, through his solid reading knowledge of French, access the literary works of innovation and experiment that were being produced. Apart from some early poems written in French and translations from the language, his facility is demonstrated by the fact that when back in Dublin in 1901 he reviewed the opening of Douglas Hyde's Irish language play *Casadh an tSúgáin* (*The Twisting of the Rope*) for the French journal *L'Européen* – in French.³

This was a period in which the major works which largely defined modern literature were being created – in Paris. These are what Roger Shattuck termed 'The Banquet Years', when, particularly following the funeral of Victor Hugo in 1895, and so right at the onset of Synge's first visit to the French capital 'all the arts changed direction as if they had been awaiting a signal. Along a discernible line of demarcation they freed themselves from the propulsion of the nineteenth century and responded to the first insistent tugs of the twentieth'.⁴ The names of Gauguin, Seurat, Rousseau in painting, Faure, Debussy, Ravel in music, Verlaine, Rimbaud, Mallarmé in literature – to name but a few – can only hint at the explosion of artistic innovation in this period. And as is clear from Synge's referencing of Mallarmé and Huysmans in his Preface to *The Playboy of the Western World*, which was published alongside the play in 1907, he was aware of innovative symbolist literature, and as demonstrated by his including the names of Ibsen and Zola in the same Preface, he was equally alert to socially engaged realist writers. The reference to Ibsen within a quartet of otherwise French writers is interesting, but as with the other arts it's also the case in terms of theatre – namely that Paris was the centre of radical theatre experiment, especially in terms of production. It was the home of André Antoine's Théâtre Libre, founded in 1887, which was the innovative centre of realist staging; also of Aurélian Lugné-Poe's Théâtre de l'Œuvre, founded in 1893, home of the symbolist reaction to realism. And it was Lugné-Poe who was instrumental in introducing Ibsen to France, for both Ibsen – and Strindberg – were more likely to be performed within these sympathetic theatres than in their native Norway and Sweden. These were the original art theatres which influenced similar movements across Europe: the Moscow Art theatre, founded in 1897, being one, and the Abbey Theatre in Dublin, established in 1904, another. And Synge was firmly located in the midst of this artistic experimentation and conservative reaction which emanated from Paris and reverberated across Europe. Indeed, 'Synge's sojourns in Paris gave him a backseat row at some of the rowdier sideshows of European civilization entering crisis – the Dreyfus affair, the Arms Race, Alfred Jarry's *Ubu Roi*,[5] which was premiered at the Théâtre de l'Œuvre and directed by the theatre's founder Aurélian Lugné-Poe on 10 December 1896, and it was the same director who, on 12 December 1913, produced *Le Baladin du Monde Occidental – The Playboy of the Western World*.

Of course, in starting to make a connection between Synge's work and that of experimental European and, above all, Paris-based theatre, I am doing nothing new. Katherine Worth's classic study, *The Irish Drama of Europe*, established the basis of such a position in 1978. However, her orientation is towards the influence of one particular strand of the avant-garde on the emerging Irish theatre, particularly that of Maurice Maeterlink and a symbolist drama which aspired to music in its attempts to create an aesthetic which was spiritual rather than material. This resulted in a style captured in Yeats's stage directions for *The Land of Hearts Desire* (1894): 'It is night, but the moon, or a late sunset glimmers through the trees and carries the eye far off into a vague, mysterious world'.[6] According to Maurice Bourgeois, Maeterlink was Synge's favourite author and his notebooks towards the end of his life see him musing about Maeterlink's *Pelléas and Mélisande* in terms of drama as a dream, wondering whether, with the exception of Maeterlink's work, 'Is the drama – as a beautiful thing – a lost art?'[7] However any inclination towards seeing Synge's aesthetic as purely meditative needs to be off-set by a comment in response to a review of *The Playboy*: 'the Rabelaisian note, the "gross" note if you will, *must* have its climax no matter who may be shocked'.[8] The reference was to François Rabelais, Jarry's favourite author, and in the dirty realism of *Playboy* which was rediscovered by the Druid Theatre Company in the 1980s we see again the 'gross' note Synge sought for. And as Druid's director Garry Hynes noted in this context: 'The play belongs to the mainstream, the European historical mainstream. Synge is also a European'.[9]

The European line I'm tracing owes less to the delicacy of symbolist theatre and far more to the aggressive, 'gross' art of Jarry, and so I'm going to focus largely on Jarry and *Ubu Roi* in relation to *Playboy*, make some references to Ibsen, and a brief cross-reference to Frank Wedekind. But it's another dimension rather than the revolution in the arts and the theatre that I first wish to address, one which Roger Shattuck describes as 'The most turbulent force of all [now] almost forgotten', namely anarchism (20).

The characteristic expression of French anarchism in the last decades of the nineteenth century was that of individual acts of violence which were often conceived on a symbolic rather than practical plane. This was a period of the so-called *l'acte gratuit*, the gratuitous, random act of aggression, directed against individual members of, and institutions expressive of, the bourgeoisie. In the period March 1892 to June 1894, and so immediately prior to Synge's first arrival in the French capital, there were eleven dynamite explosions resulting in nine fatalities, and Mari François Carnot, President of the Republic, was stabbed to death. The key characteristic of these attacks – which were not limited to Paris – is captured by the bomb attack on the restaurant of the Théâtre Bellecour in Lyon. Describing the restaurant as a meeting place for 'the fine flower of the bourgeoisie', an article in the anarchist journal *Le Droit Social* concluded that 'the first act of the social revolution must be to destroy this den'.[10] Theatres, like the Chamber of Deputies which suffered a bomb attack in 1892, or the Bourse (Stock Exchange), the brokers of which were attacked with vitriol and revolver in 1886, were places where anarchists could be confident of hitting their targets, for the nineteenth-century theatre had become an essentially bourgeois entertainment. This is what Bertolt Brecht was later to term 'culinary' theatre and, in the words of anarchist Emile Henry who had detonated a bomb in the Café Terminus at Paris's Gare Saint-Lazare, such buildings were legitimate targets as they were 'inhabited by the bourgeois; hence there would be no innocent victims'.[11]

It was in this turbulent time that Jarry's play was performed, and as is well known Yeats attended the premiere with Arthur Symons. Although Yeats didn't understand the language, the confrontational nature of the performance, in which the flimsy plot was a composite parody of Shakespeare, and King Ubu's sceptre was a toilet brush, was clear enough for him to realize that a new and brutal artistic era had emerged; 'What more is possible?' he asked, 'After us the Savage God'.[12]

Nicholas Grene has pointed out to me the paucity of information about theatre visits contained in Synge's diaries of the period, which note only a visit to a production of Ibsen's *Ghosts*, but it's clear that although Synge was in Paris at the time, having returned there from Ireland the previous month, he did not attend the premiere of *Ubu* with Yeats. The fact that the play ran for only two days would have given little other opportunity. But it was during this visit to Paris, which lasted through to the spring of 1897, that Synge met with Yeats on 21 December 1896. Unfortunately, the extent to which Jarry's play featured in that conversation is unrecorded, but given that it was premiered only two weeks earlier, and had such an effect on Yeats, it is difficult to assume it went unremarked. However it was not necessary for Synge to have been informed by Yeats about *Ubu* and the combative artistic attitude it embodied; the final version of the play had already been published in June 1896, five months before the production, and the political and artistic turbulence of the period permeated publications and conversations to which Synge's command of French would have given him unmediated access.

The point that needs to be clarified here is whether we are talking about stylistic influence – and the answer is decidedly not – or what I'll term attitude. Both plays caused riots; nominally because of a word which disturbed the audiences' sensibilities – 'shift' in *Playboy* and 'shite' (*merde*) in *Ubu*. But the plays are worlds apart in terms of style; *Playboy* observed the major tenets of dramatic realism, while Jarry's flimsy, proto-Dadaist play was a puppet-style parody of *Macbeth* and *Hamlet*. But in his description of the 'ignoble' Ubu as 'really rather a spoiled child' who, like the bourgeoisie, demands that his every appetite is granted immediate satisfaction, one starts to see a unanimity in their attitudes to their audiences, and the society from which they were drawn.[13]

The issue here is that even if Synge had been in Paris at the time, and even if he had a sufficient knowledge of French to be able to access – even participate in – these radical political and theatrical discussions, why should they have any influence on the development of his drama – or even more simply, accord with his own work? That question takes us back to the Irish context.

I've noted the overlap in time between the Aran Islands and Paris visits and Declan Kiberd astutely recognizes that '*The Aran Islands* might be read as a document in the history of 1890s anarchism, with the community on Inis Maan presented as a version of the commune, a utopian zone where most of the discontents of civilization seem to be annulled'.[14] This, however, is incomplete in its engagement with Synge's overall anarchist attitudes – particularly those which have affinities with Jarry and *l'acte gratuit*. While in Paris, Synge had attended a lecture in June 1895 by the

French anarchist Sébastien Faure and commented that it was '*trés interessant, mais fou*' ('very interesting, but daft').[15] A similar apparent rejection of active politics is seen in his 1897 decision to resign from Maud Gonne's Paris-based nationalist *L'Association Irlandaises* after a bare three months of membership, informing her, according to a draft of the letter, that he no longer wished to be 'mixed up with a revolutionary and semi-military movement' but insisting that he wanted 'to work in my own way for the cause of Ireland'.[16] But a rejection of anarchist – and any revolutionary – physical force, does not mean an attitude of acquiescence and it would be a mistake to read this as a stark choice between the worlds of active politics and reflective art. In a review of *Journal Anarchiste*, published in May 1896, Jarry established the hierarchy that existed between the revolutions of anarchism and art in stating that the anarchists were simply men who could not write. In a similar vein one might conclude that Synge's termination of his brief flirtation with practical politics was informed not so much by a rejection as an actual embrace of social change, and at the most fundamental of levels: namely, an assault on the self-image of the audience which penetrated more profoundly than any assassin. Kiberd suggests that '[Synge's] initial ambivalence towards anarchism [gave] way to an enthusiasm discernible in every section of *The Aran Islands*' (328). This is a suggestive reading which, again, projects Synge's work away from the idea of west of Ireland retreat into something far more socially and politically engaged. But the anarchism which infuses *The Aran Islands* is that of the commune that lives outside, or in Synge's terms, 'before' convention; the anarchism is pacific not combative. However, while it was not published until 1907 it was completed in 1901, and so before Synge's exposure to the full wrath of bourgeois hostility to his work as experienced around the premiere of *The Shadow of the Glen* in 1903. After that there is a discernible hardening in his attitude.

The play was condemned by Arthur Griffith. 'Norah Burke is a lie' he said. 'Men and women in Ireland marry lacking love, and live mostly in a dull level of amity. Sometimes they do not – sometimes the woman lives in bitterness – sometimes she dies of a broken heart – but she does not go away with the Tramp'.[17]

The playlet *In a Real Wicklow Glen* (probably by Griffith himself), stages the fidelity which even the unhappiest of wives would display. Dramatizations of women's position in marriage had, of course, already rocked Europe in Ibsen's *Doll's House* and *Ghosts*.

And when Synge named his rebellious wife Nora, and allowed her a triumphant exit at the play's conclusion, the aura of Ibsen was all too apparent. Ibsen had already been championed by another Irishman, George Bernard Shaw, whose *Quintessence of Ibsenism* had been published in 1891, and Edward Martyn's Ibsenite *The Heather Field* had been produced in 1899 alongside Yeats's *The Countess Cathleen*. Synge's audiences would have been all too aware of the nature of the 'problem play' in which contentious social issues were addressed on stage, especially, in Ibsen, the rights of women to exercise free choice in their relationships. This was clearly a threatening concept in an Ireland where the post-famine practice termed 'familism' by the American anthropologists, Arensberg and Kimball, positioned the father as the centre of all authority and women were, on the one hand idealized as the pure embodiment of Ireland, while on the other being economic burdens whose value lay simply in providing cheap labour and producing sons. This was not a society which could welcome a woman like Nora, who could complain that her husband was 'always cold, every day since I knew him – and every night,'[18] boast that it's 'a power of men I'm after knowing' (49), refer longingly to 'the men who do be reared in the Glen Malure' who know how to 'drive a mountain ewe' (47), entertain herself with Patch Darcy and finally leave with the tramp. With *The Shadow of the Glen*, Synge was clearly seen as trying to introduce these 'morbid' and European obsessions into Ireland and effectively to undermine the very foundations of the nascent state. And Griffith was clear as to the source of this theatrical infection; it had its source in 'the decadent cynicism that passes current in the Latin Quarter and the London salon'.[19]

Synge's 'European' antagonism to bourgeois, nationalist Ireland was moreover exacerbated by reactions to *The Well of the Saints* in 1905. The play's reception was later described by Willy Fay as marked by 'crass ignorance ... fatuity [and] malevolence' and his record of Synge's reaction underlines the point as to the aggressive intent behind *Playboy*: '"Very well, then," he said to me bitterly one night, "the next play I write I will make sure will annoy them".'[20] It was clearly Jarry's *Ubu Roi* which staged the Europe-wide brutal reality of what Synge described as an 'ungodly ruck of fat-faced, sweaty-headed swine',[21] but he was equally committed to the attack, and for reasons which, like Jarry's, can be seen to have affinities with anarchism.

It's the period between *The Shadow of the Glen* and *The Playboy of the Western World* that serves to clarify this developing hostility. During this time Synge undertook a series of visits to the west of Ireland in the company of Jack Yeats, visits commissioned by the then *Manchester Guardian* for which he wrote a series of twelve articles published in June and July of 1905. The comments Synge made on social conditions in these 'congested districts', the poorest and most deprived parts of Ireland, are instructive and take us back into the politicized realm of class. I stress class because so often Synge's social comments are seen as born of a sense of Ascendancy caste superiority. George Watson, for example, commented on Synge's 'caste contempt, amounting almost to physical revulsion'[22] when faced by the rising Irish middle class and he notes that part of Synge's attraction to the Aran Islands 'is the absence ... of any trace or taint of the bourgeoisie' (40). Phrases such as 'ungodly ruck of fat-faced, sweaty-headed swine' and 'rampant double-chinned vulgarity' certainly suggest both revulsion and contempt, but they are the consequence of what Synge clearly regards as class exploitation. Much of his ire is directed at shopkeepers who, he said, 'would rather have the people idle, so they can get them for a shilling a day' as casual sellers of turf. In his view 'the prices charged are often exorbitant' and 'keep the people near to pauperism!'[23] And these same people were, he said, 'swindling the people ... in a dozen ways and then buying out their holdings and packing off whole families to America'.[24]

This Ireland, as described by the historian F.S.L. Lyons, was one which, pre-Famine, had been distinguished by an economic system resting on a secure aristocracy and 'an impoverished and insecure peasantry', but was now seeing the emergence of a bourgeoisie.[25] And at the heart of the social and economic system was what was referred to as the 'gombeen man' – the word derived from the Irish *gaimbín*, meaning monetary interest. And in the description given by AE (George Russell) we see how powerful and pervasive was the social network they constructed:

> In congested Ireland every job which can be filled by the kith and kin of the gombeen kings and queens is filled accordingly, and you get every kind of inefficiency and jobbery. They are all publicans, and their friends are all strong drinkers. They beget people of their own character and appoint them lieutenants and non-commissioned officers in their service ... in fact round the gombeen system reels the whole drunken congested world,

and underneath this revelry and jobbery the unfortunate peasant labours and gets no return for his labour.[26]

W.B. Yeats famously denied that Synge had any political interests, stating that:

> Synge seemed by nature unfitted to think a political thought, and with the exception of one sentence, spoken when I first met him in Paris, that implied some sort of nationalist conviction, I cannot remember that he spoke of politics or showed any interest in men in the mass.[27]

Synge's comments on the conditions in the congested districts certainly disprove the last comment on 'men in the mass' but while contemporary criticism has increasingly read Synge's work as informed by politics, it has tended to run in the line indicated in the quotation about 'caste' which I quoted from George Watson. Probably the best known instance is Seamus Deane's argument that 'famine, eviction, military oppression and landlordism, the characteristic facts of late-nineteenth-century Irish rural existence for the peasantry are almost entirely repressed features' of Synge's work and, in Deane's view, he effectively creams off and idealizes an indigenous Gaelic culture which his own class, and own family, had been culpable in impoverishing.[28]

I'm not seeking to deny the Ascendancy dimension of Synge's attitude to the changing Ireland he encountered, but rather I want to stress the point made by Bruce Arnold that Synge 'wavered between socialism and communism'.[29] And while, from our contemporary standpoint, there are sharp distinctions to be drawn between those ideologies and anarchism, the late-nineteenth century reality is that these were all variants on radical, and frequently violent, means of overthrowing the status quo, and social engagement, and associated social change, were certainly part of Synge's background. While the original letter from Synge to his mother in November 1896 no longer exists, her revealing commentary on the correspondence does: 'poor Johnnie ... he says he has gone back to Paris to study socialism and he wants to do good'.[30] While the phrase 'wants to do good' suggests unfocused ineffectuality, the combination of an impulse to effective ameliorative action, coupled with an interest in socialism, clearly suggests that Synge's re-entry into the anarchist-infused air of a Paris about to experience *Ubu Roi* was fuelled by a politics which extended beyond the confines of Ascendancy 'caste': concerns which were further informed, and focused, by his *Manchester Guardian* commission. And, in a letter to his friend,

Stephen MacKenna, the relationship between his perceptions of the society of the congested districts, his politics – and the plays, come into focus. He first gave MacKenna a vitriolic verdict on what he found during his 1905 visit to Mayo, the setting of *Playboy*:

> There are sides of all that western life, the groggy-patriot-publican-general-shop-man who is married to the priest's half-sister and is second cousin once-removed of the dispensary doctor, that are horrible and awful … All that side of the matter of course I left untouched in my stuff. I sometimes wish to God I hadn't a soul and then I could give myself up to putting those lads on the stage. God, wouldn't they hop![31]

The contemporary reality was that this class sought to achieve a political power commensurate with its growing economic strength and cultural self-confidence. Central to their agenda, and increasingly Synge's despair and displeasure, was the work of the Gaelic League, established in 1893 to support the speaking of Irish and, through its Oireachtas (gatherings), the preservation of Irish dance, music, and poetry. The League was non-sectarian in its origins; indeed its founder, Douglas Hyde, was a Protestant. However, as Tom Garvin writes:

> By the middle of the first decade of the twentieth century, an organization which had been started with inter-faith cultural intentions had been transformed into a mass organization dominated by Catholics and increasingly subservient to political forces that were republican, separatist or clericalist.[32]

Synge's perception was that this nexus of interests preferred to idealize rather than analyse Ireland, and was creating a society which, in his words, feared 'any gleam of truth'.[33] His feelings are expressed in a sketch for a play which he wrote while working on *Playboy*, *National Drama: A Farce*, where an unnamed cultural nationalist group – as interested in alcohol as art – seeks to define a national Irish drama 'which contains the manifold and fine qualities of the Irish race, their love for the land of their forefathers, and their poetic familiarity with the glittering and unseen forms of the visionary world'. But, above all, 'The National Drama of Catholic Ireland must have no sex'.[34] This was decidedly neither Synge's view, nor his practice, as expressed perhaps most succinctly in his January 1904 letter to Stephen MacKenna: 'I think squeamishness is a disease and that Ireland will gain if Irish writers deal manfully, directly and decently with the entire reality of life'.[35] Although at times Synge appears to doubt his courage to address the fallen state of Irish society, he does consistently claim to engage with one denied reality – the sexual.

Writing to MacKenna, Synge observed that 'on the Irish stage the people want the other elements without the sex. I restored the sex-element to its natural place'[36] and in the draft of this letter he stresses the extent to which his knowledge of the realities of Irish sexuality are based on what can perhaps be described as field-work:

> I have as you know perambulated a good deal of Ireland in my thirty years and if I were to tell, which heaven forbid, all the sex-horrors I have seen I could a tale unfold that would wither up your blood.[37]

As is clear from *The Shadow of the Glen*, an issue which clearly engaged Synge is the denial of desire; the repression effected on the young by the old, above all in a society where economic power ensured that it was normally only the elderly males who could fully exercise choice in finding a mate. As noted, Ibsen had already engaged with the issue of a woman's position within marriage, and in *Ghosts*, which followed *A Doll's House*, showed the devastating personal and social consequences of denial – and scandalized Europe through its explicit suggestion of both syphilis and incest as the outcome. But it was probably the German playwright Frank Wedekind who engaged most provocatively with the subject of sexual denial in his plays *Spring Awakening* (1891) and the Lulu plays *Earth Spirit* and *Pandora's Box* (1895 and 1904 respectively). Synge, of course spoke German and spent time in the country – reading Ibsen in German. This was in 1893-94 and so just prior to his first Paris visit. Wedekind's *Spring Awakening* focuses on sexual denial and suicide among adolescents, and although there's no evidence as to Synge's knowledge of his work there is strong evidence of his interest at this time in what W.J. McCormack calls 'difficult reading', specifically Marx, Nietzsche, Wagner, and Schopenhauer, which 'constituted a first step towards ... the lively (and deadly) issues which would define Modernism' (112). This clearly set Synge against a national drama, and the class who supported it, which would be anything other than open, honest and, as necessary, 'gross'. For while my focus here is on Jarry, Synge's work is allied to that of an avant-garde which transcends national borders: one which, moreover, saw its rejection of conventional morality as central to its attack on the very fundamentals of bourgeois society.

In *A National Drama: A Farce* it's the character of Jameson who summarizes the vapidity of a 'national' theatre which suppressed society's harsh truths, asking rhetorically, 'In short you think that the Irish drama should hold up a mirror to the Irish Nation and it going to Mass on a fine springdayish Sunday?'[38] This echoes Synge's own distaste for what he termed 'a purely fantastic unmodern ideal breezy springdayish Cuchulainoid National Theatre',[39] a rejection of saga-sentimentality which suggests that his work will not only be modern, but unyielding in its search for truth. As he stated in 1904 'what I write of Irish country life I know to be true and I most emphattically [sic] will not change a syllable of it because A. B. or C. may think they know better than I do'.[40] *Playboy* is that truth, unremitting in its gaze and refusal to turn its back on 'the entire reality of life'.

Playboy opens with Pegeen, 'a wild-looking but fine girl of about twenty'.[41] As she is alone on stage the audience has to focus on the fact that she is writing out the order for her trousseau, but when the fact rapidly emerges that she is destined to marry the 'fat and fair' Shawn Keogh they have to be struck by the disparity between their physical and psychological characteristics (57). But the only other men of the community seen on stage apart from Pegeen's father are Philly O'Cullen, 'thin and mistrusting' and Jimmy Farrell 'who is fat and amorous, about forty-five' (60-1). In this context it is not only Shawn's youth, but also his wealth, which makes him the obvious husband for Pegeen. And Shawn in this context is wealthy, and the whole marriage project with Pegeen is based on wealth and a calculation which owes more to profit than passion. Shawn himself speaks of the match being 'a good bargain' (59). Interestingly, when Pegeen initially defends Shawn against the mockery of her father, Philly and Jimmy, asking what right they have 'to be making game of a poor fellow for minding the priest', the stage directions indicate that she is simply 'taking up the defence of her property' (65), a note which chimes with a description of her in an early draft of the play as being 'ambitious in all ways' (56). She is no innocent in this world. However, it is equally the case that this is a marriage which her father speaks of as having 'chosen' for her and one which is totally based on material transactions and which Shawn is prepared to use his wealth to defend: seeking to obtain the Widow Quin's support in the venture he offers so much in the way of live-stock, property-rights and other gifts that she interrupts him with 'That'll do, so' (117). But it's the dowry which provides the key information as to the very clear economic class point Synge wishes to make. The dowry is being provided by Shawn – the prospective husband, not Michael, the prospective father-in-law – and it is substantial. When the possibility of the marriage appears to be foundering, Shawn reminds Michael of how much he stands to lose: a 'drift of heifers' and a 'blue bull from Sneem' (155). The full significance of this is found in the cast list for the play: while both Philly and Jimmy are described as 'small farmers', Shawn is given simply as 'farmer'. This demonstrates Synge's awareness of the class divisions operating in rural Ireland in which 'small farmers', who still largely survived on the basis of an economy of potato cultivation, were subordinate to the 'strong farmers' who were progressively consolidating their land holdings and shaping the transition to an agrarian capitalism based on cattle. And Shawn clearly is part of this emerging economic elite just as he is in his piety.

Shawn's moral principles are derived from the fact that he is 'afeard of Father Reilly'. This, coupled with his preference for his bed as opposed to the drunken wake for Kate Cassidy, suggests that he is the product of the 'devotional revolution' which, inspired by Cardinal Paul Cullen, sought to replace semi-pagan practices, such as wakes, with standardized, church-approved alternatives. The emerging bourgeoisie of post-Famine Irish society embraced this morally upright lifestyle as it accorded with their general disdain for profligacy and preference for the consolidation of wealth. Indeed, as argued by Luke Gibbons, this religious 'revolution' was 'part of an overall modernizing thrust', one of several features demonstrating Ireland's 'direct integration into the capitalist world economy'.[42] Shawn's class position is reinforced throughout the text and a marginal note which Synge included in an early draft, 'work through Shawn's righteousness in contrast with Christy' (64), clearly suggests that 'righteousness' is to be seen as negative.

On the surface Old Mahon appears to be a polar opposite to Shawn and the value system he embodies. The latter is teetotal; Old Mahon is alcoholic. The attempt to force Christy into marriage with the Widow Casey was so that he would 'have her gold to drink' (103), and while Michael's reasons for arranging the marriage of Pegeen is not expressed in such overt and brutal terms it is still a match he has 'chosen' (153) for clear economic gain. Father Reilly's power over Shawn is no less complete for being driven by devotion, for what all three 'fathers' look to achieve is the removal of autonomous free-choice from their various 'off-spring'; the difference between Shawn and Christy and, to a lesser extent, Pegeen, is the extent to which they resist incorporation within the patriarchal power-structure, and it is the basis of that resistance, and its implications for the individual and society, which is of particular interest.

Michael's description of Shawn as a 'shy and decent Christian' (153) establishes one end of the spectrum on which he is viewed, by Shawn, as an 'old Pagan' (65). The idea of a pagan substratum to Irish culture was central to Synge's thinking as is made clear in a passage from *The Aran Islands* where he recounts how an old man knelt by a funeral grave-side and repeated a prayer for the dead. But, for Synge, this expression of Christian faith was a superficial accretion on a bed-rock reality:

> There was an irony in these words of atonement and Catholic belief spoken by voices that were still hoarse with the cries of pagan desperation which, more truly, expressed 'the inner consciousness of the people'.[43]

While Michael's mix of drunkenness and cupidity is a corruption of any indigenous pagan impulse, enough remains for him to, temporarily at least, prefer Pegeen's marriage to Christy as 'I liefer face the grave untimely and I seeing a score of grandsons growing up gallant little swearers by the name of God, than go peopling my bedside with puny weeds the like of what you'd breed, I'm thinking, out of Shaneen Keogh' (157). His description of Pegeen as 'a heathen daughter' (153), and her rejection of Shawn as one 'with no savagery' (153) captures the profound level at which the unrestrained expression of passion in the pursuit, or defence, of the fully-realized self is a virtue; albeit now but a flickering remnant of a reality driven to the verge of extinction through commerce and conformity. Therefore, while Christy's 'killing' of his father is a lie, and the place where the blow was struck merely a potato field, its gradual transformation by Christy into a battle of epic proportions is both parody of the sagas expressed in what Synge termed the 'old and magnificent language of our manuscripts'[44] and their profound evocation. In displacing Shawn, he vanquished an Ireland in thrall to 'squeamishness' and which recoiled from dealing 'with the entire reality of life'.[45] Moreover he strikes down modern 'authority' in all its repressive manifestations. This again is something which Synge shares with a feature of European modernism captured in Paul Gauguin's praise of Brittany in a letter to his friend Claude-Emile Schuffenecker: 'I love Brittany, I find there the savage and the primitive'.[46] And it's worth noting that Synge studied Breton while in Paris and visited Brittany several times during his stays in France, seeing in the emergent dramatic movements of Ireland and Brittany the products of the Celtic imagination and 'a limited but puissant nationality'.[47] And so fuelling Christy's blows against Old Mahon is the 'savage' desire for personal sexual choice and gratification, a blow which evokes a pagan, heroic, non-bourgeois Ireland – one perfectly captured in Yeats's *On Baile's Strand* (1904) where Cuchulain denies domesticity and proudly asserts 'I'll dance or hunt, or quarrel or make love, / Wherever and whenever I've a mind to'.[48]

So while Christy's future is projected 'from this hour to the dawning of the judgement day' (173), his transformation, and the community's response to him, is based on the heroic past. His rendition in act two of the 'killing' evokes the epic battles of the sagas, but it is the poetry, as much as the violence, which has its origins in the 'ancient manuscripts'. Declan Kiberd has shown the extent to which the love-exchange between Christy and Pegeen is derived from Synge's informed reading of Douglas Hyde's translations of ancient Irish poetry, *The Love Songs of Connacht* (1893), and his knowledge of these and other originals. As Kiberd observed: 'In [Synge's] hands, the meaning of Gaelic tradition changed from something museumized to something modifiable, endlessly open'.[49] In striking down his father, Christy frees himself from the past and starts out on his journey of liberation, but through the final reconciliation with Old Mahon Synge demonstrates that the corollary of the overthrow of the past is its necessary reintegration into the future. The process by which the community, and especially Pegeen, enabled Christy to become the Playboy is one of complementary wish-fulfilment and self-realization; he is the heroic past made flesh. But when it faces them in all its bloody reality they make the choice of mediocrity over magnificence. In this particular 'battle of two civilizations' the victor is bourgeois conformity and its associated allegiance with the law. But alongside their failure is the apparently available alternative of a cultural revivalism which provides a genuine, rather than ersatz, redemption of self and society. However, as noted by Una Chauduri in her comparison of the conclusion of *Playboy* with the exit of Nora from Ibsen's *A Doll's House*, this 'heroism of departure' is actually 'an impossible ideal'.[50] Christy's departure is 'radically transgressive' in terms of the norms of nationalist expectations and celebrates the potency of the heroic past, but at the same time is dramatizing its practical impossibility in a world now given over to the 'gombeen men'.

As Synge acknowledged, his values were dependent on a social stasis in which modernity was held at bay, and he had 'a dread of any reform that would tend to lessen their [the peasants'] individuality'.[51] The commitment to an outward-looking Ireland which was simultaneously progressive and true to its heroic and poetic past was more easily rendered through the romantic anarchism of *Playboy* in which the community's failures are dramatized, but the radical alternative occupies an off-stage infinity, than it was in any systematic socio-political programme. Only by projecting Christy beyond economic imperatives could Synge make him the embodiment of a liberation whose precise lineaments are finally more easily suggested than defined. Shawn is certainly defeated: there will be no marriage to Pegeen as she makes clear by cuffing him around the ear with an imperious 'Quit my sight' (173). The play opened with her preparation for a wedding, but it closes on her 'keening' 'wild lamentations' over the death, with Christy's departure, of all the poetry and passion he promised and, with the lack of any marriage, it also means that it ends the possibility of either 'gallant little swearers' or 'puny weeds'; this will be a barren Ireland.

The world left after the disappearance of Christy is that captured by Joseph Campbell's 1911 poem 'The Gombeen Man'.

> Behind a web of bottles, bales,
> Tobacco, sugar, coffin nails
> The gombeen like a spider sits,
> Surfeited; and, for all his wits,
> As meagre as the tally-board
> On which his usuries are scored.
> The mountain people come and go
> For wool to weave or seed to sow,
> White flour to bake a wedding cake,
> Red spirits for a stranger's wake.
> No man can call his soul his own
> Who has the Devil's spoon on loan.
> And so behind his web of bales,
> Horse halters, barrels, pucan sails
> The gombeen like a spider sits,
> Surfeited; and for all his wits,
> As poor as one who never knew
> The treasure of the early dew.[52]

This is the world of Ubu; unadorned but triumphant, a note more pervasive in its deadly implications than the emotional extremes of triumph and regret expressed by Christy or Pegeen. Alongside their charged closing lines we should set Michael's self-satisfied and profoundly Ubuesque : 'By the will of God, we'll have peace now for our drinks. Will you draw the porter, Pegeen?' (173).

---

[1] An earlier version of this paper was presented at the Irish Theatrical Diaspora conference, 'French and Irish Theatres : Influences and Interactions', University of Lille, June 2008, and published as 'Synge and the "Savage God"', *Études Irlandaises*, 33.2, Automne/Autumn 2008, 21-30.
[2] W.J. McCormack, *Fool of the Family: A Life of J.M. Synge* (Wedenfeld and Nicolson: London, 2000): 144
[3] J.M. Synge, 'Le Mouvement Intellectuel Irlandais', *Collected Works II: Prose*. Edited by Alan Price (Gerrards Cross, Colin Smythe, 1982): 378-82
[4] Roger Shattuck, *The Banquet Years* (London: Jonathan Cape, 1969): 18.
[5] McCormack, 25-6.
[6] W. B. Yeats, *The Land of Hearts Desire* , *The Variorum Edition of the Plays of W.B. Yeats*. Edited by Russell K. Alspach (London: Macmillan, 1966): 180
[7] J.M. Synge, *Collected Works IV: Plays 2*. Edited by Ann Saddlemyer (Gerrards Cross, Colin Smythe, 1982): 394.
[8] Synge, *Plays 2*, xxv.
[9] 'Roundtable Discussion with Garry Hynes' in Adrian Frazier (ed), *Playboys of the Western World: Production Histories* (Dublin: Carysfort Press, 2004): 89.
[10] Quoted in George Woodcock, *Anarchism* (Harmondsworth: Penguin, 1963): 250.
[11] Emile Henry, 'A Terrorist's Defence', *An Anarchist Reader*. Edited by George Woodcock (Glasgow: Fontana, 1978): 193.
[12] W.B. Yeats, *Autobiographies* (London, Macmillan, 1955): 349.
[13] Alfred Jarry, *Selected Works of Alfred Jarry*. Edited by Roger Shattuck and Simon Watson Taylor (New York: Grove Press, 1965): 80.
[14] Declan Kiberd, *Irish Classics* (London: Granta Books, 2000): 427.
[15] Quoted in McCormack, 138.
[16] J.M. Synge, *The Collected Letters of John Millington Synge, Volume I, 1871-1907*. Edited by Ann Saddlemyer (Oxford, Clarendon Press, 1983): 47.
[17] Quoted in Robert Hogan and James Kilroy, *The Modern Irish Drama: A Documentary History Vol II: Laying the Foundations 1902-1904* (Dublin: The Dolmen Press, 1976): 79.
[18] J. M. Synge, *Collected Works III: Plays I*. Edited by Ann Saddlemyer (Gerrards Cross: Colin Smythe, 1982): 35. Subsequent references appear in the text.

[19] Quoted in P.J. Matthews, *Revival: The Abbey Theatre, Sinn Féin, The Gaelic League and the Co-operative Movement* (Cork: Cork University Press, 2003): 139.
[20] William G. Fay, 'The Playboy of the Western World', *J.M. Synge: Interviews and Recollections*. Edited by E. H. Mickhail (London: Macmillan, 1977): 48
[21] Synge, *Prose*, 283.
[22] G.J. Watson, *Irish Identity and the Literary Revival* (Washington D.C.: Catholic University Press, 1993): 39.
[23] Synge, *Prose*, 330.
[24] Synge, *Letters 1*: 116.
[25] F.S.L. Lyons, *Ireland Since the Famine* (London: Fontana, 1973): 50.
[26] George Russell, *Co-Operation and Nationality* (Dublin: Maunsel, 1912): 13-14.
[27] W.B. Yeats, 'Synge and the Ireland of his Time', *Essays and Introductions* (London: Macmillan, 1961): 319.
[28] Seamus Deane, *Celtic Revivals: Essays in Modern Irish Literature 1880-1990* (London: Faber & Faber): 59-60.
[29] Bruce Arnold, *Jack Yeats* (New Haven: Yale University Press, 1998): 136.
[30] McCormack, 143.
[31] Synge, *Letters 1*, 116
[32] Tom Garvin, *Nationalist Revolutionaries in Ireland, 1858-1928* (Oxford: Clarendon Press, 1987): 85.
[33] Synge, *Prose*, 400.
[34] Synge, *Plays I*, 224.
[35] Synge, *Plays 1*, 74.
[36] Synge, *Plays 1*. 116.
[37] Synge, *Plays 1*, 76.
[38] Synge, *Plays I*, 224.
[39] Synge, *Letters 1*, 74.
[40] Synge *Letters 1*, 91.
[41] J.M. Synge, *Collected Works IV: Plays 2*. Edited by Ann Saddlemyer (Gerrards Cross: Colin Smythe, 1982): 57. Subsequent references appear in the text.
[42] Luke Gibbons, *Transformation in Irish Culture* (Cork: Cork University Press, 1996): 86.
[43] Synge, *Prose*, 75.
[44] Synge, *Prose*, 400.
[45] Synge, *Letters 1*, 74.
[46] Quoted in Belinda Thomson with Frances Fowle and Lesley Stevenson, *Gauguin's Vision: A Discussion of Materials and Techniques* (Edinburgh: National Gallery of Scotland, 2005): 39.
[47] Synge, *Prose*, 393.
[48] W. B. Yeats, *The Variorum Edition of the Plays of W.B. Yeats*, 477-79

49 Declan Kiberd, *Synge and the Irish Language*. Second Edition. (London: Macmillan, 1993): xxix.
50 Una Chauduri, *Staging Place: The Geography of Modern Drama* (Ann Arbor: University of Michigan Press, 1995): 62.
51 Synge, *Prose*, 286.
52 Joseph Campbell, 'The Gombeen Man', *The Field Day Anthology of Irish Writing: Volume II*. Edited by Seamus Deane (Derry: Field Day Publications, 1991): 762.

8 | THE TRANSLATOR'S PLAYWRIGHT: KAREL MUŠEK AND J.M. SYNGE

Ondřej Pilný

Writing to John Quinn on 16 September 1905, W.B. Yeats reported that, apart from the recent production of Synge's *The Well of the Saints* by the Deutsches Theater in Berlin, 'The Shadow of the Glen has been put into Czech by somebody connected with the National Theatre there'. Yeats was delighted, concluding that he 'said in a speech some time ago that [Synge] would have a European reputation in five years, but his enemies have mocked the prophecy'.[1] The Czech translator he referred to was actor-director Karel Mušek,[2] whom Yeats came to meet nine months later. Mušek then provided the Abbey Theatre directorate with detailed information concerning the management of the well-established National Theatre in Prague, which in turn served as a vital point of comparison in the development of a national theatre in Ireland.

The origins of the Irish Dramatic Movement are generally familiar. Its foundations were laid by W.B. Yeats, Lady Gregory, Edward Martyn, and George Moore, who formed the Irish Literary Theatre in 1899. The project was followed by Yeats and Lady Gregory's Irish National Theatre Society (1903-1906); the Society was provided with the Abbey Theatre building by Annie Horniman in 1904, and Synge became a joint director of the theatre with Yeats and Gregory in 1905. Finally, the INTS was reformed as the National Theatre Society, Ltd. in 1906; by then, the Abbey was generally regarded as the most important theatre with a national agenda in Ireland (although its acceptance as such was indeed less than universal).

The origins of Czech patriotic theatre, on the other hand, may be traced back to the construction of the Bouda theatre, a timber establishment erected in the Prague Old Town in 1786 (the name translates literally as 'The Hut') for performances of plays in Czech alongside those in German. The provisional building became a veritable centre of patriotic cultural activity in the three years that it lasted. Czech plays were simultaneously allowed on the stage of the Estates Theatre (*Stavovské divadlo*), alongside performances in German, and opera in Italian (this is where Mozart's *Don Giovanni* was premiered in 1797). The frequency of Czech dramatic productions and their status were greatly enhanced by the foundation of the Interim Theatre (*Prozatímní divadlo*) in 1862 as the first venue to stage plays in Czech only. Its name reflected its function, which was to stage plays until a representative building of a Czech National Theatre had finally been constructed. That happened in 1881, based on a large public collection of donations gathered over three decades. The catastrophic fire that gutted the building shortly after its inauguration did not prevent its triumphant re-opening in 1883, as one of the largest European national theatres featuring a permanent ensemble.

Given the comparable position of the Irish and the Czechs as nations striving for cultural emancipation and political autonomy from a dominant powerful neighbour, but also the differences in the respective theatre histories that I have just outlined, it is perhaps not surprising that the standard commentary of a Czech critic on Irish theatre may be epitomized as follows: 'The history of theatre in Ireland shares a lot with that of Czech theatre, the only difference being that the Irish, as regards theatre, grew up within ten years'.[3] Indeed, when looking back to the 1930s, translator and critic Frank Tetauer summarized the rapid growth of Irish theatre in a commendatory, but at the same time matter-of-fact, manner:

> A distinctive national drama was created out of nothing, and a singular theatrical tradition was established; amateurs grew into actors, enthusiasts into authors, and a romantic society was transformed into a national cultural institution.[4]

It was particularly through Karel Mušek that the work of contemporaneous Irish playwrights came to the attention of Czech practitioners in the mid-1900s. Apart from championing G.B. Shaw in Bohemia, Mušek introduced Synge to the Czechs, and provided the initial impulse for the playwright to be established as a significant presence in Czech theatres. Mušek's translations of Synge were among the earliest in Europe, and several of them were produced in prominent venues in Prague and elsewhere. Further translations of all of the plays were made, starting with the 1940s, resulting in an impressive production history: in January 2010, I was able to trace twenty-four different productions of *The Playboy* in three alternative Czech translations alone, five productions (and four translations) of *The Shadow of the Glen*, two productions (and two translations) followed by a radio adaptation of *Riders to the Sea*, three productions (in two translations) of *The Well of the Saints*, two productions (and two translations) of *The Tinker's Wedding*, and one production (and two translations) of *Deirdre of the Sorrows*.5 A substantial majority of the translations have also been published.

**Karel Mušek, National Theatre director
Courtesy of the National Theatre archive,
Prague**

The present essay explores, specifically, the interaction between Mušek and Synge and his work. As is often the case, this vital and captivating link was a result of coincidence, which brought together two people whose lives bore pronounced similarities, professional and personal alike. Both came to the theatre without any formal instruction; both served a national cause by utilizing wider European influences; moreover, they were both avid travellers, hikers, and also early photographers. The exploration, however, must negotiate notable obstacles. For one, it is a well-established fact that relatively little will ever be known about Synge's private thoughts and emotions due to the scarcity of evidence, which is one of the reasons that make the study of his work ever-intriguing and ever-frustrating at the same time. Moreover, tracing Karel Mušek truly involves detective work, as he has largely disappeared from public record, and the best part of his papers, together with his entire photographic archive, seems to have vanished.

Mušek was born on 1 January 1867 in Prague into the family of a locksmith. He was described as 'the last male offspring of a theatre dynasty',[6] since most of his extended family had been involved in travelling theatre companies. He lost both of his parents at the age of four, and ended up in an orphanage shortly after. Aged seventeen, he started acting in travelling companies in the country, largely as a means of making a living, since he had very little in terms of other qualifications.[7] Young Mušek had a stroke of luck in 1889, when, after a series of walk-on parts at the National Theatre in Prague, he was offered a chance to join the ensemble. He continued acting for the following three decades, appearing in more than 500 productions at the National; after acting in lovers' roles, he came to excel mainly in smaller comic parts. From 1900 on, Mušek also started to direct plays regularly, joining what was to be the last generation of actor-directors. His productions (of which there were over eighty) primarily included the work of Czech authors, both revivalist and contemporary, and plays he himself had translated from English.[8]

Mušek came to learn English by meeting Alice Hillstead, a young Englishwoman working as a governess to the daughter of Josef Šmaha, an established National Theatre director to whom he served as an occasional assistant. It was also due to Miss Hillstead that Mušek acquired a knowledge of English literature, while lifting himself from a state of bare literacy and gradually becoming an apt cultural commentator on British and Irish affairs. Mušek and

Hillstead got married in 1897; their only daughter Hana was born the same year.⁹

From the few existing accounts, Mušek comes across as a hard-working and reasonably modest person, who compensated for his lack of formal education by enormous enthusiasm; his associates have repeatedly described him as a 'self-made man'.¹⁰ He was known as a good companion who established rapport quickly with celebrities and country folk alike; his brilliant skills as a storyteller would have definitely contributed to that reputation. A unique anecdote provided by a prominent actor friend, Rudolf Deyl, illustrates this amply:

> During our joint trip to London he managed, for instance, to obtain endorsement for us to enter a garden party at the Thames, where the Yorks used to pick their roses. It was a Thackeray celebration to which only about 300 people from assorted London literary circles had been invited. He ushered me moreover to the dressing rooms of famous actor Beerbohm Tree and director Bourchier during a performance of *Henry VIII* at His Majesty's Theatre. Mušek managed to have us invited to take tea in G.B. Shaw's study, where he proceeded to converse with Shaw for a very long time. Mušek also introduced me to the Savage Club, so that I got acquainted with select London society. Amidst the plentiful collections of the British Museum, he effortlessly located a copy of a Shakespeare Folio. In the large temple in Richmond he took me, without a guide, to the grave of the famed Garrick. He had detailed knowledge of the English household and its customs, which was of considerable help to him in directing plays; his productions bore all features characteristic for and related to England.¹¹

Mušek seems to have met Shaw around 1906, after he had translated *You Never Can Tell* and *The Devil's Disciple*, and made such an impression on the playwright that a regular correspondence ensued. Moreover, Shaw made Mušek his exclusive agent for Czech theatres and granted him translation rights to his work. He did not allow plays previously translated by Mušek to be offered to other translators until 1950: that is, over twenty-five years after Mušek's death. When he did so, it was only after the translation agency DILIA, which was managed by the communist state, consented to pay a life-long monthly rent to Mušek's widow, who by then was an impoverished, frail, and completely blind old lady.¹²

Mušek's translations of Shaw were regarded as rather laborious by his successors, many of whom were disgruntled by the exclusivity

**Young Mušek in a Czech revivalist drama and as one of
the Dromios in *The Comedy of Errors*
Courtesy of the National Theatre archive, Prague**

of the translation rights in Shaw's lifetime.[13] His translations of Synge were initially haphazard, and acquired accuracy only through meticulous revision in rehearsal and after. Nonetheless, Mušek was swift, and extremely dedicated: his relentless efforts to promote his favourite authors included the publication of numerous articles and news items in the daily press, and many of his translations. These included Synge's plays and *The Aran Islands* in the 1920s, the printing of which he funded from his own pocket.[14] His work thus represented a lasting and multifaceted enrichment of the Czech theatrical scene.

Mušek first heard about Synge from Richard J. Kelly (1856-1931), barrister and journalist, who was editor and managing director of *The Tuam Herald*. Kelly came to Prague in June 1905 as a member of the British branch of the International Society of Journalists, a group of whom were invited to travel in Bohemia for over a week. The party included, prominently, Horace Plunkett, and Mušek and his wife were asked to guide them for part of their extensive travels. Kelly seems to have been mesmerized by the country, and summed up his impressions by a somewhat uncritical exclamation that

'Wherever one looks in the little kingdom of Bohemia, politeness, hospitality, intelligence and good will are ubiquitous.'[15]

Kelly was a friend of the architect and inveterate Abbey theatregoer Joseph Holloway, and exchanged letters with Synge.[16] It was he who forwarded Mušek a copy of *The Shadow of the Glen* – perhaps a curious thing to do by a founding member of the Catholic Truth Society who prominently authored some of its brochures.[17] Mušek rapidly set out to translate the play, while also working on a well informed article about 'The Irish National Theatre'. The article came out in *Lumír*, a highly respected Czech literary journal, in September 1905. It charts the history of theatre in Ireland from the 1630s onward and details the early activities of W.B. Yeats and Lady Gregory, quoting Yeats's views on the theatre as voiced in *Samhain*. It is likely that sources for the article were provided by Kelly, together with the copy of Synge's play, since Mušek included a full translation of Miss Annie Horniman's official letter in which she offers the Abbey Theatre building to the INTS and outlines her conditions.[18]

When the translation of *Shadow of the Glen* was completed, Mušek proceeded to direct what was to be the first ever production of the play in a foreign language. The premiere took place on 7 February 1906 at Smíchovské divadlo, an established small theatre focused on introducing the work of modern authors. A copy of the flyer for the performance reached Synge via Kelly; the playwright then wrote to Mušek, requesting copies of reviews and any other details of how the play succeeded.[19] Mušek promptly dispatched these, and summarized: 'Your play, although a little foreign to our people has met with a very good success and will be repeated.'[20]

Mušek was a realist director by disposition, opposed to gratuitous experimentation and whatever smelled of intellectual over-interpretation of drama; his unique (because explicit) directorial reflection concerning Shakespeare's *Hamlet* may serve as a good illustration of his convictions:

> The desire to achieve the greatest possible degree of scenic illusion must not be condemned ... Shakespeare did not write his plays for scholars and professors only. He wrote for the people, and the people demand at least partial, unobtrusive scenery ... Finally, the right to have an opinion of one's own must be allowed by the director to the actor, and by the critic to the director.[21]

It does not come as a surprise then that Mušek based the stage design and costumes for his production of *The Shadow* on 'cards with real Irish interiors and types of the people' that were provided, again, by Kelly. [22]

In the same letter, Mušek requested copies of *The Well of the Saints* and *Riders to the Sea*, one of which he was planning to offer to the National Theatre. Having temporarily run out of copies of *The Well*, the playwright forwarded *Riders* first. That was on 10 March 1906.[23] By May, Mušek already had a response to his translation of the one-act tragedy from the National. The theatre's reaction was nevertheless negative: in Mušek's words, the manager felt that the play was 'highly characteristic, but for our people a little too sad. Especially as we have played two years ago the Hollandish Drama "Hope" which is also taken from fisherfolk's life'.[24] One must remember that before the age of global travel, Bohemia was an even more intrinsically inland country. By way of consolation perhaps, Mušek mentioned that he had already started translating *The Well of the Saints*, which he hoped would suit the Czech audience better.

Moreover, the translator began making plans to foster his vigorous interest in Irish theatre in general and Synge's plays in particular by visiting the country. Having made arrangements with the playwright, he arrived in Dublin on 24 July 1906, and stayed for close to two weeks. Synge was well pleased to organize the visit, soliciting an invitation from Lady Gregory for Mušek to come and stay with her at Coole Park for a few days. The playwright was going through a rather turbulent period at the time, as the Abbey directors were struggling to resolve a major conflict with Annie Horniman over Willie Fay and stage management,[25] while Synge's anxious July letters to Molly Allgood amply demonstrate the fit of jealousy that he was suffering over the love of his life. Moreover, he was desperately trying to find time to finish his next play, *The Playboy of the Western World*.[26] All this perhaps explains the eventual irritable remark made in a letter to Molly the day before Mušek's departure: 'I'm fagged out with my efforts to amuse Musek [sic] all day, he goes away tomorrow evening. I like him very much but it is hard to talk to him continually as his English is so uncertain.'[27]

Mušek's visit was busy indeed. He spent the first day in Dublin with Synge, who then dispatched him to Coole Park, writing to Lady Gregory:

> I have promised that you will show him the inside of a real cottage in the West as they want to reproduce one exactly for

our plays. They have £12,000 a year *and* all scenery and lights from the government so they can afford to do things well. I have had a lot of interesting talk with him about the working of their pay system etc, and learned some things that may be useful to us by and by ... Please remind Yeats not to disparage acting qualities of the 'Well' as they talk of doing it too!²⁸

On his way to Galway, Mušek marked the scope of dereliction in the midlands which gave the countryside 'a sad, rather than a romantic appearance'. He was similarly taken aback by the dirt in railway carriages and stations – 'evidently the doing of the folk in general', with nobody taking care to restrict themselves in spitting simply anywhere – combined with a fair amount of ubiquitous drinking. Passing through the 'deserted half-wilderness' of the plains near Gort, the traveller was finally driven in a cart to what he called 'the castle'. Mušek was astonished by the spectacular landscape of the surrounding park, followed by the splendour of Lady Gregory's art collection in her marvellous residence. 'I dare say that this is likely to be the only time that I was spending the night in a bedroom with a Velasquez painting hanging over my head,'²⁹ observed the former inmate of an orphanage.

BIBLIOTÉKA V COOLESKÉM ZÁMKU

'The Library at Coole Park'. Photograph by Karel Mušek

Mušek depicted the daily regime at Coole Park as that of true gentry. The evening meal struck him as particularly ceremonious:

> At half past seven, a gong was sounded as a signal to get dressed. The bedrooms already featured hot water and evening attire at the ready. A dress suit or a dinner jacket for the gentlemen. When the entire company [consisting of Lady Gregory, her son Robert, W.B. Yeats 'and two ladies'] were gathered in the library, which was adjacent to the dining room, the butler ... entered and announced that dinner was ready. This always consisted of a soup, fish or salad, poultry, roast meat, a dessert and fruit. The food was being brought to the table by the butler, who placed it in front of the mistress of the house. She distributed it onto individual plates which were then carried to their destinations around the table by a chamber-maid ... The meal was being washed down with wine, sherry and claret ... Beer did not arrive at the table whatsoever.[30]

After dinner, the company adjourned to the library for an extensive discussion of Irish, English and Czech theatre, with Mušek translating and transcribing the titles of numerous Czech plays for his hosts. The debate was continued on the following day, when the Bohemian visitor was invited, together with Yeats, to dine at Tullira Castle by Edward Martyn. Mušek observed:

> My intimation that our theatre has been the recipient of an annual subsidy caused genuine astonishment. 'How, you receive a subsidy? From the provincial government? What else would you wish for then?'
>
> I explained that the subsidy was authorized by the provincial assembly – further astonishment. 'You have an assembly? What else do you want? *We* have been struggling in vain to get Home Rule for a whole century'.
>
> This necessitated further explanation as regards the official language, the suffering of Czech minorities, the state institutions and their power, and the lack thereof with the Czech parliament, including the parliament's dependent status.[31]

The guest's account poignantly documents at this point how a habitual grumbling of national activists may end up unexpectedly being put into perspective: an instructive instance of cultural exchange indeed.

Mušek's attempt at a justification of Czech national hardship was followed by Martyn and Yeats arguing about the dominance of

Catholicism in the Irish national movement. The course and the result of the dispute may be gathered from Mušek's conclusion that 'Mr. Yeats seems to be right. The Irish movement was never entirely national; the main motif has always been the supremacy of Rome.'[32]

In the remaining part of his visit to Coole Park, Mušek was able to take long walks in the surroundings of Gort, and take photographs. Everywhere he encountered what to him was extreme poverty, accompanied by a lack of cultivation of the land. On his way to Tullira Castle, he entered his first Irish cottage (Lady Gregory met the request made by Synge) and claimed: 'I know the Czech countryside thoroughly. However, I do not remember having seen a more miserable human abode than those here, in the West of Ireland.'[33]

NÁMĚSTÍ IRSKÉHO MĚSTEČKA
'The Square of a Country Town' (Gort)
Photograph by Karel Mušek

OPUŠTĚNÉ CHATY
'Deserted Cottages'
Photograph by Karel Mušek

CHATA IRSKÉHO TKALCE

'An Irish Weaver's Cottage'
Photograph by Karel Mušek

Back in Dublin, Mušek met members of the Irish National Theatre Society, including W.G. Fay and Sarah and Molly Allgood.[34] According to Synge, he wanted 'to hear the keen and see some of our Aran dresses etc', this being an indication that Mušek was still considering a production of *Riders to the Sea*.[35] Finally, two of his last days in Ireland were spent hiking with Synge in County Wicklow. The places they visited included Dargle Glen near Bray, where Mušek took a photograph of Synge which was later published in Maurice Bourgeois's study on the playwright.[36] They went to Carrickmines to see the nearby Kiltiernan cromlegh, passed around the cottages in Kilgobbin (apparently a favourite location of Synge's where he allegedly took all his visitors), and further down in the country, arrived in Wicklow town, walked in the 'plain between Laragh and the Great Sugar Loaf', and presumably spent the night at the house of an acquaintance of Synge's, a farmer by the name 'Menctillon' (Mc Dillon?).

The Translator's Playwright: Karel Mušek

HROB IRSKÉHO NÁČELNÍKA V KILTERNANU

'An Irish Chieftain's Tomb at Kilternan'
(The Kiltiernan Cromlegh)
Photograph by Karel Mušek

KELTSKÝ KŘÍŽ NA ROZCESTÍ

'Celtic Cross at a Crossroads
Photograph by Karel Mušek

The exact route of the trip or any further details unfortunately cannot be established with any degree of accuracy, as Mušek's published account represents an instance where the raconteur, and in this case clearly also fabricator, has taken over from the otherwise meticulous and honest observer. Mušek's version of what he called his 'rambles around Dublin and hikes into the Wicklow Mountains'[37] is largely a shameless collage of passages from Synge's essay 'The People of the Glens' and from *The Aran Islands*, in which the author pretends to have witnessed all sorts of local people narrating their stories to the playwright, including, prominently, the source story for *The Shadow of the Glen*.[38] Given the nature of such rare fabulation, it is reasonable to conclude that apart from wishing to tell a captivating tale and documenting the authenticity of Synge's sources (which was generally taken for granted by Czech reviewers and critics in any case), Mušek was anxious to present himself as *the* authentic Czech authority on Synge. Notwithstanding all that, Mušek's portrayal of Synge may likely be trusted:

> [Synge was] tall and well-built by appearance. However, he in no way exuded good health. The dark unkempt chestnut hair, sharp features, an almost entirely square jaw, and rough voice made him older than he in fact was. He was very simply clad: coarse clothes, heavy boots, a celluloid collar, soft hat, a long-collared sleeveless coat. His appearance was fully in keeping with him being a man who spent a long time on the deserted islands of Aran; a man who was taciturn and grumpy in public and came to life only in conversation with country people, herds and fishermen ... His exterior hardly differed from that of the country folk.[39]

The Abbey directorate were clearly impressed by Mušek's visit, regarding it as an important sign of recognition on the Continent. Yeats boasted to his father that although 'We have a long way to go yet ... we have gone far enough for the Stage Manager of the National Theatre of Bohemia ... to have been sent to find out particulars and report upon the plays'.[40] Some days later, he expressed his gratitude in a letter to Mušek for a 'detailed account of your theatre which tells me exactly what I want to know and will be most useful': Yeats had probably asked Mušek to write down the information conveyed during their meeting in full detail for him. An awareness of the advanced state of development of the Prague National Theatre is apparent from a warm note of thanks appended to Yeats's letter by Lady Gregory, who wrote to Mušek that 'It was a great pleasure having you here, and we all felt it a great encouragement that you who are doing such good work at home should take an interest in us, who are so to speak at the edge of the world.'[41] The technological superiority of the Czech National Theatre to the Abbey was confirmed by the Abbey benefactor Annie Horniman on her visit to Prague in August of the same year. Mušek – who acted as her guide, following a request made by Lady Gregory – expressed a similar awareness, particularly in his later writing, where he repeatedly made an equation between the Abbey and the Czech Interim Theatre concerning both its status and the basic nature of its staging conditions.[42] Nevertheless, he regarded the minimal staging options as most suited to the material performed at the Abbey, and a welcome alternative to the excesses of recent German productions.[43]

In the autumn of 1906, preparations were already under way for a National Theatre production of *The Shadow of the Glen* in Prague. It was a period of major transition for the National, which had been gradually turning away from being a conventional nineteenth-century establishment, and allowing modern plays onto its stage, together with a degree of experimentation in stage design and lighting. In the spring, the Moscow Art Theatre headed by Stanislavski made a guest appearance, and immediately exercised profound influence on the acting and staging practices at the National. Needless to say, the innovation that was making itself felt in various ways at this emblematic national institution (and in Czech theatres in general) had numerous opponents among the more conservative critics and audience members alike.[44] This context of conflicting theatrical styles and their politics then naturally had considerable bearing on the production history and initial reception of Synge's plays in Czech.

The Shadow of the Glen provides an interesting case in point: the production was postponed several times, and took place only in August 1907, amidst the holiday season, which is not an auspicious time for new work to be introduced anywhere.[45] The play was presented in the unlikely company of a slight verse comedy by Jean Richepin entitled *The Filibusterer* (*Le Flibustier*, 1888), and stayed on for two nights only, in spite of the painstaking advance work. Mušek, who directed the play and appeared in it as the Tramp, had the one-act cast by the end of the previous year already, and modelled the stage on a drawing sent to him by Frank Fay in September 1906.[46] The director's copy of the acting text reveals, in addition, the extent to which the original translation had been revised in rehearsal. Mušek was still negotiating Synge's original dialect, using the slightly archaic language of Czech revivalist peasant drama as the basis for his version. In addition to that, some local Irish references had to be revisited: for instance, the notion of the 'tramp' proved to be a particular problem, as the customary image of the Czech men of the roads did not seem to match those depicted by Synge. In the end, the 'tramp' was turned into '*potulný honák*' – that is, a 'wandering cattle-herd' in Czech.⁴⁷

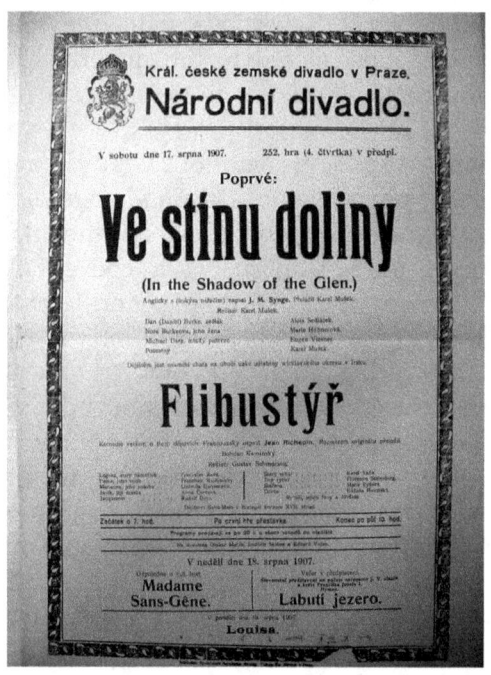

National Theatre in Prague, poster for
The Shadow of the Glen, August 1907
Courtesy of the National Theatre archive, Prague

The production received a certain degree of critical praise, despite an apathetic welcome from the summer audience. Václav Hladík, who reviewed *The Shadow* for a prominent daily, regarded the production as 'an extraordinary experiment'. According to him, the 'Irish burlesque play' opened in a 'gloomy and eerie Maeterlinckean mood', centred on the passionate longing of a lonely country wife, and came to replace 'Maeterlinck's terror with Moliére's stick' in the end. 'A degree of ancient primitivism emanates from this realistic Irish folk play,' Hladík summarized.

Almost in the same breath, he added that he could not find the slightest reason for the play to be staged at the National Theatre, clearly evidencing the current debate concerning the desirable shape of the national theatre and its cultural agenda.[48] Notwithstanding the minimal run of the play, royalties were duly dispatched to the author, together with a poster for the play, which the Abbey proudly displayed in its foyer.[49]

The work by Synge that Mušek most championed (similarly to the playwright's recent biographer, W.J. McCormack) was *The Well of the Saints*. He seems to have finished the translation already in 1906 but was unable to find a theatre willing to produce it.[50] What therefore eventually came to determine which of Synge's plays would be staged next was the fame of *The Playboy of the Western World*, which had been gradually spreading around Europe. The play quickly drew the attention of translators in various countries, although it was not performed outside of Ireland or Britain until 1913, the year of the first French production at the Théâtre Antoine in Paris. In Bohemia, Josef Julius David, an English teacher from Hradec Králové and translator of Milton, requested translation rights as early as April 1907. He was politely refused by Synge, however, who stated that he had authorized Mušek to translate *The Playboy*, for the latter had already translated some of his other plays.[51]

Nevertheless on this occasion, Mušek procrastinated. In September 1908 he notified Synge that he had postponed the work as there was little chance of placing the play, due to Prague theatres allegedly focusing on national plays at that particular time. This was an excuse that Mušek may have resorted to as a result of insufficient critical or commercial acknowledgment of his earlier translations of Synge. At the same time, Mušek's inaction perhaps also reflected his overall view of *The Playboy*. He thought that, while the play may have been vital in the Irish context, it lacked a suitable degree of relevance to Czech audiences. He seemed to regard *The Playboy* as a mere satire on the Irish people, while the elements of high Romanticism in the play were evidently alien to him.[52] Further evidence of the fact that the figurative universe of *The Playboy* remained largely closed to Mušek is provided by the translator's preface to the published playtext, which features unacknowledged extended quotations from Maurice Bourgeois, and does not attempt to enter into original interpretation in any way.[53]

Details of the first Czech translation of *The Playboy* remain unclear. When the play was premiered at the Vinohrady Theatre in Prague in 1916, it was billed as 'translated by V.A. Jung and Karel Mušek', the alleged co-translator being Václav Alois Jung (1858-1927), a lexicographer and accomplished translator of English Romantic poetry, Pushkin's *Eugene Onegin*, Wilde's *The Ideal Husband*, and many other works. However, an extant undated typescript of a translation of the play bears only Jung's name, while the published version is attributed to Mušek only. The extent, and also the circumstances of the collaboration (or its possible aftermath) are hence impossible to determine.[54] Regardless of the authorship of the translation, the Vinohrady production of *The Playboy* seems regrettably to have been a rather dreary attempt at a strictly naturalist staging of Synge's wild comedy. Still, the play thus at least finally came to the wider attention of Czech critics and practitioners: it solicited an insightful analysis from the prominent literary and theatre critic Otokar Fischer in a major daily,[55] and was eventually given a brilliant avant-garde production by Jiří Frejka and the DaDa Theatre in 1928.[56] Starting with the 1960s, *The Playboy* became one of the most frequently performed twentieth-century international dramas on the Czech stage.

Mušek's favourite play, *The Well of the Saints*, was also acted in the end, and turned out to be the last of Synge's dramas to reach the stage in Mušek's lifetime. First, the Brno National Theatre gave a successful studio-space production in 1920.[57] That was closely followed by the Prague National Theatre which had decided to have a go at the play after all. Mušek, however, was unable to participate in either of the productions, as director or actor, since he suffered a major stroke when he came to assist in the planning of activities for the newly founded National Theatre of South Bohemia in České Budějovice around that time.[58] He swiftly found his role elsewhere nonetheless: he funded the publication of his translations of Synge, and promoted the play, its author, and the Irish theatre in general in two articles that appeared around the time of the premiere.[59]

The National Theatre production of *Well* was staged, as part of its regular season, at the Estates Theatre. The play was put on a double bill with *The Hour-Glass* by W.B. Yeats.[60] It was directed by Karel Želenský and starred the popular actress Marie Hübnerová as Mary Doul. The set was designed by a prominent cubist artist and architect, Vlastislav Hofman, who seamlessly combined expressionist, symbolist, and realistic elements into an imaginative whole.

Furthermore, a perceptive essay on *The Well of the Saints* and *The Hour-Glass* was published a few days before the premiere. It discussed the influence of the Parisian Théâtre Libre on Synge, and described the playwright as a curious brand of a patriot, unwaveringly dedicated to the truth and merciless in depicting the flaws of his audience; the author of the article also drew an extended

Vlastislav Hofman, stage design for J.M. Synge, *Studnice svetcu* (*The Well of the Saints*), National Theatre, Prague at the Estates Theatre, November 1921.
Courtesy of the National Theatre archive, Prague

parallel between *The Well of the Saints* and Maeterlinck's *The Miracle of St Anthony*.[61]

All the conditions then seemed exquisitely right. Despite that, the play closed after three nights.[62] Reviews were mixed. Otokar Fischer highlighted Synge as the most accomplished Irish playwright, and considered the play very powerful. However, he observed:

> [H]ow alien is this Gaelic fantasy, cruelty and irony in comparison with the folk poetry of other peoples, how much oddity thrives, in particular, in this 'western world' of Ireland, at the western extremity of Europe, with its idioms, raciness, and paradoxes.

This heady mixture may be a little too much for the Continental sensibility, Fischer concluded, remarking also on the regrettably lukewarm acting of the entire supporting cast.[63] Another reviewer, Karel Engelmüller, treated the play likewise with serious consideration. He was nonetheless irked by what he perceived as the excessive earthiness and vulgarity of some scenes, judging that 'things are taken rather too far and there is more cynicism and roughness of edge than may be necessary', and closing with the conjecture that 'the play may have been put on the repertoire due to the major significance of its author's name rather than for its ideological or dramatic value.'[64] Mušek himself was disappointed by the production, blaming its failures on the lack of experience of its producers, and he complained that he had not been approached as advisor, despite the fact that he had visited the area where the play was set with Synge and knew it 'as the back of his hand'.[65] He was not to see what he would regard as a successful production of the play, since *The Well of the Saints* vanished from the Czech stage for more than eight decades afterwards.

Poster for J.M. Synge, *Studnice svetcu* (*The Well of the Saints*) and W.B. Yeats, *Presýpací hodiny* (*The Hour-Glass*), National Theatre, Prague at the Estates Theatre, November 1921
Courtesy of the National Theatre archive, Prague

Mušek's activity sadly came to a premature end: he was left severely disabled in his early fifties, and having to fight a speech deprivation. After a struggle that lasted several years, he passed away in a Prague sanatorium on 12 November 1924, aged fifty-seven. Numerous obituaries paid tribute to him. His contribution to Czech theatre was perhaps best described by Hanuš Jelínek, who wrote about the 'keen theatrical foresight' that Mušek possessed as an authority on English-language theatre, whose intuition 'had enabled him to recognize the significance of a number of authors before they achieved international recognition'.[66] Mušek may have gone down in the annals of Czech National Theatre as a foot-soldier: he deserves to be remembered as a determined early pioneer of Irish drama in Europe.[67]

---

[1] W.B. Yeats to John Quinn, 16 September [1905]. *The Collected Letters of W.B. Yeats, Vol. IV: 1905-1907*. Edited by John Kelly and Ronald Schuchard (Oxford: Oxford University Press, 2005): 178.

[2] Earlier English-language sources tend to refer to 'Pan Karel Mušek', presumably since this is the way he is referred to in several passages of Maurice Bourgeois's early study *John Millington Synge and the Irish Theatre* (1913): and on the basis of letters addressed to Mušek by Synge. This may confuse many a reader into considerations of the role of mythology in naming Czech offspring. 'Pan,' however, is the Czech equivalent of 'Mr'. Similarly, 'Bohemia' is used in the present context solely as the Latin geographical term for the western part of the historical Czech Lands.

[3] An anonymous review of Maurice Bourgeois, *John Millington Synge and the Irish Theatre* (1913): 'O irském divadle,' *Scena* 1: 2. půlročník (1913/1914): 236. All translations from Czech are my own.

[4] Frank Tetauer, 'Příklad irského divadla,' *Divadlo* 12 (19).1 (1932/1933): 17.

[5] For a full list of translations and productions, see the Appendix.

[6] V. Müller, 'Zakladatel prospěšné tradice,' *Lidová demokracie* 1 January 1967, 5.

[7] Jaroslav Kvapil, *O čem vím. 2. část* (Prague: Václav Tomsa, 1947): 181. Most of the biographical information comes from Kvapil (a principal director of the National Theatre) and Müller's tribute to Mušek cited above.

[8] National Theatre Archive online, item Karel Mušek. http://archiv.narodni-divadlo.cz, 16 May 2008.

[9] Hana Mušková married an American, Joseph T. Shaw, sometime in the mid-1920s and went to live with him in New York state. Together they translated several works by Czech revivalist authors into English.

10 Kvapil, 181; Frank Tetauer, obituary for Karel Mušek, *Apollon* 2:5 (1924/1925): 83.
11 Rudolf Deyl, 'Za Karlem Muškem,' *Národní politika* 14 November 1924, 4.
12 Müller, 5. Alice Hillstead-Mušková died, aged eighty-six, on 11 June 1957 in the east Bohemian town of Hradec Králové, where she lived from 1935 and taught at the local business academy (National Theatre Archive, Prague, files Karel Mušek and Alice Mušková). A photograph of GBS dedicated 'To Alice Hillstead Musek at Xmas 1937, G. Bernard Shaw' appeared recently online, being offered for purchase by a New York autographs dealer.
13 Cf. Tetauer, obituary for Karel Mušek, 83, Kvapil, 184. The famous prose writer and dramatist Karel Čapek, who knew Shaw well and greatly admired his work, indicated to him repeatedly that Mušek's translations were deficient, and shortly after the translator's death made suggestions as to a possible rectification of the situation, recommending his own agent as Mušek's successor. Shaw accepted the offer of the new agent but as regards the quality of translation retorted: 'I have never yet had a translator who was not denounced as illiterate, ignorant of English, imbecile, and fatal to my reputation.' Karel Čapek to GBS, 28 November 1924; GBS to Karel Čapek, 25 December 1924. See also Karel Čapek to GBS, 15 January 1930. All three letters as reprinted in *Zpravodaj Společnosti bratří Čapků* 46 (2008): 14-17.
14 Cf. Andrej Stankovič, *Josef Florian a Stará Říše* (Prague: Triáda, 2008): 143 and I: D77, D98, N44, N47, N48 for details. The translation of *The Aran Islands* was revised for publication by František Pastor with no objection from Mušek, since the publisher was not happy with the quality of the rendering of passages concerning nature phenomena. Cf. the selection from the correspondence of Josef Florian from the period 1920-1923 edited by Daniel Samek, *Souvislosti* 19.3 (2008): 154-57.
15 A 1905 article from *The Freeman's Journal* cited by Mušek, 'Anglický tisk o Češích,' *Národní listy* 7 July 1905, 2. The journalists stayed in Bohemia from 7 to 18 June; the visit was covered by Czech newspapers all over the country. Kelly kept on returning, and wrote about Bohemia and Czech patriotism for a number of periodicals (cf., e.g., 'Bohemia and Ireland,' *The Leader* 15 October 1910, 210-11). He may have been responsible for bringing Synge's letters to Mušek to Ireland; Ann Saddlemyer claims that copies of the letters got to the Trinity College Library due to the interest of Edward Hutchinson Synge at a time when the latter was considering publishing some of them in a new edition of the work of his uncle the playwright in the 1920s. Ann Saddlemyer (ed.), *The Collected Letters of John Millington Synge Vol. 1, 1871-1907* (Oxford: Clarendon Press, 1983): xvii. The originals are now held in the Berg Collection of the New

York Public Library. For details of the journalists' visit and Kelly's articles on Bohemia and the Czechs, see Daniel Samek, *Česko-irské kulturní styky v první polovině 20. století / Czech-Irish Cultural Relations, 1900-1950*, trans. Ondřej Pilný (Prague: Centre for Irish Studies, Charles University, 2009): 31-34.

16 Despite that, Kelly and Synge probably never met. See *Letters 1*, 118, 159.

17 For biographical information on Kelly and a list of some of his legal and journalistic work, see 'Mr. R.J. Kelly, K.C.,' *The Tuam Herald* 23 December 1922. Mušek mentions that Kelly sent the play to him in the preface to his translation of *The Playboy of the Western World*. John Millington Synge, *Hrdina západu*, trans. Karel Mušek (Stará Říše na Moravě: M. Florianová, 1921; the preface is dated 1914). This is confirmed by Kelly; cf. 'Bohemia and Ireland', 210.

18 Karel Mušek, 'Irské divadlo národní,' *Lumír* 33.12 (1904/1905): 554-60, 15 September 1905.

19 JMS to KM, 5 February 1906. *Letters 1*, 158-59. Synge was aware since July 1905 already that Mušek was translating the play: as the editors of Yeats's collected letters note, Kelly informed Holloway about the fact on 12 July 1905, and the latter in turn told the playwright on 17 July, sending him Mušek's address in Prague. *The Collected Letters of W.B. Yeats, Vol. IV*, 178 n4. Synge's letter to Mušek quoted above is, however, his first.

20 KM to JMS, 12 February 1906. Cited in *Letters 1*, 159. The full name of the theatre was *Švandovo divadlo na Smíchově*: i.e., Švanda's Theatre in Smíchov; this is mistranslated in the *Letters* (and some other sources) as Inchover Theatre, Smíchov, probably because the owner's name was taken for an ordinary noun ('švanda' is an informal Czech expression for 'fun').

21 Karel Mušek, 'Poznámky režisérovy k vypravení Hamleta' (programme note to KM's staging of *Hamlet*), National Theatre, Prague, 2 February 1920, n.p. The Archive of the National Museum, Prague, Č 1570.

22 KM to JMS, 12 February 1906. *Letters 1*, 159.

23 *Letters 1*, 109 dates the letter as 'March 10th [1905]'. *Recte* 1906, as the correspondence seems to follow from JMS's first letter of 5 February; moreover, Mušek had not met Kelly until June 1906.

24 KM to JMS, 21 May 1906. Cited in *Letters 1*, 168-69. The manager referred to was Gustav Schmoranz who, despite the rejection of *Riders to the Sea*, wrote a complimentary letter to Synge in French in July, stating that they will be happy to stage *The Shadow of the Glen* in the following season. This 'will mean royalties!' Synge rejoiced. *Letters 1*, 181.

25 For a detailed account of the controversy, see Adrian Frazier, *Behind the Scenes: Yeats, Horniman, and the Struggle for the Abbey*

Theatre (Berkeley and Los Angeles: University of California Press, 1990): 175-92.

26 Cf. *Letters 1*, 168-85. McCormack analyses Synge and Molly's relationship in detail: *Fool of the Family: A Life of J.M. Synge* (London: Weidenfeld and Nicolson, 2000): 288-305.

27 JMS to Molly Allgood, 3 August 1906. *Letters 1*, 184. Synge's view of Mušek's English interestingly differs from that of R.J. Kelly who opined in his enamoured article on Bohemia that Mušek 'writes and speaks English with wonderful fluency and accuracy'. Kelly, 'Bohemia and Ireland', 210.

28 JMS to Lady Gregory, 24 July 1906. *Letters 1*, 181. The dating of Mušek's visit in *The Collected Letters of W.B. Yeats, Vol. IV*, 465 is erroneous, although the dates given for his visit to Coole Park – 27-31 July – are most likely correct.

29 Karel Mušek, 'V zapadlém kraji. Črty z Erina, ostrova hoře,' part 1, *Zvon* 7.23 (1907): 363-65.

30 Mušek, 'V zapadlém kraji,' part 1, 365.

31 Karel Mušek, 'V zapadlém kraji. Črty z Erina, ostrova hoře,' part 3, *Zvon* 7.25 (1907): 388.

32 Mušek, 'V zapadlém kraji,' part 3, 389.

33 Karel Mušek, 'V zapadlém kraji. Črty z Erina, ostrova hoře,' part 2, *Zvon* 7.24 (1907): 379. See also 380-81 and part 3, 389-91.

34 This part of Mušek's visit is briefly outlined in David H. Greene and Edward M. Stephens, *J.M. Synge, 1871-1909* (New York: Collier Books, 1961): 209-10.

35 JMS to Molly Allgood, 24 July 1906. *Letters 1*, 181.

36 Maurice Bourgeois, *John Millington Synge and the Irish Theatre* (Constable and Co.: London, 1913): 14. The photo was sent to Synge by Mušek on 12 September 1906. *Letters 1*, 255 n.1. A further copy was sent to J. Grierson in 1937 by Mušek's widow, together with a letter of condolence from Lady Gregory written on the death of KM, both to be lodged in a museum should it be seen as opportune. Cf. UCD Archives, ref. code IE UCDA LA25.

37 Mušek, preface to Synge, *Hrdina západu*, x.

38 Karel Mušek, 'Z irských glenů,' *Zlatá Praha* 33.43 (1916): 513-15 and 33.44 (1916): 525-26. Synge's letters establish beyond any doubt that the trip took place on 2-3 August 1906, with Synge already writing to Molly from home (i.e., Glenageary) on 3 August in the evening; Mušek and Synge met for the last time on the following day when the translator was leaving Ireland. Cf. *Letters 1*, 184-85. The itinerary of the trip outlined by Mušek is, roughly, as follows: morning train to Bray – Dargle Glen – arriving in Wicklow Town by train or cart in the evening – spending the night in Rathnew (farmer Menctillon) – walking through the plain between Laragh and Great Sugar Loaf in the morning – going down through a narrow glen 'opposite the mountain' (Sugar Loaf?): reaching a rocky edge over The Devil's

Glen, and then up again – spending the night in Bray – next day to Carrickmines to see the Kiltiernan cromlegh – to cottages at Kilgobbin – night train home. This would have clearly required an additional day and some swiftness of foot, to say the very least. The passages included verbatim from 'The People of the Glens' indicate beyond any doubt that Mušek used the version of the text published in *The Shanachie* (March 1907). See J.M. Synge, *Travelling Ireland: Essays 1898-1908*. Edited by Nicholas Grene (Dublin: The Lilliput Press, 2009): 107-116.

39 Mušek, preface to Synge, *Hrdina západu*, ix-x. The final sentence of the extract comes from Mušek, 'Z irských glenů,' *Zlatá Praha* 33.43 (1916): 513. An obituary that was most likely written by Mušek characterises the late Synge's work as bearing 'a touch of Maeterlinck and being saturated in the Irish spirit; world issues were of little interest to him, he always depicted only virtuous but destitute characters from his people, as he knew them from the boggy and mountainous areas of the "Green Isle".' *Národní listy* 4 April 1909, 2.

40 W.B. Yeats to J.B. Yeats, [5] August [1906]. *The Collected Letters of W.B. Yeats, Vol. IV*, 465, 465 n6. Yeats remembered Mušek in a note of August 1929 as a 'vivid energetic man'. *The Collected Letters of W.B. Yeats, Vol. IV*, 465 n6.

41 W.B. Yeats to KM, with a note by Augusta Gregory, 24 August [1906]. *The Collected Letters of W.B. Yeats, Vol. IV*, 480-81. Lady Gregory apparently initiated a mention of Mušek's visit in *Lady's Pictorial* of 18 August. Cf. *The Collected Letters of W.B. Yeats, Vol. IV*, 465 n6.

42 Cf. *The Collected Letters of W.B. Yeats, Vol. IV*, 481 n4, which quotes Horniman's letter to Yeats of 30 August 1906: 'I went about a good deal with Dr [sic!] Musek & came to the conclusion that in Bohemia the *people* wanted the drama for itself, not merely as a means of propaganda ... How you would love to meddle with that elaborate lighting apparatus! There was a pleasantly lighted back sheet without any of that shuddering effect I object to so much & the colour of the moonlight was good.' The production she describes was Gonoud's *Faust*. According to the editors, Horniman and Mušek kept up a correspondence after the visit.

43 Karel Mušek, 'Irské literární divadlo,' *Divadelní list Máje* 3.2 (2 November 1906): 17-18, Karel Mušek, 'Irské národní divadlo,' *Divadlo* 1(8).4 (1920/1921): 4, 29 December 1920. The comparison with German theatre practice had originally been made in Mušek's first article on Irish theatre: Mušek, 'Irské divadlo národní', 560.

44 Cf., for instance, the memoirs of Rudolf Deyl which provide extensive details of the era: Rudolf Deyl, *O čem vím já* (Prague: Melantrich, 1971): particularly 136-56.

45 The last delay was reportedly caused by the Court coming to Prague which meant that theatres had to change their bills and put on lashings of opera to suit the German-speaking nobility. See Synge to

Frank Fay, 12 May 1907; JMS quotes Mušek's explication to this effect. *Letters 1*, 341.

46 Mušek dispatched photos of 'the Bohemian Nora and Dan Burke' to Synge in December 1906. JMS to Molly Allgood, 21 December 1906. *Letters 1*, 264. A letter from Mušek to F.J. Fay of 28 September 1906 expresses gratitude for sending the stage plan. Ann Saddlemyer, *Theatre Business. The Correspondence of the First Abbey Theatre Directors: William Butler Yeats, Lady Gregory and J.M. Synge* (University Park and London: The Pennsylvania State University Press, 1982):136 n.1. The play was performed on 17 and 22 August.

47 The director's copy of the text (*režijní kniha*) handwritten and including all revisions, together with a preliminary stage plan with a list of props, is lodged at the Prague National Theatre archive. No photographs from the production have survived.

48 Václav Hladík, review of J.M. Synge, *Ve stínu doliny*, trans. and dir. Karel Mušek, *Národní listy* 20 August 1907, 2.

49 Cf. Ann Saddlemyer, *The Collected Letters of John Millington Synge Vol. 2: 1907-1909* (Oxford: Clarendon Press, 1984): 88-89. Mušek mentions seeing the framed poster at the Abbey during his final visit to Ireland in July 1912. Mušek, 'Irské národní divadlo,' *Divadlo* 1(8).5 (1920/1921): 4, 14 January 1921.

50 In a letter to Synge of 9 (14?) September 1908, Mušek stated that he had translated *The Well* two years previously, sent it to Vinohradské divadlo (Vinohrady Theatre) but heard nothing back as regards the chances of production. *Letters 2*, 184-85 n.4, 199 n.1. In an earlier letter from 1907, Mušek in turn mentioned having spoken to the director of the small Urania Theatre who was considering to stage the play; however, nothing came out of that discussion either. *Letters 1*, 341.

51 J.J. David requested the rights by a letter of 30 April. Synge's refusal is dated 10 May. Mušek was forwarded a copy of the play shortly before that, sending his thanks and asking for the translation rights on 7 May. *Letters 1*, 335, 340 and 340 n.1.

52 Interestingly enough, Synge's first translator into German, Max Meyerfeld, seemed also to regard *The Playboy* as too parochial for the German audience. Cf. *Letters 2*, 184 n.1. For Mušek's views, see 'Irské národní divadlo,' *Divadlo* 1(8).5 (1920/1921): 4, 'E.J.M. Synge,' *Divadlo* 1(8).24 (1920/1921): 4, 28 October 1921, and 'Tři irské hry,' unpublished typescript, n.d (1908-9?), National Museum, Prague, Č 1570/1. In 'Irské národní divadlo,' Mušek made a curious link between *The Playboy* and Ladislav Stroupežnický's play *Naši furianti*, an 1880s piece of political satire with a rural setting that was a seminal work of the Czech national revival. *Naši furianti* nonetheless remains a much shallower play and one with very distinctly local targets.

53 Cf. Mušek, preface to Synge, *Hrdina západu*, x-xiv, and Bourgeois, 193-95, 200-212.

54 An unpublished typescript of Jung's translation, titled 'Rek západu,' is housed in the library of the Prague Theatre Institute (Divadelní ústav). Jung's biographer lists the play as co-translated with Mušek but was unable to find further information on the stages of the translation process or the extent of individual contribution either. Jiří Frýzek, *Václav Alois Jung: Život a dílo* (Rychnov nad Kněžnou: Městský úřad, 1997): 60, 76. Given Mušek's vigorous enforcement of his rights as the authorised translator of Bernard Shaw (cf. Kvapil, 184 and Müller, 5): he may have stepped in and required to co-author the translation, and eventually suppressed Jung's contribution. The gradual change of the title to *Hrdina západu* ('rek' being replaced by a less archaic synonym for 'hero') is also of note.

55 Otokar Fischer, 'Činoherní novinka,' *Národní listy* 6 December 1916, 3. Fischer's review presents an illuminating reading of multiple dimensions of the play; the production itself is discussed merely in the concluding paragraph which condemns it thoroughly. A flamboyant – but at the same time quite astute – review of the first French production was published earlier in the Czech theatre journal *Scéna*: Richard Weiner, 'Le Baladin du monde occidental,' *Scéna* 1: 2. půlročník (1913/1914): 176-80.

56 An anonymous review in the cultural monthly *Rozpravy Aventina* highlights director Frejka's 'non-realistic scenography' and 'the perfect use of stage space to facilitate a dynamic of the visual composition'. *Rozpravy Aventina* (1927-1928): 16 February 1928, 146.

57 A review in a national daily describes the production as 'one of the most accomplished in the current season' and points out that the opening performance was introduced by prominent poet and dramaturge Jiří Mahen, who outlined the literary importance of Synge in his speech. n.a., 'Národní divadlo v Brně (Původní dopis),' *Český deník* 27 April 1920, 5.

58 Deyl, 'Za Karlem Muškem'.

59 A total of four plays were published between 1921-22, followed by a posthumous publication of *The Aran Islands* (see note 14 above and the Appendix). Mušek favourably reviewed *The Aran Islands* in 1907. The fact that he regarded it as an ethnographic document may be interpreted as further proof that Mušek saw Synge as, at heart, a rural realist. Mušek's lack of a critical eye as regards the way Synge depicts the life on the islands may have likewise been influenced by his knowing little about Aran, which he never visited. Cf. Karel Mušek, review of *The Aran Islands* by J.M. Synge, *Lumír* 35.8 (1907): 383-84, 15 June. The articles mentioned were 'Irské národní divadlo' and 'E.J.M. Synge,' both referred to above.

60 The placing of the play in a double bill suggests that cuts may have been effected. The National Theatre archive holds what presumably is the director's copy of the acting text. It is a regular printed copy of the play published earlier in the year with notes and drawings penned in. No cuts are, however, indicated.

61 R., 'Synge a Yeats (K provedení 'Studánky světců' a 'Přesýpacích hodin' ve Stavovském divadle),' *Jeviště* 2.43 (1921): 638-40, 27 October.

62 These were 5, 6 and 9 November 1921.

63 Otokar Fischer, 'Večer zázraků,' *Národní listy* 8 November 1921, 4-5.

64 Karel Engelmüller, review of *Studnice světců* and *Přesýpací hodiny*, *Zlatá Praha* (1921-1922), 16 November 1921, 387.

65 Quoted in a letter by Josef Florian to the translator of *The Hour-Glass*, Jaroslav Skalický, 20 February 1922, as reprinted in *Souvislosti* 19.3 (2008): 156. The non-realistic aspects of the staging were hardly to Mušek's taste either.

66 Hanuš Jelínek, obituary for Karel Mušek, *Lumír* 51.9 (1924): 499, 27 November.

67 I wish to express my gratitude to Daniel Samek, Roy Foster, Bohuslav Mánek, and Hana Zahradníková for helpful suggestions, Matouš Kurz and Michaela Raisová for assistance with archival research, and Patrick Lonergan for enabling me to present a preliminary version of this study at the Synge Summer School in 2008. I am likewise grateful to the staff of the National Theatre archive, the National Museum archive in Prague, the Theatre Institute, Prague, and the Czech Radio archive.

9 | WELL, WELL, WELL: A QUESTION OF 'PIETY'[1]

Richard Pine

I begin by asking your indulgence for the following parody:

> Tobar
> Tobar an Bhric, Tobar na Carraige,
> Tobar an Duin, Tobar Eoin,
> Tobar Melin, Tobar na Molt,
> Tobar na Buadh, Tobhar an Rí,
> Tobar na Súl,
> Tobhar Brighde, Tobar Pádraig.
>
> All those Wicklow wells. I'd get so tense before a lecture, d'you know what I used to do? As we drove along those narrow, winding roads I'd recite the names to myself, just for the mesmerism, the sedation, of the incantation –
>
> Ballintubber, Tubbercurry,
>
> God's Well, Holy Well,
>
> Lady's Well, Kevin's Well, Tooth Well,
>
> White Well, Eye Well.
>
> Wicklow – Donegal. Over the years they became indistinguishable ... because the wells we moved among were beyond that kind of celebration.

For those of you who are wondering what that was all about, I was trying to parody Frank Hardy's opening monologue from Brian Friel's *Faith Healer*, as he recites – or 'incants' – the place-names of the villages in Scotland and Wales where his craft as a faith healer has been tried.

By substituting the names of wells in Wicklow and Donegal for those place-names, I intended to suggest that the healing power associated with so many Irish holy wells may be, today, as vulnerable to modern belief as Frank Hardy's power as a healer. And by translating Friel's line 'the *people* we moved among were beyond that kind of celebration',[2] I want to suggest that the healing wells are in most cases – but not all – beyond celebration, as our globalized culture moves away – or takes us away – from the roots of experience, from the deep structures of the psyche on which myth depends for its continuing – or discontinued – presence in our lives.

So in this lecture, I'm going to speak about the significance of *wells*, or the significance of *the* well as an archetypal affect of the human imagination. My intention is to argue that, by moving away from such affects and archetypes, we make it easier for our society – to use Synge's much debated expression – to live 'by the power of a lie', and I will look at the nature of drama as a mirror of the deceitful world in which we are increasingly tending to live. The twin poles of my argument are the relation of identity to place, and the universal or global world in which identity is acted out.

As my title suggests, I'll speak mainly about three wells as they appear – or in fact *don't* appear – in plays by Synge, Yeats, and Friel: Synge's *The Well of the Saints*, Yeats's *At the Hawk's Well* (1917), and Friel's *Translations* (1980). At the end, I'll also make some remarks about Synge's *Playboy of the Western World*.

At the risk of telling you something you already know, *The Well of the Saints* concerns the temporary restoration of sight to two people by means of holy water, the confusion that results, and their subsequent embrace of their renewed blindness. *At the Hawk's Well* shows us an old man who has waited fifty years for a miracle to occur at the well, which will endow him with eternal life; and *Translations* is a treatment of the mapping exercise in Ireland in the 1830s known as the Ordnance Survey.

In order to get directly to the core of my argument, I'll begin with the question posed by Owen O'Donnell in the map-making episode in *Translations* (this is the scene in which Owen O'Donnell, a native of Baile Beag, is working with George Yolland of the Ordnance Survey to anglicize Irish place-names):

> We call that crossroads Tobair Vree. And why do we call it Tobair Vree? I'll tell you why. Tobair means a well. But what does Vree mean? It's a corruption of B[h]rian ... an erosion of Tobair Bhriain. Because a hundred-and-fifty years ago [i.e.

around 1680] there used to be a well there, not at the crossroads, mind you – that would be too simple – but in a field close to the crossroads. And an old man called Brian, whose face was disfigured by an enormous growth, got it into his head that the water in that well was blessed; and every day for seven months he went there and bathed his face in it. But the growth didn't go away; and one morning Brian was found drowned in that well. And ever since, that crossroads is known as Tobair Vree – even though that well has long since dried up. I know the story because my grandfather told it to me ... So ... what do we do with a name like that? Do we scrap Tobair Vree altogether and call it – what? – The Cross? Crossroads? Or do we keep piety with a man long dead, long forgotten, his name 'eroded' beyond recognition, whose trivial little story nobody in the parish remembers?[3]

As with the wells of County Wicklow, with which Synge was intimately acquainted, the fictitious Tobair Vree has a significance beyond the mere person whose name it bears. Or is it fictitious? The catalogues of the Wicklow wells make it clear that, as in the case of Owen O'Donnell, the names and functions of the wells have been rescued from oblivion and re-entered into the folk memory by the slender recollection of one or two witnesses.

The key expression in Owen's speech, as far as this lecture is concerned, is the question: 'Do we keep piety with a man long dead, long forgotten, his name "eroded" beyond recognition?' It might have been just as easy for Owen to ask: 'do we keep *faith* with a man long dead?', but Brian Friel tells me that his choice of the word *piety* was quite deliberate.[4]

The *concept* of the well, rather than the well itself, is crucial to the question of 'keeping piety' – *piety* being a central word in the dialogue of *Translations*, as Owen's father, Hugh, reminds his lifelong friend Jimmy Jack: 'the *desiderium nostrorum* – the need for our own. Our *pietas*, James, was for older, quieter things' (445-6). And beyond and behind that simple word is the fundamental issue of *change*, a transfer or transitus. Hugh has already acknowledged to Yolland that his community has been reliant on 'the mythologies of fantasy and hope and self-deception ... imprisoned in a linguistic contour which no longer matches the landscape of fact' (418-9) and this is brought to a cathartic point by the Ordnance Survey.

Piety obviously conveys the sense of being *pious*, but also of fidelity to natural obligations, of dutifulness, of devoutness, of conventional belief or orthodoxy – a personification of a respectful and faithful attachment to gods, country, relations, especially parents.

At the heart of my argument – whether it concerns itself with globalization or the ritual significance of the well – is the question of what it means to keep faith or, in Friel's more emphatic word, *piety*.

How can a person in modern society continue to invoke the archetypal powers of *that time* – to refer back to events or personalities *in illo tempore*? How can we continue to connect with the ancient springs of myth and legend?

The changes which took place in Ireland during the nineteenth century, many of which could be said to have been precipitated by the Ordnance Survey project, brought an end to what Yeats called 'the Celtic Twilight', and which was chronicled to a lesser but very elegant extent by Synge in his descriptions of Wicklow, Kerry and Connemara.

In *Translations*, Owen taunts his father:

> **OWEN.** Do you know where the priest lives?
>
> **HUGH.** At Lis na Muc, over near ...
>
> **OWEN.** No he doesn't. Lis na Muc, the Fort of the Pigs, has become Swinefort ... And the new school isn't at Poll na gCaorach – it's at Sheepsrock. Will you be able to find your way? (418)

When Hugh O'Donnell acknowledges these changes he says 'we must learn where we live. We must learn to make them [the new place-names] our own. We must make them our new home' (444).

One thinks of John Montague's poem 'A Lost Tradition':

> All around shards of a lost tradition,
> The whole landscape a manuscript
> We had lost the skill to read,
> A part of our past disinherited
> But fumbled like a blind man
> Along the fingertips of instinct.[5]

And one might contrast it with Montague's poem which begins 'Like Dolmens round my childhood, the old people',[6] which suggests that ancient memories as embodied in old people can protect the innocence of the young. When Adrian Frazier speaks of Synge's experience of the 'metaphysical loneliness of place' and his witness to the 'strangeness of everything',[7] I think he could be referring to the loss of certainties that pitched Synge himself into a mode of vagrancy.

The political and economic necessity for a new Ireland which emerged in the wake of the Ordnance Survey and the Famine, and which was incorporated in the land wars and the war of independence, ran counter to the work of Synge and Yeats, even though Synge (and after him Éamon de Valera) knew that the way of life which they celebrated was already dying. The 'real Ireland' became the 'hidden Ireland' and was overlaid by a new linguistic and metaphysical contour which became the new 'reality'. The transition was commemorated by Friel not only in *Translations* but also in *Dancing at Lughnasa* (1990), and even in his early plays such as *The Enemy Within* (1962), *The Blind Mice* (1963), *The Gentle Island* (1971), *Volunteers* (1975), and his versions of Turgenev's *Fathers and Sons* (1987) and Chekhov's *Uncle Vanya* (1998).

When I described Friel in my book as 'the Diviner',[8] I intended to indicate that, as Seamus Heaney says, 'divining is a gift for being in touch with what is there, hidden and real, a gift for mediating between the latent source and the community'.[9] Heaney's apparent insistence that 'what is there [is both] hidden *and* real' brings us to the heart of the matter and the function of drama.

It is the point at which we recognize that *pietas* has become insufficient to sustain itself as an active ingredient in people's consciousness, that faith is no longer supportive and supportable. Drama is required in order to re-establish our belief in the incredible.

Owen's (or Friel's) questions – 'do we keep piety?' and 'will you be able to find your way?' – bring to the surface, and articulate, the questions implicit in Synge's and Yeats's plays. These questions are those of identity, memory, and belonging – or, conversely, the failure of memory, the loss of identity, and displacement. Above all, 'the power of a lie' and its relation to a sense of place.

And this connects intimately with the Jungian notion of the deep structures in our psyche and thus we have the prospect of a discussion not only of the *well* as a deep *physical* structure, but also of its *meta-physical* significance as a symbol of our connection with nature and the secrets of nature.

If we agree that drama is a pretence on the part of playwright and actors, and an acceptance of that pretence on the part of their audience, then it becomes possible for us to accept that what takes place is a *representation* of an action or of an exchange of words, rather than the action or words themselves.

So one of my questions is: how far is *deceit* a given in the human psyche and how far is it a modern phenomenon? Do we *lie* every time we elect a government? (I think we do.) And what is 'the power of a lie'?

How far must a 'lie' be promulgated before it becomes the 'truth'?

The plays I'm discussing are deceitful but we accept them because we know that they *are* a pretence.

If it is the nature of ritual to persuade the communicant of a mysterious truth, then the 'willing suspension of disbelief' operates so as to enable us, and the actors, to carry out the playwright's deception – that is, to persuade us, for the period of the suspension of disbelief, that the people on the stage *really are* who they purport to be – Owen O'Donnell, the custodian of the Hawk's Well, Synge's blind couple.

So the nature of drama – which we see today so closely copied in the media and political life and rhetoric – is to question our capacity for both belief and disbelief.

Central to the question of faith and piety is that of *representation*. *Blind* faith – and I use the word deliberately, of course – requires that we believe in some power that is, *in fact*, incredible. The cardinal example of such faith in the Christian world is that of transubstantiation, the transformation of bread and wine into the flesh and blood of Christ, which is known as the 'Real Presence'.

On a superficial level, we have to observe that none of the three wells is actually shown to us: Tobair Vree and the Well of the Saints are spoken of and discussed, but not represented on stage. The title of *At the Hawk's Well* suggests that the well itself is on the stage, yet Yeats's stage directions make it very clear that the well is to be *suggested* by means of a cloth on the ground of the stage, rather than physically shown, and the opening incantation is:

> I call to the eye of the mind
> A well long choked up and dry.[10]

The notion of the well is therefore suggested in the same way that the communion wafer and the wine suggest the 'real presence' of Christ. That is to say, *belief* lies at a much deeper level than the superficial discussion of these wells is capable of.

The purpose of the well is – another crucially important Frielian term – to *affirm* some of man's innate relationship with the phenomenal world. It includes the affirmation of the role of memory in establishing continuity.

The well is the container of water as a transforming, healing, and regenerative force whose symbolic power is transcendent.[11] The containing of the water in the well – the sacred spring – gives it a spiritual significance which is either productive of, or is produced by, human reaction with nature. Whether or not the significance of the well was the author or the creature of human perception of it, there is no doubt that the result of this perception is the first stage of *ritual*, the inception of a drama. The playwrights I am discussing are the high priests of this ritual that occupies our imagination, and their collected works are the bible which runs parallel to, and so often coincides with, the history of modern Ireland.

The tragedy depicted in the short discussion in *Translations* when Owen describes the failure of Tobair Vree to heal B(h)rian's distortions is a signal that when that reaction of man with the supposed healing powers of the well is less than expected or prayed for, terrible consequences occur – maybe an analogy with the current crisis in Irish politics.

Many wells throughout Ireland are associated with the power of restoring sight to the blind or those afflicted with poor eyesight. (Of the 106 holy wells catalogued in County Wicklow, fifty-six were specifically credited with curative powers, and although only four of these are said to have cured eyesight, we can infer that the *general* characteristics of being curative, in thirty-eight cases where no specific ailment was mentioned, would have included blindness and failing eyesight).[12] Furthermore, as Walter and Mary Brenneman say in their comprehensive survey of Irish holy wells, 'Eye wells are ... more important for the purpose of gaining wisdom or inner grace through "seeing" than merely for the cure for some eyes irritated by peat smoke' (18). The curative power of a well was much more profound than the amelioration of ailments, as we observe from the quest for eternal life pursued by Cuchulain and the Old Man in *At the Hawk's Well*.

It is hardly surprising that a well, as the source and container of *water*, is regarded as having 'great sacred power', as the Brennemans say in their chapter on 'Myth and Ritual at Celtic Irish Springs' (21). They say, 'Power of place is an essential element of the power and sacredness of the holy well ... The people who dwelt there ... were connected ontologically to the place and carried a name that was often associated with it' (22-3). The foundational myth of the well is that a sacred spring is located in the Otherworld, and that at certain times a communication is possible between this world and the Otherworld – it is this Otherworld, the place of the imagination, with which we no longer connect; to adopt and contort Kathleen Raine's title, we no longer worship at, or even observe, *ancient springs*.[13]

The Brennemans also draw attention to the fact that:

> [t]he symbolism of the sacred spring, its myths and rituals, the role of the well in Celtic Ireland emerges as crucial to life, both physical and spiritual ... The well ... is the source of wisdom ... that, like water itself, holds all the possibilities of life, from knowledge of the nature of things to the urge to regenerate through sacrifice and love. (41)

They go on to state that:

> The *deus loci* is the deity of a particular place; as such, it is the 'spirit' of the place in a double sense. It is the feeling of *unique power* that one experiences in a particular place, and it is the spirit abstracted from that place or thematized in the form of a supernatural being ... The *deus loci* marks off the boundaries of the place and of the people residing there. (88. Emphasis added)

Owen O'Donnell's point – that the well is *not* where one might suppose it to be – and Synge's location of the Saint's Well at a spot on an island remote from where the play's action takes place, suggest that *place* is extremely important, which makes the discussion of Tobair Vree so crucial to the mapping of places in *Translations*.

The vagueness with which, in the 1930s, Wicklow schoolchildren, often transmitting their grandparents' memories, referred to the possible or rumoured location of forgotten or neglected wells, shows that the association of *place* – in this case the wells in question – with the residual *power* of that place, had become detached.[14]

Place is crucial because it connects with the residual power associated with the *deus loci*.

It is obvious that in *Translations* the Irish language is being *dis*-placed by the mapping exercise, but it is also suggested that places themselves are being *dis*-placed and therefore that people who live in those places no longer have anywhere to live.

If the 'Otherworld' is the sacred place, the seat of power, and if the well is the medium through which the power and sacrality of the Otherworld pass into the ordinary world, then for Yolland the mystery of the place-names and the ineffable culture of Baile Beag is *his* other-world. It is something which he will never be able to enter, but with which he wishes that he could communicate.

Our modern abandoning of myth and legend is our way of allowing the Otherworld to be desecrated, or de-sanctified. (I should add that as an atheist I am totally non-religious, but that does not separate me from my fascination with the pagan and paranormal imagination.)

Yolland sees the anglicization of the place-names as an eviction, and, paradoxically, it is this which Hugh O'Donnell acknowledges and accepts. The Ordnance Survey is perhaps the earliest example of the globalization of Ireland. As Lord Salisbury would say fifty years later, 'The most disagreeable part of the three kingdoms is Ireland, and therefore Ireland has a splendid map',[15] and, by *re*-naming Ireland, a different Ireland was being brought into existence – one which answers, in English, to English voices and English perceptions.

I would like to spend some time discussing the concept of identity: firstly, the idea of an indivisible, irreducible self; secondly, the place of that self in the world; and thirdly the passage of that self through time. And I would add that *place* also requires an identity in order to be located and described.[16]

I think it worthwhile briefly to mention these three aspects of identity because, in the three plays which I am principally discussing, and in many more plays by all three of the playwrights, personal identity is problematic: let's mention the major points at which identity is, or can be, threatened.

In *Translations*, George Yolland thinks that Owen's name is 'Roland'. When the misunderstanding is pointed out to him, it gives rise to considerable amusement, but on the first occasion on which it is mentioned, it gives rise to considerable alienation between Owen and his brother Manus:

> **MANUS.** And they call you Roland! They both call you Roland!
>
> **OWEN:** Shhhh. Isn't it ridiculous? They seemed to get it wrong from the very beginning – or else they can't pronounce Owen. I was afraid some of you bastards would laugh.
>
> **MANUS.** Aren't you going to tell them?
>
> **OWEN.** Yes – yes – soon – soon.
>
> **MANUS.** But they ...

> **OWEN.** Easy, man, easy. Owen – Roland – what the hell. It's only a name. It's the same me, isn't it? Well, isn't it? (408)

That question – 'it's the same me, isn't it?' – is at the heart of the identity crisis of Baile Beag, because it marks the *translation* of Owen as a miniature of the anglicization of Baile Beag into Ballybeg, of Lis na Muc into Swinefort, and of course of Tobair Vree into ... what? It is ironic that Yolland, responsible for anglicizing the place-names, should decide that the place should continue to be known as Tobair Vree, to continue to embody all the uncertainties that Owen has pointed out, because he has recognized that without their original names these places cease to have meaning.

To reinforce this point, Friel paraphrases a few lines from George Steiner's *After Babel*:

> **OWEN.** We name a thing and – bang! – it leaps into existence!
>
> **YOLLAND.** Each name a perfect equation with its roots.
>
> **OWEN.** A perfect congruence with its reality. (422)[17]

But naming depends on both memory and the future, and the Ordnance Survey exercise is excising Irishness from the collective conscious *and* unconscious of the people of what is now called Ballybeg.

If identity changes with time (the revenant Owen, now known as Roland, insists that 'It's the same me, isn't it?') then one's perception of oneself changes, and others' perceptions of you change also. If memory is capable of maintaining *pietas*, then meaning persists in a natural state, but if memory falters, as it has in the case of Tobair Vree, and so many of the holy wells of Wicklow, meaning becomes vulnerable.

It is particularly difficult to use the word 'I' with any certainty, or to understand what is meant when one is addressed as 'you' – even more so in the languages which employ the second-person singular as well as plural – 'thou' and 'you'. Paul Ricoeur, in discussing this difficulty, says : 'it is I, Paul Ricoeur, who am, and am not, the heart of the world'. And he applies this to our understanding of the meaning of 'here' as opposed to 'there'. Ricoeur says:

> Absolutely speaking, 'here' as the place where I am, is the zero point in relation to which all other places become near or far. In this sense, 'here' is nowhere. And yet, the use of 'here' in conversation implies a *minimal topographical knowledge*, thanks to which I can situate my 'here' in relation to a system of coordinates ... The place functions therefore in the same way as

the date, namely by inscribing the absolute 'here' onto a system of *objective coordinates*.¹⁸

I do not think I am making too much play on the terms *minimal topographical knowledge* and *objective coordinates* when I suggest that, in respect of personal identity, this exactly gives us the metaphysical equivalent of the physical mapping that so excites Owen and Yolland in their quotation from George Steiner; to repeat:

OWEN. We name a thing and – bang! – it leaps into existence!

YOLLAND. Each name a perfect equation with its roots.

OWEN. A perfect congruence with its reality.

This seems to me to point to a fundamental ontological difficulty: not only is one's personal, irreducible identity subject to change through time and space, but also one's capacity for knowing *where one is* is at risk, not from the coordinates of date and place but from the weaknesses of memory and from the strength of others' perception of oneself.

There can in fact be no *objective* co-ordinates except in the skill of the cartographer, but this will elude the skill of the toponymist and the effective interpretation of the map.

The drunken certainty with which Owen and Yolland decide that 'we name a thing and – bang! – it leaps into existence' is fundamentally flawed, not by poteen but by the fact that naming Owen as 'Roland' has failed to bring him into existence. Continuing to name a crossroads 'Tobair Vree', when 'Vree' means nothing, and no-one remembers the reason for the naming, is keeping piety with what is now a myth.

The question of identity in terms of *utterance* is also crucial. When Owen, in *Translations*, supposedly 'translates' the speech by Captain Lancey, his brother asks him 'What sort of a translation was that? ... You weren't saying what Lancey was saying!' to which Owen replies 'Uncertainty in meaning is incipient poetry' (408).¹⁹ Owen, as the intermediary, has attempted to soften the fact that, as Manus has already realized, and as Yolland will shortly acknowledge, the map-making exercise is a form of military eviction, or, as one might say, evisceration. The act of translation, or, to use the Greek equivalent, of metaphor, if it is dishonest, can be brutally fatal.

One of the most difficult lines in all of Friel's work is that spoken by Owen in his return to Ballybeg: 'it's such a delight to be back here with you all again – "civilised" people' (403); we should note that in the text the word 'civilised' appears in inverted commas. Owen's remark is difficult and problematic. In one sense, the British map-making is part of the spread of one kind of civilization, a hegemonic annexation of the places and character of Ireland. In another sense (the sense in which the people of Baile Beag speak Irish, Greek, and Latin but not English) the children of the hedge-school are the 'civilised' people and the map-makers are the barbarians.[20]

Within Owen's remark we therefore encounter the classic, archetypal distinction between civilians and barbarians, between 'us' and 'them', which occurs whenever one culture is confronted by another, or more specifically when one person from that culture is presented with the image of *the* 'other'.

The difficulty is compounded by Yolland's respect for the customs and 'pieties' of Baile Beag, which he expresses in general terms to Hugh O'Donnell and specifically in relation to Tobair Vree. The attraction of the 'other', which Yolland encounters in his working relationship with Owen and in his brief liaison with Máire, is, in this instance, catastrophic for all concerned. Friel seems to be demonstrating the fact that despite the best intentions, thought is incommunicable and that differences between cultures or mindsets are insuperable.

Everywhere in Synge's work, as in Yeats's and Friel's, we find the oscillation between the real and the imagined, between what appears to be 'true' and what appears to be 'false'.

In *The Well of the Saints* we *see* a blind couple, played of course by actors who are *not* blind, just as we witness the blindness and madness of Oedipus, who we believe has killed his father and slept with his mother, but the moment we leave the theatre of make-believe we speak of the skill of actors and directors in creating that illusion. Synge cruelly juxtaposes the truth of blindness with the anti-truth of vision – or is it the other way round? Although Martin Doul believes his wife to be beautiful, because that is what he has been told and he has no means of disproving it, there is considerable doubt to his belief: 'We don't know rightly what way you have your splendour ... [and he asks himself] if you have it at all'.[21]

Martin's wish is that 'If we could see ourselves for one hour, or a minute itself, the way we'd know surely we were the finest man and the finest woman of the seven counties of the east' (73). As it is, Martin and Mary are caught between the lies they have been told – that they are fine-looking people – and the truth with which they are sometimes taunted. Blindness prevents them from knowing which is truth and which is lies, and Mary Doul, convinced of her own beauty, refuses to believe those taunts – that she is 'a fright', or 'a wrinkled wizened hag' (93). Her dark view of the world is that 'those that have their sight ... do have great joy, the time they do be seeing a grand thing, to let on they don't see it at all, and to be telling fool's lies' (73).

'Fool's lies'. One cannot escape the conclusion that the difference between the sighted and the blind is similar to the difference between politicians and the electorate. How many politicians see realities but deny that they see them? How many politicians tell the blind ugly electorate that they are beautiful? How great a burden can the 'truth' carry before it breaks under the strain? How often can a 'lie' be told before it is detected? What is 'true' and what is a 'lie'?

When Timmy the blacksmith tells Martin and Mary that with the healing water of the Saint's Well 'the two of you will see a great wonder this day, and it's no lie', he is telling a dramatic truth in so far as the gift of sight will provoke a dénouement, but he also regrets that 'it was bad work we did when we let on she was fine-looking' (92-3). The lie lies in the truth.

In this play Synge anticipates 'the power of a lie' in *The Playboy*. Mat Simons says 'it's more joy dark Martin got from the lie we told' (93). Dark Martin is – saving his doubts – happier in believing the lie than sighted Martin is in embracing the truth. 'There's no man but would liefer be blind a hundred years, or a thousand itself, than be looking on your like' (99).

The retreat of Martin and Mary back into blindness is a retreat into their kind of truth, that is, an acceptable lie.

Moving on briefly to the third example which I have chosen, the Old Man and the young Cuchulain in *At the Hawk's Well* both wear masks, and the musicians and the Guardian of the Well have faces 'made up to resemble masks'. Thus the identity of the two principal characters is permanently in question, while the four others *pretend* to have no perceivable identity. The location is also problematic, since there is only a suggestion that the well actually exists.

So the deception practised in Yeats's *At the Hawk's Well* is of a different order, much closer to the roots of symbolism in the well.

The Old Man has waited fifty years for the 'secret moment' of the ritual at which the miracle takes place and he receives the gift of immortality. During that time, the miracle has eluded him, yet he continues both to believe *and* to mistrust the miracle. He calls the dancers/musicians at the well 'deceivers of men' and rails against them at the play's close: 'Accursed dancers, you have stolen my life. You have deluded me my whole life through' (217-8). The young Cuchulain tells the truth – literally – when he says 'There is no well'. In terms of Irish holy wells, he is telling no more – or less – than the truth, when he says that all he can see is 'a hollow among stones half-full of leaves', since many wells are in fact shallow containers of water rather than (to use the appropriate Jungian term) deep structures.

And the Old Man also tells the truth when Cuchulain, hearing the Guardian of the Well giving 'the cry of the hawk', believes that he has actually heard a hawk: 'There is no bird' (214). This may be generically of the same order as 'The Emperor's New Clothes' but, I think, much more serious. There is no well, there is no hawk *at the hawk's well* – and the old man and Cuchulain tell us so. They are in fact telling the truth when, as part of a drama, they should be telling a lie, or at least mis-representing the truth.

Synge, in *The Playboy* – a play that is far more problematic than anyone seems willing to acknowledge – deceives everyone: the characters on stage are deceived, the audience is deceived, but most importantly *the play itself is a deception of itself.*

If we accept that the person on the stage *really is* Christy Mahon, then we also have to accept that he *believes* he has killed his father. Why else would he have run away? Yet first of all he is wrong (but not deceiving himself) and secondly when it is discovered that his (almost) honestly recounted story of how he dealt his father a fatal blow is found to be untrue, he is reviled for being a deceiver – which he is not.

When I say 'almost' honest, I mean that Christy embellishes his account of his attack on his father, presumably to make the account more attractive, but he still *sincerely* believes that his father is dead.

There is, therefore, no 'power of a lie' – there *is* a misconception, but that doesn't enter into the plot until Christy's father arrives: up to that point Christy has told the truth, but it is later described as a 'lie'. In fact, Christy has become a hero by the power of a *truth*, not the power of a *lie*.

Conclusion

I hope to have suggested to you:

firstly, that the pretence that takes place every time we witness a dramatic presentation – or *re*-presentation – is mirrored by a pretence that takes place in the so-called 'real' world;

secondly, that the Jungian 'deep structures' of our psyche may be in abeyance, or beyond our reach, at this stage of our age of denial, but that, whatever our religious beliefs, or lack of them, their affective powers may, at some point, reawaken our awareness of the inexplicable, of the *merveilleux*, of the way in which, it seems, we cannot escape our psyches;

thirdly, that we need to look again at the fundamental roots of myth – myth which makes most literary criticism appear so puerile and which, as all the great psychologists can tell us, continues to control the deep structures from which we suffer and which we cannot escape from celebrating;

and *fourthly*, that in a very uncomfortable but very real sense we are all displaced persons, refugees not only from the 'real' world but also, and more seriously, from ourselves and from our imaginations. The migrant mind is both vulnerable and dangerous, because it seeks a home that has been taken from it, and which it can never recover – as with the lame scholar, Manus O'Donnell in *Translations*, it can turn violent. It is predicted in Yeats's masterpiece, *Purgatory* (1938), and in Beckett it becomes inevitable – not only Vladimir and Estragon in *Waiting for Godot* (1955) but in the characters in the *Trilogy* – a type for which Lawrence Durrell coined the term *dromomania* – the tramps of Provence who may have been known to Beckett also: 'peripatetic philosophers ... [in search of] a verifiable truth, with the desire to rediscover submission as a fine art ... at heart solitaries'.[22]

The vagrant or displaced person is a solitary, separated from family and society, in search of a truth in which he or she can be at home: not only outside place but, to take Eavan Boland's title, outside history.[23] He or she is defined by their *otherness*, because they are strange not only to the rest of the world but also to themselves. Synge saw it, Yeats saw it, Friel continues to see it – where, after all, is 'the home place'?

[1] This lecture, delivered on 5 July 2007, is dedicated to the memory of John Devitt (1941-2007): teacher and memorialist of Irish drama and film.
[2] Brian Friel, *Faith Healer* in *Plays 1* (London: Faber and Faber, 1996): 332.
[3] Brian Friel, *Translations* in *Plays 1*, 420. Subsequent references appear in parentheses in the text.
[4] Brian Friel, letter to the author, 12 January 2007; he adds 'Wells have always attracted me'.
[5] John Montague, *Collected Poems* (Loughcrew: Gallery Press, 1995): 33.
[6] Montague, 12.
[7] Adrian Frazier, 'The Irish Renaissance 1890-1940: Drama in English', in Margaret Kelleher and Philip O'Leary (eds.) *The Cambridge History of Irish Literature* Volume II 1890-2000 (Cambridge: Cambridge University Press, 2006): 193.
[8] Cf. Richard Pine, *The Diviner: The Art of Brian Friel* (Dublin: University College Dublin Press, 1999).
[9] Seamus Heaney, quoted in Pine, *The Diviner*, 35.
[10] W.B. Yeats, *Collected Plays* (London: Macmillan, 1960): 208. Subsequent references appear in parentheses in the text. The idea that Yeats's well, 'long choked up and dry', could have influenced Friel's 'Tobair Vree', 'long since dried up', is attractive but Brian Friel assures the author (undated letter) that the wording was not intended as an allusion to Yeats.
[11] Walter L. Brenneman Jr and Mary G. Brenneman, *Crossing the Circle at the Holy Wells of Ireland* (University of Virginia Press, 1995): 16.
[12] Geraldine Lynch, 'The Holy Wells of County Wicklow' in K. Hannigan and W. Nolan (eds.) *Wicklow: History and Society* (Dublin: Geography Publications, 1994): 636-647.
[13] Cf. Kathleen Raine, *Defending Ancient Springs* (London: Oxford University Press, 1967).
[14] Lynch, 647-8.
[15] Quoted in J.H. Andrews, *A Paper Landscape: the Ordnance Survey in Nineteenth-Century Ireland* (Dublin: Four Courts Press, 2002): iv.
[16] This part of the lecture is indebted to Paul Ricoeur, *Oneself as Another* (Chicago: Chicago University Press, 1992).
[17] Cf. Steiner: 'Words and objects dovetailed perfectly. As the modern epistemologist might put it, there was a complete, point-to-point mapping of language onto the true substance and shape of things. Each man, each proposition, was an equation, with uniquely and perfectly defined roots, between human perception and the facts of the case'. The parallels between Steiner's work and *Translations* are catalogued in *The Diviner*, 359-363.
[18] Ricoeur, 53. Emphasis added.

[19] Cf. Steiner, 'Uncertainty of meaning is incipient poetry'.
[20] Cf. Octave Mannoni, *Prospero and Caliban: the Psychology of Colonization* (New York: Praeger, 1964): 19-28.
[21] J.M. Synge, *Collected Works III: Plays Book 1*. Edited by Ann Saddlemyer (Gerrards Cross: Colin Smythe, 1982): 71. Subsequent references appear in parentheses in the text.
[22] Lawrence Durrell, *Caesar's Vast Ghost* (London: Faber and Faber, 1990): 22-24.
[23] Cf. Eavan Boland, *Outside History* (Manchester: Carcanet, 1990)

10 | SYNGE AND TOM MURPHY: BEYOND NATURALISM

Alexandra Poulain

Tom Murphy has been a constant experimenter with theatrical form during the last fifty years, but he is also, arguably, the contemporary Irish playwright who owes most to Synge's dramaturgical style. It is commonly assumed that Tom Murphy had originally rejected Synge, only to go back to him at a later stage in his career; this view is largely based on the oft-repeated story of how Murphy became involved in playwriting, which has been recorded by Fintan O'Toole. In 1959, Murphy, then in his twenties, was standing in Tuam's Market Square with his friend Noel O'Donoghue, looking for something to do. O'Donoghue suggested they write a play. 'When Tom Murphy asked Noel O'Donoghue "What would we write about", O'Donoghue replied "One thing is fucking sure – it's not going to be set in a kitchen"'.[1] The story has been taken to suggest that Murphy's initial creative gesture was one of artistic parricide, of emancipation from Synge's overwhelming influence as the founder of a whole tradition of peasant drama which became the trademark of the Abbey. As Riana O'Dwyer has argued, 'It may however have been the formulaic plays written by successors of Synge which provoked this rejection', rather than the plays of Synge himself'.[2] In any case, in 1985 Murphy returned to that tradition when he wrote *Bailegangaire*, which is indeed 'set in a kitchen' in the west of Ireland – a play in which, as in its companion piece *A Thief of a Christmas* (1985), there are distinct borrowings from Synge. In *Bailegangaire*, Mommo obsessively tells and retells a story of misfortunes, echoing Maurya's complaints in *Riders to the Sea*. As Nicholas Grene has observed, Cathleen's rhetorical question in

Riders, 'Who would listen to an old woman with one thing and she saying it over' 'is given its grim answer in *Bailegangaire*' where Mary, Mommo's granddaughter who has returned from a nursing job in England to take care of Mommo, is forced to listen to her unfinished story every night.³ The Syngean echo contains a degree of irony, but should also be regarded as a homage that Murphy pays to Synge, whom he belatedly acknowledges as a major influence.

There is, however, another way of looking at the story. What I am going to argue in this paper is that there is a continuity from Synge to Murphy that runs throughout Murphy's dramatic career, not just in the post-*Bailegangaire* work. While the two playwrights live in different times and come from different backgrounds, they have played a similarly critical role in the Irish culture of their times. In their drama they have tried relentlessly to articulate something about the violence of the norm, the seduction of conformity and the loneliness and terrible freedom which is the lot of those who resist its appeal and look for self-expression. This they have done by working, apparently, within a dramaturgical tradition of naturalism which they have consistently questioned and destabilized, inventing a dramaturgy which points to the existence of another world beyond the known world of everyday experience.

It is commonplace to associate the bulk of Irish drama with naturalism. Although Yeats pushed in a different direction, the Abbey as a cultural institution was instrumental to the creation of a canon of national drama which was predominantly naturalistic – although the importance of the counter-tradition of non-naturalistic drama probably needs to be reassessed. Synge of course wrote for the Abbey – indeed he could be said to have been a product of the Abbey – yet while his drama has some outward elements of naturalism it really subverts the aesthetics of naturalism and invents something quite different.

As Patrick Pavis points out in his *Dictionary of Theatre*, a naturalistic performance is one in which what happens on the stage is presented as reality itself, rather than an artistic transposition, a staging, of reality. It is thus eminently paradoxical, since it strives to achieve maximum illusion, yet insists that it is the ideal medium of reality. On the stage, the aim of the naturalistic performance is to give a complete, unembellished reproduction of reality, and especially of the material conditions of human experience.⁴ Both Synge and Murphy occasionally resort to the devices and strategies of naturalistic drama, but I will argue that they both do so to engage critically with the aesthetics and ideology of naturalism.

The most immediately perceptible characteristic of naturalistic theatre concerns scenography. The set is envisaged as a faithful reproduction of the reality outside the theatre, and often importing 'authentic' props and items of scenery on the stage. A precursor in this respect was the French director André Antoine, founder of the Théâtre Libre in 1887, who famously used real pieces of meat for his production of Fernand Icres' *The Butchers* in 1888, causing an uproar. Synge of course resorted to a similar method for the staging of his plays. Ann Saddlemyer reports that for the first staging of *Riders to the Sea* 'he went so far as to order thick flannel and pampooties, the traditional Aran footgear, from the west'.[5] Some of Murphy's plays are also set in a sociologically realistic setting which is occasionally recreated faithfully on the stage, as in the 1992 Abbey revival of *Conversions on a Homecoming*, a play set entirely in a pub in the west of Ireland in 1985. In Frank Conway's set, the pub had been reconstituted with a luxury of detail as a 'real' pub on the Abbey stage, and part of the theatre's marketing plan for that production actually depended on the fact that it was 'real stout' which came out of the taps, so that the actors got 'really drunk' each night.

Indeed the second characteristic of a naturalistic performance concerns the acting style, which must be true to life. Naturalistic theatre sees the completion of the conventions of bourgeois theatre, especially that of the invisible fourth wall first theorized by Diderot, and later taken up again by Antoine. The image of the fourth wall first crops up in Diderot's advice to the playwrights of his time: 'When you write or act, think no more of the audience than if it had never existed. Imagine a huge wall across the front of the stage, separating you from the audience, and behave exactly as if the curtain had never risen'.[6] In this configuration, the spectator is like a voyeur, spying on actions which are supposed to take place independently of him or her. The actors should never break through the fourth wall, for instance to address the audience. Synge is usually associated with the naturalistic performance style which became known (perhaps erroneously, as an over-simplification) as the 'Abbey method'; yet the very structure of his plays defeats naturalism because of their self-conscious theatricality, so that they constantly point to their own artificiality. A case in point is Christy's storytelling in *Playboy*: no matter how true to life the actor playing

Christy may strive to be, there is a histrionic quality to the storytelling scenes which calls attention to itself and says, 'this is theatre'. Beyond the onstage audience (the villagers in act one, the girls in act two, Pegeen in act three), the actor playing Christy inevitably gestures towards the real audience in those scenes, and thus dispels the naturalistic illusion. This is especially true as the story becomes larger and larger with each rendition, so that we recognize it as pure performance.

Self-conscious theatricality is also essential to Murphy's aesthetics, even in the plays which are most likely to be played naturalistically. *A Whistle in the Dark* (1961), Murphy's first full-length play, is the relentless tale of a family of five Irish brothers and their father, immigrants in Coventry, caught in an unstoppable cycle of violence which culminates with the murder by the eldest brother of the youngest one, whom he was trying to protect. This happens as part of the brothers' return from a street-fight against a rival group. Before the violent climax, Dada returns to face his sons, whom he has deserted in battle: in an extraordinary scene, he improvises a story of getting caught in another fight and fending off three individuals singlehanded. The epic story, very much in *Playboy* style, becomes a performance in its own right, a scene of seduction directed at his own sons (who are not all taken in), whom he then proceeds to present with a silver cup in homage to the 'fighting Carneys'. Dada's relatedness to Christy had in fact been suggested at the beginning of act two which opens with Dada 'viewing himself from different angles in the mirror', replaying Christy's mirror scene at the opening of *Playboy*'s second act.[7] The 'trophy' scene in act three, which ends with celebratory recitations and songs, again exhibits its own theatricality and thus deliberately tampers with the naturalistic illusion. Similarly, at the end of *Conversations on a Homecoming*, Junior attempts to pacify his drunken comrades: 'We've had the complimenting stage, let that be an end to the insulting stage, and we'll get on with the singing stage'.[8] Indeed in the last part of the play songs are sung, at first loudly and drunkenly, until progressively the mood becomes quieter and more intimate and the singing becomes expressive of the delicate mixture of conflicting emotions which remain beyond the reach of words. In the context of a night out at the pub this is all very realistic, so that one might argue that the songs in *Conversations* merely contribute to the naturalistic illusion of continuity between the real world and the onstage world. However, Junior's speech points to the tripartite structure of the play, which he sees as having not three acts but three 'stages' – a polysemic word which suggests theatricality as well as temporality. He thus overtly calls attention to the fact that *Conversations* is structured like a classic well-made play (exposition/ conflict/resolution) and reveals the self-conscious theatricality of the play, dispelling rather than reinforcing the naturalistic illusion. The singing session, which again solicits the configuration of the inset performance, watched by onstage and offstage audiences, is received for what it is, as performance, not reality.

The third characteristic of theatrical naturalism concerns language: a naturalistic play will strive to reproduce the dialects and sociolects of the characters' social and geographical background. In naturalistic drama, a character's speeches reflect his or her psychology and ideology, and must be delivered accordingly, so that the actor must strive to suppress the poetic or literary qualities of the dramatic text. The claim that the language of a play should be 'authentic' thus only makes sense within a naturalistic aesthetics – for instance, nobody would think of attacking Shakespeare on the grounds that no-one really speaks in iambic pentameter, because reproducing the language of real people outside the theatre is clearly not what he was trying to do. On the contrary, it seemed a matter of course to both Synge and his initial audience that his approach to language was naturalistic. Famously, when he was attacked for linguistic inauthenticity he made no claim to poetic licence, but on the contrary defended himself by insisting that the language of his plays was straight from real life:

> When I was writing *The Shadow of the Glen*, some years ago, I got more aid than any learning could have given me, from a chink in the floor of the old Wicklow house where I was staying, that let me hear what was being said by the servant girls in the kitchen.[9]

In this oft-quoted passage from the Preface of *The Playboy of the Western World*, Synge creates a personal myth of authenticity which, interestingly, already involves a theatrical configuration: the Anglo-Irishman imagines himself as voyeuristic audience spying through the fourth wall – which in this case happens to be a floor.[10] This vertical configuration, which materializes the distance (physical and sociological) between the players and their audience, paradoxically enrols the theatrical paradigm in an attempt to construct a fiction of authenticity; yet it can also be read as an unconscious admission of the essentially theatrical, that is, artefactual nature of Synge's dramatic language. The structures and idiolects of Hiberno-English may be close enough to what Synge had heard from the servants in the Wicklow house, or the fishermen in Aran; yet the language of the play is so distinctive that it proved a real challenge for the actors who first played the parts, who felt almost as if they were acting in a foreign language. Ann Saddlemyer reports this testimony by actress Maire nic Shiubhlaigh, who played Nora in *The Shadow of the Glen* and Bride in *The Well of the Saints*:

> At first I found Synge's lines almost impossible to learn and deliver. Like the wandering ballad-singer I had to 'humour' them into a strange tune, changing the metre several times each minute. It was neither verse nor prose. The speeches had a musical lilt, absolutely different from anything I had heard before.[11]

The difficulties she reports have to do with sound-patterns, rhythm, prosody – in other words with the inherent musicality of the language, which makes it 'absolutely different from anything [she] had heard before' – a testimony diametrically opposed to Synge's claim of having heard it all before from the servants. The affinity of Synge's dramatic language to music is possibly even more striking when one looks not at individual lines, but at the texture of dialogues which contain very complex patterns of interwoven repetitions and echoes, reminiscent of the distinctive repetitive poetics of operatic libretti. Consider the following extract from *The Shadow of the Glen*:

> **MICHAEL**. (*Looking at her with a queer look*). **I heard** tell this day, Nora Burke, that it was on the path below Patch Darcy would be passing up and passing down, and **I heard** them say he'd never pass it night or morning without speaking with yourself.
>
> **NORA**. (*In a low voice.*) It was **no lie you heard**, Michael Dara.
>
> **MICHAEL**. I'm thinking it's a power of men you're after knowing if it's in a lonesome place you live itself.
>
> **NORA**. (*Giving him his tea.*) It's in a lonesome place you do have to be talking with some one, and looking for some one, in the evening of the day, and if it's a power of men I'm after knowing they were fine men, for I was a hard child to please, and a hard girl to please (*she looks at him a little sternly*), and

it's a hard woman I am to please this day, Michael Dara, and it's no lie I'm telling you.

MICHAEL. (*Looking over to see that the tramp is asleep, and then pointing to the dead man*) Was it **a hard woman to please you were** when you took himself for your man?

NORA. What way would I live and I an old woman if I didn't marry a man with **a bit of a farm, and cows on it, and sheep on the back hills**?

MICHAEL. (*Considering.*) That's true, Nora, and maybe it's **no fool you were**, for there's good grazing on it, if **it is a lonesome place**, and I'm thinking it's a good sum he's left behind.

NORA. (*Taking the stocking with money from her pocket, and putting it on the table.*) I do be thinking in the long nights it was **a big fool I was** that time, Michael Dara, for what good is **a bit of a farm with cows on it, and sheep on the back hills**, when you do be sitt<u>ing</u> look<u>ing</u> out from **a door** the like of **that door**, and see<u>ing</u> noth<u>ing</u> but the **mists roll<u>ing</u> down the bog**, and **the mists** again, and they **roll<u>ing</u> up the bog**, and hear<u>ing</u> noth<u>ing</u> but the wind cry<u>ing</u> out in the **bits of broken trees** were **left from** the great **storm**, and the **streams roar<u>ing</u>** with the **rain**.¹²

Michael's first statement depends on a binary rhythm which creates a first pattern of echoes ('I heard tell this day' and 'I heard them say'; 'would be passing up / and passing down'; 'never pass it night / or morning'). Another concatenation plays on repetition, polyptoton (the use of words derived from the same root) and paronomasia (the use of words which sound similar) to link together the words path / Patch / passing up / passing down / pass. The point of the repetition is its musicality, not the information it conveys (which is delayed until the end of the line: 'without speaking with yourself'). In Jakobson's terminology, the referential function (language's aptitude to convey information) is minimal, while the poetic function, which naturalistic drama strives to suppress, is prominent.

The structure of binary – or, occasionally, ternary – repetition recurs in the following speeches ('for I was a hard child to please, and a hard girl to please, and it's a hard woman I am to please this day'), and also weaves one line into the texture of the next one. Typically, Nora's final cue starts from the patterns of Michael's previous speech but at the end turns into something different, with its own musical coherence, based on rhythm and assonance and alliteration. Thus the *-ing* form of the gerund repeatedly echoes with 'nothing', giving the sequence: sitting / looking / seeing / nothing / rolling / rolling / hearing / nothing / crying / roaring. The end of the passage veers into hypotyposis and the storm comes alive, recreated by the alliterative, percussive quality of the rhythm. The whole passage works as a very complex operatic duet, in which musicality is expressive of the whole drama of tentative seduction which is going on below the surface of the words, and only breaks through the surface when Michael makes his proposal a few lines down.

This musical texture takes us very far from naturalism. As Riana O'Dwyer has pointed out, both Synge and Murphy have a musical background; both envisaged a musical career before settling for playwriting, and their dramatic languages are essentially musical, indeed operatic.[13] Synge had first wanted to be a violinist and a composer; Murphy was and still is a very fine tenor, and the singing voice occurs both thematically and structurally in his plays – opera in *The Gigli Concert* (1983) and *Too Late for Logic* (1989), folk songs and ballads in *Conversations on a Homecoming*, *The Wake* (1998), and so on. More importantly, the language of his plays has an inherent musicality which consistently subverts the naturalist aesthetics of even the most outwardly naturalistic plays. Take, for instance, the opening of *A Whistle in the Dark*:

> **HARRY.** (*looking for sock*). Sock-sock-sock-sock-sock? Hah? Where is it? Sockeen–sockeen–sockeen?
>
> **HUGO.** (*singing*). 'Here we go loopey loop, here we go loopey laa ...
>
> **HARRY.** Now–now–now, sock–sock!
>
> **BETTY.** Do you want to see if that camp-bed is going to be too short for you, Iggy?
>
> **HARRY.** (*without looking at her, pokes a finger in her ribs as she passes by*). Geeks! (*Continues search for sock.*). Hah? Sockeen.
>
> **BETTY.** Iggy?
>
> **IGGY.** Are we r-r-ready?
>
> **HARRY.** (*in frustration*). Stock -king!
>
> **HUGO.** Maybe you dropped it on the stairs.
>
> [IGGY *dashes up the stairs. The doorbell is ringing.* BETTY *going to answer it.* HUGO *beats her to it and admits* MUSH. HUGO *and*

MUSH *in front hall, in greeting to each other, singing 'Here we go loopey loop'*]

HARRY. (*simultaneously, finding missing sock in one of his shoes*). Aaa! Hidey-hidey, was you? (*Drops his shoes with a clatter on the floor.*)

HUGO *and* MUSH *entering.* MUSH *is about thirty, a small fella, cheapish new suit; sycophantic.*

MUSH. 'Allo-'allo-'allo!

HARRY. (*sniffing socks*). These has been dead for a year or more.

HUGO. Did you find it?

MUSH. I wasn't long, was I?

[HARRY *throws his balled-up socks at* MUSH; MUSH *catches them and throws them at* HUGO; HUGO *retaliates by throwing a cup at* MUSH *which smashes against the wall,* MUSH *shooting at it with an imaginary gun.* BETTY *exits to kitchen*].[14]

The first stage direction states that the characters are all 'preoccupied with themselves'; yet the incipit works as a nightmarish version of an operatic ensemble based on an arrangement of contrapuntal percussive sounds and cries. As in Synge, although to a widely different effect, the materiality of the signifier calls attention to itself and defeats the naturalistic illusion, by forwarding the artificial nature of the language, and thus introducing the possibility of a critical distance towards the 'reality' which is shown on the stage.

Naturalism flourished in the heyday of positivism, when artists thought the scientific method could be applied to understand social mechanisms. They tended, however, to envisage these social mechanisms in terms of determinism, the posture according to which there can be no way out of oppression and alienation for the oppressed and alienated. This is why naturalism is often criticized for its metaphysical, static conception of social mechanisms and relationships, which it tends to naturalize. As Brecht suggested, naturalistic theatre may disapprove of such mechanisms (of exploitation, oppression etc.) but ultimately it tends to present them as a necessary, ineluctable evil.

On the contrary, both Synge and Murphy articulate a dynamic critique of the established order. They do this by privileging a decentred perspective, and observing the centre from the margins. Synge's heroes are usually associated with the margins of the social order: tinkers, beggars, tramps, strangers; they may be geographically marginal, as are the women of *Riders*, or indeed as is Deirdre, who is at first kept away from Emain Macha by Conchubor, then goes into exile when he calls her to his side. They are also associated with movement: nomadism, as opposed to the sedentary status of those in the centre. For those who live on the margins, the centre always seems partly desirable; yet their desire to settle is always tinged with something of the death-wish: it involves acceptance of conformity, and loss of individual freedom or vision. This dilemma is allegorized in *The Well of the Saints*, in the fable of the two blind beggars who give up their whimsical, poetic vision when they gain plain sight and start seeing what everyone else sees, the mediocrity of the real world. They are cured not just of blindness, but of their individual vision: they are normalized and disciplined by the saint, the dispenser of ideology, and the play suggests that this process of normalization entails a form of psychic death. In the tragic world of Deirdre, this death is literalized. Act three dramatizes the end of the travelling life: when Deirdre and Naisi return to Ireland, to Emain Macha (the centre of political power) and to settled life, they discover that the house which Conchubor has prepared for them is a fresh grave:

> **DEIRDRE.** (*She pulls hanging, and it opens.*) There's new earth on the ground and a trench dug. It's a grave, Naisi, that is wide and deep.
>
> **NAISI.** (*goes over and pulls back curtain showing grave.*) And that'll be our home in Emain. 15

Yet readings of Synge which highlight only his romanticizing of the travelling life, associated with freedom, independence of mind, individuality, and creativeness, run the risk of oversimplification. The road has its sinister side too: loneliness, exposure to cold, hunger, physical pain (the travellers' bleeding feet is a recurring motif), and various dangers. While Christy's exit at the end of *Playboy* is triumphant, the threat with which the two blind beggars are sent off at the end of *The Well of the Saints* must be taken seriously:

> **TIMMY.** There's a power of deep rivers with floods in them where you do have to be lepping the stones and you going to the south, so I'm thinking the two of them will be drowned together in a short while, surely.

> **SAINT.** They have chosen their lot, and the Lord have mercy on their souls. (*He rings his bell.*) And let the two of you come up now into the church, Molly Byrne and Timmy the smith, till I make your marriage and put my blessing on you all.[16]

Clearly, the two beggars who have shunned integration into the community are being sent to their death. The play is generically ambiguous, a grim comedy emerging from the tragic feeling of ineluctable death, which manifests itself in the horror of decaying, ageing bodies. Synge's drama is literally haunted with the terror of death, envisaged not as an external danger but as something which is working its way within live bodies; Beckett was later to evolve his whole oeuvre from Synge's intuition that to be born is to start dying. The beggars' blindness, which enables them to indulge their mutual fantasy of physical beauty and eternal youth, points to the singularity of their poetic vision, but it also metaphorizes their refusal to acknowledge the imminence of death. This denial of reality, the play suggests, is in fact as deathly as the uncritical embracing of communal values. In the end, Martin and Mary are caught between two promises of death: death by conformity and slow decay on the inside is balanced against death by drowning (in their fantasy) on the outside. The final image of the play (the saint herding the community of villagers into the church to celebrate a wedding) merely parodies the happy ending of comedy, but just below the surface the play unfolds as tragedy rather than comedy. There is no escape from death, it suggests: all one can do is choose one's own death – as Deirdre who chooses to return to Emain Macha because she knows that she will grow old and that Naisi's desire will peter out.

Murphy's dramaturgical geography is strikingly similar to Synge's. I mentioned earlier the story of the genesis of *On the Outside*, yet Murphy's self-created myth of complete fortuitousness is hard to credit because his first play was so programmatic. Its title in fact contains in seed the dramaturgy of Murphy's whole career. *On the Outside* is a short one-act play, set in late 1950s rural Ireland on the threshold of a dancehall which the two male protagonists fail to access because they lack the small sum of money that would get them in. As Fintan O'Toole has argued, the inaccessible dance is a powerful metaphor of social exclusion in 1950s Ireland, just when a part of Irish society was experiencing unprecedented prosperity.[17] While the initial situation never evolves (the two protagonists never get in), the audience's interest is kept alive thanks to their energy and inventiveness as they desperately attempt to find a way in. Although it was allegedly written to pass the time, *On the Outside* provides the essential point of view for all Murphy's later theatre: he is always interested in the margins of society, in the dispossessed, or at least in those who do not conform with the moral or intellectual orthodoxies of the day. His protagonists include the family of immigrant thugs in *A Whistle in the Dark*, failed circus artists in *The Sanctuary Lamp* (1975), a failed actor (*Conversations on a Homecoming*), a failed quack doctor (*The Gigli Concert*), and a whole array of sex-workers and small-time criminals in *The Morning After Optimism* (1971) *The Blue Macushla* (1980), *The Wake*, and *The House* (2000). Murphy's theatre conveys the poignancy of their desire for normality, respectability or at least recognition, and the violence of the normative social order which exploits and expels the misfits. Francisco's story in *The Sanctuary Lamp* of 'the critic's ball', delivered from the pulpit in a church, relates the circus artists' final engagement, during a private party at a reputed critic's house, where all the literati of the day have gathered. The story first reports their deluded sense of integration in what Francisco derisively calls 'civilization', followed by a scene of brutal lynching and expulsion – a sequence strikingly reminiscent of the structure of *The Playboy of the Western World*, except that the outcome (the death of the female member of the company) is tragic rather than comic.

Again the tension between the centre and the margins implies notions of the sedentary against the nomadic. Murphy's heroes often set out on a quest for identity, yet find out that their identity cannot be defined or stabilized, but that it is instead rather inchoate, always in the process of becoming what it is. Murphy's privileged theatrical metaphor for this perpetual movement of the self is travelling, the impossibility of settling down in any one place. Several plays use the very Irish trope of homecoming, with an ironic twist. In all these plays, the protagonist comes home to a house which exile has made him or her idealize, and endow with a sense of authenticity. The house is a complex symbol; amongst other resonances it works as a metonym of Ireland, and a metaphor of self: to come home is to regain a sense of belonging and an identity long lost to the estranged traveller. Homecoming, however, proves to be the beginning of a new journey of the soul, in the course of which the idealized construct of the house is confronted with reality, and exposed as an illusion. Most of these plays (*The Blue Macushla*, *Conversations on a Homecoming, The Wake*), end when the hero leaves the house behind him or her, and takes to the road again, giving up the lure of a stabilized identity and embracing a life of open possibility. In *The House*, however, the hero, ironically named Christy like Synge's playboy, refuses nomadism and clings to the house of his dreams, which closes in upon him like a tragic trap. The house is a Big House which belongs to the De Burcas, an Anglo-Norman family for whom Christy's mother used to work as a cleaning lady. When Christy comes home from England and finds out the house is for sale, he decides to buy it, indulging an old fantasy of belonging, respectability, and ownership, and bragging that 'I would kill for here'.[18] The play takes him up on his word as in the process of securing the house he actually murders one of the De Burca daughters, breaks Mrs. De Burca's heart, and destroys any chance he ever had of marrying Mary, the victim's sister and his lifelong love. Synge and Murphy's decentred perspective enables them to articulate a critique of the social order, the institutions which sustain it (the family, the church, the educational system, the market, the intellectual elite, and so on), and the modes of production of ideology. But perhaps more crucially, their emphasis on the interplay between the centre and the margins makes it clear that whatever is shown on the stage at any one moment is not the only reality: in their drama there is always more than one world, which constitutes the ultimate subversion of naturalism.

In Synge's plays the recognizable 'reality' carefully reconstructed onstage is challenged by the storytellers. As Lionel Pilkington has argued, there is a performative dimension to the culture of storytelling: storytellers actually make another reality exist in parallel to the known, familiar world.[19] In *Playboy*, Christy's attraction is that he brings the promise of another world to Pegeen, a way out – of Shawn Keogh's bed, and of the unimaginative, one-dimensional world into which she was born. Her keening in the final moments strikes a genuinely tragic note as she finds herself back where she was in the first place, stuck within the limits of the known world forever, as if caught eventually within a naturalistic aesthetics which denies the possibility of an elsewhere. The tramp in *The Shadow of the Glen*, and the two blind beggars in *The Well of the Saints*, perform similar functions, conjuring up alternative fictitious worlds beside the solid, familiar reality shown on the stage. This ability of stories to emulate reality is the very subject of *Bailegangaire*, one of Murphy's most powerful plays. As Mommo tells and retells her tale, impersonating all the roles, the archaic, grotesque world of the story (set in 1950s Ireland) takes over, displacing the present of 1985. Two realities, two historical moments thus compete for the audience's attention, the past pervading the present and paralysing it, preventing the two sisters from getting on with their lives, so that the naturalistically constructed 'reality' of 1985 is displaced by the ghost of past tragedy. Mommo's story constantly interferes with the dialogue between Mary and Dolly, and comments sarcastically on their present situation:

> **MOMMO.** Good man Josie!
>
> **MARY.** I'm trying to stop it!
>
> **MOMMO.** And that was the second greeting he uttered that night.
>
> **MARY.** Talk to her!
>
> **DOLLY.** That's what I try to do!
>
> **MOMMO.** He got no answer.[20]

Only when Mommo and Mary finish the story at the very end of the play is the present freed from the hold of the past. While in *Bailegangaire* the co-existence of several worlds has a tragic import, other plays challenge naturalism by fulfilling the utopian promise of Synge's poet-figures who assert the possibility of another world. When JPW sings 'like Gigli' at the end of *The Gigli Concert*, he challenges the rules of naturalistic theatre and fashions a new aesthetic according to dynamatology's dictum that 'anything is possible'. Reality, or at least the sort of reality which naturalism is concerned with, is not given the final word.

So what is left of Synge's inheritance one hundred years later? In his own drama Murphy remembers both Synge's compassionate fascination with reality, and his passionate refusal to accept that reality is given to us once and for all, that we are 'stuck with it'. In true Syngean fashion Murphy's theatre reaches beyond naturalism, and places itself under the auspices of the God of infinite possibility who appears in JPW's personal version of Genesis:

> God taking his stroll in the Garden, as we were told, and passing by innocent Adam, he would nod and say (He nods and winks.) 'I am who am'. And that was fine until one day, Adam, rather in the manner of Newton, was sitting under a tree and an apple fell on his head, jolting him into thought. 'Whatever

can he mean, said Adam, 'I am who am'?' And he waited until
the next time God came strolling by, and he said, 'Excuse me' –
or whatever they said in those days. 'I must find out'. And he
put the question to God. But God said, 'Out, out!' 'I only asked',
said Adam, but God said 'Out!' And, naturally, after such rude,
abrupt and despotic eviction, the wind was taken out of Adam's
intellectual sails: not surprising that he was not up to pursuing
the matter. Which is a pity. Because, the funny thing, God had
got it wrong. Because what does it mean, 'I am who am'? It
means this is me and that's that. This is me and I am stuck with
it. You see? Limiting. What God should have been saying of
course, was 'I am who may be'. Which is a different thing,
which makes sense – both for us and for God which means, I
am the possible, or if you prefer, I am the impossible.[21]

JPW's God is the God of theatre, a theatre which rejects the
'limiting' constraints of naturalism and conjures up alternative,
'impossible' worlds on the stage. In Synge and Murphy's non-
naturalistic dramaturgy, theatre is not so much a 'mirror held up to
nature', as the discloser of the unsuspected, hidden potential of
reality. This makes for a profoundly political, indeed radical theatre,
which passionately refuses to endorse the claim that 'there is no
alternative' to the unsatisfactory status quo.

---

[1] Fintan O'Toole, *Tom Murphy: The Politics of Magic* (Dublin: New Island Books, 1994): 22.
[2] Riana O'Dwyer, 'Synge and Murphy: Insiders and Outsiders', in Christopher Murray (ed), *Alive in Time, The Enduring Drama of Tom Murphy* (Dublin: Carysfort Press, 2010) (103-122): 103.
[3] Nicholas Grene. 'Talking, Singing, Storytelling: Tom Murphy's *After Tragedy*'. *Colby Quarterly*, 27-4, 4 December 1991 (204-217): 251.
[4] Patrick Pavis, *Dictionnaire du théâtre* (Armand Colin, 2004): 228-9
[5] Ann Saddlemyer, 'Introduction' to J.M. Synge, *The Playboy of the Western World and Other Plays* (Oxford: Worlds Classics, 1995): xv.
[6] Denis Diderot, *Discours sur la poésie dramatique*. In *Livres, tome IV, Esthétique-Théâtre*, éd. L. Versini (Laffont: Bouquins, 1996): 1309-10. Translated by the author.
[7] Tom Murphy, *Plays 4* (London: Methuen, 1997): 33.
[8] Tom Murphy, *Plays 2* (London: Methuen, 1993): 68.
[9] J.M. Synge, *Collected Works IV: Plays 2*. Edited by Ann Saddlemyer (Gerrards Cross: Colin Smythe, 1982): 53.
[10] This configuration is strikingly reminiscent of that used in Diderot's *The Illegitimate Son* (1757), in which Diderot imagines himself as the only spectator of a play, spying on the actors (who are re-enacting the

real story of their lives and playing their own parts) from a hidden corner of the drawing- room.

[11] Saddlemyer, 'Introduction', xi.
[12] J.M. Synge, *Collected Works III: Plays 1*. Edited by Ann Saddlemyer (Gerrards Cross: Colin Smythe, 1982): 47-9. Emphases added.
[13] O'Dwyer, 106
[14] Murphy, *Plays 4*, 3-4.
[15] Synge, *Plays 2*, 240.
[16] Synge, *Plays 1*, 151.
[17] O'Toole, 36.
[18] Tom Murphy, *The House* (London: Methuen, 2000): 43.
[19] Cf. Lionel Pilkington, *Theatre & Ireland* (Basingstoke: Palgrave, 2010)
[20] Murphy, *Plays 2*. 105.
[21] Tom Murphy, *Plays 3* (London: Methuen, 1994): 211.

11 | LIVING WITH GHOSTS: SYNGE AND MARINA CARR

Emilie Pine

Twentieth-century Irish drama is peopled by ghosts, or as Michael Billington puts it, 'In Irish drama the dead are always with us'.[1] Indeed, Anthony Roche argues, 'Ghosts are a strong and recurrent feature of Irish drama ... [where] the past is always living as a potential to be resurrected in the endless present of the theatre'.[2] Irish theatre is not merely marked by the perpetual eruption of the ghostly figure into the present, but also by its tendency to provide a home for these ghosts, in which death and the past, as imagined spaces, co-exist with life and the present. A critical mapping of this haunted space must necessarily explore the drama of Synge, as well as his theatrical inheritors, in particular the work of Marina Carr.

In Synge's second play *Riders to the Sea*, the old woman Maurya has lost five of her six sons to the vagaries of the sea. Her last remaining son, Bartley, is about to set off on a voyage and the shadow of death hangs over him in the first scene – a shadow which engulfs him when he is drowned, and his prone, drenched body is carried onstage and waked. Maurya is convinced from the beginning that Bartley will suffer the same fate as her other sons, and this is underlined when she has a vision of him before he sets sail. In the vision, Bartley leads a grey pony, astride which sits his drowned brother Michael. The local women later report that it was the grey pony that 'knocked [Bartley] over into the sea, and he was washed out where there is a great surf on the white rocks'.[3] Maurya's vision is thus confirmed as a premonition of Bartley's death. When Bartley's body is laid out onstage and the women gather round keening, Maurya laments the loss of 'a husband, and a husband's father, and six sons ... six fine men' (21) and she catalogues their deaths, all of them taken by the sea. Though there is only one body onstage, Maurya's words create a company of dead men who ghost the stage.

In *Riders to the Sea* there are thus many layers of haunting – as the play opens Maurya is still mourning the death of Michael. Bartley, though alive when the audience first sees him, is a marked man. Maurya's vision suggests that Michael's spirit not only haunts her, but is a malign presence, which claims his living brother. Maurya's keening for her dead husband, father-in-law, and sons demonstrates the role of Bartley's death in igniting the memory of earlier traumas, as if all Maurya's losses were suddenly made contemporaneous. Though the ghost of Michael may have been a figment of Maurya's morbid imagination, the physical reality of death is underlined by the presence of Bartley's dead body onstage – a shocking signifier of the power of the sea, that other haunting presence in this island community's life. Bartley's body finally also represents the limbo of death – he is between the here and the after – as his body, not yet nailed in its white-board coffin, represents both his presence and his absence.

The reality of the dead body on stage and the wake is also used to strong effect in *The Shadow of the Glen*, in which Dan Burke is laid out for his wake in the cottage he shared with his wife Nora. In this play Synge uses both the idea of the dead haunting the present, with destructive results, as well as playing on the in-between-status of the recently dead. The Tramp, who has called late to the cottage, speaks of Dan's soul 'going up naked to the saints of God', imagining the experience of death as a separation of body and soul, while the motif of the journey acknowledges the present/absent limbo of death.[4] When Dan's body seemingly starts back to life and claims the status of a 'man that's dead', he exists as both ghost and living man (41). His demand for 'a drop' confirms the needs of his living body, while his 'black stick' further grounds him in physical reality, at the same time as his 'cold' and 'queer' nature suggest his ghostliness. Though the shadow of death hovers over Dan Burke at the end of the play, as Nora promises him 'it's not long, I'm telling you, till you'll be lying again under that sheet, and you dead surely' (57), he has also brought Nora closer to death by rendering her homeless: as she says, 'it's myself will be wheezing that time with lying down under the Heavens when the night is cold' (57). Dan Burke thus embodies the fear at the heart of Maurya's vision of Michael returning as a spiteful spirit.

The return to life of a tyrannical old man is again a central trope in *The Playboy of the Western World* as Christy's father, Old Mahon, is resurrected to haunt Christy and destroy the new life he has created for himself. In their insistent physical reality, the 'ghosts' of Dan and Old Mahon are neither the unknown nor unknowable, but rather are all too familiar and tangible. For both Christy and Nora the deaths of these tyrannical old men represent freedom from oppression, opening up the possibility of a new life. The refusal of both Dan Burke and Old Mahon to be dispatched, however, consigns both Christy and Nora to be subject to their ghosts and, ultimately, to be wanderers of limbo themselves.

In these three plays, then, Synge identifies different attitudes towards death – from Maurya's despair to Nora and Christy's liberation. In all three plays, death is not the final frontier, but is a permeable boundary between worlds, and for all three characters the overlap of the dead and the living brings catastrophe upon them. All three characters, as a result, share a fear of the dead, and all three plays thus show the destructive power of being haunted. Synge identifies the ambivalence of the living towards the dead, as the living both fear and regret their dead, though Maurya bemoans her loss, whereas both Nora and Christy are set free. Yet even in Maurya's mourning there is an ambivalence as, having lost all her sons, she is now beyond the point when the sea can take anything further from her.

Two themes that recur in Irish drama are the complex attitude towards the ghosts of the past, and the ties that bind the living and the dead. Ghostly presences abound in many of the key plays of twentieth-century Irish drama: W.B. Yeats's *Purgatory* (1938), Hugh Leonard's *Da* (1973), Brian Friel's *Faith Healer* (1979), Frank McGuinness's *Observe the Sons of Ulster Marching Towards the Somme* (1985), Stewart Parker's *Pentecost* (1987), Sebastian Barry's *The Steward of Christendom* (1995), and Mark O'Rowe's *Terminus* (2007) are all haunted plays. And that is not even to include the plays in which the past, or the memory of trauma, metaphorically haunts the present. The ghosts in these plays are actual figures, presented to the audience, and the audience must decide what to invest in these hauntings, and what to make of them. The ghosts are not homogenous, though they all signal some deep, underlying anxiety and fear. In Yeats's late play, the ghosts are shadows of light and dark, a projection, and reflection, of the Old Man's bitterness about the past. In Barry's *Steward*, the ghost has physical form, as the young Willie comforts his aged and isolated father, though he is still a figure from his father's imagination. Rather than representing the schism with the past as in *Purgatory*, however, this haunting, as in Parker's *Pentecost*, enables a healing of wounds. Healing is impossible in both Friel's *Faith Healer* and O'Rowe's *Terminus*, where the characters onstage are only slowly revealed as ghosts, their deaths the result of personal betrayals, their resurrection made possible by the power of monologue. The father in Leonard's *Da* and the soldier ghosts in McGuinness's *Observe the Sons* are both welcome and errant spirits, ghosts who should be laid to rest but who still pursue relationships with the living, relationships that were left unresolved.

Though they are varied, these ghosts, like Synge's, follow one of two types, a pattern of haunting, be it either the malevolent ghosts who return to stymie the present and claim the future, or the longed-for ghosts who are held to the breasts of the living so that the future is arrested, in a paralysed moment in which the present is always looking backwards. This rich lineage of ghostliness has thus shifted shape and yet remained remarkably similar, from the moment when Synge's Christy first let fall the loy on his father's head in a field, to the fall of O'Rowe's un-named woman (known only as 'C' in the script) from the arm of a crane, high over Dublin.

One of the features of Synge's dramas is that the ghosts and the sense of ghostliness infect and inhabit the landscape. We can apply Beckett's line, 'outside of here it's death', to the sea in *Riders to the Sea*, and to the lonesome valley of *The Shadow of the Glen*.[5] In *The Playboy*, the first mention of Christy is as a 'fellow above in the furzy ditch, groaning wicked like a maddening dog'.[6] Shawn Keogh's fearful description of Christy illustrates his anxiety over who may be abroad in the 'great darkness', as well as his dread of the landscape itself.

The sense in Synge's drama that the landscape itself is haunted and has a haunting power over individuals also recurs in Irish drama, and is most resonant in the plays of Marina Carr. Carr's heroines are intimately connected to the landscape and this connection is a destructive force so that they end up, like Synge's Maurya and Nora, tragically dispossessed.

In Carr's Midlands plays – especially *The Mai*, *Portia Coughlan* and *By the Bog of Cats...* – each of the central women is so haunted by the past that she is unable to conceive of, let alone create, a future for herself. In *The Mai* (1994), there are two revenant figures: Robert, the errant husband of The Mai, and Millie, her daughter, whose adult self returns obsessively to her memories of her childhood and the period leading up to her mother's breakdown and suicide. The play opens in The Mai's home, which she has built on the edge of Owl Lake, in an attempt to woo Robert back. The strategy works, but it is not as successful as The Mai had hoped, and Robert does not transform into the faithful husband that she needs. Though she fights to win him to her forever, her actions are futile and, in despair, she drowns herself.

This fate, however, has been foretold by the very mythology surrounding Owl Lake. The myth tells that the lake was created by the tears of Coillte, who, separated from her lover Bláth by an evil witch, cried so much that the land flooded. The witch finds Coillte on the shore of the lake, pushes her in, and Coillte drowns. This myth is typical of Carr's work, which imagines a culturally haunted landscape. By occupying this haunted landscape of lakes and ghostly stories, Carr's characters become haunted in turn. In addition to the place lore, The Mai must also contend with the personal mythology of her mother, Grandma Fraochlán, who was so passionately dedicated to her lover that she says, 'I would gladly have hurled all seven of [my children] down the slopes of hell for one night more with the nine-fingered fisherman'.[7] The Mai's suicide, then, represents a similar sort of sacrifice for the sake of unrequited love, killing herself, and also killing her children's futures. Carr sets out the idea that the culture of love and life that we inherit from our mothers and grandmothers is fundamentally damaging and, indeed, haunting. As Millie says, she is haunted by memories of her mother that persist 'on and on till I succumb and linger among them there in that dead silent world that tore our hearts out for a song' (184). In this image, it is Millie – the living character – who becomes ghostly, haunting the past, rather than living in the present.

Carr's heroines are essentially lost women, associated with the fluid – and deadly – element of water, women who feel a greater connection with death than with life, who take their own lives despite, or perhaps because of, the shame and destruction they will bring to their own families, because it is the last selfish, taboo-breaking and perversely self-preserving act they see left open to them. Above all else, Carr creates the certainty within each of them that her fate is inescapable and in all three plays that fate is suicide.

The structure of both *The Mai* and *Portia Coughlan* (1996) makes their deaths a certainty as the non-linear chronology of each play reveals their suicides in the middle, rather than at the end, so that the women's characters become ghosts in the machine in the final stages of both plays. In *The Mai*, Millie both witnesses and narrates her mother's death at the end of Act One, as Robert carries The Mai's prone, drowned body onstage. Likewise, Portia's drowned body is raised out of the Belmont River at the beginning of Act Two. Although, in an allusion to Greek drama, the audience does not see the actual deaths of either of these women, this death-in-life structure ensures that there is no escape for them.

Portia is haunted by her brother's ghost and her guilt at his death. Fifteen years earlier, her twin brother Gabriel deliberately waded into the Belmont River and drowned himself. Portia stayed on the bank and survived, but she now has to live not only with the guilt at Gabriel's suicide, but her own sense that she wrongly escaped death. As she tells her husband Raphael, to 'stay in' the world 'has always been the battle for me'.[8] Like The Mai, Portia's fate is inscribed in the landscape around her. She tells one of her consorts, Finbar, about the mythology behind the name of the river: a local woman was once branded a witch, staked there, and left to die by the community. However, she was rescued by the river god Bel, who 'came down the Belmont Valley and taken her away from here, and the river was born' (219). Yet, unlike this unnamed woman who is rescued by a heroic, pagan god, there is no rescue coming for Portia and she follows a fate much closer to that of Coillte and The Mai, drowning herself in her beloved river. Though Portia imagines the source of her destiny to be mythic, her aunt Maggie May sees the situation differently. At Portia's wake, Maggie May reveals the incest in Portia's family history as her parents were half-siblings, leading Maggie May to conclude that Gabriel was 'insane from too much inbreedin' ... and walked into the Belmont River be accident' (245). Portia is not simply haunted by a ghost – though as the audience we both see and hear Gabriel and so witness the power of this haunting – but by her own share of this congenital madness.

Portia tells Finbar that when Gabriel was alive he 'used hear the girl when the river was low; he said she sounded like a aria from a cave' (219). Now, however, it is Gabriel's ghost who has become the mythical presence lingering on the river's banks, and it is his voice that haunts Portia. She hears his singing constantly and such is its power that it can '*come over and take her away*' (200). This siren call seems to Portia to be summoning her back to the river and to a death that she wrongly escaped when she was fifteen.

At first Portia seems to want to shut out the sound of Gabriel's voice, drinking or putting on a CD to '*drown*' it out with noise if not with water (195). By act three, however, Portia is increasingly out of touch with Gabriel; in stage directions his voice '*grows fainter, she strains to hear it*' (232). When Portia pursues the sound of his voice to the river, Gabriel disappears and his singing stops completely so that she is left with nothing. The fading of Gabriel's voice points up to Portia how much she needs this contact, and thus the fear is not that she cannot forget Gabriel but rather that his ghost will forget her.[9] When, at the end of the play, Portia admits that she cannot be without Gabriel, his voice sounds, '*triumphant*' (255). Gabriel at last claims Portia as his own, finally sealing their incestuous love, having haunted her to the extent that she has ruined her living family and there is only him left; the triumph of his voice at the end betrays the extent to which ghosts of the past can manipulate the present.

If The Mai and Portia are to some extent aware of the need to move on, to leave the past behind, in order to ensure their survival, then to Hester Swane in *By the Bog of Cats...* (1998), this need is blindingly obvious. Hester Swane lives on the edge of the bog in a house built for her by her long-time lover Carthage Kilbride, who is the father of her child Josie, but who has left her for the younger, richer, and more conventional Caroline Cassidy. Hester is rejected by Carthage because of her drinking and violence, and by the settled community because she is a Traveller. She refuses to accept the fact that Carthage has left her for good: she disrupts his wedding reception, burns his house and his cattle and, finally, kills both herself and her daughter Josie, in an echo of the Greek tragedy *Medea*.

Catwoman is the first to warn Hester directly about the destruction that lies ahead: 'Lave this place now or ya never will'.[10] Catwoman's words are echoed later by Hester: the 'only way I'm lavin' this place is in a box' (324). Catwoman's is not the only warning; Hester is besieged by signs of her impending death. The play opens at dawn, with Hester dragging the body of the dead swan Blackwing across the bog. When she encounters the Ghost Fancier, who has mistaken the liminal time of dawn for dusk, Hester discovers that dusk is the appointed time for her death. At this, she reacts angrily, shouting after him that 'I can't die – I have a daughter' (267). But the corpse of the swan that Hester holds insists upon her death, as her mother Josie Swane had placed her in the bird's nest when she was a baby, telling Catwoman that Hester 'will live as long as this black swan, not a day more, not a day less' (275). Despite Catwoman's attempt to break the connection by taking the baby out of the swan's nest, the curse still seems to have power – though as the play progresses we might argue that curses only have the power that we give them ourselves. But although Hester has the strength to avoid the curses put upon her by her mother and the Ghost Fancier, she instead becomes an active agent in her own death. Hester's courting of the curse is reminiscent of Synge's Deirdre, who refuses to pay heed to the disasters foretold about her. Despite Hester's protestations that she needs to survive for Josie's sake, she sets out on a wilfully destructive path: drinking, baiting Xavier when he threatens her with a gun, and provoking Carthage by burning his cattle.

Hester may at first seem to resist the idea of death but in the same scene as she tells the Ghost Fancier that she is alive and aims 'to stay that way', she also tells her neighbour Monica Murray that she wishes the ice age would return and 'do away with us all like dinosaurs' (267). Hester's comment to Monica suggests that she accepts her own extinction as a 'dinosaur' and much later in the play she tells the ghost of her brother Joseph Swane that she feels she is 'already a ghost' (321). In this Hester mimics Millie in *The Mai* as they are both made ghostly by the continued trauma of having been abandoned by their mothers as children. Like Millie, Hester has never recovered from the trauma of separation, so that in her adult life she cannot commit to living in the present. This is added to, of course, by the presence of her brother Joseph's ghost, whom she murdered years earlier in an act of jealousy at his closer relationship with their mother. Joseph's return, and the guilt and trauma surrounding his death, represents what Catwoman intuits early in the play as 'some fierce wrong ya done that's caught up with ya' (274). However, in an echo of Maurya's sense of impending doom, while Hester is aware of the danger she is driving towards, at the end of the play, as she cradles the dead body of Josie, whose throat she has just cut open, she confesses that 'I knew somethin' terrible'd happen but I never thought it'd be this' (339).

Though Hester kills Josie, it is ostensibly an act of mercy and love as she refuses to condemn her daughter to the years of ghostly longing for a mother that Hester herself has had to endure. Yet Hester is nothing if not contradictory and, while Josie's murder seems driven by pity rather than anger, it is also consistent with her earlier assertion to Carthage that she would keep his daughter from him 'if it's the last thing I do' (290). There is thus perhaps more of Medea's revenging spirit in Hester than admitted by her in the final scene. But death, Carr suggests, will not in fact be the end, as Hester promises Carthage that she and Josie will haunt him and the Bog of Cats: like a 'purlin' wind', elusive and inescapable, 'Ya won't forget me now' (340). Hester recognizes that she can be more powerful as a ghostly memory than she ever was in life. Furthermore, in death Hester will become part of the landscape. Again, the presence of Synge's drama can be felt in Carr's creation of the theatrical landscape as a dangerous and haunting cultural space.

Beyond the general sense that Synge and Carr's ghosts embody a deeply held anxiety, the ghosts that appear in their work are seeking something specific – an answer, a moment of fulfilment or revenge – from the act of haunting. In *The Mai*, Millie haunts the past, returning obsessively to the traumatic memories of losing her mother. Millie's quest, and her remembering and re-enactment of the days leading up to her mother's death, seek to answer the horror and to fill the space left by The Mai. Instead, however, it simply dooms Millie to be a living ghost. This ambivalent status – between life and death – recalls the doomed figure of Bartley in *Riders to the Sea*, as well as echoing the dead-and-alive status of both Dan Burke and Old Mahon in *Shadow of the Glen* and *The Playboy*. Millie's ghostliness also establishes the framework for reading both Portia and Hester as half-ghosts, unable to be fully alive in the world, always aware of that other world, of the dead.

In *Portia Coughlan*, Gabriel has a clear intention to reclaim Portia as his own, much as Michael appears in Maurya's vision to be claiming Bartley. Gabriel appears on the banks of the river at the opening of the play and when Portia's body is recovered from the river. Perhaps most importantly his voice sings triumphantly when she finally acknowledges that she cannot forget him and, implicitly, accepts that she will join him in the river. In this, Gabriel is a vengeful ghost, jealous of the living. Joseph, in *Bog of Cats*, is not a directly malevolent presence, but he too has a negative relationship to the present, as he appears at exactly the point at which Hester's self-destruction takes hold. Though Hester's actions seem self-motivated, Joseph's ghost represents the return of the repressed memories of her past, with disastrous consequences.

The motif of the return of the 'murdered' victim resonates, of course, with Synge's *Playboy*. However, although Old Mahon refuses to be permanently despatched, he is not, by the end of *The Playboy*, a powerful or haunting figure. Christy asserts the power of the living and the young, by accepting Old Mahon as his travelling companion on the basis that he functions as his 'heathen slave' (173). If it is impossible to exorcize the ghosts of the past, then the living must respond in one of two ways. Nora unwillingly, but defiantly, chooses the lonesomeness of the road, just as decades later, Portia and Hester at first unwillingly accept and then embrace their own deaths. However, Christy's actions suggest another response; Old Mahon cannot be easily dismissed and so Christy finds a way to live with him, by subjecting the 'dead' to the living. In this, Synge's characters adapt in a way that Carr's do not, or cannot, and this ability to find a way of living with ghosts is, finally, what Carr's heroines could – and perhaps should – learn from Synge's playboy.

---

[1] Michael Billington, Review of *There Came a Gypsy Riding*, *The Guardian*, 19 January 2007.

[2] Anthony Roche, 'Ghosts in Irish Drama', *More Real Than Reality: The Fantastic in Irish Literature and the Arts*. Edited by Donald E. Morse and Csilla Bertha (New York; London: Greenwood Press, 1991) (41-66): 63.

[3] J.M. Synge, *Collected Works III: Plays 1*. Edited by Ann Saddlemyer (Gerrards Cross: Colin Smythe, 1982): 23. Further references to the play appear in the text.

[4] Synge, *Plays 1*, 18. Further references appear in the text.

[5] Samuel Beckett, *Endgame* in *The Complete Dramatic Works* (London: Faber and Faber, 1990): 96.

[6] J.M. Synge, *Collected Works Volume IV: Plays 2*. Edited by Ann Saddlemyer (Gerrards Cross: Colin Smythe, 1982): 61. Further references to the play appear in the text.

[7] Marina Carr, *The Mai* in *Plays One* (London: Faber and Faber, 1999): 182. Further references appear in the text.

[8] Marina Carr, *Portia Coughlan* in *Plays One* (London: Faber and Faber, 1999): 255. Further references appear in the text.

[9] As Colin Davis argues, the only thing greater than the fear of ghosts is the fear that we have been deserted by the dead. See *Haunted Subjects* (Basingstoke and New York: Palgrave Macmillan, 2007): 158-9.

[10] Marina Carr, *By the Bog of Cats...* in *Plays One* (London: Faber and Faber, 1999): 276. Further references appear in the text.

12 | RE-LOCATION AND RE-LOCUTION: ADAPTING SYNGE

Melissa Sihra

Adaptations of well known plays are most successful when the new work pulsates with a life of its own while also revitalizing the source-text. The adaptation should illuminate the original in new ways, re-imagining rather than being dependent upon it. Achieving this balance can be challenging and sometimes more confining than anticipated. However, adapting a classic play provides an opportunity to flex linguistic and creative muscles and to explore one's capabilities in new ways. At its most exceptional, adaptation becomes an act of transcendence which moves beyond one-dimensional or derivative mimesis. Ideally, adaptation should be a dynamic two-way process of expression, where the original play offers insights into the creative impulses of the adaptor-dramatist and the new setting, while the new play reveals latent mysteries in the familiar.

This essay looks at the ways in which Ugandan playwright Erisa Kironde has transplanted Synge's *The Shadow of the Glen* into an African setting in his one-act play *The Trick* (1965), as well as Mustapa Matura's re-working of *The Playboy of the Western World* into a Caribbean context in 1984. Since around 1975, many Irish writers have adapted classic plays into localised situations in a process which operates metonymically, poetically, and politically as a means of obliquely exploring a variety of historical events such as the political conflict in the North of Ireland. The Field Day Theatre Company produced a number of versions of Classical Greek dramas such as Tom Paulin's 1984 play *The Riot Act* (an adaptation of Sophocles's *Antigone*) and Seamus Heaney's *The Cure at Troy*

(1990), a re-working of Sophocles's *Philoctetes*. Heaney's adaptation of Sophocles' *Antigone, The Burial at Thebes* was produced at the Abbey Theatre in 2004 (and revived in 2008) and *Antigone*, in particular, has had a number of treatments by Irish writers, such as Brendan Kennelly, Aidan Matthews, and Paulin. Of his first adaptation of Sophocles for Field Day, Heaney observes:

> It was the conflict in the young man between truth to himself, his own self-respect, and his sense of loyalty to the tribe. In a way there was something analogous there for each person in Northern Ireland, dwelling within their own sense of justice and at the same time a sense of loyalty to the tribe.[1]

Marina Carr's *By the Bog of Cats...* (1998) is a response to Euripides's *Medea*, set in the Irish midlands and exploring Traveller culture and the breakdown of the family. *By the Bog of Cats...* has been translated into many languages and produced in countries such as South Korea, Hungary, the United States, and Iceland, and has also appeared in London's West End. With each locality, the play has brought forth new resonances: in Hungary for instance, Carr's version of Euripides's story became a reflection upon the oppression of Romany gypsy women. There are many variations in the ways in which each writer approaches the source-text. In some cases it is a metaphoric template for a political context, while in others, it functions as more of an aesthetic frame upon which to weave and build the story. Carr's play is inspired by *Medea*, whilst Heaney in contrast 'may not see himself as a playwright,' according to Peter Crawley.[2] Heaney makes the distinction: 'a playwright would take *Antigone* and hit it a few clouts and knock it out of shape and restructure it: my versioning was strictly verbal'.[3] Heaney regards himself thus as a poet reinvigorating the writing of a dramatist, writing along *with* the dramatist so to speak, whereas *By the Bog of Cats...* is a new play by Carr, loosely based on the original.

A number of complicated issues merge in the process of adaptation. Brian Friel, the 'Irish Chekhov', has become well known for the ways in which he adapts the Russian playwright and infuses his plays, such as *Three Sisters* in 1981 and *Uncle Vanya* in 1998, with his own speech rhythms, idioms, and so on. In 1980, Friel stated:

> I was doing a translation of *Three Sisters*. Although I do not speak a word of Russian, I had been working on the play with the help of five standard English translations. It was a kind of act of love, but after a while I began to wonder exactly what I

was doing ... I felt that the translations which we have received and inherited in some way have not much to do with the language which we speak in Ireland. 4

With Friel's use of no less than five 'standard' English translations, we can deduce that in fact 'standard' does not in any way *mean* standard. Further, Friel is saying that these translations are culturally removed from the Irish experience, being quintessentially English in rhythm and cadence, something which he reads politically as being 'neither healthy nor valuable to us' (84). With the five English translations that Friel is using, there occurs then a cultural as well as linguistic filtering of Chekhov, far-removed from Russia and more redolent, he observes, of 'either Edwardian England or the Bloomsbury set' (84). Thus Friel's own version, which he calls a translation, is multiply removed from the Russian context, five-times filtered already through English linguistic patterns and inflections. The political implications of translating are of course the subject-matter of his play *Translations* and he states: 'The work I did on *Three Sisters* somehow overlapped into the working of the text of *Translations* (84).

Friel's earlier use of the term 'translation' for what he is doing brings forth some of these questions. Friel does not speak Russian, yet his adaptations are referred to as 'translations' in parentheses in the play-title listings of the Faber & Faber *Plays Two* collection (1999). The action of retaining the same title as the original work, something which Friel has done with his 2008 version of Ibsen's *Hedda Gabler*, is also a bold move. We know that many Irish playwrights who adapt from European classics use what they call 'literal translations', and indeed the programme for the Gate Theatre premiere of Friel's *Hedda Gabler* states that 'A literal translation of Ibsen's *Hedda Gabler* was provided by Toril Solvang'.[5] However, the very notion of a 'literal translation' is oxymoronic. In Friel's *Translations*, the central message is that every act of translation is a politically motivated act of re-writing and re-telling: one which can never be neutral, predicated as it is by necessary exclusion. *Translations* dramatizes the brutal erosion and cultural defilement that can take place in any act of translation, particularly in the colonial context. Friel has come to admit that his earlier versions of Chekhov are not translations, but indeed a re-working from translations. His version of *Hedda Gabler* states on the program cover: 'Henrik Ibsen's *Hedda Gabler* in a new version by Brian Friel'. However, The Gallery Press publication of the play, states:

'Hedda Gabler, Brian Friel'. Then in small italics at the bottom: 'after Ibsen'.[6] It gets more complicated as on the back-cover of this edition where *Three Sisters* is listed as '(*after Chekhov*)', while in the Faber collection it is called a 'translation'.[7]

Apart from negotiating the mine-fields of language and translation, finding a way 'into' a source-text can also be challenging for the writer seeking to adapt. Infusing a sense of one's own voice and creativity, of re-imagining and transforming, is essential, just as there needs to be empathy with the characters and their plight. A playwright can be drawn to a work instinctually, as Carr was with Euripides and Friel with Chekhov. But playwrights are often commissioned to do adaptations, where their relationship with the primary text might not be so intimate. When adapting for the stage, there needs to be a desire to go on that journey with the characters as well as a compulsion to take them somewhere *new*. Friel was commissioned to adapt *Hedda* rather than coming to the play of his own accord. He persevered to navigate her path and the outcome is as much a journey of Friel's as it is of Hedda's.

Frank McGuinness has adapted plays by Spanish dramatists Federico Garcia Lorca and Ramon Maria del Valle-Inclan as well as Euripides' *Hecuba* (2004), Sophocles' *Electra* (1997) and *Oedipus* (2008), Brecht's *The Caucasian Chalk Circle* (1997) and *The Threepenny Opera* (1991), Chekhov's *Three Sisters* (1990) and *Uncle Vanya* (1995), and Ibsen's *Hedda Gabler* (1994), *Rosmersholm* (1987), *Peer Gynt* (1988), *The Wild Duck* (2003), *Ghosts* (2007), and *A Doll's House* (1996), which won four Tony Awards. His adaptation of Strindberg's *Miss Julie* had its Irish premiere in 2008, at which time McGuinness spoke passionately about his process:

> If you really want to annoy me, when you ask what am I doing and I say *Miss Julie,* if you go, 'Oh, when are you going to write a play?', that really does annoy me, because I absolutely look at it all as new writing... It's important to me – you can get very slack, and very sure of yourself, when you get to a certain age of writing, and you just need to have the scare of looking at these other plays, because the hard fact is that there's enough in us all for about two or three plays, and then you've got to be very careful. You have to be terribly careful not to take the advice of certain critics, [in order] to remain with your naïve genius – you begin to start cannibalizing yourself and other people. [8]

McGuinness's *Oedipus* premiered at the National Theatre, London, in 2008. He explains how this version is a very personal narrative about his relationship with his father: 'It's the first time I feel I've written about my father in the theatre,' he told Mick Heaney. 'I didn't know when I wrote it that this is what I'm drawing on, my farewell to my father, my father's farewell to me. But that's what sometimes happens in versions – you suddenly get your own life speaking to you, in a way that you wouldn't dare in a new play' (2). In terms of the emotional landscape that McGuinness traverses in his version of *Oedipus,* we see how writers are drawn to adapt classic plays for myriad, often very personal, reasons.

While many Irish playwrights have adapted international classics, it is fascinating also to explore the ways in which foreign playwrights have reconceived Irish dramas. In 1965, Ugandan playwright and political activist Erisa Kironde wrote *The Trick,* a little-known adaptation of *The Shadow of the Glen.* In works such as *The Trick* we gain insight into other cultures and political contexts, as well as observing how foreign evocations elucidate upon the familiar. Similarly, Caribbean playwright Matura's *The Playboy of the West Indies* is a striking rendition of Synge's *The Playboy of the Western World,* set in the richly evoked Trinidadian fishing village 'Mayaro' in August 1950. Matura's play was first produced by the Oxford Playhouse in 1984 and subsequently toured the UK, finishing at the Tricycle Theatre, London. It also toured the United States and has had a couple of Trinidadian productions, as well as one in Galway by Druid Theatre, and was adapted for BBC television in 1985. Both Matura and Kironde were compelled to adapt Synge's plays of their own accord and that immediacy of connection, that affinity with Synge's language and characters, can be felt pulsating throughout their adaptations.

More recently, Bisi Adigun's and Roddy Doyle's version of *The Playboy of the Western World* was produced in 2007 by the Abbey Theatre to celebrate the centenary of the premiere of Synge's play. Here, characters, plot, and language are transposed to a contemporary west Dublin pub and a new urban register and dialect is rendered. The most significant act of 'creative intervention' within Adigun and Doyle's version in their interrogation of the outsider through their deeply politicized figure of Christy who here becomes Nigerian immigrant Christopher Malomo – polite, well-educated, and looking for work. In a pre-show discussion, the authors stated that they did not wish to make a comment about race. However, in their strategic choice of the outsider as *African* outsider, dressed at one point in a girl's pink velour track-suit with the word 'bitch' emblazoned on the posterior, issues of race, difference, exile, and immigration cannot be avoided.9 The version is further politicized by the fact that it is co-authored by an Irish-based Nigerian man and an Irish man, showing a kind of indigenous intercultural reading and re-writing of an Irish text within an Irish setting. While Adigun's and Doyle's adaptation can perhaps also be described as 'intra-cultural', Matura's and Kironde's versions of Synge are clear-cut intercultural renderings, where the original plays become something else, in new settings with new titles, looking back Janus-like, nodding to the original story whilst leaping forth from it.

Intrinsic to the adaptation of a dramatic work from one country to another is the process of 'cultural translation' – how to make the play sing and be meaningfully expressive in its new setting. In his discussion of McGuinness's adaptations of Spanish Drama, David Johnston considers the importance of what he calls 'cultural enablement'.10 He observes how the translator or adaptor must create:

> the conditions by which the audience is transported into the world of the play. Translation [and adaptation] does not solely take place at the level of words. Within the world of the play the translator [and adaptor] ha[ve] to mediate all necessary extratextual information or informing intratextual assumptions so that the play can be experienced organically (184).

Johnston discusses McGuinness's process in terms of translation; however, McGuinness, not being a fluent Spanish speaker, writes, like Friel, from so-called literal translations of the original. Every act of translation, as Friel attests in *Translations,* is an act of interpretation, a politically-motivated value-judgment implicated within the subjective authority of language. McGuinness's process then is one of adaptation – that is, the transposing of a dramatic narrative from one context to another through one's poetic vision and personal narrative.

When considering how Kironde adapts *The Shadow of the Glen* to a Ugandan setting, replete with contemporaneous cultural signifiers, characters, and references, we can observe what Johnston refers to, in general terms, as an act of 'otherness transposed' (184). Kironde and Synge both wrote in English, where that language in each case, as in Matura's *The Playboy of the West Indies,* is the legacy of colonial oppression. Synge invented lyrical modes of expression through a tenacious renegotiation of Standard English in his unique interpretation of the deeply ingrained poetic cadences and liberating syntactical fibres of thinking in one tongue and speaking in another, known as Hiberno-English. Synge's lively rhythmic dialect reveals his ear for music and his ability to speak Irish, enabling the words and phrases to reverberate with an energy that performs and transforms the characters' identities and realities through the speech act. For Synge, in *The Playboy of the Western World,* language *is* action, linguistic form *is* content; where the act of storytelling facilitates transformation or, certainly, *gestures* to transcendence.

Matura too, brings an exceptional dynamism to his phonetic Creole dialect in *The Playboy of the West Indies,* stretching and bending Standard English into the freshest of elasticated speech-music. In 1980 Friel observed that:

> [W]e must make these English language words distinctive and unique to us ... The only person who did so in this country was Synge. Nobody since has pursued this course with any persistence or distinction ... Apart from Synge, all our dramatists have pitched their voices for English acceptance and recognition.[11]

Matura comments on what he calls the 'common use of language' in Synge's play as well as his own, and states that

> subverting or distorting the English language or making it fit your particular way of expressing yourself is a political statement ... There is an element of not wanting to speak the master's tongue ... It's a form of expression; how you choose to speak. And by not following the norm – it's like the last freedom there is; to speak in the way you can, or want to, [from] an anti-colonial point of view.[12]

Matura felt liberated by Synge's play in terms of cultural parallels, the political contexts of colonization, and the irreverence and freshness of Synge's language. He reflects as follows:

> I thought the way of paying respect and homage to the original is to keep the spirit of it but somehow apply the Caribbean coat of paint to it ... I thought I'd keep the original structure and set, just transplant it to the Caribbean. With the *Three Sisters,* I also tried to do that and it didn't work. I think I was trying to find too close a parallel with Russia. I was being too respectful to the original and I thought 'Oh Chekhov, I must be true to Chekhov and respect him' and then I did another version of it where I said 'to hell with Chekhov, this is my version'. And it was much more successful.[13]

The idea of 'the anti-hero' appealed to Matura, which is 'an aspect of anti-colonialism; the outlaw, the one who breaks the rules, who flaunts against authorities was a hero in Trinidad' (61). Perhaps most interesting for Matura in Synge's play was the fact that, 'in pretending to be something, you become the something' – 'a very interesting assumption to make – by pretending to be something you can become it' (64). Other transpositional resonances included:

> The sense of isolation. The sense of village community ... I remember as a kid my aunts used to take me to a beach every summer for a holiday. And it was a fishing village way up ... very hard to reach in those days ... called Mayaro. Which is where I set *The Playboy* – my *Playboy*. And all sorts of memories, the collections of people, of growing up in Trinidad started coming back. I started recognizing the Irish characters in Trinidad and vice versa. (59)

An affinity with the original text is certainly what propels the new work along and this can vary enormously from writer to writer. Matura observes that, for him, it was

> the pitch of the language, of the Irish [rhythms] which allowed me to use and draw on the Trinidadian pitch of their language as well. The colour, the telling of a story with words and painting pictures with words, it just kind of opened a treasure chest of Caribbean language which allowed me to adapt it to *The Playboy*. It was like a coat – it just fitted. (66)

The Playboy of the West Indies is written phonetically in Creole dialect and, like the original, is best experienced when heard aloud.

Unsurprisingly, Matura's adaptation of *The Playboy* comes with a glossary, showing the ways in which his local language, like Synge's, is 'fully flavoured as a nut or apple'. For example, he explains that 'Sapats' are a cheap type of footwear, 'Picong' is a type of teasing, 'Packoti House' is a brothel, 'Garraing' is 'talking for the sake of it', 'Jab-Jab' is a type of demon, 'Saga boy' is a flashy fellow, 'Jumbie' is a type of ghost, 'Wajank' is a hooligan, 'Mama Pools' is a simpleton, 'Crapeaux Smoke he pipe' means 'your fate is sealed', 'Bazodee' means crazy and 'Totie' is a penis.[14] Matura's stage-directions in act one describe '*A fishing village in Mayaro on the east coast of Trinidad – a rum shop. Evening. A counter. Tables. Chairs. Bags of rice stacked to one side. A door leading to room inside. Large, main, propped-up window. Shelves of bottles on wall behind counter*'.[15] Here, Pegeen becomes Peggy, Shawneen Keogh is

'Stanley', Christy becomes 'Ken' and the Widow Quin is 'Mama Benin'. In her opening speech, Peggy enunciates her trousseau:

> And a pair a good sappats, wit strong rubber, no bicycle type ting, but motor car, a hear dem is de bess. A dozen fine lice comb, six yards a cotton print either flowers or just print, yes, an a wide-brim straw hat for a wedding, all dis... (78)

When Ken enters, he is described as being *'of African origin'* (18). The ensuing tension-building scene, with its climax of questions from the chorus of local men, culminates as follows:

> **KEN.** (*turning around and putting up his hands*) Alright, I kill me ole man. Me ole man, a kill 'im, last Saturday a do it ... He was a wicked man, and de older he get de more wickeder he get. A reach me limit ... A had a cutlass. A just raise it up and drop de blade on de edge a he skull, here (*shows*) an he dead like a ripe mango, squash like one too, blood all over de place, an not a sound come outa him. (21-2)

Old Mahon is 'Mac' in this script – a walking 'jumbie', who enters in act two to dismantle Ken's fable: 'Me own flesh an blood. Me son, me own son do it. He en no wajank or notting. Just a dry dottish excuse for a man' (54). Fantasy and reality pull back and forth with the dual dramatic urgency of comedy and violence, as in Synge's play, and in the final scene of power-reversal, Ken victoriously declares to Mac and all around: 'Boy, I en no boy, but I go come wit you like Robinson Crusoe an he Friday, an you go cook me food an buy me rum, because a could beat you in any fight from now. Go on you' (81). In the final line, Peggy turns her back on Stanley, coming to terms with her stultifying future of mediocrity: 'Oh Lord, oh Lord, oh Lord. A lose 'im, a lose 'im, a lose de real Playboy a de West Indies'(82).

Details about Erisa Kironde's life are sketchy but it is known that he was born in Uganda and died in the 1980s. Like many African intellectuals, activists, poets, and dramatists of the twentieth century who grew-up under colonial regimes (such as Nigerians Wole Soyinka and Femi Osofisan, Ugandan Robert Serumaga, and Kenyan Ngugi wa Thion'go), Kironde moved for a time to the West. David Apter tells us that Kironde 'represented the most enlightened wing of the nationalist groups in Uganda ... having read English literature and anthropology at Cambridge [and that he was] for a time, Acting Secretary General of the Uganda National Congress'.[16] Kironde was also Chairman of the Uganda Red Cross Society, working to stop the spread of AIDS in Africa and a Fellow of

Harvard University. While he is cited in a number of books on African and Ugandan theatre, there is not much information given and he is not referred to in the extensive African theatre entry of the two-volume *Oxford Encyclopaedia of Theatre and Performance*.[17]

Kironde wrote a number of plays, such as *Kintu*, about the origin-myth of the pre-contact Baganda people, co-authored with academic and theatre practitioner Margaret Macpherson in Uganda. He wrote *The Trick* in 1965 and it is possibly while at Cambridge University that he first came across Synge's plays. *The Trick* was first staged at Makerere University in Kampala by the Makerere Free Travelling Theatre (under the direction of either Macpherson or David Cook). Kironde was a well-known figure in Uganda and his adaptation of *The Shadow of the Glen* was a very popular piece of theatre, being toured and staged far and wide in Uganda and also in Kenya at the University of Nairobi. Adrian Roscoe states: 'So successful was the transplant that when the play crossed the border into Kenya it became a cherished acquisition of University College Nairobi, and was performed with ritual regularity for many years'.[18] In their Introduction to the published play in 1968 David Cook and Miles Lee state:

> *The Trick* stands on its own. Erisa Kironde has taken Synge's *Shadow of the Glen* and transplanted it, lock, stock and barrel into Uganda, so that it appears to have grown there. It is not easy to make this kind of adaptation without falling into mere wooden translation or losing entirely the spirit of the original. Kironde's success points to a fruitful field for extending East African drama, both in English and in the vernaculars. [19]

That sense of having appeared 'to have grown there', is what marks out Kironde's play as worthy of attention. When something 'grows' somewhere, it is classed as indigenous. In terms of indigenous performance modes, scripted drama is not a traditional practice of African cultural histories and expressions. Yet Kironde enables Synge's vision to breathe with ease. African writers who chose to write scripted dramas in the twentieth century, or indeed to adapt Western canonical dramas – such as Soyinka's reworking of Classical Greek tragedies – have been criticized for employing, and thus appearing to endorse, colonial forms of expression. Writing in English is a politically fraught and complex action for an African (or indeed any colonized) writer and one that has been condemned from within. However, the critic's understandable allegiance to the pre-contact period is complicated by the fact that under colonial rule, English was the *lingua franca* and was compulsory in schools until the 1950s, with vernacular languages such as Swahili only being taught post-Independence. Thus, just as it was in Ireland, English was the dominant language of the people, albeit with its own inflections, rhythms, and so on. Friel's ironic dramaturgic deployment of the English language in *Translations* is the meta-theatrical comment *par excellence* on this reality. Soyinka's student Femi Osofisan, now a major playwright in his own right, has vociferously critiqued what he regards as Soyinka's valorization of colonial dramatic forms at the expense of indigenous African performance traditions. In African performance histories, and East African communities in particular, dance – the medium of movement – is an integral part of expression, linked to sacred rites and ritual, as well as music, song and an emphasis on the storyteller who tells his tale with the help of accompanying music and dance. Cook and Lee observe that:

> East Africans have been writing down play scripts in English for a good many years now. There are objections that can be raised against this practice. Drama is a fluent expression of the performer's whole being, and there is no doubt that the majority of people can interpret emotion more fully and freely in their mother tongue than they can in a second or foreign language. Furthermore, it may be said that scripted drama is an alien form which should not be allowed to overshadow performances growing more directly from East African tradition. (vii)

However, although 'alien' to an extent, a significant number of scripted plays have caught African audiences' imaginations where 'experiments with travelling theatres have more than confirmed what has been discovered in many widely separated places, that language is not an insuperable barrier to popular communication'.[20] Although the well-known and popular Makerere Travelling Theatre presented plays in English, Swahili, Luganda, Lwo, and Runyoro/Rutoro, often varying the language medium within any one programme, 'A synopsis of plays in English [was] given verbally in Swahili and the local vernacular before each performance' and this would have occurred when playing and touring *The Trick*, according to Cook and Lee (x).

Kironde's play needed to strike home for his audiences and his adaptation brings about a fascinating dialogue with Synge, where the East African experience, at a time of immensely turbulent decolonization, becomes something that can be understood, from the original story. What occurs with Synge and Kironde is a double interrogation of the process and impact of colonization, through the lenses of pre- and post-Independence: one story within the seams of imperialist rule, the other dealing with its unravelling and the new, fraught decolonized socio-political fabric. Matura's and Kironde's dramas challenge the linguistic legacy and imposition of colonization, being filtered once already through Synge. This 'twice-performed' or 'doubly-articulated' act of resistance, vocalized in times of Independence and during processes of decolonization in the case of both adaptations, again offers new political resonances as well as poetic possibilities to Synge's plays in terms of the transformative yet precarious, joyous yet fraught, necessary liberation that occurs at the end of both *The Shadow of the Glen* and *The Playboy of the Western World*. It is no surprise that Synge's voice communicates easily to marginalized or oppressed peoples, where the valorization of independence and individual spirit is the central dramatic through-line.

How did Erisa Kironde build the bridge between Synge and his Ugandan and Kenyan audiences during the violently turbulent, politically strife-ridden 1960s and '70s? What were the 'ways in' and what were the obstacles? In a short essay from 1978, Macpherson observes, in relation to Synge's play, that:

> Kironde read J.M. Synge's play *The Shadow of the Glen* and was fascinated by this story of married life between a couple unequal in age and attitudes to living in a remote Irish glen ... Kironde was struck by the relevance of this play but felt that the Anglo-Irish [sic] language and setting needed adaptation for full understanding in Uganda.[21]

At such a time of intense post-colonial conflict, Kironde brings his own exuberant and deeply-felt sense of place, context, rhythm and expressiveness to play, wholly domesticating the action and characters of *The Trick*, such that few audiences realized that this was an adaptation of a classic Irish drama. Not realizing that a work is an adaptation is the mark of its success, showing that the playwright has made the work live in a meaningful way, of its own accord.

Uganda gained independence in 1962 and *The Trick* premiered in 1965; however the 1960s were a period of successive brutal regimes under the leadership of Milton Obote from 1966-71, followed by Idi Amin's genocidal 'reign of terror', until Obote came back into power in the 1980s. Rather than making his play explicitly political, Kironde simply indigenizes Synge's folktale, letting the relevance of the story resonate figuratively as well as literally in terms of domestic brutality and confinement. While I do not want to overstate the political resonances of the play, it cannot be divorced from its historical, political contexts, in either Synge's Ireland or Kironde's Uganda. And we must remember how the gift of metaphor here allows for a coded resistance to autocratic rule and the life and death realities of censorship at this time in Uganda. The play also resonates in another way: the popular humorous folk-tale of a mock-death and eavesdropping is multi-cultural, with a number of variations found around the world, and certainly was not even unique as a dramatic device to Synge's play in Ireland (as is discussed by Éilis Ní Dhuibhne elsewhere in this book).

For Kironde, like most who look at Synge's work with an eye to adaptation, the Hiberno-English idiom and dialect and the comic timing were both compelling and challenging. Interwoven with language also is the complex issue of comedy. Humour, like language, is a deeply ingrained cultural experience, historically moulded with rhythms, patterns, expectations and familiar 'short-hands' that vary from one country to the next. In terms of adapting Synge's perfectly-timed orchestration of comedy (and pathos), there is an intrinsic requirement to 'know your audience' in order to pitch, phrase, and construct sentences that enable their moments of laughter and sympathy. If humour and comedy are largely culturally-specific, then moments of recognition must operate to facilitate the laughter, which comes from a subtle but significant adjustment of content, signifiers, attention to pitch, register and all-important timing down to punctuation and syllable count. For example, Cook and Lee explain that:

> An East African audience laughs not only at things which an average European spectator would recognize as 'funny', but also whenever it is surprised, especially if the surprise is under emotional tension. This is probably a universal human reaction which has been inhibited in recent centuries by European social conventions, except perhaps in the music hall and the circus. (x)

In his 'transplantation' Kironde brings us richly into the Ugandan world of the time. His stage directions reveal *'The inside of a rectangular hut',* with a fire-place in one corner, made of stones, with a kettle nestling in it.[22] In this one-room hut, a pot of *waragi* –

an intriguing-sounding locally-made gin, sits on a pad of banana leaves. There are scattered logs serving as stools, a reed table with cups on it and one entrance of a reed door. There is a bed of reeds at one end of the hut, on which lies the covered body of Kalekezi, the man of the house. His wife Kamuli, is first seen in the hut, lit only by firelight, counting money. Synge's Tramp is known here only as 'Musician'. He is heard softly calling from outside, to which Kamuli quickly hides her money and lights a lamp. For Kironde, Synge's recurring fascination with the figure of the Tramp posed perhaps the greatest challenge in terms of cultural specificity and the necessity of 'transposing otherness'. George Seremba explains:

> The idea of the itinerant character or the tramp was, perhaps far more than the language, a formidable obstacle in Kironde's quest to adapt Synge's play. Tramps quite simply did not exist in Uganda or East Africa: certainly not during the 1950s and the 1960s.[23]

Synge's tramp is closely identified with poetry, freedom of spirit and the imagination. He is in possession of valiant strength against adversity and the elements, with privileged communion with the natural world, and is wholly recognizable to the fabric of Irish cultural history and folk-traditions, from the pre-contact era of travelling bards and *seanachai*, as well as the Travellers or itinerant tin-smiths and balladeers from the eleventh and twelfth centuries. The tramp was a figure to be admired for what was regarded as his authentic state of being and embodiment of independence. Thus the wanderer or tramp-figure has become a central trope of Irish drama and literature (look at the work Boucicault, Gregory and Yeats, Beckett, Friel, Carr – all filled with wanderers, travellers, tinkers), and with Synge himself signing his letters affectionately to Molly Allgood as 'Ever your Tramp', or 'Your old Tramp'. Kironde, thus needing to find a dramatic counterpart, did so with his character simply called 'Musician'.

Music and dance are essential to the performance rituals of African peoples. Thus, Kironde takes a real character from Kampala's social fabric who enters the new narrative. In Uganda there lived a man named 'Majangwa', who was a colourful part of life in Kampala, well-known to the people of the city from the 1940s to the 1960s, never seen without his long drum. Macpherson gives us a good pen-picture:

> He often moved at a sort of trot and yet he never seemed to be in a hurry. In the later years he often mumbled to himself or he

sang snatches of song as he moved 'from Nalubabwe to Nalubabwe'. He was unshaven. His hair was wild and long and grey, or at least grizzled. He often wore a tattered barkcloth and sometimes his feet were done up in bits of old sacking. [...] Always he carried his *ngalabi* [drum]. [He] was undoubtedly strange but he had a kind of poetry about him. Perhaps because his drumming was compelling. Perhaps because of the unselfconsciousness of his songs. Perhaps because he didn't live like the rest of us. He was frightening. He was challenging ... Because of its linking with the strange figure of the real Majangwa the Kironde adaptation spelled out the issue very clearly for the play's first Uganda audience, particularly the link between poetry and joy and free existence ... this strange magic attached to the character imposes itself upon reader or audience. (68, 69)

Kironde's evocative transformation of Synge's Tramp, into the initially nameless 'Musician', is, by the end of the play, named as 'Majangwa'. In the familiar echoes of the closing moments of the play, Musician says:

> We'll be leaving you now. Come on, Kamuli. The rain is falling but the air is kind and it'll be fine tomorrow ... You'll not feel the lack of a roof when you're with me for I know all the ways a man can get food for his stomach. We'll be going now and you'll learn how to live. You were lonely married to an old man – and afraid. Come, I will teach you to dismiss loneliness. We'll move from market to market, and I'll play on my drum and you will dance and the lonely, the bigger fools with homes, will pay for our act.
>
> **KALEKEZI.** (*impatiently*): Get out of that door, I tell you, and make your plans outside.

The Musician replies:

> (*at the door*): Come along with me and it's not only my plans you'll hear but the laughter of the world will be ringing in your ears. There'll be hard times of course. We'll get turned away many a time from markets, and, when times are hard and the cotton price has fallen, they'll let us sing and dance and send us away with a dry lump of lumonde, but the next market will put us straight. We'll be with people who want to be happy and we'll delude them for a little time longer into forgetfulness of their troubles, and, if the rain wets us through, we'll see the sun rising over the hills and the white mists flat over the swamps and the stars shining till the shadow of every tree is plain. We'll watch the fools who are afraid of life and we'll be living and you

won't have time to sit watching an old man snoring in his drunken sleep and wheezing in his age.

KAMULI. I'll be wheezing myself by then in the cold swamp air, I think. But you've a fine tongue, Majangwa, and a kindly face. I'll come with you, Majangwa, and get away from this detestable old... yes, you are old, Kalekezi, an old, old, old man. And how do you think you're going to live now with no one to look after you? Next time you lie under that blanket you'll be really dead and with none to be sorry for you either.

Exit with Majangwa, drumming. Kazungu (the herdsman) begins to slink out too but Kalekezi stops him. (113-4)

Apart from Kamuli's departure, Majangwa's intoxicating drumming at the end of the play is perhaps the most significant action, communicating an affirmation of life wordlessly into a Ugandan cultural context. Nora's spirit too, manifests in the character or Kamuli, as the real Majangwa's wife - Nakirijja, was a familiar figure in Kampala, dancing to his drum on the streets with their pet dog.

Kironde's colourful rendering of local life comes through in the text. Upon first entering the hut, the Musician says: 'I walk from Nalubabwe and back to Nalubabwe ... and when I see a house, I call, and say to myself, 'Maybe they'll give me a piece of cassava and a corner for my drum, and maybe they'd enjoy my jesting' (104). Kamuli, Synge's Nora – the beleaguered woman of the house, sighs:

> No matter, stranger. No matter, bring your drum in ... He has died on me. And I in a foreign land and with all the cotton ready to be picked and the coffee trees just ready to start yielding. (104)

Kironde's play, like Synge's, is a moving testimony to individual human triumph over brutality, fear, loneliness and exile. When Kamuli asks the Musician if he is ever scared, he replies:

> Me. Afraid? Lonely? I am too poor and homeless to feel lonely, and walking the roads at night, turned away from doors, where would I be if I felt afraid? If I were easily frightened, walking in the night with every bush a lion, every falling leaf a leopard, and every stray branch a snake and all the town robbers on the road every night. If I were afraid, I'd be a madman... shouted at by all the village children or maybe dead... like Mukasa who was found on the hills. (106)

As in Synge's play, the humour of the piece emerges with the revelation that Kalekezi is not dead. Kironde writes, '*The blanket is drawn slowly off the body. Kalekezi looks out. Musician moves uneasily, then looks up and springs to his feet with a movement of terror'* (107). After a brief exchange, Kalekezi shouts 'I'm not dead but dying of thirst. Bring me a drop quickly before she comes back'. We can see how the same joke of trying to cadge a drink behind your wife's back is universal! Musician replies: 'Then you're not dead?' Kalekezi asks 'How could I die and I as dry as a rubbing stone?' Musician then goes *'behind firewood and bringing out a bottle, pouring out liberal measure of waragi in a cup'* before saying 'What will she say if she notices you smell like a beer-boat? You must have a reason for pretending to be dead' (107).

> Kalekezi: 'I have ... and I shall show myself soon, for my joints are going to sleep and there's been a fly on my nose as big as a bat and making me want to sneeze... and you two nattering away like weaver birds about leopards and Mukasa (curse him) and coffee. Give me that waragi ... Go over now to where those spears are and fish out that stick. (108)

Although this is all very humorous, Kironde is more explicit than Synge about the issue of domestic abuse, as when Kamuli says: 'What good is rich land and cows and cotton when there's nothing to do but hoe in the garden, feed the fire and him, an old drunk man and a wife-beater. I just sit watching life go by' (110).

Kironde's play is not written phonetically but is subtly permeated from time to time with a flavour of Hiberno-English syntax, such as 'How could I *and I as dry as* a rubbing stone?' (107, emphasis added). Also, there are echo-chambers of Synge's language, where Kironde has retained his choice of word in a subtle homage that does not overpower, such as 'stranger', 'queer' and, indeed, the final line, which is, in part, identical to Synge's - 'may you have a long and quiet life and good health with it'(114). It is important to remember though that it would all be spoken in local accents, just like Matura's version, and this would further imbue the powerful re-location and re-locution.

From the works referred to in this essay we can see that, whether it is an Irish re-working of a classic play or a foreign 'transplant' of an Irish drama, the act of adaptation is always a complex interplay of linguistic association and cultural identification. 'These creative reflections can yield both expected and unforeseen resonances which can symbiotically enrich both works. Erisa Kironde's *The Trick* engages with Synge's vision, not only to communicate to other times, places and peoples, but also to inspire new expressions of hope, emancipation and imagination, just as the Tramp inspires Nora, and Majangwa offers hope to Kamuli through taking the road less travelled.

---

[1] Peter Crawley, 'Conflicts, sacred rites and themes as old as time', *The Irish Times*, 5 April 2008: 7.

[2] Crawley, 7.

[3] Crawley, 7.

[4] 'Brian Friel in interview with Paddy Agnew (1980)', in *Brian Friel: Essays, Diaries, Interviews: 1964-1999*, Edited by Christopher Murray (London: Faber & Faber, 1999): 84. Subsequent references appear in the text.

[5] Gate Theatre, *Hedda Gabler Show Programme* (Dublin: Gate Theatre, 2008).

[6] Brian Friel, *Hedda Gabler* (Meath: The Gallery Press, 2008).

[7] Brian Friel, *Plays Two* (London: Faber & Faber, 1999): ii.

[8] Mick Heaney, 'Adapting to Harsh Realities', *The Sunday Times*, 20 January 2008: 4. Subsequent page references are included in the text.

[9] 'Meet the Makers: Bisi Adigun and Roddy Doyle', Abbey Theatre, 16 October 2007.

[10] David Johnston, 'En Otras Palabras: Frank McGuinness and Spanish Drama', in Melissa Sihra and Paul Murphy (eds.), *The Dreaming Body: Contemporary Irish Theatre* (Gerrards Cross & New York: Colin Smythe & Oxford University Press, 2009): 184. The subsequent reference appears in the text.

[11] Friel, *Essays*, 85-6.

[12] Kirsty Blake-Knox, ' "The Coat That Fitted": A Comparative Study of John Millington Synge's *The Playboy of the Western World* and Mustapha Matura's *The Playboy of the West Indies*', Unpublished undergraduate dissertation, School of Drama, Film and Music, Trinity College, Dublin, 25 April 2007: 59.

[13] Blake-Knox 67. Subsequent quotations from the interview with Matura are included in the text.

[14] Glossary of *The Playboy of the West Indies*, Blake-Knox, 77.

[15] Mustapha Matura, *The Playboy of the West Indies* (London: Oberon Books, 2010): 9. Subsequent references appear in the text.

[16] David E. Apter, *The Political Kingdom in Uganda: A Study in Bureaucratic Nationalism* (London: Routledge, 1997): 317.

[17] Dennis Kennedy (ed.), *The Oxford Encyclopaedia of Theatre and Performance* (Oxford: Oxford University Press, 2003).

[18] Adrian Roscoe, *Uhuru's Fire, African Literature East to South* (Cambridge: Cambridge University Press, 1977): 262.

[19] David Cook & Miles Lee (eds.), *Short East African Plays* (London: Heinemann, 1968): ix. Subsequent references appear in the text.

[20] Cook and Lee, viii.

21 Margaret Macpherson, 'What Happened to Majangwa?', *Mawazo*, vol. 4, No. 4, 1969: 69. Subsequent references appear in parentheses in the text.
22 Erisa Kironde, *The Trick,* in David Cook & Miles Lee (eds.), *Short East African Plays* (London: Heinemann, 1968): 103. Subsequent references appear in parentheses in the text.
23 George Seremba in conversation with Melissa Sihra, Trinity College, Dublin, 8 April 2007, unpublished.

13 | EVOLVING *PLAYBOYS* FOR THE GLOBAL WORLD

Sara Keating

From its first production in 1907, *The Playboy of the Western World* has occupied a fascinating and contentious role in the construction of Irish cultural identity. Both nationally and internationally, the performance history of the play over the last century has allowed theatre-makers to assert the relationship of *Playboy* to Irish cultural realities. Indeed, it has become *the* definitive play in the Irish theatrical canon, while Synge's influence – and the influence of *The Playboy* in particular – continues to haunt the work of contemporary Irish playwrights.

In the early years of the twenty-first century, the discourse surrounding the production and reception of Synge shows evidence of an ongoing anxiety about identity. This is evident from three major productions of *The Playboy of the Western World* – by Druid Theatre in 2004 and 2005, and Pan Pan Theatre in 2006 – all of which exemplify concerns about Ireland's cultural identity in the context of an increasingly globalized society. Therefore, in this paper, I want to suggest that, by considering Synge's work in the context of contemporary theatre practice, we can identify some of the problems that arise when we use dramatic and/or literary texts as models for understanding Irish cultural identity.

Although many of his contemporaries contested Synge's representation of the west of Ireland, a discourse of authenticity surrounded the first productions of his plays. That discourse went on to have a significant impact on the subsequent reception of his work. The Abbey theatre's founders' proposition that an Irish national theatre should reflect 'the deeper thoughts and emotions of

Ireland' defined an emergent artistic ideology that was concerned with dramatic representation as a synecdoche of reality.[1] That ideology has been prominent in the development of the Abbey since 1904, and continues to shape the theatre's activities today. In content, this ideology was reflected in the rural setting of almost the entire repertoire, and in the predominance of social realist themes. In form, the Abbey's developing aesthetic was committed not just to the physical illusion of reality on the stage, but also to the heightened symbolic reality of the naturalist school of theatre. The detailed sets and costumes of productions did not merely reflect authentic peasant dress and furniture; they were authentically sourced too.[2]

Meanwhile, the distinctive Abbey style of acting also emphasized the authenticity of the company's realistic presentational style, as Frank Fay makes clear:

> The [Abbey] actors have most of them peasant blood, if they are not the children of peasants, and instinctively talk, move and act as peasants would, and are familiar with the habits of country folk.[3]

Although the acting company included middle-class nationalists from Dublin, the performers were encouraged to change their accents and to learn Irish, subsuming their portrayal of peasant life within the naturalistic discourse of authentic representation.

The controversy surrounding the first production of *The Playboy of the Western World* illustrated this problematic relationship between the Abbey's realist representational ideology and contemporary social reality. Synge of course claimed that the play was inspired by true stories, and famously declared that:

> I have used one or two words only that I have not heard among the country people of Ireland ... [I]n countries where the imagination of the people and the language they use is rich and living it is possible for a writer to be rich and copious in his words and at the same time to give the reality which is the root of all poetry ... [O]n the stage one must have reality.[4]

The controversy that resulted from the premiere of the play was specifically directed at this claim to realism, with the audience's well-known objections focussing on its authenticity, as evident in such responses as 'that's not the West' and 'that's not Western life'.[5]

Yet, despite the initially negative reaction, *The Playboy* gradually became the touchstone of the Irish dramatic tradition. The nationalist resistance to the play became the catalyst for subsequent readings of it, which negotiated the tragicomic elements of Synge's text to reinterpret and project it as a realistic representation of the social conditions in Ireland at the turn of the century. In politically divided, civil-war-torn Ireland, *The Playboy* became indelibly associated with a romantic yesteryear, where a community was unified against a common threat,[6] and between 1924 and 1934, Synge's play was produced at the Abbey Theatre on an annual basis; in the following ten years, it was produced 6 times.[7]

Furthermore, the naturalist aesthetic of the first production set the template for ethnographic readings of it as an embodiment of a particular cultural identity in 1907: that is, an understanding of Irish culture as a wild, rural, linguistically idiosyncratic, peasant-based culture, not far removed from the original nationalist ideals that it once offended.[8] If the great lesson of *Playboy* can be summarized as involving the need to understand 'the great gap between a gallous story and a dirty deed',[9] the play itself became part of the idealistic ideological rhetoric used to avoid the impoverished reality of post-independence Ireland. However, the persistent ethnographic understanding of the play has limited the way in which it has been interpreted throughout the twentieth century – and continues to ghost twenty-first-century productions.

The 2004 and 2005 productions of *The Playboy of the Western World* by Druid Theatre Company provide an interesting example of the limitations of this continued association between Synge's play and Irish cultural identity, although the passage of time has given the cultural construction of Irish identity in Synge's text an entirely different significance. National cultural identification at the turn of the twentieth century might be seen as an internalized discourse that was projected outwards for political effect. In contrast, cultural identity at the turn of the twenty-first century became an externalized discourse with economic significance. Because that discourse was directed outside of the country rather than being conducted within it, it gave Irish cultural identity a global presence, as a highly attractive, international commodity, 'creating a tension between Ireland as it is presented to the world (through culture) and Irishness as it is experienced and expressed within the country itself', as Patrick Lonergan puts it in his study of the effects of globalization on Irish theatre.[10]

If Irish cultural identity has evolved from having local significance to acquiring global reach, that evolution has not, however, been accompanied by an expansion in our understanding of what that identity actually entails. Thus, instead of a rejuvenated version of Irish identity that might encompass a broader understanding of Irishness – one that includes the lacunae revealed by historical revisionism, while also making space for Ireland's significant new immigrant population – we instead have the old version of Irish cultural identity being recycled and exported. That conservative version of identity may meet economic imperatives for cultural and heritage organizations, but it leaves the ideological imperatives of cultural representation behind. What we are left with, then, is a repackaged version of the Celtic Twilight, a canny combination of history and contemporary wealth that is embedded with contradictions. As Cronin, Gibbons and Kirby comment, in this context 'culture as social critique has given way to culture as economic commodity'.[11]

Druid embodied these contradictions in their sophisticated marketing campaigns, first for the 2004 production of the play, starring Cillian Murphy and Anne Marie Duff, and then for the 2005 *DruidSynge* cycle, the company's ambitious production of the entire Synge canon. During the production's run at the Town Hall Theatre, Galway and the Gaiety Theatre in Dublin, Murphy was also starring in Christopher Nolan's Hollywood blockbuster *Batman Begins*; in international press interviews to promote that movie, Murphy's involvement with the theatre production was often cited. Meanwhile, Duff was familiar to Irish and British audiences from her leading role in Paul Abbott's television serial *Shameless*.

The juxtaposition of the two productions displays the company's understanding of modern media culture and global branding. The 2004 production – which we might see as 'Celebrity Synge' – received enormous international attention, providing a platform (and thus a wider potential audience base) for the less-saleable *DruidSynge* project, both nationally and internationally. For both productions, the Galway-based company's marketing campaign positioned itself within the inherited discourse of authenticity that featured in the play's original production, and which dominated its subsequent life on the Irish and international stage. It did so in a number of ways.

First, in media coverage of both events, the company projected itself as having a unique and 'historic' relationship with Synge.[12] Druid's first ever production in 1975 was of *The Playboy of the Western World*. They produced the play a second time in 1977, and their most celebrated production took place in 1982, in a version that travelled to the Aran Islands (the first time Synge's work had been professionally staged there), before touring internationally for three years. Hence, Synge was the foundation stone upon which the company, their repertoire, and their international reputation were built. As Garry Hynes commented, in an interview conducted in 1982, Synge was Druid's 'house playwright'.[13]

Second, Druid established a discursive relationship involving the landscape of the west of Ireland, which was construed as the place where Synge had found his inspiration, and as the location in which Druid's work was grounded. The company's marketing campaign stressed that this geographical relationship made them the natural inheritors of Synge's canon: that the rural history of their company made their relationship with Synge's plays an organic one and that their productions were thus authentic representations of Synge's work. This relationship was reinforced by the visual imagery in the advance publicity for the productions. During the rehearsal period for the 2004 staging of the play, the company of actors visited many of the places that influenced Synge's work – the cottage in which he lived on the Aran Islands, the pub in which he drank, the cliff where he sat and looked out into the sea. Hynes wanted the actors to absorb the atmosphere – the 'lonesome scruff of the hill', as she commented in an interview in the *New York Times*.[14] Images from this trip were used as part of the publicity campaign. Pictures of the windswept actors frolicking on the cliffs in tweed caps and knit jumpers further projected the 'natural' relationship between the company and the plays they were staging, and these images appeared in international titles like the *New York Times* and *The Financial Times*.[15] Meanwhile, following its Galway opening and a subsequent Dublin run, the production began a pilgrimage across the west of Ireland: to Geesala, Co Mayo (where *The Playboy of the Western World* is thought to have been set), to each of the three Aran islands, and to Dún Chaoin in the Kerry Gaeltacht. While the local touring sites commendably brought the professional productions to audiences that might not ordinarily have the opportunity to see such high quality theatre, there was also an undeniable strategic significance in the sites that Druid chose to visit.

This regional tour – a longstanding feature of the work of Druid Theatre – was repeated in 2005 for *DruidSynge*. A scene shot on the Aran Islands from the documentary *Mighty Talk*, filmed by Wildfire Films in 2005 during the build-up to *DruidSynge*, features a hand-painted sign outside the building known as Synge's cottage. It reads 'Failte Abhaile Synge' ('Welcome Home, Synge'). As the discourse surrounding the event suggested, Druid were bringing Synge home.[16] The use of the Irish language, meanwhile, suggests another layer of association between the authenticity of Druid's relationship with a native audience and the writer.

Indeed, as Hynes revealed in an interview with Ann Saddlemyer at the 2007 Synge Summer School, the spectre of Synge himself appeared on stage in a variety of crowd scenes throughout the cycle, as if confirming his approval of Druid's project.[17] Meanwhile, the closing gesture of *DruidSynge* brought Synge's problematic unfinished *Deirdre of the Sorrows* to a more definitive conclusion: as the action ended, one of the child actors advanced to the front of the stage, revealing a picture of Synge to the audience before the lights went down. This act again sought to suggest the writer's complicity in the event.

However, as well as bringing Synge home, Druid were also bringing Synge to a new international audience, touring his work to Edinburgh, New York, and Tokyo. The tour confirmed and expanded the company's international profile and also enhanced the status of Synge's work in a global context.

Strikingly, both Druid productions stayed within the bounds of the traditional naturalist aesthetic that we associate with *The Playboy of the Western World*, providing a largely authentic (that is, a familiar) version of Synge's play to contemporary audiences, albeit one rooted in a grittier realism than the diluted comic buffoonery that the play had become known for. It was 'more Dickensian realism than "Oirish" blarney-blah', critic Michael Coveney wrote of the 2004 production, referencing the deflated, sterilized place of the play in the Irish theatrical canon.[18] Karen Fricker in *The Guardian* commended Garry Hynes for 'scraping away the vestiges of romanticism from stage depictions of rural Ireland'.[19] Significantly, the major criticism of the 2004 production was that the star presence of Cillian Murphy distracted from the overall authenticity of the 'superbly detailed set' and its lighting which '[has] the warmth and intensity of real sunlight'. His 'movie-star locks ... give the impression that the western boreens come with complimentary shampoo'.[20]

The 2005 *DruidSynge* production, which used the same set for all six of Synge's plays, brought a symbolic quality to the realism of the play. Francis O'Connor's blue-wash design was centred by a bare-earth floor, which, in the case of *The Playboy* in particular, saw the actors get dirtier and their costumes more worn as the action progressed. The stage environment thus metaphorically mirrored the dramatic action. As Michael Billington commented, 'the walls and doors of Francis O'Connor's adaptable permanent set became even more unhinged than the characters';[21] the stage almost became a character too.

The universally positive critical commentary about *DruidSynge* further reinforced the authenticity of Druid's production. It was variously described as 'much more realistic than usual',[22] and 'as close to perfection as dammit'.[23] Druid's *Playboy* had become the definitive version of the play. This sort of rhetoric inadvertently illustrated the problematic relationship between the realistic representation of *Playboy* and its signification in a global internationalized context. The production performed a confirmation of the continued contemporary understanding of Irish cultural identity as something historic. Yet with its high production values and international mobility, it simultaneously projected an Irish identity that was sophisticated and contemporary too. The national and international success of *The Playboy of the Western World* and the rest of the *DruidSynge* project suggests that this simultaneously historic and contemporary understanding of Irish cultural identity operates with potent force in both a local and a global context.

The 2006 production of *The Playboy of the Western World* by Pan Pan Theatre provides a more complex and empowering version of Synge's play, and offers an interesting engagement with the ideas of cultural authenticity which the play has come to stand for. Premiering in Beijing in March 2006 with an all-Chinese cast, Pan Pan's *Playboy* was a global project both in its inception and in its reach. The company's translation of the work for a Chinese audience provided an invigorating engagement with contemporary Irish cultural identity in its globalized reality, where an immigrant population has radically changed the cultural landscape of Ireland since the beginning of the twenty-first century.[24] Where *DruidSynge* exploited traditional understandings of Irish cultural identity to market their production, Pan Pan's production interrogated the very idea of Synge's play as an authentic cultural text. They did so by translating it for an entirely different cultural context.

The idea of staging a play so uniquely associated with Ireland's rural and nationalist heritage for a contemporary Chinese audience seems an unlikely one. The radical difference between the cultures of Ireland and China needs little elaboration, so it may not be surprising to note the company's claim that Synge's work had never before been translated into Mandarin. Meanwhile, the text was an unusual choice for Pan Pan, who have usually associated themselves with the postmodern European avant-garde tradition that remains largely foreign to mainstream Irish theatre culture.25 However, the themes of Synge's play translated well into the context of modern-day China. The conflict between rural and urban cultures that dominated the play's original production, for example, is particularly relevant in a contemporary Chinese context. The Chinese economy has lately undergone rapid reform and rampant economic growth, forcing traditional cultural and social structures to adjust to its demands. As the *Irish Times* China correspondent Clifford Coonan suggested, the play also had 'parallels with classical Chinese philosophy', particularly in relation to Confucian teaching on father-son relationships.26 Furthermore, Christy's outsider status was given political weight as he was transformed into a bedraggled migrant worker from the Xinjiang province who ends up in Beijing, his dual characterization as a Muslim and a rural farm worker who ends up in the city reinforcing his status as an outsider in the community.27

In attempting to draw cultural parallels between Synge's play and contemporary Chinese culture, translator Yue Sun and director Gavin Quinn made radical changes to traditional stage versions of the play. First, they relocated the action from a Mayo shebeen at the turn of the twentieth century to a 'whoredressers' – a hairdresser's shop that is a front for a brothel – in present day Beijing. This relocation of the action made the play seem contemporary to a Chinese audience, while also developing the themes of sexuality in Synge's original. The heightened peasant dialect of Synge's text was translated into contemporary Mandarin argot, using a mix of Beijing dialect and slang to produce an effect for Chinese audiences similar to that which Synge's use of language had on its original audience.

Apart from changing the play's setting, there were also formal differences in Pan Pan's approach to the play, not least in their condensation of Synge's three-act structure into a pacey eighty-minute romp. More significantly, however, the traditional realistic setting that has dominated the play's production history was transformed by designer Aedin Cosgrove's slick postmodern aesthetic. Using strategically placed television screens, which showed the actors in the dressing rooms preparing to go on stage, and mirrors that reflected the audience watching the play, the production pushed the traditional stage realism of Synge's play into the contemporary cultural context of reality television, while also highlighting the theme of performance, which runs throughout Synge's original.

Despite the use of these techniques, Pan Pan's *Playboy* was not framed as a realist piece, as Quinn's direction of the actors made clear. The actors often used direct address to the audience, and they were clearly seen stepping in and out of their roles on the televisions that displayed their presence backstage. However, Quinn also incorporated traditional elements of Chinese performance tradition – such as stylized physical movement adapted from Chinese opera – to clarify the line between the reality effect of the theatrical performance and the representational construct.

The critical response to the Beijing production was very positive. Although the audience had little or no knowledge of the original play or its history, Pan Pan's production allowed them to view it entirely through their own cultural lens. It was not without controversy, however, as a small number of audience members registered complaints with the Chinese Ministry of Culture about the highly sexualized nature of the performance.[28] (The police were sent in to investigate, but found nothing objectionable). That such rhetoric and response echoed that of the original production was a reminder of the faithful connection between both versions, despite the radical difference in cultural context.

The production's transfer to Dublin later that year initiated an opportunity for Irish audiences to consider the ways in which such global cultural interchange might be used to interrogate a repertoire founded on traditional cultural identifications. That is, it provided audiences with a chance to witness how an engagement with the repertoire outside of traditional Irish constraints might create room for expanding versions of Irish cultural identity. That identification may have occurred on a participatory basis (by encouraging Chinese audiences in Beijing to imagine their own experience through another culture and by inviting an Ireland-based Chinese audience to participate in cultural exchange in Irish theatre). And it also can be seen as having occurred on a broader ideological level (by forcing Irish audiences to reconsider the significance of *The Playboy of the Western World* outside of the traditional framework in which the canon has placed it). It also provided an unusual opportunity for potential Chinese audiences in Ireland to see their own culture on the Irish stage. What was involved then was, as Patrick Lonergan observed, not merely a theatre performance but 'a social performance about Ireland's attitude to multiculturalism and immigration'.[29]

However, the discourse surrounding the Irish premiere of Pan Pan's production, and the key issue of linguistic re-translation that the production faced in its transfer, threatened the potential social value that the production might wield. Instead of questioning the cultural identities embodied in Synge's text by performing an alternative version of these identities, as the Chinese production did, the production on the Irish stage was re-mediated through the discourse of authenticity associated with Synge's play. This dilution of the production's originally radical stature was triggered by the surtitles that were specifically prepared by Pan Pan for the Irish production. The surtitles were given deliberate physical prominence behind and above the stage. As Quinn explained, this decision was made in order to provide an 'aesthetic of language' to the non-Chinese-speaking audience: 'The words will be large and prominent ... like an artistic installation,' he stated.[30] Quinn believed that this decision would highlight the constructedness of language within the play (it is language after all that enables Christy's transformation) and, more obviously, that it would allow Irish audiences to understand what is going on on-stage. However, where the Chinese translation used the colloquial contemporary language of Bejingese slang, the surtitles that framed the Irish performance used the 'distinctive heightened diction' of Synge's play almost verbatim, although Synge's play was occasionally peppered with necessary references to the contemporary Chinese context (such as names) and swearwords.[31]

Hence, the production juxtaposed the action on stage against the historical Hiberno-English of Synge's play. On the one hand it self-consciously placed the original text in dialogue with the contemporary Chinese reality. However, while performing in an Irish context where audiences are almost over-familiar with Synge's play, the verbatim reproduction of *The Playboy* in the form of surtitles simultaneously confirmed the authenticity of Pan Pan's version of the play: that is, its faithfulness to the original text. The surtitles thus worked both to confirm and undermine our expectations of the classic play. It created a sort of double vision for the audience in which text and performance competed with each other rather than acting as complementary forces. The textual stability of the surtitles thus projected Synge's text *above* the fluidity of the ephemeral performance context of the production. The result was to fetishize the Chinese elements of the production in their performative context, while also creating a textual space for an Irish audience to reconfirm their own fixed ideas about *The Playboy of the Western World*. The unresolved nature of their intercultural experiment was a provocative challenge to the audience, denying intellectual closure while at the same time stimulating a genuine response to the idea of cultural globalization as a process rather than a *fait accompli*.

These three productions of *The Playboy of the Western World* illustrate two different features of globalization. If the *DruidSynge* production highlights the function of Irish cultural identity as a successful international marketing brand that might be exploited on a global economic scale, Pan Pan's production engages with the actual social process of globalization, suggesting how these social processes have impacted upon the cultural construction of Irish identity. However, the contradictions inherent in both performances suggest the unresolved and evolving nature of contemporary Irish cultural identity. Where Pan Pan's production in Beijing provided a fine example of how globalization brings Irish culture into contact with new cultures through immigration (among other cultural exchanges), its Irish transfer suggested the continued necessity of reformulating the (textual) boundaries upon which Irish cultural identity has been traditionally constructed. As the character of Hugh suggests in Friel's *Translations* (1980), 'it is not the literal facts of history that shape us, but images of the past embodied in language … we must never cease renewing those images, because once we do, we fossilize'.[32] The suspended duality of Pan Pan's production suggests that it is in the ephemeral forum of the theatre that this reality of cultural identity as a process rather than a fixed reality finds its perfect expression. It seems more than fitting that this is the ultimate lesson of Synge's play about the transformational Christy Mahon too.

---

[1] Lady Gregory, 'Our Irish Theatre' in John P Harrington (ed), *Modern Irish Drama*, First edition (New York: Norton, 1991): 378.

[2] As Fintan O'Toole has commented, 'naturalism grew out of the need to convince the audience of the reality of rural life … If you were producing a play about the West of Ireland, it was essential that the Dublin actors convince themselves and others that there really were peasants, that you went to the Aran Islands to get real pampooties

and real three legged stools to dress the actors and the stage'. Fintan O'Toole, *Critical Moments* (Dublin: Carysfort Press, 2003): 286.
3 Frank Fay, 'An Irish National Theatre', in Harrington, 392-393.
4 J. M. Synge, *Collected Works Volume IV: Plays 2*. Edited by Ann Saddlemyer (Gerrards Cross: Colin Smythe): 53-4.
5 Joseph Holloway, '27 January 1907' in Robert Hogan and Michael J. O'Neill (eds), *Joseph Holloway's Abbey Theatre Diaries* (Southern Illinois University Press: Feffer & Simons, 1967)
6 See Daniel Corkery, *Synge and Anglo Irish Literature* (Cork, 1931).
7 As stated on the Abbey Theatre online archive.: www.abbeytheatre.ie/archives
8 See Corkery.
9 Synge, *Plays 2*, 169.
10 Patrick Lonergan, *Theatre and Globalization: Irish Drama in the Celtic Tiger Era*, (Basingstoke and New York: Palgrave Macmillan, 2009): 189.
11 Michael Cronin, Luke Gibbons, Peadar Kirby (eds), *Reinventing Ireland: Culture and the Celtic Tiger* (London: Pluto Press, 2002): 2
12 Brian Lavery, 'Irish Masterpiece Returning to its Bleak Home', *The New York Times*, 17 March 2004: 9
13 Patrick Lonergan, 'Druid and Synge' http://syngecycle.com/aboutdruidsynge/druid-theatre-and-john-millington-synge
14 Lavery, 9.
15 Lavery, 9.
16 RTÉ, 'Mighty Talk: A Journey With *DruidSynge*', *DruidSynge: The Plays of John Millington Synge* (RTE, Wildfire Films and Druid Theatre, 2007).
17 'Garry Hynes and Ann Saddlemyer in Conversation at the Synge Summer School', *DruidSynge: The Plays of John Millington Synge*.
18 Michael Coveney, 'Playboy Passion with an Emerald Hue' in *The Daily Mail*, 12 February 2004: 54.
19 Karen Fricker, 'Review' in *The Guardian*, 11 February 2004: 30.
20 Gerry McCarthy, 'Dramatic Shifts', *The Sunday Times*, 22 February 2004: 19.
21 Michael Billington, 'Synge for your Supper', *The Guardian*, 19 July, 2005.
22 Benedict Nightingale, 'The Synge Cycle', *The Times*, 30 August, 2005.
23 Emer O'Kelly, 'Unleashing a Chariot of Dramatic Fire, *The Sunday Independent* 24 July, 2005.
24 According to 2006 census in Ireland, there were 414,412 non-Irish nationals living in Ireland. http://www.cso.ie/census/documents/vol4_t36_40.pdf This included a total of 11, 161 Chinese people, an increase of ninety-one percent on the figure recorded in 2002.

25 Pan Pan Theatre was founded by Gavin Quinn and Aedin Cosgrove in 1991. Their productions, which include *Macbeth 7* (2004), *Oedipus Loves You* (2006) and *Playing the Dane: The Rehearsal* (2010), are typified by postmodern practices that include textual deconstruction and multimedia performance.
26 'The philosopher Confucius said there are five core relationships that maintain social order, and one is that between father and son'. Clifford Coonan. 'Synge's greatest play transfers well to modern China', *The Irish Times*, 21 March 2006: 13.
27 Notably, all references to Christy as a Muslim were taken out before the Chinese production and re-inserted for the production's tour to Dublin; references to Islam were thought to be too controversial for a Chinese audience. Gavin Quinn. Interview with Sara Keating, September 2007.
28 See Gary Meneely, 'Peking at Your Knickers', *The Sun*, 24 March, 2006: 7; and Helen Bruce, 'The Actress' Skirt is Too Short Call the Police', *The Daily Mail*, 24 March, 2006: 23 for particularly entertaining accounts of the censor's interventions.
29 Patrick Lonergan. 'Review of *The Playboy of the Western World*', *Irish Theatre Magazine*, Vol. 7. no 30, Spring 2007: 94.
30 Gavin Quinn. Interview with Sara Keating, September 2007.
31 Karen Fricker. 'Review', *The Guardian*. 18 December 2006.
32 Brian Friel, Translations in *Plays One* (London: Faber and Faber, 1996): 419

14 | RE-WRITING SYNGE'S *PLAYBOY* – CHRISTY'S METAMORPHOSIS, A HUNDRED YEARS ON

Bisi Adigun

'Oh my grief, I've lost him surely. I've lost the only playboy of the western world', goes the last line as uttered by Pegeen Mike, played by Molly Allgood in J.M. Synge's original *The Playboy of the Western World*.[1] The play was first produced on the Abbey stage in 1907. A hundred years on, the same line has been modernized.[2] It is now simply: 'Fuck off!' I can still hear it rendered as only Eileen Walsh can. Pin-drop silence; lights went down gradually. It is blackout. Or is it that I have blacked out? No! Wait! The stage lights are coming up again; so is the audience. The few seconds it took for the stage lights to be brought back up for the curtain call was long enough for all in the audience to rise on their feet in unison and applaud thunderously. What a sight! What a night! It was simply marvellous to behold. The production, as writer/director Terry Mc Mahon would later write, 'had people laughing so much that there has been one, as yet unconfirmed, report that an Irish member of the audience was so overwhelmed by the insidious merriment, they unintentionally urinated on one of the Abbey's sacred theatre seats'. And in the words of Emer O'Kelly, 'The only riot at the opening of the new version of *The Playboy of the Western World* was riotous laughter'.[3]

Each time I cast my mind back to that night, the saying that always springs to mind is: *que sera, sera*. Why? Because that was the night that my long-held vision turned into reality. The vision that I had in 2004 was to have a modern version of *The Playboy*, in which the iconic Irish character of Christy Mahon is a Nigerian refugee, staged on the Abbey stage to coincide with the centenary of the original production. In this article, I retrace my steps to how it all began: how the journey of the modern version of *The Playboy*, which my company Arambe Productions commissioned Irish award-winning author Roddy Doyle and me to co-write, ended up on the Abbey stage. It is apt for me to begin at the beginning because the journey of a hundred years begins with a step.

I am originally from Nigeria where I lived before I travelled in 1993 to the UK. In the UK, I quickly established myself as a performing artist and a workshop facilitator. I came to Ireland in 1996 with the sole plan of spending a few months in the country in order to regularize my stay and return to the UK. But when man plans, God laughs. In 1997, I enrolled for a Master's degree in Drama Studies at University College Dublin and Eric Weitz was then one of my lecturers. It was Weitz who asked me some time in 2003 to contribute to his book of essays titled *The Power of Laughter*. He suggested that I provide an outsider's view of the Irish comedies that I had seen since I arrived in Ireland. The productions which I had seen that I decided to discuss in the essay were Tom Murphy's *Bailegangaire* (1985), Martin McDonagh's *The Beauty Queen of Leenane* (1996), Jim O'Hanlon's *The Buddhist of Castleknock* (2003), Marie Jones's *A Night in November* (1994), and *The Playboy of the Western World*.

Although I first came across *The Playboy* as a drama undergraduate student of Obafemi Awolowo University, Ile Ife in Nigeria in the late 1980s, the first time I ever saw a production of it was in 1998 in St Patrick's College, Dublin. It was this production that I wrote about in the essay. In the essay, which I titled 'An Irish joke, A Nigerian Laughter', I discuss how I taught myself how to laugh at Irish jokes. The premise of my essay is based on the notion that although tragedy is universal, comedy is culture-specific. In other words, to get a people's joke, one needs to be familiar with the cultural context of the joke. And by extension, it is important to be able to understand a people's joke in order to find their comedy funny. I did not find that particular production of *The Playboy* funny at all. I therefore decided to read the play to see if it was funnier on page than stage.

It was when I was reading the text of *The Playboy* that the idea of a modern version of the play with a Nigerian Christy Mahon struck me. It occurred to me that Synge's Christy is the archetypal 'asylum seeker'. It is exactly what Christy Mahon does in Synge's masterpiece that asylum seekers must do to be allowed to stay in Ireland. Like Christy, an asylum seeker must have a story to back up his/her refugee application. It does not matter whether the story is true or not, but it must be compellingly convincing. I see Christy Mahon as the epitome of the majority of immigrants constantly searching for who they are in a foreign land. As I have written in my essay, 'for any immigrant to fit into a new environment ... a lot of reinvention is necessary as Christy Mahon has demonstrated'. It is for this reason that I see *The Playboy* 'as more of a prophesy than a comedy'.[4]

Art's relationship with reality is intrinsically symbiotic. Reality inspires art and art in turn influences reality. From the early 1990s, Ireland began to experience an economic boom and this made it more attractive to people from various parts of the world. Within a decade, Ireland changed from an ostensibly homogenous society to a culturally diverse society. It did not come as a surprise that from the late 1990s, Irish theatre became increasingly preoccupied with Ireland's changing cultural landscape. Multiculturalism became the buzzword with a specific focus on cultural diversity and racialism. It became a trend among Irish dramatists and theatre companies to write and produce plays that required the 'other', best amplified by black actors. Some productions that had come to pass or were in the making around the time I was writing the essay were Donal O'Kelly's *Asylum! Asylum!* (Peacock, 1994), Beckett's *Catastrophe* (Tall Tales 1999); Donal O'Kelly's *Farawayan* (Calypso, 1998); Bernard-Marie Koltes's *Quay West* (Bedrock, 1997); Eithne McGuinness's *Limbo* (Queen of Sheba Productions, 2000); Ken Harmon's *Done Up like A Kipper* (Peacock, 2001); Jim O'Hanlon's *The Buddhist of Castleknock* (Fishamble 2002); Charlie O'Neil's *Hurl* (Barrabas, 2003); Athol Fugard's *My Children My Africa* (Galloglass, 2003); and Maeve Ingoldsby's *Mixing it on the Mountain* (Calypso Productions, 2003).

Without any doubt, these productions were well-meant contributions to the emergent discourse of new 'multicultural' Ireland, in the sense that they required black and Irish actors to work together creatively. Therefore, they provided the much needed platform to encourage intercultural exchange. I was in a few of them. However, it is often the case that most, if not all, the black characters in these plays lack agency. More often than not, they are asylum seekers or outsiders who must leave at the end for the Irish to live. So you would often see these characters come on stage with gusto and hope at the beginning, but by the end they disintegrate into oblivion. And this is probably why Patrick Lonergan remarks that:

> The problem of racism is rarely analysed or treated with any complexity on the Irish stage – instead, it's usually just a lever in a melodramatic plot. The genuinely racist are punished, the ignorant learn a lesson, and order is restored.5

Naturally, as time went on I began to get nervous whenever I went to see an Irish drama that had a black character in it. I began to see an ugly pattern of consistently presenting the 'other', especially black characters, as helpless victims at the mercy of the kind-hearted Irish. Then I recalled the advice an aunt proffered when I informed her in 1986 that I had secured a university place to study drama. 'Don't play the part of a slave', she advised. 'If they ask you to do a play, and there is a part for a king or a rich man, play that,' she concluded with a wink. It was that golden advice, among other things, that inspired me to begin to think of setting up a theatre company in 2003. It was obvious that there was a dearth of Irish plays with roles for a king or a rich person who is black. In obedience to my aunt's advice I felt compelled to create plays which would give black actors like myself the opportunity to play roles that are not only challenging but also influential. In my view, Christy Mahon is singularly the quintessence of that challenging and influential role. But can it be played by a black actor? That is the question.

Due to time and space constraints, I am not able to go into the details of all the aims and objectives of Arambe here.6 Suffice it to say however that it was born out of the need to create an avenue through which African immigrants can express themselves through art. And I felt this can be achieved by producing African plays as well as reinterpreting relevant plays in the Irish canon. *The Playboy* was on the agenda at the very first meeting of the board of Arambe, which was held in 2004. But prior to holding that meeting, I knew that it was inevitable that my vision of a modern version of *The Playboy* would be a reality by 2007. I recall that I actually contacted the Abbey Theatre for the first time in August 2004 to set up a meeting with Ali Curran, the then Director of the Peacock, to discuss my idea of the modern version of *The Playboy*. I told her that I would like to stage it at the Abbey. When I did not get an appointment I contacted the Abbey again by email correspondence in January 2005, saying:

> Come 2007, there will be a contemporarized production of *Playboy* to celebrate the centenary of the first production of this Irish masterpiece. As impossible or rather unimaginable as it may seem, my wish is to see this production on the national stage.

In fact, with the benefit of hindsight now I could be accused of being obsessed with my idea of modernizing *The Playboy*, because every opportunity to publicly express my opinion about Irish theatre that presented itself then was employed to convince myself that the mission of creating a modern version of Synge's classic must be accomplished. A few examples of such opportunities will be useful here.

I did an interview with *Sunday Tribune* journalist Rachel Andrews towards the end of 2003 and it was headlined 'All the World's A stage: A Black Actor Playing Pegeen? Having talked to Bisi Adigun, why not?'[7] Then in the summer 2004 issue of *Irish Theatre Magazine* I was asked to write how I envisaged Irish theatre in the next 100 years. In the article, entitled 'Living Colour', I said that I believed Ireland was changing fast and the country was ready for a Nigerian play on the Abbey Stage. To conclude I raised the question: 'So what will you say if I tell you I am looking forward to a production of *The Playboy of the Western World* with Nigerian actor Kunle Animashaun as Christy Mahon?'[8] Also in the *Sunday Tribune* edition of 19 September 2004, I was asked, among many others working in the theatre industry, to suggest who would be ideal to be appointed the Artistic Director of the Abbey Theatre to replace the then outgoing Ben Barnes. In my contribution to the piece entitled 'A Terrible Beauty: What Now for the Abbey' I named Jimmy Fay as an ideal choice to head the Abbey because he had been multicultural before it became a fad. I concluded: 'What I would love is for the Abbey to commission Arambe to produce a version of *The Playboy of the Western World*'.[9]

So I actually did talk the talk about the idea of a modern version of *The Playboy* for over two years before the time finally came, at the beginning of 2005, to walk the walk. Heeding the suggestion of Rupert Murray, a founding board member of Arambe who passed away in 2006, I contacted Irish writer Roddy Doyle to ask if he would be happy to co-write the play with me. In fact it was the same Rupert Murray who had, in 2004, informed me at a Board meeting of Arambe that the centenary of *The Playboy* at the Abbey was coming up in 2007: hence my initial contact with the Abbey and my subsequent determination to dedicate the premiere production of the modern version to Rupert Murray.

The idea of co-writing the modern version of *The Playboy* with Roddy Doyle was an exciting one. I met Doyle for the first time in 2000 when I was invited to take part in a week-long workshop organized by Calypso Productions to see if Doyle's series of short stories with the title 'Guess Who's Coming to Dinner' published in *Metro Eireann*, could be turned into a stage play. Since then I had stayed in touch with him. I would later interview him for an episode of *Mono*, the RTE intercultural flagship television magazine programme that I co-presented between 2000 and 2003. When I launched Arambe, he was the Chief Launcher on the night. Because Mr Doyle was already acquainted with my work, it was not too difficult for me to convince him, by showing him my essay, to embark on a creative journey of modernizing *The Playboy* with me.

As soon as Doyle agreed to come on board, my next stop was the Arts Council. On behalf of Arambe Productions, I applied to the Arts Council for a commission grant of €10,000. The short summary of the proposal in the application is worth quoting here:

> Arambe proposes to commission its Artistic Director, Nigerian Dramatist Bisi Adigun and acclaimed Irish Writer Roddy Doyle to jointly create a new work by adapting John Millington Synge's comic masterpiece *The Playboy of the Western World*.
>
> Designed to commemorate, and to coincide with, the centenary of the first production of *The Playboy* at the Abbey Theatre on 27 January 1907, this proposed adaptation is intended to, in the context of the recent phenomenon of refugee-seeking in Ireland, explore the original play's theme of identity construction through narratives of self-invention.
>
> By reworking Christy Mahon's role, the crucial power of storytelling, in a situation where acceptance is dependent on narrative credibility, will be demonstrated. While reception of the stranger demands a clear differentiation between truth and fiction, the central insight to be developed is how the relations between a refugee and a host community could hinge upon conflicting interpretation of heroism and victimhood.
>
> The adaptation will also reflect how notions of virtue and decorum have changed so dramatically in Ireland since the

Playboy riots of 1907, so that the spectacle of females standing in their shifts – deemed scandalous a century ago – has now become an accepted feature of our urban shopscape.

I have taken the liberty of reproducing excerpts from this application for two main reasons. Firstly I believe it helped Arambe, in no small way, to articulate to the Arts Council why the idea of a modern version of *The Playboy* deserved to be funded. Arambe got an offer of €10,000, without which the company would not have been in a position to commission the work. Secondly and perhaps more pertinently, it served as my manifesto when I was writing the modern adaptation of *The Playboy* with Mr Doyle.

In fact I recall that before we started writing on Monday, 16 January 2006, Mr Doyle was really concerned about how we were going to end our adaptation in such a way that it would be comparable to the famous ending in the original. Based on my view, as I have articulated it in the summary quoted above, that 'the sense of decorum and decency have changed so dramatically in Ireland since a riot broke out at the mention of females standing in their shifts' when the original *The Playboy* was first staged, I said to Mr Doyle that if our Pegeen ends the play with 'fuck off', it shall suffice. I was not wrong.

That was how we got the end of our new version out of the way. So in a way, we actually began the process from the end. It was like being asked to solve a mathematical equation after being presented with the solution. With the words 'fuck off', it was not too difficult to come up with the appropriate ending for our adaptation. The challenge then was how to justify this ending. In other words, we knew exactly where we were going, but were not sure how to get there. But for me that was not the only challenge. Since our Christopher is meant to be a Yoruba from western Nigeria and he has to 'kill' his dad in Nigeria before fleeing, we had to come up not only with a good reason why any Yoruba person would kill his dad but also the appropriate weapon with which the deed is done. I prayed to God for inspiration.

One night, less than two weeks after we started writing, I was reading Nigerian news online when I came across a very interesting story in the Nigerian *Punch* of 23 January 2006. It was manna from heaven. With the headline 'Son Kills mother with Pestle' the article written by one Emmanuel Obe tells the story of how somewhere in a suburb of Benin in the south-east of Nigeria, a man allegedly beat his 65 year-old mother to death with a pestle. The second paragraph of the article reads:

> Trouble between mother and child was allegedly ignited by the refusal of the deceased to let her son sell off a piece of the family land and travel abroad with the proceeds from the sale.

I could not believe it! Who says prayers are never answered? Could I have come across such a story at a better time? But as I have said already, reality and art are symbiotically linked. In a less than one-hundred-word newspaper article about a real life story, the reason why our fictional Christopher will kill his dad and the weapon he will use is presented to me on a platter of gold. And, to cap it all, pestle sounds like pistol. My God is good! That was how the headache of the motive for Christopher's patricide and the murder weapon was solved. And so we began to write; word-by-word, phrase by phrase and scene by scene until we completed a first draft in June 2006. After the reading of the first draft which was facilitated by the Abbey Theatre, Mr Doyle and I went back to work on the second draft of our modern version, which upon completion at the end of October 2006, was promptly submitted to the Abbey with the hope that the national theatre would produce its premiere in January 2007.

It was not until shortly before Christmas of 2006 that Arambe got the news that the Abbey had decided not to produce the play. However they changed their mind about four months later. And the rest, as they say, is history. In my humble view, the process of writing the modern version of *The Playboy* is perhaps one of the only genuinely intercultural creative collaborations in the world. In my view it is akin to the process of conceiving a life. In an article published in the *The Irish Times* weekend magazine, I said that, like Barack Obama, the modern *Playboy* is an epitome of the 'wow theory'.[10] I shall cherish the experience of co-writing the play for the rest of my living days.

If co-writing the modern version of *The Playboy* in 2006 genuinely epitomized the beauty of interculturality, you can imagine my joy when the Abbey Theatre finally agreed to produce its premiere in 2007. The opening night was one of the most joyous moments of my life. But 'Joy has a slender body that breaks too soon' as Ola Rotimi has said in his play *The Gods Are Not To Blame*. 'There is trouble now in the land. Joy has broken and scattered. Peace too is no more'.[11] If someone had told me that Ireland is a place where a dramatist's carefully constructed castle of words (to borrow Ulick O'Connor's phrase) could be commandeered, occupied, poked at and deconstructed the moment his back is turned, I would have said: 'You're joking me'. However that is what has happened to the modern version of *The Playboy,* which I have paraded proudly as the epitome of interculturalism at its best.

But this is neither the time nor the space to go into the trauma and hardship which the huge success of the modern version of *The Playboy* has caused me. It is a story for another day: a chapter in another book. What is important for me here is to retrace all the steps that I took before I was able to accomplish the mission of creating a platform, at the Abbey, for Synge's iconic Irish Christy to metamorphose into a Nigerian Christopher Malomo a hundred years on. Now a black character can come on stage tired and timid and leave at the end bold and brave. This might be a small step for me; it is a giant leap for black actors and Africans living in Ireland. For 'While fiction', as Ellison has pointed out, 'is a form of symbolic action, a mere game of "as if"', therein lies its true function and its potential for effecting change.'[12]

---

[1] J.M. Synge, *The Playboy of the Western World* in *Collected Works, Volume IV: Plays 2.* Edited by Ann Saddlemyer (Gerrards Cross: Colin Smythe, 1982): 173.

[2] The original production of *The Playboy of the Western World* premiered on 27 January 1907. Bisi Adigun and Roddy Doyle's version of the play premiered at the Abbey Theatre in October 2007. The part of Pegeen was played by Eileen Walsh.

[3] Terry McMahon, 'Arambe Theatre Company'. http://www.terrymcmahon.org/TERRY_MCMAHON_Miscellaneous_Wr/TERRY_MCMAHON__Arambe_Producti/ARAMBE_PRODUCTIONS.doc and Emer O'Kelly, Review of *The Playboy of the Western World, Sunday Independent,* 7 October 2007.

[4] Bisi Adigun, 'An Irish Joke; A Nigerian Laughter' in Eric Weitz (ed.) *The Power of Laughter* (Dublin: Carysfort Press, 2003) (76-86): 82

[5] Patrick Lonergan, Review of *The Cambria, Irish Theatre Magazine,* 5/23: 63

[6] More information about the company may be found at http://www.arambeproductions.com/

[7] Rachel Andrews, 'All the World's A Stage', *Sunday Tribune,* September 2003.

[8] Bisi Adigun, 'In Living Colour' *Irish Theatre Magazine,* 4/19: 31.

[9] Sunday Tribune, 'What Now for the Abbey?' *Sunday Tribune,* 19 September 2004.

[10] Bisi Adigun, 'Why + how = Wow' *Irish Times Magazine,* 1 November, 2008.

[11] Ola Rotimi, *The Gods Are Not to Blame* (Oxford: Oxford University Press, 1971): 8.
[12] Ralph Ellison in the Introduction to *Invisible Man*

AFTERWORD

Adrian Frazier

1

After creating the Synge School in 1990, and running it for ten summers in Rathdrum not far from the family home, Nicholas Grene, reasonably enough, wanted a break. His baby was well grown now, and ought to be able to walk on its own. It was then that he passed the child into my hands for the summer of 2001.

I had just relocated to Ireland, and was working at the National University of Ireland in Galway. I wasn't unfamiliar with the country. Wasn't I now married to an Irishwoman, and father of an Irish citizen? I could find my way to Wicklow, even to Rathdrum— with a map and extra time for wrong turns.

Still, the School survived its first year under my direction.

It took me two years to kill it off.

Well, not kill it off. There was life enough left for Tony Roche to revive it in 2005.

2

The lives of these little Irish summer schools are more touch and go than one might think. Even if a county council annual grant comes through, you need thirty students to pay for the full week, and attract ten day-trippers a day. The number of students coming may be affected by advertising, the fluctuating prices of transatlantic flights, the currency exchange rate, terrorism and rumours of terrorism (these heavily affect the US market), the willingness of current and former international speakers to bring along students, etc. The programme of speakers appears not to be that important; not many people know about even the most famous academics.

3

One of the great successes of the Synge School in its first decade was to build up a corps of students who came every year; about a dozen of them. A clutch of highly educated women came from Edinburgh; Nicholas Grene teasingly called them the 'Tartan Brigade'. They were great. One ebullient and eloquent member of the brigade (the name Helen comes back to me) was an expert on Irish actresses who had toured the 'provincial theatres', and she had seen many performances herself. She asked what I knew about the Allgood sisters. At the time, my knowledge began and ended with their names, but I have since become very interested in them (plug: I have a book coming out on the subject), and many times I wished I had asked Helen a lot of questions about Molly and Sara Allgood when I had the chance.

The Tartan Brigade were joined by a number of other literary adults, several of them by profession teachers, by pastime theatergoers. They had become great friends with one another through the Synge School, and with the stalwart members of the local committee, then led by Irene Parsons, Nicky Grene's neighbour up the hill.

After so many summers in Wicklow listening to talks on Synge, by 2002 a lecturer would have a hard time telling them something about the playwright that was worth knowing that they did not already know.

4

During the first week of the School under my direction, there was a fine line-up of scholars.

W.J. ('Bill') McCormack, the Synge biographer and a Wicklow Protestant himself, was one of them. His friends Deirdre Toomey and Warwick Gould of London were others; they are the husband-and-wife editors of the *Yeats Annual*. Bill McCormack gave a talk on 'The Silence of Barbara Synge'. She was someone somewhere in the

Synge family tree around about the end of the eighteenth century, and it appears that she utterly disappeared from the historical record not long into her adulthood. That was the silence in the title of the talk. Bill was brilliant. And incomprehensible. You should have heard the silence of the Tartan Brigade.

The next afternoon, Bill, Deirdre, and I all got in a barney about some point Warwick Gould was making about the textual history of Yeats's edition of Synge's poems. We went at it hammer and tongs. We were having the greatest time.

Afterwards, Helen of Edinburgh took me by the elbow, and reminded me, as director of the school, I ought not to forget the existence of the actual students of the school. We had been talking, she pointed out, only to one another. Fair point.

5

It is a feature of the Synge School to have a poetry reading. Actually, that year we had two, as Bill McCormack one afternoon along the trip up the glen (*Shadow of the* ...) morphed into 'Hugh Maxton', and recited his Swiftian verses.

The evening event was Tom Mac Intyre, playwright, fiction writer, and that night's poet. In a hotel in the vale of Avoca, below the 'meeting of the waters', we all gathered. Tom got on a jag about the power of the Muse. He was reading a selection of poems about his encounters with the tooth-mother. Synge once wrote an article (discussed by Mary Burke in this volume) entitled 'Can We Go Back Into Our Mother's Womb?' Alas, we can, and with Tom we did. It was scary to do so. Time slowed down; stopped.

Irene Parsons caught my eye at one point. I must have been glancing around nervously. She did not have to mouth her words like that; I could already see what she meant. 'Can you not make him stop?' But there was no stopping him. He was in his element.

Liz Tottenham – a member of the committee in whom resides the wisdom of old stock (after all, she has spent her life planting trees) – I looked to for comfort. There I found understanding, complete understanding in a glance, but not really comfort. Socially, it was not good.

Sometimes it is doubted if audiences can still be shocked as Synge once shocked them. Aren't we all now so modern and jaded? Well, they can be, and that night they were.

6

In spite of my own unsteadiness as the director of an Irish summer school, there were a great set of lectures that summer. Particularly memorable were Lucy McDiarmid's 'Secular Relics: the boat, the dinnerplate, the bones, & other remnants of a life' (what a title!), and James Pethica's 'Synge's Ghost', about the various séances in the course of which Yeats tried (and sometimes succeeded) in evoking his dead friend.

7

Still, as good as the talks were, I was aware that as director of 'the School', I had to do better the next year. And look at it yourself in the list of talks published in this volume – the line-up for the coming year was unbeatable: Roy Foster, Ben Levitas, Garry Hynes, Declan Kiberd, Nicholas Grene, Lucy McDiarmid, Riana O'Dwyer, Paul Mercier (he was great on the day). Myself! How can you beat that?

In the meantime, Notre Dame University had set up a summer school under the direction of Seamus Deane, who was nearly as famous then as the 'Famous Seamus'. It was held at Newman House, on Stephen's Green. Particularly targeted at our American friends, it offered course credits, the virtual equivalent of large amounts of cash in the USA. At the Synge School we had seminars for students (taught by Ben Levitas and myself that year, I think), but they weren't academic courses with attendance taken, papers written, grades given, etc. That was not the summer school as understood hitherto in Ireland. Notre Dame was bullying its way into a rather internationally naïve subculture, or so I jealously conceived the situation.

Furthermore, Nine Eleven of historical fame occurred in 2001, and Americans had become nervous about foreign travel. Flying to a summer school in Ireland had become a risk in their minds.

Finally, *The Irish Times* helpfully publishes an annual guide to Irish summer schools. As our early numbers of applications were running low, I was hoping for more than the usual small number of Irish participants. So I furnished the paper with ample information about our brilliant list of speakers. But when the relevant issue came out, while it included twenty-five or thirty summer schools and their highlights, there was, incredibly, nothing about the Synge School.

I inquired. A mere accident. No malice.

Come the end of June when the summer school opened, we had between twenty and twenty-five paid up students. Not as many county councillors showed up. We were not far below the historical average, but it had always been a close-run affair.

8

Ben Barnes kicked off the summer school in late June 2002 and the new Minister of the Arts, John O'Donoghue of Kerry, was there to shed his blessings. The lectures in that summer were as good as anyone could have hoped. And those present heard John McGahern read from *That They May Face the Rising Sun*. Alone, worth the price of the week. On top of that, there was a long interview with Garry Hynes about her plans for the forthcoming *DruidSynge*. That was great. For those that were there.

I had another programme set up for the summer of 2003 when it was decided that really the running of the Synge School was too nip-and-tuck; the stress was overwhelming. Rather than a plus for the community, it had become a drain.

And truly it is hard on the local committee to keep a summer school going. They carry the load.

So it is wonderful to see so many of the original committee came together again under Tony Roche and still serve under Patrick Lonergan. The old-timers include Nicky Kirwan, Enda Fitzpatrick, Michael Brennan, and Elizabeth Tottenham. It is a tribute to them that in spite of its directors, or I should say, and must in honesty say, this one particular director, that the Synge School still thrives.

THE SYNGE SUMMER SCHOOL, 2001-2010

Directors: Adrian Frazier (2001-2), Anthony Roche (2005-2007), Patrick Lonergan (2008-2010). The School did not take place in 2003 and 2004.

Biography and Irish Drama

1-7 July 2001

James Pethica, 'Synge's Ghost: Yeats, Lady Gregory and the 1914 Detroit Seance'
Fintan O'Toole, 'Alternative Lives: Reality and Imagination in Irish Theatre'
Deirdre Toomey, 'A Young Man's Ghost'
W.J. McCormack, 'The Silence of Barbara Synge'
Warwick Gould, 'Synge's Textual Self'
Lionel Pilkington, 'Synge and the Politics of Irish Unionism'
Lucy McDiarmid, 'Secular Relics: the Boat, the Dinnerplate, the Bones and other Remnants of a life'
Adrian Frazier, 'Literature as Life: Synge in his Plays'
Ann Saddlemyer, 'Unlikely Successors: Ezra Pound and Georgie Hyde Lees'
Guest speaker: Sebastian Barry
Performance: *Bat the Father Rabbit the Son* by Donal O'Kelly
Readings by Hugh Maxton and Tom Mac Intyre

Plays and Controversies

30 June – 6 July 2002

Roy Foster, 'Ten Years of Purgatory'
Lucy McDiarmid, 'Anger, Apologies, Statues: the form of Cultural Controversy'
Ben Levitas, 'Staging a Riot: Synge and the *Playboy* controversy'

Riana O'Dwyer, 'Whistling in the dark: responses to the early plays of Tom Murphy'
Paul Mercier, 'Thoughts of a Director in the Thick of Production'
Karen Fricker, 'No More Riots? The Possibility of Controversy in Twenty-First Century Irish Theatre'
Adrian Frazier, *The Shadow of the Glen* and the Three Kinds of Ignorance'
Declan Kiberd, 'Crossing the Border: McGuinness and the Sons of Ulster'
Nicholas Grene, 'Reality Check: Authenticity from Synge to McDonagh'
Garry Hynes, 'Staging Synge'
Reading: John McGahern

101 Years of Irish Theatre

26 June – 2 July 2005

Anthony Roche, 'Postcolonial *Playboy*'
Anne Fogarty, 'Tragedy and Feminism in Lady Gregory's History Plays'
Nicholas Grene, 'Place in Irish Drama'
Adrian Frazier, 'Hollywood Irish: Abbey Actors in the Movies'
Declan Kiberd, 'Different Deirdres'
Mary C. King, 'Intimates and Others: Identity and Community in the drama of Synge, McDonagh and Carr'
Robert Tracy, 'Brian Friel's Rituals of Memory'
Paul Murphy, 'Woman As Fantasy Object in Synge's *When the Moon has Set*'
Melissa Sihra, 'Transformative Moments of Being and Becoming in the Theatre of Marina Carr'
Readings by Marina Carr and Brendan Kennelly

Synge and His Influences

2-8 July 2006

Anthony Roche, 'Synge and His Influence: Beckett, Friel, McDonagh'
Stephen Watt, 'Synge and Melodrama: The Nature of the "Syngean"'
Thomas Kilroy, 'Synge in Our Time'
Riana O'Dwyer, 'Tom Murphy with Synge in the Western World'
Mary Luckhurst, 'Negotiating Tactics: Irish Drama in England'
Ronan McDonald, 'Synge and Darwin'
P.J. Mathews, 'Synge and Parnell'
Christopher Murray, 'Western World or Eastern World: Who Owns Synge's Plays Today?'
Christina Hunt Mahony, 'Lyrics for Saints and Sinners: Language in the Plays of Synge and Sebastian Barry'
Reading: Seamus Heaney

Synge and his Contexts

1-7 July 2007

Anthony Roche, 'Synge's *Playboy*: The Oral and the Written'
Fiona McIntosh, 'The Abbey and the Court: Yeats, Synge and the Greek Theatre of Gilbert Murray'
Harry White, 'Synge and Music'
Anna McMullan, 'Protean Bodies in Beckett and Synge'
Ann Saddlemyer, 'The Poeticizing of Synge'
Richard Pine, 'Well, Well, Well: Synge, Yeats and Friel'
Eilís Ní Dhuibhne, 'Synge and Folklore'
Ben Levitas, 'Synge and Meta-Theatre'
Patrick Lonergan,'"Mirror(s) Up to Nature": Druid Theatre's Productions of Synge, McDonagh and Keane'
Panel discussion with Ann Saddlemyer and Garry Hynes
Opening address: Fiach Mac Conghail
Reading by Eavan Boland

'Irish Theatre and the World Stage'

29 June – 5 July 2008

John P. Harrington, 'Synge, Irish Theatre, and the New York Stage'
Emilie Pine, 'The Backward Look: Ghosts and Memories in Marina Carr and Conor McPherson'.
Ondřej Pilny, 'Translating Synge'
Ros Dixon, '"Oh Chekhov! Thou Art Translated": Brian Friel's Three Sisters'
Nicholas Grene, 'Is Beckett an Irish Playwright?'
Shaun Richards, 'Synge and the European Avant-Garde'
Mark Phelan, 'Performing History – Stewart Parker'
Melissa Sihra, 'Irish Theatre and World Stages – Reflections on Recent Developments'
Patrick Lonergan, 'Internationalising Irish Drama: Sheridan, Synge, McPherson'
Bisi Adigun, ' Re-writing Synge's Playboy – Christy's Metamorphosis, A Hundred Years On' followed
Opening Address by Lynne Parker
Reading by Sebastian Barry

'Irish Drama: 100 Years After Synge'

28 June – 3 July 2009

Melissa Sihra, 'The Eye of the Dream: Marina Carr's *Marble*'
Patrick Lonergan, 'The Ethics of Irish Storytelling – Synge and Tom Murphy, Beckett and Martin McDonagh'

Lionel Pilkington, 'Synge and Ireland's Performance Culture'
Mary Burke, 'After Synge: 100 years of the "stage tinker"'
Aoife Monks, 'Kiss Me, I'm Irish: Performing Gender in St Patrick's Day parades and Irish Dance Shows'
Alexandra Poulain, 'Synge and Tom Murphy'
Karen Fricker, 'Irish Theatre Criticism Today '
Paige Reynolds, 'Synge's Things: Material Culture in Modern and Contemporary Irish Drama'
PJ Mathews, 'Re-Thinking Synge'
Irish Writers in Conversation: Christina Reid, Billy Roche
Irish Practitioners in Conversation: Colin Dunne
Reading by Joseph O'Connor
Opening Address by Nicholas Grene

'Re-Imagining Irish Drama'

1-4 July 2010
Anne Fogarty, '"I met a fool i' the forest"': James Joyce and the Legacy of Synge'
Shaun Richards, 'Space as Form and Theme in Irish Drama'
Christopher Murray, 'The Outsider and the Pastoral in Irish Drama from Synge to Barry'
Sara Keating, 'Evolving *Playboys* for the Global World' – Recent Productions of *The Playboy of the Western World*'
Graham Saunders, 'The Beckettian World of Sarah Kane'
Mark Phelan, 'Fair Play Synge'
Patrick Lonergan, '"The Chap That Writes Like Synge" – Shakespeare and the Irish Theatre'
Lisa Fitzpatrick, 'Women Writing Violence: Rape, Murder and Mayhem on the Contemporary Irish Stage'
Reading by Patrick McCabe
Public Address by Bernard Farrell

TEXTS CITED

Adigun, Bisi, 'In Living Colour', *Irish Theatre Magazine*, Volume 4, Number 19: 31.
--- 'Why + how = Wow' *The Irish Times Magazine*, 1 November, 2008.
American Railroad Journal, 'Dreadful Affray and Wholesale Slaughter in Kerry', *American Railroad Journal and Advocate of Internal Improvements*, 9 August 1834: 491.
Andrews, J.H., *A Paper Landscape: The Ordnance Survey in Nineteenth-Century Ireland* (Dublin: Four Courts Press, 2002).
Andrews, Rachel, 'All the World's A Stage', *Sunday Tribune*, September 2003.
Apter, David E., *The Political Kingdom in Uganda: A Study in Bureaucratic Nationalism* (London: Routledge, 1997).
Archer, William, *About the Theatre: Essays and Studies* (London: Fisher Unwin, 1886).
Arnold, Bruce, *Jack Yeats* (New Haven: Yale University Press, 1998).
Barnard, Toby, *A Guide to Sources for the History of Material Culture in Ireland, 1500-2000* (Dublin: Four Courts Press, 2005).
--- *Making the Grand Figure: Lives and Possessions in Ireland, 1641-1770* (New Haven, CT: Yale UP, 2004).
Beckett, Samuel, *The Complete Dramatic Works* (London: Faber and Faber, 1990).
Beer, Gillian, 'Darwin and the Uses of Extinction', *Victorian Studies* 51: 2 (2009): 321-31.
Bertha, Csilla and Donald E. Morse (eds), *More Real Than Reality: The Fantastic in Irish Literature and the Arts* (New York; London: Greenwood Press, 1991).
Billington, Michael, 'Synge for your Supper', *The Guardian*, 19 July 2005.
--- Review of *There Came a Gypsy Riding*, *The Guardian*, 19 January 2007.
Birmingham, George, *The Lighter Side of Irish Life* (London and Edinburgh: T.N. Foulis, 1914).

Blake-Knox, Kirsty, '"The Coat That Fitted": A Comparative Study of John Millington Synge's *The Playboy of the Western World* and Mustapha Matura's *The Playboy of the West Indies*', Unpublished dissertation, School of Drama, Film and Music, Trinity College, Dublin, 2007.

Boland, Eavan, *Outside History* (Manchester: Carcanet, 1990).

Bourgeois, Maurice, *John Millington Synge and the Irish Theatre* (Constable and Co.: London, 1913).

Brenneman Jr, Walter L. and Mary G. Brenneman, *Crossing the Circle at the Holy Wells of Ireland* (University of Virginia Press, 1995).

Brown, Bill (ed.), *Things* (Chicago: University of Chicago Press, 2004).

Browne, Eamon, 'Faction Fighting in Kerry, Ballyeagh Strand 1834', *Kerry Archaeological and Historical Society Magazine* No. 9 (1998): 39-42.

Bruce, Helen, 'The Actress' Skirt is Too Short Call the Police', *The Daily Mail*, 24 March 2006: 23.

Burke, Mary, 'Evolutionary Theory and the Search for Lost Innocence in the Writings of J.M. Synge' in *The Canadian Journal of Irish Studies* 30: 1 (2004): 48-54.

--- *'Tinkers': Synge and the Cultural History of the Irish Traveller* (Oxford: Clarendon Press, 2009).

Caird, Donald, 'A View of the Revival of the Irish Language' *Éire-Ireland*, 25: 2 (1990): 96-108.

Cairns, David and Shaun Richards, 'Reading a Riot: the "Reading Formation" of Synge's Abbey Audience', *Literature and History* 13, no. 2 (Autumn 1987): 219 -37.

Campbell, J.F. *Popular Tales of the West Highlands* (London: Gardner, 1890).

Carleton, William, *Traits and Stories of the Irish Peasantry, vol. 1* (Dublin: William Curry Jun. and Co., 1843)

Carr, Marina, *Plays One* (London: Faber and Faber, 1999).

Cashman, Ray, *Storytelling on the Northern Irish Border, Character and Community* (Bloomington: Indiana University Press, 2009).

Censorship and Licensing (Joint Select Committee), *Verbatim Report of the Proceedings and a Full Text of the Recommendations* (London: The Stage, 1910).

Chauduri, Una, *Staging Place: The Geography of Modern Drama* (Ann Arbor: University of Michigan Press, 1995).

Christiansen, Reidar Th and Seán Ó Súilleabháin, *The Types of the Irish Folktale* (Dublin, 1966).

Clark, Samuel and James S. Donnelly Jr. *Irish Peasants: Violence and Political Unrest, 1780-1914* (Madison: University of Wisconsin Press, 1983).

Colum, Padraic, *The Road Round Ireland* (New York: Macmillan, 1926).

--- *Three Plays: The Fiddler's House, The Land, Thomas Muskerry* (Boston: Little, Brown and Co., 1916).

Conley, Carolyn A., *Melancholy Accidents: The Meaning of Violence in Post-Famine Ireland* (New York & Oxford: Lexington Books, 1999).
--- 'The Agreeable Recreation of Fighting', *Journal of Social History*, 33:1 (1999): 57-72.
Cook, David and Miles Lee (eds), *Short East African Plays* (London: Heinemann, 1968).
Coonan, Clifford, 'Synge's Greatest Play Transfers Well to Modern China', *The Irish Times*, 21 March 2006: 13.
Corkery, Daniel, *Synge and Anglo-Irish Literature* (Cork, 1931).
Coveney, Michael, 'Playboy Passion with an Emerald Hue', *The Daily Mail*, 12 February 2004: 54.
Crawley, Peter, 'Conflicts, Sacred Rites and Themes as Old as Time', *The Irish Times*, 5 April 2008: 7.
Crofton Croker, Thomas, *Researches in the South of Ireland: Illustrative of the Scenery, Architectural Remains, and the Manners and Superstitions of the Peasantry* (Dublin: John Murray, 1824).
Cronin, Michael, Luke Gibbons, Peadar Kirby (eds), *Reinventing Ireland: Culture and the Celtic Tiger* (London: Pluto Press, 2002).
Curtin, Jeremiah, *Tales of the Fairies and the Ghost World* (London, 1895).
Danaher, Kevin, *In Ireland Long Ago* (Cork: Mercier Press, 1964).
Dasenbrock, Reed Way, *Imitating the Italians* (Johns Hopkins University Press, 1991).
Davis, Alex and Ruth Connolly, 'J. M. Synge's "Vita Vecchia": An Autobiographical Palimpsest'. *The Long Room*, 50-51 (2005): 46-63.
Davis, Colin, *Haunted Subjects: Deconstruction, Psychoanalysis and the Return of the Dead* (Basingstoke and New York: Palgrave Macmillan, 2007).
Day, Angélique and Patrick McWilliams (eds), *Ordnance Survey Memoirs of Ireland* (Belfast: Institute of Irish Studies, 1990).
Dean, Joan Fitzpatrick, *Riot and Great Anger: Stage Censorship in Twentieth Century Ireland* (Madison: University of Wisconsin Press, 2004).
Deane, Seamus (ed.), *The Field Day Anthology of Irish Writing*. Three vols. (Derry: Field Day Publications, 1991).
--- *Celtic Revivals: Essays in Modern Irish Literature 1880-1980* (London: Faber and Faber, 1985).
Derrida, Jacques, *Given Time: 1. Counterfeit Money*, trans. Peggy Kamuf (Chicago: University of Chicago Press, 1992).
Dewar, Daniel, *Observations on the Character, Customs, and Superstitions of the Irish and on Some of the Causes which have Retarded the Moral and Political Improvement of Ireland* (London: Gale and Curtis, 1812).
Deyl, Rudolf, 'Za Karlem Muškem,' *Národní politika* 14 November 1924, 4.
--- *O čem vím já* (Prague: Melantrich, 1971).

Diderot, Denis, *Livres, Esthétique-Théâtre*, éd. L. Versini (Laffont: Bouquins, 1996).
Durrell, Lawrence, *Caesar's Vast Ghost* (London: Faber and Faber, 1990).
Eliot, T.S. *On Poetry and Poets* (London: Faber, 1957).
Engelmüller, Karel, review of *Studnice světců* and *Přesýpací hodiny*, *Zlatá Praha* (1921-1922): 16 November 1921, 387.
Evans, E. Estyn, *Irish Folk Ways* (Mineola, New York: Dover Publications Incorporated, 2000).
Eyler, Audrey S. and Robert F. Garratt (eds): *The Uses of the Past* (Newark: University of Delaware Press; London and Toronto: Associated University Presses).
Fischer, Otokar 'Večer zázraků,' *Národní listy* 8 November 1921.
Foster, John Wilson and Helena C.G. Chesney (eds), *Nature in Ireland: A Scientific and Cultural History* (Dublin: Lilliput, 1997).
Frazier, Adrian, *Behind the Scenes: Yeats, Horniman, and the Struggle for the Abbey Theatre* (Berkeley and Los Angeles: University of California Press, 1990).
--- (ed.), *Playboys of the Western World: Production Histories* (Dublin: Carysfort Press, 2004).
Freeman's Journal, 'Irish National Theatre, Synge's New Play', *Freeman's Journal*, 6 February 1905.
Freyer, Grattan, 'The Little World of J.M. Synge', *Politics and Letters* 1, no. 4 (1948): 50-52.
Fricker, Karen, 'Review. *The Playboy of the Western World*', *The Guardian*, 11 February 2004: 30.
Friel, Brian and Charles McGlinchy, *The Last of the Name* (Dublin: Collins, 2007).
Friel, Brian, *Essays, Diaries, Interviews: 1964-1999*. Edited by Christopher Murray (London: Faber and Faber, 1999)
--- *Hedda Gabler* (Oldcastle: The Gallery Press, 2008).
--- *Plays 1* (London: Faber and Faber, 1996).
--- *Plays 2* (London: Faber and Faber, 1999).
Frýzek, Jiří, Václav Alois Jung: *Život a dílo* (Rychnov nad Kněžnou: Městský úřad, 1997)
Gamble, John, *Sketches of History, Politics and Manners: Taken in Dublin and the North of Ireland in the Autumn of 1810* (London: C Cradock and W Joy, 1811).
Garrigan Mattar, Sinéad, *Primitivism, Science, and the Irish Revival* (Oxford: Clarendon Press, 2004).
Garvin, Tom, *Nationalist Revolutionaries in Ireland, 1858-1928* (Oxford: Clarendon Press, 1987).
Genet, Jacqueline and Richard Allen Cave (eds), *Perspectives on Irish Drama and Theatre* (Gerrards Cross: Colin Smythe, 1991).
Gibbons, Luke, *Transformation in Irish Culture* (Cork: Cork University Press, 1996).

Gonalez, Alexander G. (ed.), *Assessing the Achievement of J. M. Synge* (Westport.: Greenwood Press, 1996).
Gonne, Maud and W.B. Yeats, *The Gonne-Yeats Letters*. Edited by Anna MacBride White and A. Norman Jeffares (Syracuse: Syracuse University Press, 1994).
Greene, David H. and Edward M. Stephens, *J.M. Synge, 1871-1909* (New York: Collier Books, 1961).
Gregory, Lady Augusta, *Collected Plays 4: Translations, Adaptations and Collaborations* (Gerrards Cross: Colin Smythe, 1979).
--- *Seven Short Plays* (Dublin: Maunsel, 1911).
Grene, Nicholas, *Synge: A Critical Study of the Plays* (London: Macmillan, 1975).
--- 'Talking, Singing, Storytelling: Tom Murphy's *After Tragedy*'. *Colby Quarterly*, 27-4, 4 (December 1991): 204-217.
--- (ed.), *Interpreting Synge: Essays from the Synge Summer School 1991-2000* (Dublin: Lilliput Press, 2000).
Hannigan, K. and W. Nolan (eds), *Wicklow: History and Society* (Dublin: Geography Publications, 1994).
Harmon, Maurice (ed.), *J. M. Synge Centenary Papers* (Dublin: Dolmen Press, 1972).
Harrington, John P. (ed.), *Modern Irish Drama*. First edition (New York: Norton, 1991).
--- *The English Traveller in Ireland. Accounts of Ireland and the Irish Through Five Centuries* (Dublin: Wolfhound Press, 1991).
Harris, Susan Cannon, *Gender and Modern Irish Drama* (Bloomington: Indiana University Press, 2002).
Hart, Peter, *The I.R.A. and its Enemies: Violence and Community in Cork 1916-1923* (Oxford: Clarendon Press, 1998).
Heaney, Mick, 'Adapting to Harsh Realities', *The Sunday Times*, 20 January 2008: 4.
Heidegger, Martin, *Poetry, Language, Thought*, trans. Albert Hofstadter (New York: Harper Perennial, 2001).
Hladík, Václav review of J.M. Synge, *Ve stínu doliny*, trans. and dir. Karel Mušek, *Národní listy* 20 August 1907, 2.
Hogan, Robert and James Kilroy, *The Modern Irish Drama: A Documentary History, Volume 3, The Abbey Theatre: The Years of Synge 1905-1909* (Dublin: Dolmen Press, 1978).
--- *The Modern Irish Drama: A Documentary History Volume 2: Laying the Foundations 1902-1904* (Dublin: The Dolmen Press, 1976).
Holbek, Bengt, *Interpretation of Fairytales* (Helsinki, 1987).
Holloway, Joseph, *Joseph Holloway's Abbey Theatre: A Selection from his Unpublished Journal Impressions of A Dublin Playgoer*. Edited by Robert Hogan and Michael J. O'Neill (Carbondale: Southern Illinois University Press, 1967).
Houlihan, Michael, *Puck Fair. History and Traditions* (Limerick: The Treaty Press, 1999).

Hurley, John W., *Irish Gangs and Stick-Fighting in the Works of William Carleton* (Pipersville: The Caravat Press 2006).
Hurley, John W. *Shillelagh: The Irish Fighting Stick* (Pipersville: The Caravat Press, 2007)
Inglesby, Elizabeth 'Expressive Objects: Elizabeth Bowen's Narrative Materializes', *Modern Fiction Studies* 53:2 (Summer 2007): 306-333.
Irish Times, The, 'Fair Play in Lanesboro, but no Faction Fighting', 14 January 1999.
Jarry, Alfred, *Selected Works*. Edited by Roger Shattuck and Simon Watson Taylor (New York: Grove Press, 1965).
Jones, Greta, 'Contested Territories: Alfred Cort Haddon, Progressive Evolutionism and Ireland,' *History of European Ideas* 24.3 (1998).
Joyce, James, *Occasional, Critical and Political Writing*. Edited by Kevin Barry (Oxford: World's Classics, 2002).
Karel Mušek, 'V zapadlém kraji. Črty z Erina, ostrova hoře,' part 2, *Zvon* 7.24 (1907).
Keefe, Robert, 'Literati, Language, and Darwinism', *Language and Style* 19: 2 (1986): 123-38.
Kelleher, Margaret and Philip O'Leary (eds), *The Cambridge History of Irish Literature Volume II 1890-2000* (Cambridge: Cambridge University Press, 2006).
Kennedy, Dennis (ed.), *The Oxford Encyclopaedia of Theatre and Performance* (Oxford: Oxford University Press, 2003).
Kiberd, Declan, *Irish Classics* (London: Granta, 2000)
--- *Synge and the Irish language*. 2nd ed (London: Macmillan, 1993).
Kiely, David M. *John Millington Synge, A Biography* (Dublin: Gill and Macmillan, 1994).
King, Mary C. *The Drama of J. M. Synge* (Syracuse: Syracuse University Press, 1985).
Kinmonth, Claudia, *Irish Country Furniture, 1700-1950* (New Haven: Yale UP, 2003).
--- *Irish Rural Interiors in Art* (New Haven: Yale UP, 2006).
Knapp, James, 'Primitivism and Empire: John Synge and Paul Gauguin', *Comparative Literature* 41:1 (1989): 52-68.
Kvapil, Jaroslav, *O čem vím. 2. část* (Prague: Václav Tomsa, 1947).
Lavery, Brian, 'Irish Masterpiece Returning to its Bleak Home', *The New York Times*, 17 March 2004: 9
Levitas, Ben, *The Theatre of Nation: Irish Drama and Cultural Nationalism, 1890-1916* (Oxford: Oxford University Press, 2002);
Logan, Patrick, *Fair Day: The Story of Irish Fairs and Markets* (Belfast: Appletree Press, 1986).
Lonergan, Patrick 'Review of *The Cambria*' *Irish Theatre Magazine* Volume 5 , number 23: 63.
--- 'Druid and Synge' http://syngecycle.com/aboutdruidsynge/druid-theatre-and-john-millington-synge

--- *Theatre and Globalization: Irish Drama in the Celtic Tiger Era*, (Basingstoke and New York: Palgrave Macmillan, 2009).
--- 'Review of *The Playboy of the Western World*', *Irish Theatre Magazine*, Volume 7, number 30, Spring 2007: 94.
Lyons, F.S.L., *Ireland Since the Famine* (London: Fontana, 1973).
Lyons, Patrick, 'Miscellanea', *Béaloideas* Vol. 13, No. 1/2 (1943).
Macpherson, Margaret, 'What Happened to Majangwa?' *Mawazo*, vol. 4, No. 4, 1969.
Mannoni, Octave, *Prospero and Caliban: the Psychology of Colonization* (New York: Praeger, 1964).
Marx, Karl, *Capital*, Volume 1, trans. Ben Fowkes (New York: Penguin Classics, 1990).
Masefield, John, *John M. Synge: A Few Personal Recollections with Biographical Notes* (New York: Macmillan, 1915).
Mathews, P.J. 'Hyde's First Stand: The Irish Language Controversy of 1899' *Éire-Ireland*, 35:1 (2000): 173-187;
--- *Revival: The Abbey Theatre, Sinn Fein, The Gaelic League and the Co-operative Movement* (Cork: Cork University Press, 2003).
Mauss, Marcel, *The Gift: The Form and Reason for Exchange in Archaic Societies*, trans W. B. Halls (New York: W. W. Norton, 1990).
McCarthy, Gerry, 'Dramatic Shifts', *The Sunday Times*, 22 February 2004: 19.
McCormack, W.J., *Fool of the Family: A Life of J. M. Synge* (London: Weidenfeld and Nicholson, 2000).
McDonagh, Martin, *The Beauty Queen of Leenane and Other Plays* (New York: Vintage, 1998).
McDonald, Ronan, *Tragedy in Irish Literature: Synge, O'Casey, Beckett* (London: Palgrave, 2002).
Meneely, Gary, 'Peking at Your Knickers', *The Sun*, 24 March, 2006: 7;
Mercier, Vivian, *Modern Irish Literature: Sources and Founders*. Edited by Eilís Dillon (Oxford: Clarendon, 1994).
Mickhail, E.H., *J.M. Synge: Interviews and Recollections* (London: Macmillan, 1977).
Montague, John, *Collected Poems* (Loughcrew: Gallery Press, 1995).
Moore, James, *The Post-Darwinian Controversies* (London: Cambridge UP, 1979).
Müller, V. 'Zakladatel prospěšné tradice,' *Lidová demokracie* 1 January 1967, 5.
Murphy, James H. and Betsey Taylor FitzSimon (editors), *The Irish Revival Reappraised* (Dublin: Four Courts Press, 2004).
Murphy, James H., *Ireland: A Social, Cultural and Literary History, 1791-1891* (Dublin: Four Courts Press, 2002).
Murphy, Tom, *Plays 2* (London: Methuen, 1993).
--- *Plays 3* (London: Methuen, 1994).
--- *Plays 4* (London: Methuen, 1997).
--- *The House* (London: Methuen, 2002).

Murray, Christopher (ed.) *Alive in Time, The Enduring Drama of Tom Murphy* (Dublin: Carysfort Press, 2010).
--- *Twentieth Century Irish Drama: Mirror up to Nation* (Manchester: Manchester University Press, 1997).
Mušek, Karel, 'Irské divadlo národní,' *Lumír* 33.12 (1904/1905): 554-60, 15 September 1905.
--- 'Irské literární divadlo,' *Divadelní list Máje* 3.2 (2 November 1906).
--- 'Irské národní divadlo,' *Divadlo* 1(8).4 (1920/1921).
--- 'Poznámky režisérovy k vypravení Hamleta', National Theatre, Prague, 2 February 1920, n.p. The Archive of the National Museum, Prague, Č 1570.
--- 'V zapadlém kraji. Črty z Erina, ostrova hoře,' part 1, *Zvon* 7.23 (1907).
--- 'Z irských glenů,' Zlatá Praha 33.43 (1916): 513-15 and 33.44 (1916): 525-26.
--- review of *The Aran Islands* by J.M. Synge, *Lumír* 35.8 (1907): 383-84, 15 June.
--- V zapadlém kraji. Črty z Erina, ostrova hoře,' part 3, *Zvon* 7.25 (1907).
Nerlich, Brigitte, 'The Evolution of the Concept of 'Linguistic Evolution' in the 19th and 20th Century', *Lingua* 77: 2 (1989): 101-12.
Ní Dhuibhne, Eilís , 'Synge's Use of Popular Material in *The Shadow of the Glen*', *Bealoideas*, 1990, 141-80
--- 'Dublin Modern Legends: an intermediate Type List', *Bealoideas* (1983): 55–69.
--- 'Ex Corde', *Bealoideas* (1980): 86–134
Nic Shiublaigh, Maire, *The Splendid Years* (Dublin: J. Duffy, 1955).
Nicholson, Steve, *The Censorship of British Drama 1900- 1968, vol. 1, 1900-1932* (Exeter: University of Exeter Press, 2003).
Nightingale, Benedict, 'The Synge Cycle', *The Times*, 30 August, 2005.
Ó Conchubhair, Brian, *Fin de Siècle na Gaelige: Darwin, An Athbheochan agus Smaointeoireacht na hEorpa* (Indreabhán: Cló Iar-Chonnachta, 2009).
O'Brien Johnson, Toni, *Synge: The Medieval and the Grotesque* (Gerrards Cross: Colin Smythe, 1982).
O'Donnell, Ian, 'Lethal Violence in Ireland, 1841-2003: Famine, Celibacy and Parental Pacification', *British Journal of Criminology* 45:5 (2005).
O'Donnell, Patrick, *The Irish Faction Fighters of the 19th Century* (Dublin: Anvil Books, 1975).
O'Kelly, Emer, 'Unleashing a Chariot of Dramatic Fire, *Sunday Independent*, 24 July, 2005.
--- Review of *The Playboy of the Western World*, *Sunday Independent*, 7 October 2007.
O'Toole, Fintan, *Critical Moments* (Dublin: Carysfort Press, 2003).
--- *Tom Murphy: The Politics of Magic* (Dublin: New Island Books, 1994).

Pavis, Patrick, *Dictionnaire du théâtre* (Paris: Armand Colin, 2004).
Pearse, Padraic, 'What Is a National Language?' *An Claidheamh Soluis*, January 28,1905, 6-7.
Pilkington, Lionel, *Theatre & Ireland* (Basingstoke: Palgrave Macmillan, 2010).
--- *Theatre and State in Twentieth Century Ireland: Cultivating the People* (London: Routledge, 2001).
Pine, Richard, *The Diviner: The Art of Brian Friel* (Dublin: University College Dublin Press, 1999).
Porter, Raymond J. and James D Brophy (eds.), *Modern Irish Literature: Essays in Honor of William York Tindall* (New Rochelle, N.Y.: Iona College Press, 1972).
Power, Tyrone, *The Lost Heir and the Prediction* (New York: J and J Harper, 1839).
Raine, Kathleen, *Defending Ancient Springs* (London: Oxford University Press, 1967).
Reynolds, Paige, 'Colleen Modernism: Modernism's Afterlife in Irish Women's Writing,' *Éire-Ireland* 44:3&4 (Fall/Winter 2009): 94-117.
Ricoeur, Paul, *Oneself as Another* (Chicago: Chicago University Press, 1992).
Roche, Anthony, 'Synge, Brecht, and the Hiberno-German Connection, *Hungarian Journal of English and American Studies*, 10.1-2 (2004): 9-32.
Roscoe, Adrian, *Uhuru's Fire, African Literature East to South* (Cambridge: Cambridge University Press, 1977).
Rotimi, Ola, *The Gods are not to Blame* (Oxford: Oxford University Press, 1971).
RTE, 'Garry Hynes and Ann Saddlemyer in Conversation at the Synge Summer School' *DruidSynge: The Plays of John Millington Synge* (RTE, Wildfire Films and Druid Theatre, 2007). DVD.
---'Mighty Talk: A Journey With DruidSynge', *DruidSynge: The Plays of John Millington Synge* (RTE, Wildfire Films and Druid Theatre, 2007). DVD.
Russell, George, *Co-Operation and Nationality* (Dublin: Maunsel, 1912).
Ryan, W.P. 'A Singer 'O the Green', *Daily Chronicle*, 4 February 1911.
Saddlemyer, Ann (ed.), *Theatre Business. The Correspondence of the First Abbey Theatre Directors: William Butler Yeats, Lady Gregory and J.M. Synge* (University Park and London: The Pennsylvania State University Press, 1982)
Saddlemyer, Ann and Robin Skelton (eds): *The World of W.B. Yeats* (Seattle: University of Washington Press, 1965).
Samek, Daniel, *Česko-irské kulturní styky v první polovině 20. století / Czech-Irish Cultural Relations, 1900-1950*, trans. Ondřej Pilný (Prague: Centre for Irish Studies, Charles University, 2009).
Shattuck, Roger, *The Banquet Years* (London: Jonathan Cape, 1969).

Shaw, George Bernard, *The Quintessence of Ibsenism* (London: W. Scott, 1891).
Sihra, Melissa and Paul Murphy (eds.), *The Dreaming Body: Contemporary Irish Theatre* (Gerrards Cross & New York: Colin Smythe & Oxford University Press, 2009).
Sofer, Andrew, *The Stage Life of Props* (Ann Arbor, MI: University of Michigan Press, 2003).
St John-Stevas, Norman, *Obscenity and the Law* (London: Secker & Warburg, 1956).
Stankovič, Andrej, *Josef Florian a Stará Říše* (Prague: Triáda, 2008).
Stewart, Bruce, 'The Bitter Glass': Postcolonial Theory and Anglo-Irish Culture: A Case Study', *The Irish Review* (No. 25 (Winter, 1999 – Spring, 2000).
Stewart, Susan, *On Longing: Narratives of the Miniature, the Gigantic, the Souvenir, the Collection* (Baltimore and London: Johns Hopkins University Press, 1984).
Storgaard Jorgensen, Annette, 'Mission Impossible? An Account of the Role of Schooling in the Revival of Irish' in Student Foreign Language Projects at RUC (Roskilde: Roskilde Universitetscenter, 1988): 16-39.
Sunday Tribune, 'What Now for the Abbey?' *Sunday Tribune*, 19 September 2004.
Sweeney, Frank, *The Murder of Connell Boyle, County Donegal, 1898* (Dublin: Four Courts Press, 2002).
Synge, John Millington, *Collected Letters, Volume 2*. Edited by Ann Saddlemyer (Oxford: Clarendon Press, 1984).
--- *Collected Letters Volume 1*. Edited by Ann Saddlemyer (Oxford: Clarendon Press, 1983).
--- *Collected Works, Volume I: Poems*. Edited by Robin Skelton (Gerrards Cross: Colin Smythe, 1982).
--- *Collected Works Volume II: Prose*. Edited by Alan Price (Gerrards Cross: Colin Smythe, 1982).
--- *Collected Works, Volume III: Plays 1*. Edited by Ann Saddlemyer (Gerrards Cross: Colin Smythe, 1982).
--- *Collected Works, Volume IV: Plays 2*. Edited by Ann Saddlemyer (Gerrards Cross: Colin Smythe, 1982).
--- *Hrdina západu*, trans. Karel Mušek (Stará Říše na Moravě: M. Florianová, 1921).
--- *Letters to Molly*. Edited by Ann Saddlemyer (Cambridge: Belknap Press of Harvard University Press, 1971).
--- *Playboy of the Western World and Other Plays*. Edited by Ann Saddlemyer (Oxford: World's Classics, 1998).
--- *Travelling Ireland: Essays 1898-1908*. Edited by Nicholas Grene (Dublin: The Lilliput Press, 2009).
Tetauer, Frank, 'obituary for Karel Mušek', *Apollon* 2:5 (1924/1925): 83.
--- 'Příklad irského divadla,' *Divadlo* 12 (19).1 (1932/1933).

Thomson, Belinda with Frances Fowle and Lesley Stevenson, *Gauguin's Vision: A Discussion of Materials and Techniques* (Edinburgh: National Gallery of Scotland, 2005).
Thorning, J. *En moderne irsk dramatiker* (Copenhagen, 1921).
Thornton, Weldon, *J. M. Synge and the Western Mind* (Gerrards Cross: Colin Smythe, 1979).
Tuam Herald, 'Mr. R.J. Kelly, K.C.,' *The Tuam Herald* 23 December 1922.
Turkle, Sherry, *Evocative Objects: Things We Think With* (Cambridge, MA: MIT Press, 2007).
United Irishman, 'All Ireland', *United Irishman*, 11 February 1905.
Walcott, Derek, *Conversations with Derek Walcott*. Edited by William Baer (Mississippi: University Press of Mississippi, 1996).
Watson, G. J. *Irish Identity and the Literary Revival* (Washington DC: CUA Press, 1994).
Watt, Stephen, *Beckett and Contemporary Irish Literature* (Cambridge: Cambridge UP, 2009).
Weiner, Richard, 'Le Baladin du monde occidental,' *Scéna* 1: 2. půlročník (1913/1914).
Weitz, Eric (ed.) *The Power of Laughter* (Dublin: Carysfort Press, 2003).
Wilde, Lady Francesca (Speranza), *Ancient Legends, Mystic Charms, and Superstitions of Ireland* (London: Ward and Downey, 1888).
Wood, James, *The Broken Estate* (New York: Picador, 1999).
Woodcock, George (ed.) *An Anarchist Reader* (Glasgow: Fontana, 1978).
--- *Anarchism* (Harmondsworth: Penguin, 1963).
Wright, William, *The Brontes in Ireland: Or Facts Stranger than Fiction* (London: Hodder and Stoughton, 1893).
Wulff, Helena, *Dancing at the Crossroads* (Oxford, 2008).
Yeats, John Butler, *Early Memories: Some Chapters of Autobiography* (Dublin: Cuala Press, 1923).
Yeats, W. B. *Autobiographies* (London, Macmillan, 1955).
--- *Collected Letters, Volume IV 1905-1907*. Edited by John Kelly and Ronald Schuchard (Oxford: Oxford University Press, 2005).
--- *Collected Letters Volume III, 1901-1904*. Edited by John Kelly and Ronald Schuchard (Oxford: Oxford University Press, 1994).
--- *Collected Plays* (London: Macmillan, 1960).
--- *Essays and Introductions* (London: Macmillan, 1961).

CONTRIBUTORS

Bisi Adigun is a Yoruba man from western Nigeria. He holds a BA in Dramatic Arts (1990), MA in Drama Studies (1999), MA in Film/Television (2002) and currently is on the doctoral programme in Drama Studies in Trinity College Dublin. Bisi is the founder and artistic director of Arambe Productions for which he has produced and directed *The Gods Are Not To Blame*, *The Kings of the Kilburn High Road*, *The Dilemma of A Ghost*, *Through A Film Darkly* and *Pantomime;* co-written, with Roddy Doyle, a modern version of J.M. Synge's *The Playboy of the Western World*; and written, directed and produced *African Voices, Once Upon A Time & Not So Long Ago*, a modern version of *The Trials of Brother Jero* and *The Butcher Babes*. He is also the author of *The Playboy of the Sunny South East*, *White Bread and Black Skin (*a skit*)* and *Home, Sweet Home*, a Nigerian adaptation of Jimmy Murphy's Irish emigrant play *The Kings of the Kilburn High Road*. For more on his work, visit: www.arambeproductions.com

Mary Burke is an Associate Professor of English at the University of Connecticut. She was the 2003-04 NEH Keough-Naughton Fellow at the Institute for Irish Studies, University of Notre Dame and the 2010 Boston College-Ireland Visiting Fellow. She is the author of *'Tinkers': Synge and the Cultural History of the Irish Traveller* (Oxford University Press, 2009). She also writes creatively and was nominated for a Hennessy Irish Writing award in 2008.

Sara Keating writes about theatre for the *The Irish Times* among other publications. In 2006 she completed a PhD on twentieth-century Irish theatre at the Samuel Beckett Centre, Trinity College Dublin. She has published essays on Tom Murphy, Martin

McDonagh, Brian Friel and Samuel Beckett and currently teaches courses on Irish theatre at Trinity College, University College Dublin and New York University, Dublin.

Adrian Frazier teaches at the National University of Ireland, and is the author, most recently, of *Hollywood Irish: John Ford, Abbey Actors, and the Irish Revival in Hollywood* (Lilliput Press, 2011)

Ben Levitas teaches in the Department of Drama at Goldsmiths, University of London. He is author of *The Theatre of Nation: Irish Drama and Cultural Nationalism 1890-1916* (Oxford: Clarendon Press, 2002) and co-editor, with David Holdeman, of *W.B. Yeats in Context* (Cambridge, 2010)

Patrick Lonergan teaches at National University of Ireland, Galway. He is the author of *Theatre and Globalization*, which won the 2008 Theatre Book Prize and a 2010 ESSE Book Prize. He was appointed director of the Synge Summer School in 2008, and is currently writing a book about Martin McDonagh, for publication by Methuen Drama in 2012.

Éilís Ní Dhuibhne was born in Dublin in 1954. She was educated at Scoil Bhríde, Scoil Chaitriona, and UCD, where she studied English, Old Irish and Folklore. In 1978-9 she spent a year as a graduate student, studying Folklore, at the University of Copenhagen and in 1982 was conferred with a PhD in Irish Folklore by UCD. As well as many research articles, mainly on oral narrative, she has written several collections of short stories, many novels, books for children, and plays for stage and radio. Her literary work has won many awards and is widely anthologized and translated. She reviews regularly for the *The Irish Times*. Eilís worked as a librarian and archivist in the National Library of Ireland for many years. She is currently Writer Fellow at UCD and teaches on the MA in Creative Writing there. She is a member of Aosdána, the Irish Academy of Artists.

Mark Phelan is Director of the Postgraduate Programme and currently Head of Drama Studies at Queen's University Belfast, where he has worked since 2001. He has published widely on Irish theatre and photography.

Ondřej Pilný is Associate Professor of English and Director of the Centre for Irish Studies at Charles University, Prague. He is the author of *Irony and Identity in Modern Irish Drama* (2006) and editor of *Global Ireland: Irish Literatures in the New Millennium* (with Clare Wallace), *Time Refigured: Myths, Foundation Texts and Imagined Communities* (with Martin Procházka), and an annotated volume of J.M. Synge's works in Czech (2006). His translations include plays by J.M. Synge, Brian Friel, Martin McDonagh, Enda Walsh, and Flann O'Brien's *The Third Policeman*.

Emilie Pine lectures in modern drama in the School of English, Drama and Film at University College Dublin. Emilie is assistant editor of the *Irish University Review*, and is the recipient of the 2011 Irish Studies Fulbright Scholar award. Her book *The Politics of Irish Memory: Performing Remembrance in Contemporary Irish Culture* is published by Palgrave Macmillan. She is currently writing a cultural history of Ireland in the 1930s.

Richard Pine is founder and Director Emeritus of the Durrell School of Corfu, where he now lives. His books include *Lawrence Durrell: the Mindscape* (1994), *The Thief of Reason: Oscar Wilde and Modern Ireland* (1995), *The Diviner: the Art of Brian Friel* (1999), *2RN and the Origins of Irish Radio* (2002), *Music and Broadcasting in Ireland* (2005) and *Charles: the Life and World of Charles Acton* (2010). A former secretary of the Irish Writers' Union, co-editor of the *Irish Literary Supplement* and consultant to the Council of Europe on cultural development programmes, he holds an honorary fellowship of the Royal Irish Academy of Music.

Alexandra Poulain is Professor of Irish Literature and Drama at Charles de Gaulle University (Lille 3). Her published works include articles on Yeats, Synge, Lady Gregory, Beckett and Tom Murphy. Her latest book is *Endgame ou le théâtre mis en pièces*, co-authored with Elisabeth Angel-Perez (CNED/Presses Universitaires de France, 2009). She is co-editor of *Tombeau de Beckett*, a collection of new essays to be published by Editions Aden in 2011.

Paige Reynolds is an associate professor in the English Department at the College of the Holy Cross in Worcester, Massachusetts. She is the author of *Modernism, Drama, and the Audience for Irish Spectacle* (Cambridge UP, 2007) and editor of a 2011 special issue of the journal *Éire-Ireland* focused on material culture. She has published on topics including modernism, Irish drama and performance, and film and is currently writing a study of the playwright, novelist, and cultural critic Mary Manning.

Shaun Richards is Emeritus Professor of Irish Studies at Staffordshire University. He is the author, with David Cairns, of *Writing Ireland: Colonialism, Nationalism and Culture* (MUP, 1988), the editor of *The Cambridge Companion to Irish Drama* (CUP, 2004), and has published widely on Irish drama in major journals and edited collections.

Anthony Roche is an Associate Professor and the Head of Subject for Drama Studies in the School of English, Drama and Film at University College Dublin. From 2004 to 2007 he was Director of the Synge Summer School in Wicklow. He has published widely on Irish drama and theatre of the twentieth and twenty-first centuries. Recent publications include *The Cambridge Companion to Brian Friel* (2006) and *Contemporary Irish Drama* Second Edition (2009). His *Brian Friel: Theatre and Politics* and *J.M. Synge and the Making of a Modern Irish Drama* will be published in 2011.

Ann Saddlemyer is Professor Emeritus of the University of Toronto, where she was Master of Massey College. She has written extensively on both Canadian and Irish literatures. Her previous editions include the works of Lady Gregory, the plays of J.M. Synge and the award-winning 2-volume *Collected Letters of John Millington Synge* (OUP, 1983, 1984). She is one of the General Editors of the Cornell Yeats series and of the *Selected Irish Drama* series published by Colin Smythe. Her most recent books are the biography *Becoming George: the Life of Mrs W.B. Yeats* (OUP 2002) and the edition *W.B. Yeats and George Yeats: the Letters* (OUP 2011).

Melissa Sihra is Lecturer in Drama at the School of Drama, Film and Music, Trinity College Dublin and President of the Irish Society for Theatre Research. She is editor of *Women in Irish Drama: A Century of Authorship and Representation* (Palgrave 2007), co-editor (with Paul Murphy) of *The Dreaming Body: Contemporary Irish Theatre* (Colin Smythe and Oxford University Press) and co-editor (with Pirkko Koski) of *The Local Meets the Global in Performance* (Cambridge Scholars Press, 2010). She is currently writing a monograph on the plays of Marina Carr.

APPENDIX

A) Czech Translations of J.M. Synge

The Shadow of the Glen
Ve stínu doliny, trans. Karel Mušek (Stará Říše na Moravě: M. Florianová, 1921).
Ve stínu doliny, trans. Gabriela Nová (Praha: Dilia, 1964).
Stinné údolí, trans. Zdeněk Mahler (in fact: Josef Topol), unpublished (1973).
Stín doliny, trans. Hana Zahradníková. John Millington Synge, *Hrdina západu: dramata a próza*, ed. Ondřej Pilný (Praha: Fraktály, 2006).

Riders to the Sea
Jezdci k moři, trans. Karel Mušek, design and engravings by Antonín Václav Slavíček (Stará Říše na Moravě: M. Florianová, 1922).
Jezdci k moři – radio adaptation, trans. and adapt. Jiří Strnad; unpublished (1998).
Jezdci k moři, trans. Daniela Furthnerová. Synge, Hrdina západu: dramata a próza (2006).

The Tinker's Wedding
Drátenická svatba, přel. Gabriela Nová (Praha: Dilia, 1964).
Drátenická svatba, trans. Zdeněk Mahler (in fact: Josef Topol), unpublished (1973).

The Well of the Saints

Studnice světců, trans. Karel Mušek (Stará Říše na Moravě: M. Florianová, 1921).

Studna světců, trans. Ondřej Pilný, Druhý břeh (Časopis Švandova divadla) 1.3 (2003): 37-51; Synge, Hrdina západu: dramata a próza (2006).

The Playboy of the Western World

Rek západu, trans. V.A. Jung, unpublished MS in the library of the Prague Theatre Institute (n.d.).

Hrdina západu, trans. Karel Mušek (Stará Říše na Moravě: M. Florianová, 1921).

Hrdina západu, trans. Vladislav Čejchan (Praha: Dilia, 1961).

Hrdina západu, trans. Vladislav Čejchan, 2nd ed. (Praha: Orbis, 1961).

Hrdina západu, trans. Martin Hilský (Praha: Národní divadlo, 1996); Synge, *Hrdina západu: dramata a próza* (2006).

Deirdre of the Sorrows

Královna žalu, trans. Aloys Skoumal, unpublished (1946).

Deirdre, královna smutků, trans. Daniela Furthnerová. Synge, Hrdina západu: dramata a próza (2006).

The Aran Islands

'Věrná žena' (A Faithful Wife; extract from *The Aran Islands*), trans. Josef Hrůša, *Tribuna*, 16.6.1927: 2.

Aranské ostrovy, trans. Karel Mušek, translation revised by František Pastor (Stará Říše na Moravě: M. Florianová, 1929).

Aranské ostrovy, trans. Mariana Housková. Synge, Hrdina západu: dramata a próza (2006).

Poems

'V Glencullen' (In Glencullen), trans. O.F. Babler, *Hlas (List československé strany lidové)*, 14.6. (recte 15.6.) 1946: 3.

'Ve vzpouře...,' 'Přání,' 'Zima,' 'Kletba' (?, A Wish, Winter, The Curse), trans. Daniel Dobiáš, *Tvar* 4 (21.2.2002): 12.

Essays

'Útisk pahorků,' 'Na cestě' (The Oppression of the Hills, On the Road), trans. Frank Tetauer, *Apollon* 1.7 (1923/1924): 122-24.

'Uspán éterem' (Under Ether), trans. Miloš Komanec (translator's name omitted), *Babylon* 13.2 (28.10.2003), 'Literární a výtvarná příloha': 5.

'Ve Wicklow a v Connemaře' (In Wicklow and in Connemara – selected essays), trans. Miloš Komanec. Synge, *Hrdina západu: dramata a próza* (2006).

Miscellanea

'Poznámky o literatuře' (Notes about Literature), trans. Ondřej Pilný. Synge, *Hrdina západu: dramata a próza* (2006).

B) Czech Productions of J.M. Synge's Plays

The Shadow of the Glen

Ve stínu doliny, trans. Karel Mušek

7 February 1906, Smíchovské divadlo (Švandovo divadlo na Smíchově), Praha

17 and 22 August 1907, Národní divadlo, Praha

15 February 1927, Neodvislé jeviště group, Umělecká Beseda, Praha

19 December 1940, Národní divadlo moravskoslezské, Ostrava, dir. Karel Palouš

Stinné údolí, trans. Zdeněk Mahler (in fact: Josef Topol)

1973, Činoherní studio, Ústí nad Labem

Riders to the Sea

Jezdci na moři, trans. Karel Mušek (?)

19 November 1929, Národní divadlo v Brně – Reduta, Brno

Jezdci k moři, trans. Karel Mušek

1934 (?), Národní divadlo moravskoslezské, Ostrava

Jezdci k moři – radio adaptation, trans. and adapt. Jiří Strnad

1998 (recorded), 1999 (broadcast), Český rozhlas

The Tinker's Wedding

Drátenická svatba, trans. Zdeněk Mahler (in fact: Josef Topol)

1973, Činoherní studio, Ústí nad Labem

Krásné vyhlídky: John M. Synge, Drátenická svatba, trans. Zdeněk Mahler (in fact: Josef Topol)
29 May 1987, Činoherní klub, Praha

The Well of the Saints
Studnice světců, trans. Karel Mušek
12 April 1920, Národní divadlo v Brně – Reduta, Brno
5, 6 and 9 November 1921, Národní divadlo, Praha
Studna světců, trans. Ondřej Pilný
18 November 2003, Švandovo divadlo na Smíchově, Praha

The Playboy of the Western World
Rek západu (?Hrdina západního kraje), trans. V.A. Jung and Karel Mušek
2 December 1916, Vinohradské divadlo, Praha
Hrdina západu, trans. Karel Mušek
9 February 1928, The DaDa company, Theatre Na Slupi, Praha
19 December 1940, Národní divadlo moravskoslezské, Ostrava, dir. Karel Palouš
19 March 1947, Divadlo DISK (Státní konzervatoř), Praha
1969 (translations by Mušek and Čejchan adapted by Z. Kočová), Maringotka, Praha
1971 (translation adapted by Jaroslav Hornát), Divadlo DISK, Praha
1995, Divadlo Na zábradlí, Praha
25 November 2000, Studio Marta – JAMU, Brno
Hrdina západu, trans. Vladislav Čejchan
1962, Městská divadla pražská (Divadlo komedie), Praha
1963, Divadlo Petra Bezruče, Ostrava
1969, Divadlo bratří Mrštíků, Brno
1970, Městské divadlo, Příbram
1977, Státní městské divadlo, Šumperk
1978, Divadlo Petra Bezruče, Ostrava
1978, Divadlo Vítězslava Nezvala, Karlovy Vary
1982, Západočeské divadlo, Cheb
12 June 1993, Městské divadlo, Zlín
1996, Národní divadlo moravskoslezské, Ostrava

18 April 1997, Divadlo F.X. Šaldy, Liberec
3 February 2001, Západočeské divadlo, Cheb
Hrdina západu, trans. Martin Hilský
1996, Národní divadlo, Praha
25 September 2004, Divadlo v Dlouhé, Praha
10 September 2007, Činoherní klub, Praha
13 December 2008, Těšínské divadlo, Český Těšín
Prowincjonalny Playboy – Hrdina západu
26 March 1999, Těšínské divadlo, Český Těšín – Polish scene

Deirdre of the Sorrows
Královna žalu, trans. Aloys Skoumal
23 January 1946, Divadlo DISK (Státní konzervatoř), Praha

INDEX

A

à Kempis, Thomas, 11, 44
Abbey Theatre, 24, 49, 53-54, 118, 134, 150, 153, 159, 176, 178, 226, 229, 242, 247, 256, 262-67, 282-83, 285, 287
Adigun, Bisi, 4, 229, 242, 259, 263, 264, 267, 277, 279, 291
Allgood, Molly (Maire O'Neill), 17, 23, 50, 160, 164, 176, 178, 238, 259
Allgood, Sara, 270
Antoine, André, 134, 201
Arambe Productions, 260, 264, 291
Aran Islands, 9, 15, 94-99, 101-102, 105, 109, 112, 119, 133, 137-38, 140, 179, 249, 255
Archer, William, 37, 52
Arensberg, Conrad and Solon Toothaker Kimball, 139
Arnold, Bruce, 141, 150
Arts Council (Ireland), 264, 265

B

Barnard, Toby, 74, 92, 279
Barnes, Ben, 3, 263, 273
Barry, Sebastian, 217, 275-77
Baudelaire, Charles, 11
Beckett, Samuel, 53, 81, 91, 195, 209, 218, 224, 238, 261, 276, 277, 279, 285, 289, 291, 293
Beer, Gillian, 70, 162, 279
Billington, Michael, 215, 224, 251, 256, 279
Birmingham, George, 118, 129
Blake-Knox, Kirsty, 242, 280
Bliss, Alan, 7
Boccaccio, 27, 96
Boland, Eavan, 195, 197, 277
Bopp, Franz, 62, 70
Bouda theatre, 154
Bourgeois, Maurice, 135, 164, 169, 173, 176
Brecht, Bertolt, 2, 44, 53, 136, 207, 228, 287
Brenneman, Walter and Mary, 187, 196, 280
Brittany, 9, 12, 94, 111, 146
Brno National Theatre, 170, 297-98
Brontë, Emily, 127
Brown, Bill, 73, 91
Browne, Eamon, 129

Bryars, Gavin, 28
Burke, Mary, 5, 52, 55, 271, 278, 291

C

Caird, Donald, 67, 71, 280
Cairns, David, 53, 294
Calypso Production, 261, 264
Campbell, Joseph, 148, 151
Campbell, Mrs Patrick, 24
Carleton, William, 123, 126-31, 280, 284
Carnot, Mari François, 136
Carr, Marina, 4, 215, 218-19, 223-24, 226, 228, 238, 276-77, 280, 294
  By the Bog of Cats..., 218, 221, 224, 226
  Portia Coughlan, 218, 220, 223-24
  The Mai, 218-24
Cashman, Ray, 96, 108, 110
Cave, Richard Allen, 31, 282
Chauduri, Una, 147, 151, 280
Chekhov, Anton, 185, 226-28, 231, 277
Chesney, Helena C.G., 70, 282
Chopin, Frederic, 11
Christiansen, Reidar Th, 101, 110, 280
Clark, Samuel, 130
Colum, Padraic, 54, 114, 119, 120, 128-29
Conley, Carolyn, 117, 124, 129-30, 281
Connolly, Ruth, 11, 29, 281
Conrad, Joseph, 24
Conway, Frank, 201
Cook, David and Miles Lee, 234, 242-43, 281
Coole Park, 160, 162-63, 176

Coonan, Clifford, 252, 257, 281
Corkery, Daniel, 107, 110, 256, 281
Cosgrove, Aedin, 252, 257
Coveney, Michael, 250, 256
Crawley, Peter, 226, 242, 281
Crofton Croker, Thomas, 128, 281
Cronin, Michael, 256
Cuala Press, 19, 29, 75, 125, 289
Cullen, Paul (Cardinal), 144-45
Curtin, Jeremiah, 96, 101, 110
Czerny, Carl, 11

D

DaDa Theatre, 170
Danaher, Kevin, 130, 281
Dante, 5, 10, 11, 20, 23
Darwin, Charles, 58-63, 66, 69-70, 276, 279, 286
Dasenbrock, Reed Way, 31, 281
Davis, Alex, 11, 29
Davis, Colin, 224
Day, Angélique, 128
de Búrca, Proinnsias, 103
De Jubainville, Marie Henri d'Arbois, 94
de Valera, Éamon, 185
Dean, Joan Fitzpatrick, 39, 53
Deane, Seamus, 43, 53, 141, 150-51, 272
Debussy, Claude, 11, 134
Derrida, Jacques, 83, 92, 281
Deutsches Theater, Berlin, 153
Dewar, Daniel, 116, 128, 281
Deyl, Rudolf, 157, 174, 177, 179, 281
Dickens, Charles, 76
Diderot, Denis, 201, 213, 282
Dirane, Pat, 14-15, 77, 95, 96-110

Dixon, Ros, 277
Donnelly Jr, James S., 130, 280
Doyle, Roddy, 4, 229, 242, 260, 263-64, 267, 291
Druid Theatre Company, 2-4, 54, 135, 229, 245-51, 256, 277, 284, 287
DruidSynge, 2-3, 54, 248-51, 255-56, 273, 287
Dublin Theatre Festival, 4
Duff, Anne Marie, 248
Dunne, Colin, 278
Durrell, Lawrence, 195, 197, 282, 293

E

Eliot, T.S., 8, 13, 29, 282
Euripides, 226, 228
Evans, E. Estyn, 129, 282

F

Farrell, Bernard, 278
Faure, Sébastien, 138
Fay, Frank, 45, 167, 178, 246, 256
Fay, Willy, 9, 139
Fischer, Otokar, 170-71, 179-80
Fitzpatrick, Lisa, 278
Flower, Robin, 108
Fogarty, Anne, 276, 278
Foster, John Wilson, 70
Foster, Roy, 180, 272, 275
Frazier, Adrian, 53, 149, 175, 184, 196, 269, 275-76, 282, 292
Frejka, Jiří, 170, 179
Freyer, Grattan, 53, 282
Fricker, Karen, 250, 256-57, 276-78, 282

Friel, Brian, 4, 114-15, 118, 128, 181-85, 190-92, 195-96, 217, 226-31, 235, 238, 242, 255, 257, 276-77, 282, 287, 292-94
Dancing at Lughnasa, 114, 185
Faith Healer, 181, 196, 217
Translations, 12, 19, 21, 27, 30, 129, 182-89, 191, 195-96, 227, 230, 235, 255, 257, 283, 295
Fugard, Athol, 261

G

Gaelic League, 53-59, 63, 65, 67, 69-70, 118, 142, 150, 285
Galway, 2-3, 14, 80, 93, 98-105, 119, 161, 229, 248-49, 269, 292
Gamble, John, 116, 128, 282
Garrigan Mattar, Sinéad, 58, 69, 112, 128, 282
Garvin, Tom, 142, 150, 282
Gaskell, Elizabeth, 76
Gauguin, Paul, 111, 128, 134, 146, 150, 284, 289
Geesala, County Mayo, 249
Genet, Jacqueline, 31
Gibbons, Luke, 145, 150, 248, 256, 281-82
Gonne, Maud, 24, 30, 75, 138, 283
Gould, Warwick, 28, 270-71, 275
Greene, David H., 1, 176, 283
Gregory, Lady Augusta, 9, 12, 14, 23, 35, 37, 80, 111-12, 120-21, 129, 153, 159-63, 166, 176-78, 238, 255, 275-76, 283, 287, 293-94

Grene, Nicholas, 1-2, 7, 12, 29-30, 54, 136, 177, 199, 213, 269-72, 276-78, 283, 288
Griffith, Arthur, 46, 47, 54, 75, 107, 138

H

Harmon, Ken, 261
Harmon, Maurice, 1, 29, 109
Harrington, John P., 129, 255-56, 277, 283
Harris, Susan Cannon, 3, 53
Hart, Peter, 48, 54, 283
Heaney, Seamus, 185, 196, 225, 276
Hearn, Lafcadio, 9
Heidegger, Martin, 76, 92, 283
Henry, Emile, 136, 149
Hiberno-English, 65-68, 204, 231, 237, 241, 254
Hillstead, Alice, 156, 174
Hladík, Václav, 168, 178, 283
Hogan, Robert, 1-5, 54, 149, 256, 283
Holbek, Bengt, 283
Holloway, Joseph, 45, 50, 54, 159, 256, 283
Horniman, Annie, 53, 153, 159-60, 167, 175, 177, 282
Houlihan, Michael, 130
Hugo, Victor, 134
Hurley, John W., 126, 130, 284
Huysmans, Joris-Karl, 11, 134
Hyde, Douglas, 13, 16, 55, 65, 69, 81, 119, 134, 142, 147, 275, 285
Hynes, Garry, 54, 135, 149, 249-50, 256, 272-73, 276-77, 287

I

Ibsen, Henrik, 37-38, 134-38, 143, 147, 227-28
Ghosts, 37-38, 136, 138, 143, 215, 224, 228, 277
Icres, Fernand, 201
Inglesby, Elizabeth, 91, 284
Ingoldsby, Maeve, 261
Irish Folklore Commission, 101
Irish Literary Theatre, 9, 128, 153
Irish Theatre Magazine, 257, 263, 267, 279, 28-85
Irish Times, The, 6, 129-30, 242, 252, 257, 266-67, 272, 279, 281, 284, 291, 292
Isherwood, Christopher, 94

J

Jarry, Alfred, 135-39, 143, 149, 284
John, Augustus, 24
Jones, Greta, 71
Jones, Marie, 260
Joyce, James, 28, 31, 56, 69, 278

K

Kavanagh, Patrick, 115
Keane, John B., 118
Keating, Geoffrey, 4, 14, 245, 257, 278, 291
Keefe, Robert, 66, 71, 284
Kelly, Richard J., 158
Kennedy, Dennis, 242
Kennelly, Brendan, 226, 276
Kerry, 19, 56, 95, 98, 101, 102, 110, 114, 119, 121-22, 125, 129, 184, 249, 273, 279-80

Kiberd, Declan, 2-3, 7, 11, 16, 29, 56, 68-71, 94, 108-12, 128, 137, 147, 149, 151, 272, 276, 284
Kiely, David, 94
Kilroy, Thomas, 276
King, Mary C., 29, 53, 276
Kinmonth, Claudia, 74, 92
Kirby, Peadar, 256, 281
Kironde, Erisa, 2, 225, 229, 233-34, 236, 241, 243
Knapp, James, 111, 128, 284
Koltes, Bernard-Marie, 261

L

Le Braz, Anatole, 94
Leonard, Hugh, 217
Leopardi, Giacomo, 22-23
Lévi-Strauss, Claude, 112
Levitas, Ben, 3-4, 33, 53, 272, 275, 277, 284, 292
Logan, Patrick, 127, 131, 284
Lonergan, Patrick, 1, 91, 180, 247, 254, 256-57, 262, 267, 273, 275, 277-78, 292
Lorca, Federico Garcia, 2, 228
Lugné-Poe's, Aurélian, 134
Lumír, 159, 175, 179-80, 286
Lyons, F.S.L., 140, 150
Lyons, Patrick, 130

M

Mac Conghail, Fiach, 277
Mac Intyre, Tom, 271
MacDonagh, Thomas, 51
MacKenna, Stephen, 8, 49, 53, 142
MacMahon, Bryan, 118
MacNeill, Eoin, 55
MacNeill, Máire, 114

Macpherson, Margaret, 234, 236, 238, 243, 285
Maeterlinck, Maurice, 11, 168, 171, 177
Mahony, Christina Hunt, 276
Makerere Travelling Theatre, 234-35
Mallarmé, Stéphane, 11, 134
Martyn, Edward, 139, 153, 162
Marx, Karl, 92
Masefield, John, 18, 30, 285
Mason, Patrick, 3
Matheson, Cherrie, 12
Mathews, P.J., 3, 53, 69, 276
Matthews, Aidan, 226
Matura, Mustapha, 2, 28, 242, 280
Mauss, Marcel, 83, 86, 92, 285
Mayne, Rutherford, 119
McCabe, Patrick, 278
McCarthy, Gerry, 256
McCormack, W.J., 3, 5, 10, 12, 29, 53, 59, 92, 133, 143, 149-50, 169, 176, 270-71, 275, 285
McDiarmid, Lucy, 272, 275
McDonagh, Martin, 68, 71, 260, 277, 292-93
McDonald, Ronan, 49, 53, 276
McGahern, John, 2, 273, 276
McGlinchey, Charles, 115, 128
McGuinness, Eithne, 261
McGuinness, Frank, 217, 228, 242
McIntosh, Fiona, 277
McMullan, Anna, 277
McWilliams, Patrick, 128, 281
Mercier, Paul, 272, 276
Mercier, Vivian, 69
Meynell, Agnes, 24
Mickhail, E.H., 150, 285
Milton, John, 169, 236

Molloy, M.J., 118
Monks, Aoife, 278
Montague, John, 184, 196, 285
Moore, George, 127, 130, 153
Moore, James, 70
Morash, Chris, 3
Morse, Donald, 224, 279
Moscow Art theatre, 134
Mozart, 154
Murdoch, Iris, 108
Murphy, Cillian, 248, 250
Murphy, Paul, 242, 276, 288, 294
Murphy, Tom, 4, 118, 199, 213-14, 260, 276-78, 283, 286, 291, 293
   Bailegangaire, 199, 200, 211, 212, 260
   Gigli Concert, The, 206, 210, 212
   House, The, 210-11, 214, 285
   Whistle in the Dark, A, 202, 206, 210

Murray, Christopher, 53, 213, 242, 276, 278, 282
Murray, Rupert, 263
Mušek, Karel, 153-80, 283-88, 295-98
Muset, Colin, 21-23

N

National Theatre of South Bohemia, 170
Nerlich, Brigitte, 62, 70, 286
Ní Dhuibhne, Éilís, 5, 93, 110, 237, 277, 286, 292
Nic Shiublaigh, Maire, 54, 286
Nolan, Christopher, 248

O

Ó Conchubhair, Brian, 58, 69, 94, 109, 286
Ó Conghaile, Mairtín ('Mourteen'), 95
Ó Maolliadh, Colm, 103
Ó Súilleabháin, Sean, 94-95, 100-101, 109-10, 280
O'Connor, Francis, 250
O'Connor, Joseph, 2, 278
O'Connor, Ulick, 267
O'Donnell, Ian, 117, 129
O'Donnell, Patrick, 129
O'Donoghue, John, 273
O'Donoghue, Noel, 199
O'Dwyer, Riana, 199, 206, 213, 272, 276
O'Hanlon, Jim, 260-61
O'Kelly, Donal, 261, 275
O'Kelly, Emer, 256, 259, 267
O'Neil, Charlie, 261
O'Rowe, Mark, 217
O'Toole, Fintan, 2, 6, 199, 209, 213, 255, 275
Osofisan, Femi, 233, 235

P

Pan Pan Theatre Company, 4, 245, 251-57
Paris, 3, 8-18, 25, 36, 111, 133-37, 141, 143, 147, 169, 287
Parker, Lynne, 277
Parker, Stewart, 217, 277
Pater, Walter, 15-16
Paulin, Tom, 225
Pavis, Patrick, 200, 213, 287
Pearse, Patrick, 51, 64, 70, 96
Pedersen, Holger, 96
Pethica, James, 272, 275
Petrarch, 9, 23, 25, 27-28

Phelan, Mark, 5, 111, 277-78, 292
Pilkington, Lionel, 53, 211, 214, 275, 278, 287
Pilný, Ondřej, 5, 153, 175, 287, 292, 295-98
Pine, Emilie, 4, 215, 277, 293
Pine, Richard, 4, 181, 196, 277, 293
Plunkett, Horace, 158
Poulain, Alexandra, 4, 199, 278, 293
Power, Tyrone, 130
Prozatímní divadlo, 154
Pushkin, 170

Q

Quinn, Gavin, 252, 257
Quinn, John, 25, 153, 173

R

Rabelais, François, 11, 21, 44, 53, 113, 135
Racine, Jean, 24
Raine, Kathleen, 188, 196, 287
Ravel, Maurice, 134
Reid, Christina, 278
Reynolds, Paige, 5, 73, 91, 278, 293
Richards, Shaun, 5, 53, 133, 277-80, 294
Richepin, Jean, 167
Ricoeur, Paul, 190, 196, 287
Rimbaud, Arthur, 134
Roche, Anthony, 3, 53, 215, 224, 275-77, 294
Roche, Billy, 278
Roscoe, Adrian, 234, 242
Rossetti, Dante Gabriel, 20-21
Roth, Philip, 2

Rotimi, Ola, 266, 268, 287
RTÉ, 256
Russell, George (AE), 81, 113, 140, 150

S

Saddlemyer, Ann, 1, 5, 7, 29-30, 52-54, 70, 92, 99, 110, 113, 129, 149-50, 174, 178, 197, 201, 204, 213-14, 224, 250, 256, 267, 275, 277, 287-88, 294
Samhain, 52, 69, 120, 159
Saunders, Graham, 278
Schleicher, August, 62
Schopenhauer, Arthur, 22, 143
Schuffenecker, Claude-Emile, 146
Seurat, Georges, 134
Shakespeare, William, 96, 136, 157, 159, 203, 278
Shattuck, Roger, 134, 136, 149, 284, 287
Shaw, G.B., 37-39, 52, 139, 154, 157-58, 173-74, 179, 288
Sinn Féin, 46, 54, 150
Skelton, Robin, 1, 14, 29, 130, 287-88
Šmaha, Josef, 156
Sofer, Andrew, 79, 80, 92, 288
Sophocles, 225, 228
Soyinka, Wole, 233-34
Spencer, Herbert, 11, 58-59
Spinoza, Baruch, 11
Stavovské divadlo, 154
Steiner, George, 190-91
Stephens, Edward M., 176, 283
Stevenson, Robert Louis, 23, 150, 289
Stewart, Bruce, 131
Stewart, Susan, 77, 92

Strindberg, August, 134, 228
Sun, Yue, 252
Symons, Arthur, 24-25, 136
Synge Summer School, 5, 30, 91, 180, 250, 256, 275, 283, 287, 292, 294
Synge, J.M.
  'A Landlord's Garden in County Wicklow', 60-64
  'The Old and New in Ireland', 57, 62-65, 69
  'The People of the Glens', 166, 177
  Aran Islands, The, 28, 68, 74-89, 94-99, 137-38, 146, 158, 166, 174, 179, 286, 296
  Deirdre of the Sorrows, 18, 22, 27, 50, 155, 250, 296, 299
  National Drama: A Farce, 142, 144
  Playboy of the Western World, 2, 14, 17, 31, 55, 73-74, 80, 85, 90, 95, 118, 134, 140, 150, 160, 169, 175, 182, 203, 210, 213, 217, 225, 229, 231, 236, 242, 245-67, 278, 280, 282, 285-86, 288, 291, 296, 298
  Poems and Translations, 12, 19, 21, 27
  Riders to the Sea, 14, 16-17, 28, 40, 50, 65, 74, 79-83, 88, 95, 118, 155, 160, 164, 175, 199, 201, 215-16, 218, 223, 295, 297
  Shadow of the Glen, The, 14, 17, 28, 39-45, 50, 53, 65-66, 95, 98-99, 103-10, 118, 138-40, 143, 153, 155, 159, 166-67, 175, 203-204, 211, 216, 218, 223, 225, 229-30, 234, 236, 276, 286, 295, 297
  Well of the Saints, The, 3, 28, 41-44, 49, 53, 95, 118-19, 139, 153, 155, 160, 169-72, 182, 186, 192, 204, 208, 211, 296, 298
  When the Moon Has Set, 2, 12-18

T

Tang Kristensen, Evald, 97
Tetauer, Frank, 154, 173-74, 288, 297
Théâtre Bellecour, 136
Théâtre de l'Œuvre, 134
Théâtre Libre, 134, 171, 201
Thornton, Weldon, 60, 70
Tobin, Agnes, 5, 23-27, 30
Toomey, Deirdre, 270, 275
Tracy, Robert, 276
Trinity College, Dublin, 1, 9, 11, 56, 69, 99, 174, 242-43, 280, 291, 294
Turkle, Sherry, 73, 92, 289

U

University College Dublin, 101, 196, 260, 287, 292-94

V

Velasquez, Diego, 161
Villiers de l'Isle-Adam, Jean-Marie-Mathias-Philippe-Auguste, 11
Vinohrady Theatre, 170, 178

von der Vogelweide, Walter, 8, 21
Von Sydow, Carl Wilhelm, 108

W

Wagner, Richard, 143
Walcott, Derek, 2, 28, 31, 289
Watson, George, 140-41
Watt, Stephen, 91, 276
Wedekind, Frank, 135, 143
Weitz, Eric, 260, 267, 289
White, Harry, 277
Wicklow, 10, 12, 14-17, 60-64, 95, 105, 118-19, 121, 125, 133, 138, 164, 166, 176, 181-88, 190, 196, 203-204, 269-70, 283, 294, 297
Wilde, Oscar, 16, 293
Williams, Vaughan, 28
Wood, James, 110

Woolf, Virginia, 88
Worth, Katherine, 135
Wulff, Helena, 108, 110

Y

Yeats, Jack B., 5, 140, 150, 279
Yeats, Lolly, 19
Yeats, W.B., 9, 29-34, 39, 52-53, 69, 75, 96, 111, 129, 141, 149-50, 153, 159, 162, 170, 173, 175-77, 196, 217, 283, 287, 292, 294
  At the Hawk's Well, 182, 186-87, 193
  Purgatory, 119, 195, 217, 275

Z

Želenský, Karel, 170
Zola, Émile, 134

Carysfort Press was formed in the summer of 1998. It receives annual funding from the Arts Council.

The directors believe that drama is playing an ever-increasing role in today's society and that enjoyment of the theatre, both professional and amateur, currently plays a central part in Irish culture.

The Press aims to produce high quality publications which, though written and/or edited by academics, will be made accessible to a general readership. The organisation would also like to provide a forum for critical thinking in the Arts in Ireland, again keeping the needs and interests of the general public in view.

The company publishes contemporary Irish writing for and about the theatre.

Editorial and publishing inquiries to:
Carysfort Press Ltd.,
58 Woodfield,
Scholarstown Road,
Rathfarnham,
Dublin 16,
Republic of Ireland.

T (353 1) 493 7383
F (353 1) 406 9815
E: info@carysfortpress.com
www.carysfortpress.com

HOW TO ORDER

TRADE ORDERS DIRECTLY TO:
Irish Book Distribution
Unit 12, North Park, North Road,
Finglas, Dublin 11.

T: (353 1) 8239580
F: (353 1) 8239599
E: mary@argosybooks.ie
www.argosybooks.ie

INDIVIDUAL ORDERS DIRECTLY TO:
eprint Ltd.
35 Coolmine Industrial Estate,
Blanchardstown, Dublin 15.
T: (353 1) 827 8860
F: (353 1) 827 8804 Order online @
E: books@eprint.ie
www.eprint.ie

FOR SALES IN NORTH AMERICA AND CANADA:
Dufour Editions Inc.,
124 Byers Road,
PO Box 7,
Chester Springs,
PA 19425,
USA

T: 1-610-458-5005
F: 1-610-458-7103

Constellations - The Life and Music of John Buckley

Benjamin Dwyer

Benjamin Dwyer provides a long overdue assessment of one of Ireland's most prolific composers of the last decades. He looks at John Buckley's music in the context of his biography and Irish cultural life. This is no hagiography but a critical assessment of Buckley's work, his roots and aesthetics. While looking closely at several of Buckley's compositions, the book is written in a comprehensible style that makes it easily accessible to anybody interested in Irish musical and cultural history.   *Wolfgang Marx*

As well as providing a very readable and comprehensive study of the life and music of John Buckley, Constellations also offers an up-to-date and informative catalogue of compositions, a complete discography, translations of set texts and the full libretto of his chamber opera, making this book an essential guide for both students and professional scholars alike.

ISBN: 978-1-904505-52-5   €20.00

'Because We Are Poor':
Irish Theatre in the 1990s

Victor Merriman

"Victor Merriman's work on Irish theatre is in the vanguard of a whole new paradigm in Irish theatre scholarship, one that is not content to contemplate monuments of past or present achievement, but for which the theatre is a lens that makes visible the hidden malaises in Irish society. That he has been able to do so by focusing on a period when so much else in Irish culture conspired to hide those problems is only testimony to the considerable power of his critical scrutiny." Chris Morash, NUI Maynooth.

ISBN: 978-1-904505-51-8   €20.00

'Buffoonery and Easy Sentiment':
Popular Irish Plays in the Decade Prior to the Opening of The Abbey Theatre

Christopher Fitz-Simon

In this fascinating reappraisal of the non-literary drama of the late 19th - early 20th century, Christopher Fitz-Simon discloses a unique world of plays, players and producers in metropolitan theatres in Ireland and other countries where Ireland was viewed as a source of extraordinary topics at once contemporary and comfortably remote: revolution, eviction, famine, agrarian agitation, political assassination.

The form was the fashionable one of melodrama, yet Irish melodrama was of a particular kind replete with hidden messages, and the language was far more allusive, colourful and entertaining than that of its English equivalent.

ISBN: 978-1-9045505-49-5   €20.00

The Fourth Seamus Heaney Lectures, 'Mirror up to Nature':

Ed. Patrick Burke

What, in particular, is the contemporary usefulness for the building of societies of one of our oldest and culturally valued ideals, that of drama? The Fourth Seamus Heaney Lectures, 'Mirror up to Nature': Drama and Theatre in the Modern World, given at St Patrick's College, Drumcondra, between October 2006 and April 2007, addressed these and related questions. Patrick Mason spoke on the essence of theatre, Thomas Kilroy on Ireland's contribution to the art of theatre, Cecily O'Neill and Jonothan Neelands on the rich potential of drama in the classroom. Brenna Katz Clarke examined the relationship between drama and film, and John Buckley spoke on opera and its history and gave an illuminating account of his own *Words Upon The Window-Pane*.

ISBN 978-1-9045505-48-8   €12

The Theatre of Tom Mac Intyre: 'Strays from the ether'

Eds. Bernadette Sweeney and Marie Kelly

This long overdue anthology captures the soul of Mac Intyre's dramatic canon – its ethereal qualities, its extraordinary diversity, its emphasis on the poetic and on performance – in an extensive range of visual, journalistic and scholarly contributions from writers, theatre practitioners.

ISBN 978-1-904505-46-4 €25

Irish Appropriation Of Greek Tragedy

Brian Arkins

This book presents an analysis of more than 30 plays written by Irish dramatists and poets that are based on the tragedies of Sophocles, Euripides and Aeschylus. These plays proceed from the time of Yeats and Synge through MacNeice and the Longfords on to many of today's leading writers.

ISBN 978-1-904505-47-1 €20

Alive in Time: The Enduring Drama of Tom Murphy

Ed. Christopher Murray

Almost 50 years after he first hit the headlines as Ireland's most challenging playwright, the 'angry young man' of those times Tom Murphy still commands his place at the pinnacle of Irish theatre. Here 17 new essays by prominent critics and academics, with an introduction by Christopher Murray, survey Murphy's dramatic oeuvre in a concerted attempt to define his greatness and enduring appeal, making this book a significant study of a unique genius.

ISBN 978-1-904505-45-7 €25

Performing Violence in Contemporary Ireland

Ed. Lisa Fitzpatrick

This interdisciplinary collection of fifteen new essays by scholars of theatre, Irish studies, music, design and politics explores aspects of the performance of violence in contemporary Ireland. With chapters on the work of playwrights Martin McDonagh, Martin Lynch, Conor McPherson and Gary Mitchell, on Republican commemorations and the 90th anniversary ceremonies for the Battle of the Somme and the Easter Rising, this book aims to contribute to the ongoing international debate on the performance of violence in contemporary societies.

ISBN 978-1-904505-44-0 (2009) €20

Ireland's Economic Crisis - Time to Act. Essays from over 40 leading Irish thinkers at the MacGill Summer School 2009

Eds. Joe Mulholland and Finbarr Bradley

Ireland's economic crisis requires a radical transformation in policymaking. In this volume, political, industrial, academic, trade union and business leaders and commentators tell the story of the Irish economy and its rise and fall. Contributions at Glenties range from policy, vision and context to practical suggestions on how the country can emerge from its crisis.

ISBN 978-1-904505-43-3 (2009)   €20

Deviant Acts: Essays on Queer Performance

Ed. David Cregan

This book contains an exciting collection of essays focusing on a variety of alternative performances happening in contemporary Ireland. While it highlights the particular representations of gay and lesbian identity it also brings to light how diversity has always been a part of Irish culture and is, in fact, shaping what it means to be Irish today.

ISBN 978-1-904505-42-6 (2009)   €20

Seán Keating in Context: Responses to Culture and Politics in Post-Civil War Ireland

Compiled, edited and introduced by Éimear O'Connor

Irish artist Seán Keating has been judged by his critics as the personification of old-fashioned traditionalist values. This book presents a different view. The story reveals Keating's early determination to attain government support for the visual arts. It also illustrates his socialist leanings, his disappointment with capitalism, and his attitude to cultural snobbery, to art critics, and to the Academy. Given the national and global circumstances nowadays, Keating's critical and wry observations are prophetic – and highly amusing.

ISBN 978-1-904505-41-9   €25

Dialogue of the Ancients of Ireland: A new translation of Acallam na Senorach

Translated with introduction and notes by Maurice Harmon

One of Ireland's greatest collections of stories and poems, The Dialogue of the Ancients of Ireland is a new translation by Maurice Harmon of the 12th century *Acallam na Senorach*. Retold in a refreshing modern idiom, the *Dialogue* is an extraordinary account of journeys to the four provinces by St. Patrick and the pagan Cailte, one of the surviving Fian. Within the frame story are over 200 other stories reflecting many genres – wonder tales, sea journeys, romances, stories of revenge, tales of monsters and magic. The poems are equally varied – lyrics, nature poems, eulogies, prophecies, laments, genealogical poems. After the *Tain Bo Cuailnge*, the *Acallam* is the largest surviving prose work in Old and Middle Irish.

ISBN: 978-1-904505-39-6 (2009)   €20

Literary and Cultural Relations between Ireland and Hungary and Central and Eastern Europe

Ed. Maria Kurdi

This lively, informative and incisive collection of essays sheds fascinating new light on the literary interrelations between Ireland, Hungary, Poland, Romania and the Czech Republic. It charts a hitherto under-explored history of the reception of modern Irish culture in Central and Eastern Europe and also investigates how key authors have been translated, performed and adapted. The revealing explorations undertaken in this volume of a wide array of Irish dramatic and literary texts, ranging from *Gulliver's Travels* to *Translations* and *The Pillowman*, tease out the subtly altered nuances that they acquire in a Central European context.

ISBN: 978-1-904505-40-2 (2009)   €20

Plays and Controversies: Abbey Theatre Diaries 2000-2005

Ben Barnes

In diaries covering the period of his artistic directorship of the Abbey, Ben Barnes offers a frank, honest, and probing account of a much commented upon and controversial period in the history of the national theatre. These diaries also provide fascinating personal insights into the day-to- day pressures, joys, and frustrations of running one of Ireland's most iconic institutions.

ISBN: 978-1-904505-38-9 (2008)   €35

Interactions: Dublin Theatre Festival 1957-2007. Irish Theatrical Diaspora Series: 3

Eds. Nicholas Grene and Patrick Lonergan with Lilian Chambers

For over 50 years the Dublin Theatre Festival has been one of Ireland's most important cultural events, bringing countless new Irish plays to the world stage, while introducing Irish audiences to the most important international theatre companies and artists. Interactions explores and celebrates the achievements of the renowned Festival since 1957 and includes specially commissioned memoirs from past organizers, offering a unique perspective on the controversies and successes that have marked the event's history. An especially valuable feature of the volume, also, is a complete listing of the shows that have appeared at the Festival from 1957 to 2008.

ISBN: 978-1-904505-36-5 €25

The Informer: A play by Tom Murphy based on the novel by Liam O'Flaherty

The Informer, Tom Murphy's stage adaptation of Liam O'Flaherty's novel, was produced in the 1981 Dublin Theatre Festival, directed by the playwright himself, with Liam Neeson in the leading role. The central subject of the play is the quest of a character at the point of emotional and moral breakdown for some source of meaning or identity. In the case of Gypo Nolan, the informer of the title, this involves a nightmarish progress through a Dublin underworld in which he changes from a Judas figure to a scapegoat surrogate for Jesus, taking upon himself the sins of the world. A cinematic style, with flash-back and intercut scenes, is used rather than a conventional theatrical structure to catch the fevered and phantasmagoric progression of Gypo's mind. The language, characteristically for Murphy, mixes graphically colloquial Dublin slang with the haunted intricacies of the central character groping for the meaning of his own actions. The dynamic rhythm of the action builds towards an inevitable but theatrically satisfying tragic catastrophe. ' [The Informer] is, in many ways closer to being an original Murphy play than it is to O'Flaherty...' Fintan O'Toole.

ISBN: 978-1-904505-37-2 (2008) €10

Shifting Scenes: Irish theatre-going 1955-1985

Eds. Nicholas Grene and Chris Morash

Transcript of conversations with John Devitt, academic and reviewer, about his lifelong passion for the theatre. A fascinating and entertaining insight into Dublin theatre over the course of thirty years provided by Devitt's vivid reminiscences and astute observations.

ISBN: 978-1-904505-33-4 (2008) €10

Irish Literature: Feminist Perspectives

Eds. Patricia Coughlan and Tina O'Toole

The collection discusses texts from the early 18th century to the present. A central theme of the book is the need to renegotiate the relations of feminism with nationalism and to transact the potential contest of these two important narratives, each possessing powerful emancipatory force. Irish Literature: Feminist Perspectives contributes incisively to contemporary debates about Irish culture, gender and ideology.

ISBN: 978-1-904505-35-8 (2008) €25

Silenced Voices: Hungarian Plays from Transylvania

Selected and translated by Csilla Bertha and Donald E. Morse

The five plays are wonderfully theatrical, moving fluidly from absurdism to tragedy, and from satire to the darkly comic. Donald Morse and Csilla Bertha's translations capture these qualities perfectly, giving voice to the 'forgotten playwrights of Central Europe'. They also deeply enrich our understanding of the relationship between art, ethics, and politics in Europe.

ISBN: 978-1-904505-34-1 (2008) €25

A Hazardous Melody of Being:
Seóirse Bodley's Song Cycles on the poems of Micheal O'Siadhail

Ed. Lorraine Byrne Bodley

This apograph is the first publication of Bodley's O'Siadhail song cycles and is the first book to explore the composer's lyrical modernity from a number of perspectives. Lorraine Byrne Bodley's insightful introduction describes in detail the development and essence of Bodley's musical thinking, the European influences he absorbed which linger in these cycles, and the importance of his work as a composer of the Irish art song.

ISBN: 978-1-904505-31-0 (2008) €25

Irish Theatre in England: Irish Theatrical Diaspora Series: 2

Eds. Richard Cave and Ben Levitas

Irish theatre in England has frequently illustrated the complex relations between two distinct cultures. How English reviewers and audiences interpret Irish plays is often decidedly different from how the plays were read in performance in Ireland. How certain Irish performers have chosen to be understood in Dublin is not necessarily how audiences in London have perceived their constructed stage personae. Though a collection by diverse authors, the twelve essays in this volume investigate these issues from a variety of perspectives that together chart the trajectory of Irish performance in England from the mid-nineteenth century till today.

ISBN: 978-1-904505-26-6 (2007) €20

Goethe and Anna Amalia: A Forbidden Love?

Ettore Ghibellino, Trans. Dan Farrelly

In this study Ghibellino sets out to show that the platonic relationship between Goethe and Charlotte von Stein – lady-in-waiting to Anna Amalia, the Dowager Duchess of Weimar – was used as part of a cover-up for Goethe's intense and prolonged love relationship with the Duchess Anna Amalia herself. The book attempts to uncover a hitherto closely-kept state secret. Readers convinced by the evidence supporting Ghibellino's hypothesis will see in it one of the very great love stories in European history – to rank with that of Dante and Beatrice, and Petrarch and Laura.

ISBN: 978-1-904505-24-2 €20

Ireland on Stage: Beckett and After

Eds. Hiroko Mikami, Minako Okamuro, Naoko Yagi

The collection focuses primarily on Irish playwrights and their work, both in text and on the stage during the latter half of the twentieth century. The central figure is Samuel Beckett, but the contributors freely draw on Beckett and his work provides a springboard to discuss contemporary playwrights such as Brian Friel, Frank McGuinness, Marina Carr and Conor McPherson amongst others. Contributors include: Anthony Roche, Hiroko Mikami, Naoko Yagi, Cathy Leeney, Joseph Long, Noreem Doody, Minako Okamuro, Christopher Murray, Futoshi Sakauchi and Declan Kiberd

ISBN: 978-1-904505-23-5 (2007) €20

'Echoes Down the Corridor': Irish Theatre - Past, Present and Future

Eds. Patrick Lonergan and Riana O'Dwyer

This collection of fourteen new essays explores Irish theatre from exciting new perspectives. How has Irish theatre been received internationally - and, as the country becomes more multicultural, how will international theatre influence the development of drama in Ireland? These and many other important questions.

ISBN: 978-1-904505-25-9 (2007) €20

Musics of Belonging: The Poetry of Micheal O'Siadhail

Eds. Marc Caball & David F. Ford

An overall account is given of O'Siadhail's life, his work and the reception of his poetry so far. There are close readings of some poems, analyses of his artistry in matching diverse content with both classical and innovative forms, and studies of recurrent themes such as love, death, language, music, and the shifts of modern life.

ISBN: 978-1-904505-22-8 (2007) €25 (Paperback)
ISBN: 978-1-904505-21-1 (2007) €50 (Casebound)

Brian Friel's Dramatic Artistry: 'The Work has Value'

Eds. Donald E. Morse, Csilla Bertha and Maria Kurdi

Brian Friel's Dramatic Artistry presents a refreshingly broad range of voices: new work from some of the leading English-speaking authorities on Friel, and fascinating essays from scholars in Germany, Italy, Portugal, and Hungary. This book will deepen our knowledge and enjoyment of Friel's work.

ISBN: 978-1-904505-17-4 (2006) €30

The Theatre of Martin McDonagh: 'A World of Savage Stories'

Eds. Lilian Chambers and Eamonn Jordan

The book is a vital response to the many challenges set by McDonagh for those involved in the production and reception of his work. Critics and commentators from around the world offer a diverse range of often provocative approaches. What is not surprising is the focus and commitment of the engagement, given the controversial and stimulating nature of the work.

ISBN: 978-1-904505-19-8 (2006) €35

Edna O'Brien: New Critical Perspectives

Eds. Kathryn Laing, Sinead Mooney and Maureen O'Connor

The essays collected here illustrate some of the range, complexity, and interest of Edna O'Brien as a fiction writer and dramatist. They will contribute to a broader appreciation of her work and to an evolution of new critical approaches, as well as igniting more interest in the many unexplored areas of her considerable oeuvre.

ISBN: 978-1-904505-20-4 (2006) €20

Irish Theatre on Tour

Eds. Nicholas Grene and Chris Morash

'Touring has been at the strategic heart of Druid's artistic policy since the early eighties. Everyone has the right to see professional theatre in their own communities. Irish theatre on tour is a crucial part of Irish theatre as a whole'. Garry Hynes

ISBN 978-1-904505-13-6 (2005) €20

Poems 2000-2005 by Hugh Maxton

Poems 2000-2005 is a transitional collection written while the author – also known to be W.J. Mc Cormack, literary historian – was in the process of moving back from London to settle in rural Ireland.

ISBN 978-1-904505-12-9 (2005) €10

Synge: A Celebration

Ed. Colm Tóibín

A collection of essays by some of Ireland's most creative writers on the work of John Millington Synge, featuring Sebastian Barry, Marina Carr, Anthony Cronin, Roddy Doyle, Anne Enright, Hugo Hamilton, Joseph O'Connor, Mary O'Malley, Fintan O'Toole, Colm Toibin, Vincent Woods.

ISBN 978-1-904505-14-3 (2005) €15

East of Eden: New Romanian Plays

Ed. Andrei Marinescu

Four of the most promising Romanian playwrights, young and very young, are in this collection, each one with a specific way of seeing the Romanian reality, each one with a style of communicating an articulated artistic vision of the society we are living in. Ion Caramitru, General Director Romanian National Theatre Bucharest.
ISBN 978-1-904505-15-0 (2005) €10

George Fitzmaurice: 'Wild in His Own Way', Biography of an Irish Playwright

Fiona Brennan

'Fiona Brennan's introduction to his considerable output allows us a much greater appreciation and understanding of Fitzmaurice, the one remaining under-celebrated genius of twentieth-century Irish drama'. Conall Morrison

ISBN 978-1-904505-16-7 (2005) €20

Out of History: Essays on the Writings of Sebastian Barry

Ed. Christina Hunt Mahony

The essays address Barry's engagement with the contemporary cultural debate in Ireland and also with issues that inform postcolonial critical theory. The range and selection of contributors has ensured a high level of critical expression and an insightful assessment of Barry and his works.

ISBN: 978-1-904505-18-1 (2005) €20

Three Congregational Masses

Seoirse Bodley

'From the simpler congregational settings in the Mass of Peace and the Mass of Joy to the richer textures of the Mass of Glory, they are immediately attractive and accessible, and with a distinctively Irish melodic quality.' Barra Boydell

ISBN: 978-1-904505-11-2 (2005) €15

Georg Büchner's Woyzeck,

A new translation by Dan Farrelly

The most up-to-date German scholarship of Thomas Michael Mayer and Burghard Dedner has finally made it possible to establish an authentic sequence of scenes. The wide-spread view that this play is a prime example of loose, open theatre is no longer sustainable. Directors and teachers are challenged to "read it again".

ISBN: 978-1-904505-02-0 (2004) €10

Playboys of the Western World: Production Histories

Ed. Adrian Frazier

'The book is remarkably well-focused: half is a series of production histories of Playboy performances through the twentieth century in the UK, Northern Ireland, the USA, and Ireland. The remainder focuses on one contemporary performance, that of Druid Theatre, as directed by Garry Hynes. The various contemporary social issues that are addressed in relation to Synge's play and this performance of it give the volume an additional interest: it shows how the arts matter.' Kevin Barry

ISBN: 978-1-904505-06-8 (2004) €20

The Power of Laughter: Comedy and Contemporary Irish Theatre

Ed. Eric Weitz

The collection draws on a wide range of perspectives and voices including critics, playwrights, directors and performers. The result is a series of fascinating and provocative debates about the myriad functions of comedy in contemporary Irish theatre. Anna McMullan

As Stan Laurel said, 'it takes only an onion to cry. Peel it and weep. Comedy is harder'. 'These essays listen to the power of laughter. They hear the tough heart of Irish theatre – hard and wicked and funny'. Frank McGuinness

ISBN: 978-1-904505-05-1 (2004) €20

Sacred Play: Soul-Journeys in contemporary Irish Theatre

Anne F. O'Reilly

'Theatre as a space or container for sacred play allows audiences to glimpse mystery and to experience transformation. This book charts how Irish playwrights negotiate the labyrinth of the Irish soul and shows how their plays contribute to a poetics of Irish culture that enables a new imagining. Playwrights discussed are: McGuinness, Murphy, Friel, Le Marquand Hartigan, Burke Brogan, Harding, Meehan, Carr, Parker, Devlin, and Barry.'

ISBN: 978-1-904505-07-5 (2004) €25

The Irish Harp Book

Sheila Larchet Cuthbert

This is a facsimile of the edition originally published by Mercier Press in 1993. There is a new preface by Sheila Larchet Cuthbert, and the biographical material has been updated. It is a collection of studies and exercises for the use of teachers and pupils of the Irish harp.
ISBN: 978-1-904505-08-2 (2004) €35

The Drunkard

Tom Murphy

'The Drunkard is a wonderfully eloquent play. Murphy's ear is finely attuned to the glories and absurdities of melodramatic exclamation, and even while he is wringing out its ludicrous overstatement, he is also making it sing.' The Irish Times

ISBN: 978-1-90 05-09-9 (2004) €10

Goethe: Musical Poet, Musical Catalyst

Ed. Lorraine Byrne

'Goethe was interested in, and acutely aware of, the place of music in human experience generally - and of its particular role in modern culture. Moreover, his own literary work - especially the poetry and Faust - inspired some of the major composers of the European tradition to produce some of their finest works.' Martin Swales

ISBN: 978-1-9045-10-5 (2004) €40

The Theatre of Marina Carr: "Before rules was made"

Eds. Anna McMullan & Cathy Leeney

As the first published collection of articles on the theatre of Marina Carr, this volume explores the world of Carr's theatrical imagination, the place of her plays in contemporary theatre in Ireland and abroad and the significance of her highly individual voice.

ISBN: 978-0-9534257-7-8 (2003) €20

Critical Moments: Fintan O'Toole on Modern Irish Theatre

Eds. Julia Furay & Redmond O'Hanlon

This new book on the work of Fintan O'Toole, the internationally acclaimed theatre critic and cultural commentator, offers percussive analyses and assessments of the major plays and playwrights in the canon of modern Irish theatre. Fearless and provocative in his judgements, O'Toole is essential reading for anyone interested in criticism or in the current state of Irish theatre.

ISBN: 978-1-904505-03-7 (2003) €20

Goethe and Schubert: Across the Divide

Eds. Lorraine Byrne & Dan Farrelly

Proceedings of the International Conference, 'Goethe and Schubert in Perspective and Performance', Trinity College Dublin, 2003. This volume includes essays by leading scholars – Barkhoff, Boyle, Byrne, Canisius, Dürr, Fischer, Hill, Kramer, Lamport, Lund, Meikle, Newbould, Norman McKay, White, Whitton, Wright, Youens – on Goethe's musicality and his relationship to Schubert; Schubert's contribution to sacred music and the Lied and his setting of Goethe's Singspiel, Claudine. A companion volume of this Singspiel (with piano reduction and English translation) is also available.

ISBN: 978-1-904505-04-4 (2003) €25

Goethe's Singspiel, 'Claudine von Villa Bella'

Set by Franz Schubert

Goethe's Singspiel in three acts was set to music by Schubert in 1815. Only Act One of Schuberts's Claudine score is extant. The present volume makes Act One available for performance in English and German. It comprises both a piano reduction by Lorraine Byrne of the original Schubert orchestral score and a bilingual text translated for the modern stage by Dan Farrelly. This is a tale, wittily told, of lovers and vagabonds, romance, reconciliation, and resolution of family conflict.

ISBN: 978-0-9544290-0-3 (2002) €20

Theatre of Sound, Radio and the Dramatic Imagination

Dermot Rattigan

An innovative study of the challenges that radio drama poses to the creative imagination of the writer, the production team, and the listener.
"A remarkably fine study of radio drama – everywhere informed by the writer's professional experience of such drama in the making...A new theoretical and analytical approach – informative, illuminating and at all times readable." Richard Allen Cave

ISBN: 978- 0-9534-257-5-4 (2002) €20

Talking about Tom Murphy

Ed. Nicholas Grene

Talking About Tom Murphy is shaped around the six plays in the landmark Abbey Theatre Murphy Season of 2001, assembling some of the best-known commentators on his work: Fintan O'Toole, Chris Morash, Lionel Pilkington, Alexandra Poulain, Shaun Richards, Nicholas Grene and Declan Kiberd.

ISBN: 978-0-9534-257-9-2 (2002) €15

Hamlet: The Shakespearean Director

Mike Wilcock

"This study of the Shakespearean director as viewed through various interpretations of HAMLET is a welcome addition to our understanding of how essential it is for a director to have a clear vision of a great play. It is an important study from which all of us who love Shakespeare and who understand the importance of continuing contemporary exploration may gain new insights." From the Foreword, by Joe Dowling, Artistic Director, The Guthrie Theater, Minneapolis, MN

ISBN: 978-1-904505-00-6 (2002) €20

The Theatre of Frank Mc Guinness: Stages of Mutability

Ed. Helen Lojek

The first edited collection of essays about internationally renowned Irish playwright Frank McGuinness focuses on both performance and text. Interpreters come to diverse conclusions, creating a vigorous dialogue that enriches understanding and reflects a strong consensus about the value of McGuinness's complex work.

ISBN: 978-1904505-01-3. (2002) €20

Theatre Talk: Voices of Irish Theatre Practitioners

Eds Lilian Chambers, Ger Fitzgibbon and Eamonn Jordan

"This book is the right approach - asking practitioners what they feel." Sebastian Barry, Playwright "... an invaluable and informative collection of interviews with those who make and shape the landscape of Irish Theatre." Ben Barnes, Artistic Director of the Abbey Theatre

ISBN: 978-0-9534-257-6-1 (2001)   €20

In Search of the South African Iphigenie

Erika von Wietersheim and Dan Farrelly

Discussions of Goethe's "Iphigenie auf Tauris" (Under the Curse) as relevant to women's issues in modern South Africa: women in family and public life; the force of women's spirituality; experience of personal relationships; attitudes to parents and ancestors; involvement with religion.

ISBN: 978-0-9534257-8-5 (2001)   €10

'The Starving' and 'October Song':

Two contemporary Irish plays by Andrew Hinds

The Starving, set during and after the siege of Derry in 1689, is a moving and engrossing drama of the emotional journey of two men.

October Song, a superbly written family drama set in real time in pre-ceasefire Derry.

ISBN: 978-0-9534-257-4-7 (2001)   €10

Seen and Heard: Six new plays by Irish women

Ed. Cathy Leeney

A rich and funny, moving and theatrically exciting collection of plays by Mary Elizabeth Burke-Kennedy, Síofra Campbell, Emma Donoghue, Anne Le Marquand Hartigan, Michelle Read and Dolores Walshe.

ISBN: 978-0-9534-257-3-0 (2001)   €20

Theatre Stuff: Critical essays on contemporary Irish theatre

Ed. Eamonn Jordan

Best selling essays on the successes and debates of contemporary Irish theatre at home and abroad. Contributors include: Thomas Kilroy, Declan Hughes, Anna McMullan, Declan Kiberd, Deirdre Mulrooney, Fintan O'Toole, Christopher Murray, Caoimhe McAvinchey and Terry Eagleton.

ISBN: 978-0-9534-2571-1-6 (2000)   €20

Under the Curse. Goethe's "Iphigenie Auf Tauris", A New Version

Dan Farrelly

The Greek myth of Iphigenie grappling with the curse on the house of Atreus is brought vividly to life. This version is currently being used in Johannesburg to explore problems of ancestry, religion, and Black African women's spirituality.

ISBN: 978-09534-257-8-5 (2000)   €10

Urfaust, A New Version of Goethe's early "Faust" in Brechtian Mode

Dan Farrelly

This version is based on Brecht's irreverent and daring re-interpretation of the German classic. "Urfaust is a kind of well-spring for German theatre… The love-story is the most daring and the most profound in German dramatic literature." Brecht

ISBN: 978-0-9534-257-0-9 (1998)   €10

www.ingramcontent.com/pod-product-compliance
Lightning Source LLC
Chambersburg PA
CBHW050836230426
43667CB00012B/2018